ANGER

ANGER

The Struggle for Emotional
Control in America's History

Carol Zisowitz Stearns
Peter N. Stearns

The University of Chicago Press

Chicago and London

CAROL ZISOWITZ STEARNS, M.D., has a private practice in psychiatry and is clinical instructor in psychiatry at the University of Pittsburgh School of Medicine. She also holds a Ph.D. in history. PETER N. STEARNS is Heinz Professor and department head of history at Carnegie Mellon University. He is the author of numerous books and is the editor of the *Journal of Social History*.

The University of Chicago Press, Chicago 60637
The University of Chicago Press, Ltd., London
© 1986 by The University of Chicago
All rights reserved. Published 1986
Printed in the United States of America
95 94 93 92 91 90 89 88 87 86 54321

Library of Congress Cataloging-in-Publication Data

Stearns, Carol Zisowitz.
  Anger : the struggle for emotional control in America's history.

  Bibliography: p.
  Includes index.
  1. United States—Civilization—Psychological
aspects. 2. Anger. 3. United States—Social life
and customs—Psychological aspects. I. Stearns,
Peter N. II. Title.
E169.1.S7696   1986   973'.01'9   86-1470
ISBN 0-226-77151-2

Contents

Acknowledgments   vii

1   Introduction   1

2   Background   18
When the Gods Were Angry

3   The Early Victorian Synthesis   36
Domestic Idealism

4   A New Approach to Anger Control   69
1860–1940, The American Ambivalence

5   Anger at Work   110
A Contemporary Approach

6   The Managerial Style   157
Raising Cool Kids

7   The Managerial Style   190
Fighting Fair in Marriage

8   Conclusion   211
Keeping the Lid On

Appendix A   241

Appendix B   243

Notes   245

Index   291

In gratitude, to Gert

In nostalgia, to Elizabeth, Raymond, and Milton

In joy, to our other mutual project: Cordelia, Clio, Julie, Wendy, Deborah, Duncan

Acknowledgments

A number of people have aided in the preparation of this book, and in various ways. We are particularly grateful to John Demos, Randolph Trumbach, and Howard Kushner for their thorough and helpful reading of the initial manuscript; their comments and encouragement have been invaluable. We also wish to thank Michael Gordon and Theodore Kemper, for sharing bibliographical suggestions, and Laraine Flemming, Rudolph Bell, Andrew Achenbaum, John Gillis, Donald Sutton, Andrew Barnes, Chuck Lidz, and David Klahr, for helpful advice. Seminar papers by several graduate students at Carnegie-Mellon University were extremely useful to specific sections of this book; we have benefited from the intelligence and industry of Shelley Giordano, Helen Sobehart, Robert Veto, Joan Francis, Judy Bosch, and June Ladd. Sincere thanks also to Erica Van Sickel, Annette Giovengo, Stephanie Washburn, Wendy Wiener, Donna Scheuble, and Stephen Woehrl for assistance in manuscript preparation.

For released time toward the research on which this study is based, we are grateful to the Department of History of Carnegie-Mellon University. A portion of the research on anger at work was supported by the Program in Technology and Society, Carnegie-Mellon University. Dr. Peter Henderson, of Western Psychiatric Institute and Clinic, was very helpful in arranging a flexible work schedule.

We profited greatly from the ideas and stimulus provided by Dr. Joseph Campos and our other new colleagues in the International Society for Research on Emotion. Carol Stearns would like to thank two special people, Rex Speers, who taught her more than any other psychiatrist, and Donald Olsen, first and best history teacher.

We appreciate finally the patience of our children in sitting through frequent discussions of our subject, which only occasionally took on the air of laboratory experiment, and Linda Couts, whose reliable help with the smaller children made it possible to devote more time to this project.

1 Introduction

Anger at work has a history. James Franklin, the eighteenth-century Boston printer, indulged his temper freely against those in his employ, with scant sign of compunction or restraint. His apprenticed younger brother, Benjamin, though resentful of the resultant beatings and loud arguments and most eager to escape the shop, saw nothing noteworthy or unusual about James's emotional style, commenting only that his brother was "passionate."

A foreman, interviewed a decade ago by Studs Terkel, sees himself above all as a human relations expert, his own emotions geared toward creating a friendly atmosphere. So thoroughly has he internalized his mission that he deplores the occasional moodiness of his workers, not because it hampers productivity, but because grumpiness is so distasteful in itself: "If we could get everybody to feel great . . . ?" And a middle manager with a similar emotional mission: "You have to keep peace with people on all levels. Sometimes I get home worn to a frazzle over all this."[1]

Anger in marriage has a history too. Victorian thoughts: "I do not see how it is possible to pass . . . 50 years of married life . . . and not, sometimes, feel those risings of temper to which the best of manhood, have, in general, been more or less subject. Nor can I say that I should envy those, who were so indifferent—so wanting in sensibility—as never to have a single feeling of displeasure towards each other"; "Tom was spirited and quick tempered—great, lovinghearted men always are."[2] And a thought from the 1940s: "Most bickering in marriage would stop if husbands and wives would just be polite and 'behave like adults.'"[3]

Ideas about anger in marriage have changed, and sometimes real people have been caught in the crunch of altered expectations. Consider Ted, described in the popular series "Can This Marriage Be Saved" in the *Ladies Home Journal* of April 1965. The marriage counselor felt the couple was in trouble, mostly because of the husband's angry ways. The diagnosis—Ted had been raised by an old-fashioned father: "Although Ted decried his bad temper, he was secretly proud of it. He

1

regarded his temper as a heritage from his father.'' As a child, Ted recalled smashing a plate over his brother's head to retaliate for a piece of stolen cake: "My mother was furious. My father was tickled, ignored her demands that I be punished, and took me downtown for ice cream." The counselor, understanding but not at all condoning the older approach, suggested that the unfortunate Ted was "what we call an 'angry' man" and that the marriage's only hope was for him to learn to take out his feelings on inanimate objects.[4]

Americans today worry about their emotions more than Ben Franklin's brother and his contemporaries, or indeed most Victorian husbands, ever did. And there is no emotion about which we fret, amid greater confusion, than anger. While our founding fathers felt relatively free to storm and rage when the mood seized them and even took temper to be a sign of manliness, we have become embarrassed by such displays today. Though our ancestors were certainly concerned about suppressing some behaviors that might result from anger, such as insubordination by servants or children, they saw no need to attack the emotional basis of those behaviors directly. Contemporary Americans have gone much further; they seek to regulate not only behavior but the feeling itself.

Indeed, during the past two hundred years, Americans have shifted in their methods of controlling social behavior toward greater reliance on direct maniuplation of emotions and, particularly, of anger. This is not to argue that contemporary society imposes more social control than has been imposed in the past, for in part the effort to restrain anger replaces earlier forms of behavioral control, particularly tight, intimate community supervision. But control through emotions, including firm restraints on anger, has some distinctive effects, in confusing individual grasp of emotional response, and may easily be carried to undesirable lengths. This is why the system deserves scrutiny. A first step toward such scrutiny is an understanding of how, in several discrete stages, Americans moved from relative unconcern with anger per se to an increasing insistence that the emotion be denoted and reproved.

A history of the growing restraint of anger, as a significant theme in American history, may come as a surprise. Americans easily imagine themselves a rather angry people, heirs to a passionate past ranging from the righteous zeal of the Puritans who served a wrathful God, to Southern flashes of temper in defense of personal honor, through the quick-triggered Western frontiersmen with tempers to match. More recently, collective protest and widespread individual violence during the 1960s and early 1970s reminded us that our history has been peppered with angry acts of force, sometimes on the side of the law as well as against it.[5] Surely, major tides of American history have prepared us to be too angry rather than unusually restrained. A recent and well-received book on anger, playing to this theme, argued that anger has become a major American problem: not only has it become a national tradition, but contemporary therapeutic advice based on popularized-Freudian injunctions against the dangers of repression has also produced a dangerous penchant for letting angry feelings "hang out," regardless of the consequences.[6] It is easy to believe, in this context, that anger is wrecking our domestic lives as well as prompting some of the larger social tensions that concern us still. Even the august *New York Times* thunders against anger, as op-ed columnists excoriate anger as a danger to health—whether the emotion is expressed or not—and as a social menace, a "form of public littering."[7] Christopher Lasch, in his stinging indictment of contemporary culture, worries about the intense and unsocialized rage that shallow parental styles now produce among American children. A school official notes that "perhaps the emotion that causes the most problems, especially in the schools, is anger."[8]

But are we, indeed, as freely angry as we imagine ourselves? Studs Terkel's foremen are hardly quick-tempered gunslingers transported into the contemporary world of work. Rather they appear—correctly—more intensely concerned with repressing this emotion than many of their premodern antecedents were. Of course we can point to acts of anger in our past and in our present, and without question some of these cause legitimate dismay. But in the main Americans' worried preoccupation with anger is in fact a symptom of the national effort to repress and not the consequence of a particularly angry culture. We exaggerate our penchant for ventilating wrath in order better to prevent ourselves and others from recognizing how vigilant we are against the emotion. The myth of a blithely angry people is simply that—a myth, more useful in describing the way we were than the way we are today, and even then obscuring the long and complicated war against anger that many Americans have waged for a full two centuries. For at least a century past Americans have been characterized not by unusual readiness to express their tempers but by a complicated ambivalence that has focused on the need for control. Indeed, one reason for the popularity of cultural presentations of unfettered anger—the western or the street-tough detective, the athletic performance in which the coach exhorts his charges to "get mad"—lies in their fantasy value, their escapist portrayal of freedom from real-world American restraints. Some astute European observers, getting beneath surface stereotypes, have thus noted, not unusual American bluster, but a peculiar vulnerability to displays of anger on the part of others, a counterpart to the national desire for affectionate approval that may even affect the American style of diplomacy.

Yet the American stance toward anger, its real subtlety and constraint, has rarely been explored. Lloyd Warner, in the 1950s, wrote that anger constituted one of two basic dilemmas in American middle-class child rearing, the other being sex.[9] The sexual complexity has hardly gone unremarked, as a national pastime has developed of identifying revolutions and counterrevolutions in this area. But Warner's equally correct identification of anger as dilemma has passed virtually unnoticed, essentially because American scholars largely have shared a wider public desire to keep the problems of anger carefully beneath the surface. Thus recent comment not only has failed to grasp the American ambiguities of the 1950s but has also neglected an inquiry into subsequent attempts to reduce the ambiguity through further restraint. The central challenge of a historical inquiry into American anger is to grasp the development of growing anxiety about this emotion and, in the most contemporary period, of a series of attempts to introduce new levels of repression. Only through such inquiry can we understand why we no longer feel about anger as James Franklin did and why we retain the myth that we are an angry people when the evidence runs the other way.

Why History? Approaches to Anger

The need to use history to understand American anger is hardly common currency. It results from the fact that the national perception of anger, and of efforts to deal with it and even to direct expressions of it, has changed over time. We best see what we are now, in this aspect of our emotional makeup, by understanding where we have come from. And this involves, of necessity, a historical approach. But the historical approach results also from certain weaknesses in other approaches to anger, from disciplines more commonly associated with exploration of emotions than history is.

Psychology, without question, generates knowledge about emotions such as anger, though psychologists are not normally equipped to handle problems of change over time because of their preoccupation with constants of human nature. Yet in fact, even aside from the key problem of change, psychologists have not had a great deal to say about anger during the past several decades. A central psychological approach, continuing an effort begun by Darwin, has focused on the biological substrates of all emotions, including anger—and no one would contest that a strong biological element is involved.

Inevitably, the biological approach is primarily concerned with somatic constants, such as predictable changes in body chemistry or brain waves associated with particular emotional responses. Researchers have recognized individual variations in levels of anger, regarding high anger scores as a key index of maladjustment. They have also granted the possibility of deflecting anger through socialization, so that anger might seek indirect outlets. But the dominant interest in this approach has been in essentially innate human responses, comparable to aggressive responses in other animals.[10] This research contributes substantive biological knowledge and certainly reminds any social scientist working in the area of an irreducible animal component in certain emotional sensations or responses. But the approach is not conducive to a grasp of changes in the cultural valuation or actual use of anger[11] and, unfortunately, has not even answered the nagging question of whether anger is somehow a fixed quantity—if not in each individual, at least in each large grouping of individuals—so that we can count on anger's flaring up in certain situations and concern ourselves merely with variations in the manner of its expression.[12]

Social and cognitive psychologists have modified the biological approach somewhat. One important result, bearing on the understanding of emotions in general, is a renewed effort at definition, with an emphasis on emotion as a mixture of subjective and objective factors. Thus anger is seen as a physical experience, mediated through the nervous and/or the hormonal system, that gives rise to feelings of displeasure or pleasure but that is also caused by and leads to general cognitive processes that appraise the experience; emotions in this sense lead both to physiological adjustments to the conditions that aroused response and to expressive and adaptive behavior.[13] Here, clearly, is an important link between the biological and the social, a recognition of both ingredients insofar as social standards will play a major role in guiding the cognitive element of emotion. The social/cognitive psychological approach has also produced useful recent reminders about the dearth of current research on the subject of anger; this, too, is grist for the mill of a researcher attempting a novel approach to the subject.[14]

But the substantive empirical contributions of even cognitively oriented psychological study of anger have been rather meager, at least to date. Many discussions seem trapped by a fascination with abstract definitions, bent on counting how many emotions there are, arguing about which are the most basic and which the result of socialization, or speculating on even more complex theories to refine distinctions between linked emotions such as fear and anger.[15] Other limitations result from the constraints of the laboratory setting. Researchers can demonstrate that exercise heightens an immediate disposition to anger rather than draining the emotion off; thus a winded jogger is more likely to take offense than a sedentary slob (unless, perhaps, the slob eats chocolates, which have been found to promote aggressive sentiments). This is surely an interesting finding, against long-standing popular wisdom that urges exercise as a means of draining off aggression. But it is also a limited finding, in that it says nothing about the longer-range effects of exercise on propensity to anger—effects, in other words, that inevitably escape the laboratory setting. Researchers can also demonstrate that male subjects who view pornographic films, compared with control-group males who watched a Disney cartoon, display an increased propensity to administer electric shocks to women in a laboratory setting. This may imply some larger effect of pornography on aggression, but it certainly does not prove such a linkage in the real world. [16]

More promising, perhaps, has been the approach of cognitive and constructivist psychologists and sociologists in emphasizing that emotion is mediated through intellect. For instance, Stanley Schachter attempted to show that the actual feelings people reported after receiving an injection of adrenaline and being exposed to highly charged emotional situations depended on their understanding of what the content and purpose of the injection had been. [17] James Averill argues that anger is felt in response to ''judgments regarding intentionality and justification . . . with respect to the behavior of the instigator.'' In other words, anger is based on an intellectual evaluation. [18] For a historian such approaches have the appeal of reminding one that man, though surely an animal, is a thinking animal and that this may make a big difference. Unfortunately, however, social scientists have not broadened the work of cognitive and constructivist psychologists to inquire empirically about how a general worldview or a set of sociocultural assumptions may moderate emotional responses to the immediate environment. The cognitive psychologists leave us adrift in a laboratory, not in the real world, and with little appreciation for the cultural determinants of emotion. The constructivists, and the growing group of sociologists interested in describing current social expression of emotion, do acknowledge a cultural context for emotion, but they have not yet produced any work that explains how this cultural context develops or how and why it changes. [19]

A second large approach to the study of anger has been the anthropological. [20] Here there is little question that anger is treated as a social variable, differing greatly between cultures or, for the sociologists of the first half of the twentieth century, between social classes. Much of the available anthropological literature deals with fairly primitive societies, though some work on child-rearing standards touches on Western Europe, India, and the United States. Some anthropologists, including those who obliquely comment on Western choler, turn the biological approach on its head and exaggerate the variability of the emotion. Thus the Utku Eskimo group, which socializes children from age two to avoid any expression of anger by means of shunning (rather than angrily reprimanding) any pugnacious behavior, has been put forth as evidence that careful upbringing can virtually expunge what might otherwise be regarded as a normal emotion.[21] In fact, the Utku do display angry behavior against animals—by Western standards, they cruelly mistreat dogs—and exhibit moroseness when confronted with annoyances from the outside world. Thus any picture of a society without anger must be qualified. Studies of this sort unquestionably prove extreme variations in expressions of anger; however, insofar as they confuse the targets and the expression of emotion with emotion per se, they do no more to resolve nature versus nurture controversies in this area than do biological studies.

The historian is naturally attracted to the anthropological approach because of its demonstration of the social role in guiding emotions. Yet the approach cannot be taken over completely, and not only because of some exaggerations about the role of environment. Most of the postwar anthropologists who have studied anger have focused on primitive cultures that may have little bearing on the emotional behavior of people in complex industrial societies. Many, indeed, used their studies to confirm stereotypes about American anger. Thus Jean Briggs, studying her Eskimo "people without anger," frequently contrasts her harmonious adoptive community with the wilder culture from which she stemmed. Americans are indeed more ambivalent about anger than the forty-odd members of the Utku group are, but a precise comparison would involve far more subtlety than this kind of anthropological mirroring permits. Furthermore, few anthropologists in this area have displayed a sensitivity to problems of causation or change. Their approach is largely static and descriptive: a cultural approach is a given. Yet the historian of anger must take the emotion as a (partial) cultural variable and apply it to emotional expressions over time. Emotions may, in certain circumstances, change slowly. It is fascinating to learn that, among modern peoples, Greeks are unusually unconcerned about anger when one recalls the celebrations of the sweetness of angry feelings in the Homeric epics.[22] Yet the American experience shows that anger values can change rapidly, if not completely, at least under pressure of such massive changes in environment as those brought by industrialization. Americans today, by the same cultural measurements that found Greeks anger tolerant, are unusually eager to conceal anger and unusually uncomfortable with its expression; this would not have been found in a comparable international comparison around 1750. Thus while welcoming the anthropologists' insistence on variation by culture, the student of American anger cannot accept its characteristic limitations.

A third, and widely accepted, approach to emotions has been fashioned by psychoanalysis. This approach posits a relationship between frustration in childhood and an angry personality in later life. Such a view has had wide appeal to historians, for it allows for a discussion of change over time. In theory at least, as child-rearing practices evolve over history, so will anger wax and wane. The difficulties with this approach are twofold. First, psychoanalysis has long confounded anger and aggression and has never been entirely clear on the meaning of aggression. Anger, an emotion, as opposed to aggression, one of many possible overt expressions of emotion, has never been carefully examined in its own right. Second, psychoanalysis has assumed a fixed relationship between frustration and aggression, and historians who accept this hypothesis have applied it as though it were proven fact. For the most part, they have neglected to use the opportunity to test that hypothesis against historical material. In fact, there has been a great deal of recent criticism of the frustration-aggression hypothesis, and some exploration of the possibility that other aspects of child rearing, for instance, education in language development, may be as important in socializing emotion as the factors considered by Freudians. Thus psychoanalysis may offer interesting hypotheses about anger, hypotheses to be tested, but it does not give historians fixed answers.[23]

So a history of American anger becomes essential, despite the novelty of identifying a specific emotion for historical study. A grasp of changing American attitudes to anger can, among other things, explain some of the limitations of other recent approaches. Anthropologists, as we have seen, have often been trapped by myths about American anger into quests for primitive alternatives, quests that are fascinating in themselves but misleading in their comparative implications. Many psychologists and sociologists, working after the shattering experience of World War II, have been misled into an easy equation of anger and aggression and thus have centered definitional and laboratory efforts on the biological bases of aggressive action rather than on the broader subject of the emotional experience of anger.

A history of anger does far more, however, than simply throw into perspective the assumptions of other researchers. An exploration of changes in anger, and the causes of these changes, in the American past promises three results. First, it offers new insight into the nature of past periods. Relations among neighbors in colonial New England differ from those prevailing in later periods, and the differences relate to changes in the expression of anger. Fifty years ago boxing gloves were standard equipment in the closets of middle-class American boys; they are no longer, and the change relates to alterations in the way boys are socialized to deal with anger. The point here is not simply to insist on important anger-related changes in culture and behavior as a means of grasping how different our ancestors were from us and, often, from their own ancestors. The historian must also shed light on why expressions of anger have changed and how these changes are connected, not only as cause but also as effect, to some of the larger shifts in America's past. Anger, then, can illuminate aspects of the historical past that have not been well considered.

The second product of a historical inquiry is a new understanding of contemporary American anger. Given the limitations of other approaches and the continued mythologizing about American anger, an approach that traces the present as a result of the past provides a much-needed clarification not only about why we are as we are but also about what we are in terms of anger. The point can be simply put. Many social psychologists and individual therapists know, as a result of their own experience or comparative study, that Americans are peculiarly restrained in their tolerance of anger. But they have not been able to disseminate their understanding widely because they lack the tools to place myth in its proper place and to see present conditions as a result of identifiable causes in the past.

Finally, given the incompleteness of existing approaches to anger, the historian can hope to improve the terms of discussion between those who focus on biological constants and those who deal with social variability when dealing with anger and other emotions. This is not a pledge that history, or at least this history, can finally determine the limits of heredity and environment. But the historian of anger must confront these limits to some extent, recognizing that anger is partly biological, involving changes in hormonal balance and the nervous system that evolutionarily served as a preparation for fight reactions, and also partly cognitive and therefore social, in that forms, perceptions, and, possibly, levels of anger vary considerably from one society to another and, we will show further, over time within a single society. Except, recently, at the abstract definitional level, those who emphasize biological constants have taken little heed of the demonstrations of social variation, while anthropologists in this area have given scant credit to any biological fundamentals. A history of anger allows some recasting of the terms of debate, as part of its clarification of why American anger is as it is.

The Historical Framework

The history of American anger flows in part from a number of recent advances in historical approach and method. For two decades social historians, particularly those dealing with the United States and Western Europe, have steadily advanced our understanding of the behaviors and outlooks of ordinary people and aspects of society in addition to the political, military, and formal-intellectual. Many social historians have been at pains to emphasize the rational and strictly measurable features of their subjects, holding popular protest, for example, to be a supremely calculated enterprise in which emotion was present by the merest accident. During the past decade, however, social historians have broadened their reach and become willing to undertake inquiries that pose inherent limits to precise measurement. Thus historians of the family have turned from concern with structure and demographic behavior to an interest in changing levels of affection. The result has been a considerable, if not always coherent, history of the development of romantic and parental love in the modern period—and, as we will see, some speculation on the effects of these emotional developments on levels of anger within the family.[24] Thus Randolph Trumbach, writing on the origins of a new stress on love in the British aristocracy, directly claims that "the quality of attachment dramatically improved in the eighteenth century, and among other things, decreased the level of aggressive violence.[25]

If the history of anger relates to an existing body of historical scholarship—and, among other things, responds to long-standing appeals by pioneer French social historians for serious inquiry into changes in emotional context[26]—it is nevertheless a novel undertaking and demands some clear guidelines. The first of these guidelines is chronological; the second, slightly more complex, is topical; and the third, by far the most complex, though linked to familiar historical problems of sources and evidence, is definitional.

The stages of the American discovery of anger as a problem and of subsequent attempts to limit the emotion are reasonably clear. (See Appendix A for a periodization). Colonial society showed few signs of concern about anger in itself, with a few notable exceptions; a similar nonconcern prevailed in Western Europe. This situation began to change toward the middle of the eighteenth century, when among other things shifts in vocabulary denoted an attempt to identify anger more clearly. This transition in turn produced the first modern period in the history of American anger, which lasted until the middle of the nineteenth century and which focused on an ideal of an anger-free family. This focus became closely associated with the new conditions of industrial life from about 1830 on; new anger standards formed a vital part of the attempt to use the family as a refuge.

The second modern period in the effort to reevaluate and limit anger opened toward the middle of the nineteenth century and extended for at least seven decades. The focus remained on familial control of anger, but ideas of socializing children became more elaborate and complex. It was this period, indeed, that produced the most distinctive American ambivalence about anger, which signaled among other things, that the attempt to harness anger was taking more widespread hold in actual, and not just idealized, national values.

From the 1920s, a third modern stage began to take shape that at once sought to extend anger-control efforts to wider spheres—beyond the family, into work—and redefined family values themselves. In child rearing, attempts to repress anger more fully paralleled efforts in the world of work, while in marriage, anger control goals were balanced by new needs to use the family for emotional release from restraints at work. This period in America's anger history continues to the present day.

The periodization of the American history of anger into a premodern and three modern periods is of course highly generalized. We will see some important fuzziness; school standards of anger control, for example, often lagged behind changes in child-rearing goals within the family. Certainly, the chronological divisions are not meant, at least at this stage of our knowledge, to suggest tight links to some of the more precise periods in American history. We do not aspire to a precision that would allow discussions of Jacksonian anger, Reconstruction anger, and so on. But the major periods do convey some linkages with major developments. The second modern period bore some relationship to the excitement of the Civil War and certainly helped set an emotional basis for aspects of Progressivism. More consistently, stages in the development of anger-control efforts related to the steady unfolding of American industrialization and its consequences for organizational and family behavior.

The history of American anger and the changes and continuities that relate its major periods unfold most vividly in several key settings. New anger norms first developed within the family and, from an initial emphasis on husband-wife relations, spread gradually to child-rearing standards. The family and child rearing, then, form a central focus for this study. But anger standards spread to other areas of activity as well—to schooling, almost inevitably, given the interest in training children, and then, particularly in the most recent modern period, to work. This extension, important in itself, also encouraged the development of new control mechanisms that reverberated back on the family. Once the central threads of the evolution of anger in family, child rearing, and work are clarified, we will suggest some connections to other aspects of behavior, such as social protest and politics, sports, and even consumer outlook.

This study does not, however, seek to identify anger as some free-floating theme to be addressed by a random selection of illustrations from every aspect of life. The progression from family through child rearing to work is its core. There is no attempt to link changes in anger to specific events such as behavior in wars—though the effort deserves to be made, as part of a fuller use of the history of emotions that will come with time—save as a few major wars helped set in motion changes in anger standards in family or work. At the same time, the history of anger is not an isolated subject in American's past, another in the parade of separate topics that social historians have unearthed in recent years. Changes in anger do connect to other developments, including political behaviors, both as causes of change in these areas and as effects. Several of the connections can already be suggested. Ultimately, an understanding of changes in anger and other emotions may be one of the central historical linkages between personal and public spheres; and the history of anger already suggests some of the ways that family values came to intrude on impersonal relationships and that bureaucratic control mechanisms came to intrude on family and friendship ties in turn. However, at this stage in the historiography of emotion, our effort is directed first and foremost to the personal sphere, that of the ordinary man and woman. We are directing the bulk of our attention toward the everyday experiences of common folk. By concentrating on family and the work world, we touch on the spheres in which most people spend the overwhelming portion of their hours, and we bear in mind Freud's suggestion that emotional health is defined as competence in the central areas of love and work.

Definition

Anger, though a vital ingredient in individual and social life, is inherently a somewhat elusive emotion. No group or society can encourage a fully free indulgence in anger, for no coherent social life could ensue from such indulgence. Thus social variations in anger, including changes over time, involve shifts in balance, not total reversals. Anger also has many gradations, from petty annoyance to magnificant wrath, yet it is difficult to deal with these gradations in any systematic way. Most important, anger is almost always at least partly repressed or concealed, unless some magic of temperament or upbringing manages to produce low levels of the emotion in the first place. As any good therapist will note, we are rarely fully aware of all our anger even today, in our own lives; much less can we presume completely to understand the manifestations of anger in other people, in other societies, or in the past. The problem of concealment or displacement of anger raises the final set of preliminaries essential to any inquiry, historical or otherwise, into the way anger actually works in society.

A firm theory about innate amounts of anger would, of course, allow a historian or a social scientist simply to look for evidence about how innate anger is expressed. A few historians, such as Christopher Lasch, do in fact posit, from a base in Freudian theory, set amounts of anger that must be worked through one way or another. Our judgement of existing theory does not permit such luxury, and indeed we intend a history as a contribution to better theoretical understanding of anger and its social-biological components. We certainly do not assume, as have some modern theorists who have tried to bypass anger by pretending that it is simply aggression, that the history of anger can be measured precisely from evidence of violence, scapegoating, or, through displacement, intense competitiveness. Even contemporary efforts to relate basic physical symptoms, such as high blood pressure, to definable emotional states have been fraught with difficulty, in part because the measurers are trapped by their own assumptions about emotion.[27]

Any society produces some, if only implicit, standards by which it seeks to evaluate and regulate emotions. American society has certainly produced abundant, though changing, evidence about how it views anger and other emotions, particularly in such central functions as family and work. But many social analysts have confused these standards or rules with actual emotional experience. Thus most historians dealing with love have rushed from changes in the formal conventions for romance, in the eighteenth century, to statements that actual married life became more loving. Some have even concluded that, before this time, husbands and wives rarely loved each other or that, in one dramatic phrase, family life contained about as much affect as one would expect to find in a bird's nest.[28] Anthropologists dealing with anger have often similarly confused standards with actual experience. We have seen that Jean Briggs translated undoubted antianger standards among the Utku Eskimos into oversimple claims that actual Utku life, after infancy, contained no anger. In making this sort of error, such analysts have ignored the contribution of biological psychologists and postulated an almost infinitely malleable human nature. By confusing standards for emotion with emotion itself, they have ignored the recurring human effort to grapple with conflicts between social demands and feeling. How different and simple the world would actually be if emotions changed as readily as the rules for expressing them did!

The following study seeks to avoid this confusion by introducing a basic distinction and a new term. We call the conventions and standards by which Americans evaluated anger, and the institutions they developed to reflect and encourage these standards, *emotionology*.[29] Emotionology is not the same thing as emotional experience. A society may organize courtship to discourage love, but that does not prove that love does not exist or even flourish. A family may discountenance anger, but there may be much anger in that family's operations.

The idea of norms that describe and to some extent regulate emotions such as anger is by no means novel. Societies use norms for legal purposes, in defining, for example, which emotions can be censored and which freely expressed in speech and writing. They use norms to organize personal reactions to other people's emotions and personal regulation and perception of one's own emotions. Recent sociological work has produced considerable new comment on these norms, which Arlie Hochschild has defined as "feeling rules." We use this newer term for much the same purpose, to emphasize the distinctions that must be made between norms—emotionology—and emotion, particularly given the neglect of this distinction in historical work to date. We wish also to avoid the blurring between even internalized emotional "rules" and unmediated biological reactions that still bedevils aspects of the perceptive sociological work of late, and we find the concept so essential as to require a convenient adjectival form despite the initial drawbacks of neologism.[30]

Emotionology is important in itself. It normally governs what people think they should be experiencing. It governs key institutions or practices, such as childhood training in boxing or personnel procedures on the job. Emotionology also produces relatively abundant sources of evidence, and in this study heavy reliance on marital advice articles and child-rearing manuals obviously yielded emotionological findings above all.[31] As a result of both the documentation and the importance of changing valuations of anger, each of our substantive chapters on the development of American anger control contains considerable, and clearly labeled, discussions of emotionology.

Yet we also, though carefully and as a partially discrete topic, discuss anger itself. And we argue that it, too, changes in American history, if not in total levels, at least in the manner and intensity of its expression in certain key settings such as the workplace. Actual emotions, surely, are less susceptible to change than is emotionology because they do include some constant biological factors and because they reflect conservatism in personal behavior—in the actual ways by which children are socialized, for example, as opposed to the ways parents wish they were behaving—from one generation to the next. In the long run, emotionology, by shaping articulate expectations, does influence actual emotional experience. A new emotionology about anger, created first in the eighteenth century, launched a long learning period for many Americans, during which the new values gradually began to affect some aspects of the actual experience of anger. By the later nineteenth century, at least, the experience of anger itself was beginning to show the effects of a century of emotionological emphasis on the importance of control. Analysis of the effect of emotionology on emotion forms one means of beginning to tackle the interaction between social values and biological basics, and this interaction can be sketched, if often cautiously, in the history of American anger.

Since we claim to discuss emotion as well as emotionology, it seems desirable to offer a definition, and yet it is harder to define *emotion* than *emotionology* since the field has been so fraught with controversy between those who emphasize either biological or cognitive aspects. A recent working definition, seeking to encompass all the ways in which *emotion* is used normally, defines it as "a complex set of interactions among subjective and objective factors, mediated by neural/hormonal systems, which a) give rise to affective experiences such as feelings of arousal, pleasure/displeasure b) generate cognitive processes . . . c) activate widespread physiological adjustments . . . d) lead to behavior."[32] We adopt this working definition. In our discussion of the emotion anger, as opposed to the emotionology, we will seek to consider all the aspects of emotion raised by the definition. Although as historicans we will have little to say about biology, which has not changed significantly in our brief time span, we will talk about the changing ways in which anger was expressed as behavior. We will also talk about changing cognitive frameworks for appraisal of anger. In fact, this may be the most interesting part of our work, for it is the nexus between emotion and emotionology. As Silvan Tomkins has pointed out, people have very strong feelings about their feelings.[33] In our consideration of emotion, we will demonstrate how a changing emotionology led people to change their emotional perceptions of their own emotions. Anger we refuse to define, in the abstract, except to say that it is an emotion, biologically related to a "fight" response and usually aroused in a situation judged as antagonistic. If we were to define anger further at this stage, we would run the risk of reifying as a fixed entity a response that we feel varies over time. Thus we hope that we may understand anger more clearly by seeing how its meaning has evolved than by pretending that it has existed, unchanging, throughout human history.

We also provisionally shun definitional refinements that subdivide anger not only into degrees, from annoyance to rage, but also into types, from instrumental, in which anger is used to gain an external end, to narcissistic, in which anger reacts to a slight to self. Some of these distinctions are too fine or too contemporary to be applied to a historical setting. Too much preliminary distinction risks further abstraction in a field that, in the behavioral sciences, has of late been unduly bent on definitional niceties. Anger expresses a biological core related to combativeness, but beyond this its use and degree vary immensely with context, and changing contexts are one of the key subjects of this history.

Discussion of the actual experience of anger raises one other analytical problem, one more familiar to students of history. Emotionology tends to be dominated by the values of certain key groups in a society—in American history, the middle class and, particularly, its northeastern Protestant spokespeople. Emotional values specific to social groups or regions do exist, and further inquiry into their relationship to the most commonly articulated American emotionology is certainly desirable. This study deals primarily with an emotionology produced by the Protestant middle classes, one widely preached to other groups but not necessarily so widely adopted. Ethnic variations, including anger reactions and suppressions in the black experience, and certainly variations in actual emotional experience are subjects that deserve further attention (even in a purely contemporary setting). Historians of love have often assumed that new values initially produced in the upper classes gradually trickled down, but they have not traced this process with particular clarity. The dominant emotionology of anger certainly bore on lower-class American experience, particularly in the twentieth century, when institutions designed to repress anger spread to the workplace. Evidence directly from non-middle-class groups, such as protest rates, suggests the impact that dominant anger values had on key aspects of behavior. But the problem of comprehending variant emotional experiences, particularly in behaviors more remote from public scrutiny, must be recognized. This study, focused first on emotionology and then on changes in the actual experience of anger particularly in middle-class groups, acknowledges the problem but does not claim to resolve it.

Yet, for all the caveats, what follows is a history of American anger in a number of key respects. Changes in the dominant emotionology do help explain class relationships in American society, particularly in the twentieth century.[34] In this sense an emotionology initially issuing from middle-class (rural as well as urban) concerns has taken on certain hegemonic qualities, with considerable though incomplete effect on the experience of other groups. In the middle class and, probably, beyond, emotionology has also increasingly shaped the experience of anger itself. It has altered the expression of anger, shifted the outlets through which anger is most commonly expressed, and, clearly, progressively generated rising anxiety about the emotion when it is expressed, in oneself or by others. We have feelings about feelings, and here emotionology conjoins with emotion. For the reactions to emotional experience, which in fact form part of this experience in providing a sense of pain or pleasure when the emotion is sensed, are shaped primarily by cognitive functions themselves conditioned by emotionology. The increasing pain that anger causes many Americans, through the nineteenth and twentieth centuries, becomes a central ingredient of a pervasive emotional context. Quite simply, as the emotionology of anger has demanded ever more rigorous suppression of the feeling and spread from personal relationships to more public spheres, the experience of anger itself has shifted, and the discomfort of the emotion, by no means entirely excised, has become steadily more obvious.

Seeing the pain of anger in ourselves, we fight the emotion still, misreading our own past in the process. In an era seemingly devoted to rebellions against nineteenth-century restrictions, vowing its devotion to emotional liberation and the importance of feelings, we continue, indeed enhance, a long battle against one of the basic emotions. It is high time that we begin to understand how we became involved in this campaign and what consequences it has had.

2 Background

When the Gods Were Angry

The modern history of anger begins in the seventeenth and eighteenth centuries. It took shape amid a tradition of relatively unspecific standards for the emotion and relatively frequent opportunities for angry expression that predominated in Western Europe and North America into the eighteenth century. Then, particularly in the second half of the eighteenth century, a new set of standards was clearly promulgated, signaled by, among other things, a more precise terminology. This in turn launched a campaign against anger that continues to characterize American life, a campaign necessary not only because of the many occasions for anger that modern life unquestionably affords but also because of contrasting ideas and experiences in the Western tradition.

The idea of a revolution in emotions that separates the modern from the premodern is a beguiling one. Although anger has not been studied extensively as a discrete historical subject, we would not be the first historians to claim that premodern American and West European life was filled with angry displays and acrimony while the rise of modern society produced increasing efforts to repress and divert the angry emotion. Precisely because this contrast has already been implied, particularly by historians bent on showing the rise of a loving and thus anger-free family, the traditional pole of the contrast needs to be stated with care.

Traditional emotionology toward anger did differ from the standards that began to emerge in the eighteenth century. The traditional standards were less precise and were targeted differently, with less emphasis on family relations, than their modern counterparts were. But the idea of an angry past from which modern attempts at repression emerged must be qualified in several respects.

First, we are far from knowing enough about any aspect of premodern emotional life, quite definitely including anger. What follows is based on existing secondary work, with a few exceptions (notably, the attempt to deal with changes in vocabulary); our own research relates to the nineteenth and twentieth centuries, the period that saw an attempt to extend and apply the modern emotionology of anger. Although historians concerned with emotion have done more with the early modern period than with any other, there is much still to be learned. Considerable confusion has resulted from an attempt to apply Freudian or Eriksonian theories mechanically or to assume that emotionology—for example, the absence of encouragements to romantic love or modern-style maternal affection—fully describes actual emotional experience. Historians who initially assumed sharp contrasts between premodern and modern emotional styles have recently been attacked by revisionists bent on showing that basic emotional experience does not change at all.[1] It is essential to find some middle ground between these two inaccuracies.

Premodern society manifested important concern about anger, and this is the second qualification to any traditional angry/modern loving contrast. No society can allow untrammeled anger, and Western communities in the seventeenth century manifested a number of attempts to control.

Wrath was one of the seven deadly sins. The New Testament offered advice on anger control that would be repeated in many a twentieth-century marriage manual: "Be ye angry and sin not; Let not the sun go down on your anger."[2] Invocations of humility, so common in character recommendations in Puritan New England, could imply anger control, though they were directed more explicitly against pride. Puritan divines may have increased their concern about anger in the seventeenth century, foreshadowing more general anxiety that developed a century later. John Robinson, in a widely noted passage, thus termed a wrathful man "a hideous monster": "If a wrathful man saw himselfe in glass when his fit was upon him, his eyes burning, his lips fumbling, his face pale, his teeth gnashing, his mouth foaming, and other parts of his body trembling, and shaking . . . he would, and worthly, loathe himself." Robinson urged restraint as part of the battle against Satan's evil and for the sake of harmonious human society: "Few . . . have proved sound or profitable members in societies, which have nourished in themselves that touchy humor." Even for Robinson, anger had its place, as the "strongest of all affections," when it "intends the driving away and dispelling of the evil, at and against which it riseth."[3] Man serving God could legitimately express righteous wrath, particularly of course against sinners or unbelievers. But in Robinson's thought, and in Christian thought generally, the overall stance was ambivalent and by no means thoroughly approving.

Anger was indeed, in the seventeenth-century Christian view, one of the evils that Satan could visit on humankind. Witches were sometimes identified by their own uncontrolled anger, and angry fits in others were one of the symptoms that provoked suspicion of witchly intervention. "Diabolical distemper," along with anxiety and depression, were unacceptable human passions often attributed to witches in New England.[4] Anger, in other words, could be a problem that had to be explained, its sources, if possible, rectified.

More generally, of course, premodern society included a variety of measures to minimize anger or its effect in human relations. Communities had the responsibility of supervising against excessive angry abuse of wives or children.[5] Various community mechanisms existed to try to reconcile angry disputes among neighbors without recourse to formal court trials. In no sense did anger run unrestrained in premodern society, not was it as uninhibited as in a few more blatantly angry societies that anthropologists have studied.[6]

Colonial American society may indeed have seen some attempts at anger control that were more vigorous than the standards of early modern Western Europe. John Demos has argued that the peculiar importance of the family in a strange land caused New Englanders to try to encourage familial affection and anger restraint; this was not a generalized reprobation of anger, for the emotion was more freely directed against neighbors, in part to provide outlets that would safeguard the family. American nervousness about the decivilizing potential of the frontier, plus a certain degree of democracy that entered into social relations in the New Land even before modern times, may also have caused greater attention to problems of restraining anger.[7] These were themes that would emerge much more clearly in a later age, feeding, for example, some peculiarly American distinctions between family and others in expressions of anger, but the possibility that they were prepared in the seventeenth century cannot be ignored.

Without question, a number of premodern anger themes would continue into modern times; anger history exhibits continuities as well as change. The ambivalence that John Robinson, or indeed Saint Thomas Aquinas, demonstrated toward anger—seeing it as bad but useful on occasion—set a framework that modern American responses would amplify. References to anger as diabolical crop up still in twentieth-century advice manuals, secular as well as Christian fundamentalist. The premodern impulse to see anger resulting from one of the bodily humors continues to influence the characteristic Western vocabulary used to describe an angry person, with veins swelled, face red, "exploding" with passion.[8] Concern about anger, its effects on individual and society, and the ways it can be designated are by no means simply modern inventions, and we continue to use some of the standards developed in traditional Western culture.

Premodern Emotionology toward Anger

Nevertheless, the seventeenth- and early eighteenth-century approach to anger differed from what came later; standards were less precise, concern about the emotion less great. Anger served key functions in premodern society. It reflected and enforced a social hierarchy, particularly in the relatively intimate contexts of neighborhood, family, or workshop. Anger also helped create personal space in a society that was rather intrusive. In most respects, premodern communities strike us by their cohesion and lack of privacy. But in tolerating significant anger, these same communities provided some balance and outlet. In this sense, the modern effort more rigorously to control emotion replaces (and perhaps surpasses) premodern efforts at social discipline. Finally, anger served a key function in regulating social relations in a society based heavily on concepts of honor and shame. Anger defended the integrity of individual and family, and it attacked unacceptable behavior and attitudes in others. Modern society, relying less on shaming and defense of honor and more on individual conscience and sense of guilt, might generate as much anger as its premodern counterpart, but it would express the emotion differently and, on the whole, less frankly and overtly.[9]

Traditional Western attitudes toward anger were shaped in part by considerable esteem for the emotion. Both classical and Teutonic mythologies stressed the angry behavior and low levels of frustration of key gods. Homer's *Iliad* described the positive pleasures of anger: "Sweeter wrath is by far than the honeycomb dripping with sweetener, and spreads through the hearts of men."[10] Classical figures might err in anger and might suffer when anger could not be fully expressed; but the emotion was not only acceptable but often desirable. Christianity modified this approach, as we have seen. It created a second godly image along with the often-angry Yahweh. As a religion it took a middle position on the subject of anger, between the absolute prohibitions of Buddhism and Confucian reasonableness and the considerable praise for anger in Islam. But the Jewish God and to a substantial extent the Christian, and particularly the Protestant, God the Father was angry, indignant over man's sin, an exemplar of righteous wrath. Jewish emphasis on God's anger at his chosen people carried over into the early Christian apocalyptic tradition and extended through the Middle Ages to the God of early Protestantism. Revealingly, after about the twelfth century, Catholic emphasis on humility in saints, particularly that sort of humility that would entail anger control, declined markedly; holiness and anger were often quite compatible.[11]

With this background, it is not surprising that seventeenth-century moralists did not identify anger as a normal human problem—if it cropped up as a problem in specific cases, this was because of humoral imbalance or the intervention of Satan's minions. Early moralists were more concerned with preventing the "excessive" violence that anger might provoke; husbands should not become "too" angry at their wives or masters at their servants.[12] This advice focused more on excesses in behavior than on emotional control per se. Anger was not high on the list of problems to which moralists attended in any event. Other concerns—purity of religious faith, even proper sexual behavior—loomed far larger. Wrath was one of the sins least noted in advice on character or family behavior, falling well below pride as well as lust. Western people before the eighteenth century were not particularly conscious of emotions, among other things lacking a vocabulary to discuss emotional experience articulately.[13] As a result, emotional ills most commonly occurred as a vague melancholia, the kind of generalized malaise that in twentieth-century Western society occurs most often among the less well educated. And while this lack of attention to emotions began to change in the more individualistic seventeenth century, leading to greater sophistication about feelings and, ultimately, to the application of ethical concepts to emotional experience and inner control,[14] the results, save in the writings of individual moralists such as John Robinson, were not quickly applied to anger.

Premodern Western society did not, in sum, produce the clear codes of anger control developed in many Asian agricultural societies. The emotionology remained vague as well as ambivalent. Children were not, as a result, schooled directly in identifying and restraining their anger. Emphasis rested on obedience rather than emotional control. Both in theory, through Christian exhortations to obedience, and in practice, parents in seventeenth-century West European society and colonial American society attempted to subordinate their children's will to their own. Methods included physical punishment and frequent denial of gratification. Thus Henry IV of France frequently took toys away from his son, the future Louis XIII, as well as exacting daily whippings. In this case, childish rage was matched by parental wrath, so that a father could easily believe that the punishment he had received as a boy was good for his son. Successful will breaking did prevent the expression of anger against parents, but it did not explicitly teach that anger itself was wrong. A childish tantrum, as we would call it, was met by parental discipline, sometimes angry discipline; if a child became more enraged, he was punished further, with insistence on apologies for disobedient behavior. This taught that anger should find outlets other than attacks on family superiors (and, by extension in many cases, social superiors), but it did not teach general emotional control.[15]

The simple fact was that traditional Western society lacked the mechanisms and even the vocabulary to socialize children against anger in any general way. A certain amount of anger was expected in children, part of their animal-like, obstinate natures; there was no need for comment when anger cropped up unless it proved truly unusual and so roused suspicions of devilish intervention. And certainly there was no need to comment on parental control over their own anger, save when it led to behavioral excess; advice literature mentioned few parental obligations beyond the instilling of piety and proper faith.[16]

Some historians have read the premodern record to argue that characteristic child-rearing methods actually provoked unusual anger. Some of the clashes described in will breaking may indeed have had that effect. But many parents provided affection as well as angry discipline. Not all children produced tantrums that required will breaking of the most active sort in any event. Some children learned a distaste for angry discipline precisely because occasional experience of parental anger was so unusual and shocking, though it is fair to note that the resultant views were also unusual for the time.[17] It is vital, in this complex area, not to assume greater uniformity of behavior and reaction than we assume today, not to ignore variations in the moods of parents and children alike, and not to neglect signs of affectionate bonding that did exist even if expressed in a somewhat different vocabulary from that produced by modern emotionology. It is vital, also, not to be trapped by rigid Freudian or Eriksonian models. Will-breaking methods, where they involved fairly consistent discipline, did not necessarily provoke unusual anger in children.[18] Finally, to the extent that parental behavior did inspire anger—perhaps more anger than contemporary parenting inspires, though again there is no real proof of this claim—its expression was controlled through the instillation of obedience. The point is not that premodern society generated hideously angry children, for it had its own varieties of style and most assuredly its own methods of social control, but that it did not effectuate control through focus on anger directly. Anger's results might matter if they entailed disobedience or undue violence; anger itself did not. Here was concrete expression of the vagueness of premodern emotionology in child rearing.

This meant, in turn, that outside the hierarchical relations within which the control of obedience was meant to operate, there were no real standards for anger restraint. The distinction between anger control and obedience might seem far too precious were it not for the fact that there were abundant signs of relatively uninhibited expression of anger in seventeenth- and eighteenth-century life, the fruit of an emotionology that prescribed scant explicit reproof.

Premodern Anger: Emotional Symptoms

Behavioral evidence of anger abounded in the premodern world. Western society was long rather violent. It had, by modern standards, a high murder rate. Indeed, our modern concern about murder—which makes the fact of higher rates in the close-knit societies of our past so surprising—reflects less the actual incidence of the crime (though this exhibits interesting and sometimes troubling fluctuations) than our heightened sensitivity to what can be an ultimate act of rage. Westerners long preached the virtues of revenge, in response to many crimes; anger, in other words, could answer anger. Renaissance efforts to replace revenge with more state control of response to crimes largely failed. Anger at offenses to personal or family honor was ritualized in the practice of dueling, which survived into the nineteenth century. Pockets of Western society that preserved the older notions of honor into modern times, such as the American South or the German aristocracy, continued to value the angry response to affront.[19] The street life of many preindustrial cities included frequent quarrels and loud arguments, not only social superiors (or their servants as surrogates)[20] belaboring hapless lowlifes, but also conflicts between shopkeepers and wealthy patrons. Recreations in Western society, at the popular as well as at the elite level, were often violent, which might suggest the need for outlets for unusual anger or a willingness to sanction relatively direct expressions of aggressive impulses. Rural festivals, for example, allowed youths to let off steam by minor acts of vandalism or by angry charivaries directed at wayward adult members of the community. Here, too, traditions would continue into the nineteenth century, as in the angry brawling recently examined in the American South.[21] More broadly, Western traditions of popular protest supported periodic expressions of moral indignation, which demonstrated among other things a belief that certain forms of anger were socially legitimate.

Community restraint of anger, like child rearing, focused on diverting behavior rather than attacking the emotion itself. Efforts to limit violence thus encouraged a tradition of angry verbal assault. Many peasant communities of Western Europe produced an array of nicknames and traditional curses that modern people have largely abandoned because of a more rigorous set of emotional controls. Few latter-day ethnic slurs, often slightly embarrassed, can rival the richness of traditional outlets: ''May a donkey copulate with you!'' ''May a donkey copulate with your wife!'' ''May your child copulate with your wife!''[22] Use of angry insult in societies conditioned to the defense of honor and discipline through shame was not confined to the Mediterranean peasantry or the American south. It reverberated also in Puritan New England, among neighbors and strangers alike, filling courts with trials for slander. "I shall make a fool of you before I have done with you." "She said . . . that the teacher [minister] was fitter to be a lady's chambermaid than to be in the pulpit." "He said he would humble him, for he had always been a pimping knave to him." "He said that his dog's tail would make as good a church member as she." "He challenged us [to get] off our horses to try our manhood, and said that he would take me by the eyelids and make my heels strike fire against the element."[23]

Anger against outsiders poured even more freely. Westerners had long indulged a righteous wrath against foreign or religious opponents and had scared their children with tales of evil strangers. Religious and ideological turmoil raised this use of anger to a high level in the sixteenth and seventeenth centuries. Protestants easily abused Catholics and other Protestant sects, and of course witches and other deviants drew the wrath of the just.[24] Ritual attacks on outsiders and sources of evil expressed the freedom of premodern anger while helping to channel some of it. Contemporary Americans, of course, also allow themselves anger against political or religious enemies, such as Communists or right-to-lifers, but there is a difference of style. Where the premodern man prided himself on his angry crusade, viewing tolerance as a dangerous error, we, even in our crusades, are more likely to find the zealot an embarrassment to our cause and to admire some restraint and moderation. In other words, in the premodern world anger at an enemy was by modern standards peculiarly self-righteous and unembarrassed; intensity was not as troublesome as it has become, even in a just cause, in modern times.

Symptoms of violence, political anger, and even angry insult are of course highly generalized, their precise emotional bases hard to pinpoint. More relevant to our purposes are signs of personal anger and displays in family and at work. Public temper tantrums, along with frequent weeping and boisterous joy, were far more common in premodern society than they were to become in the nineteenth and twentieth centuries. Adults were in many ways, by modern standards, childlike in their indulgence in temper, which is one reason that they so readily played games with children. Modern anger standards, by contrast, involve increasing separation between child and adult emotional worlds.[25] Revealingly, accounts of mental disturbance in the seventeenth century, though they display a rich array of problems, including frequent frustrations in romantic love, do not cite anger as an issue even in excess. This omission is consistent with the frequent expressions of anger freely accepted. Anger was too normal, too anticipated to be seen as a problem.[26]

Many historians have commented on the contentious, often litigious tone of many personal relationships in premodern society.[27] Angry dispute over property was one common theme, dividing neighbors and sometimes family members and demonstrating the use of anger to create space in a tight community. While abundant property relieved certain strains in seventeenth-century America (less in the eighteenth century), anger in property defense remained common. Quarrels among neighbors became virtually endemic in New England, and while authorities worried about the social and legal implications, they did not voice explicit disapproval of the anger involved. In Plymouth, Massachusetts, for example, Peter Pitts encountered an incensed property owner when he tried to drive his oxen through a field not his own; the owner threatened to strike Pitts down with a pitchfork "although he should be hanged for it."[28] There was no one to say that this kind of reaction was anything but emotionally natural.[29]

Anger within the family was common. This is not to argue that it was more common than it is today, though there are some reasons to believe this may be so; but it was more open, more likely to be public, less likely to be followed by anguished guilt. Hierarchy was a key to familial use of anger. We have already noted that child-rearing styles permitted rather free expression of anger against children, though this was by no means invariable. Angry outbursts by husbands against wives have been noted by a number of students of the premodern European family.[30] Another interesting case involves the frequent hostility between adults and their own older parents, when these were finally in decline and no longer able to enforce obedience. Here, standards of veneration were not adequate in the absence of more generalized constraints against anger. Disputes over property frequently prompted anger between generations, and in some cases a long-concealed rage generated initially by will breaking may have played a role as well. One result was a pervasive need, among the elderly, to defend themselves contractually against angry dealings by their offspring.[31] Another result was frequent comment on the querulousness of older people themselves. A final result was a good bit of outright anger. A Virginia son quarreled with his father, in 1766, initially over the old man's indulgence in tea, which the son found wasteful. "He said abundance more and I replied tauntingly," the old man noted in his diary, admitting that both might be "unhappy in temper." Fights continued for years, prompting the father later to write, "Surely it is happy our laws prevent parricide, or the devil that moves to this treatment, would move to put his father out of the way. Good God! That such a monster is descended from my loins."[32] This kind of dispute, driving many children out of the house until their parents' death and fostering no little outright violence, is one case of an open familial anger that, though by no means the rule, was more common in premodern society than it was to become in more modern times when, among other things, new views of familial anger would constrain it.

Anger at work was also common. Here, as with families, the crucial point is that there were no explicit reproving standards; there is no evidence that anger actually felt at work was more or less common than it was to become in modern times. Outright disputes were frequent enough, despite legal and practical barriers. Reports of recurrently angry employers were legion in accounts of personal service and apprenticeship. Precisely because premodern work was so often an extension of household and involved a highly personal hierarchy between master and subordinate, whim and personal temper predominated. As in family relations, advice and law—most obviously embodied in apprenticeship contracts—sought to prevent unusual abuse, not what was seen as normal emotion.[33] As in families also, affection and acquaintance might cushion emotional relations at work, making them warmer than they were to become in the industrial setting.[34] But there was no general standard to inhibit the abrasive artisan master (joined often by his equally demanding wife) or to make any of the parties involved find an angry emotional context unusual. Benjamin Franklin as an apprentice, as noted earlier, certainly knew that his brother's emotional style was unpleasant, and he had the means to escape, but he had no basis for finding curses and beatings particularly out of the ordinary.[35] Luck of the draw, not clear standards of anger restraint, governed the preindustrial workplace. The insistence of obedience by subordinates, an extension of earlier child-rearing experience, might reduce occasions for outright confrontation, but they could also facilitate indulgence in anger by those in charge.

Thus the impression deepens of a society in which anger was not specifically reproved save when its expression contravened hierarchy, a society, then, in which control of anger was not highly valued for its own sake and in which public expression of the emotion was relatively common. It is not necessary to claim the unprovable, that there was more anger in this society than in more modern times; it is clear that it was more open than it would later become, perhaps particularly among neighbors, in certain family relationships, and in work hierarchies. In the vigorous insults and frequent brawling there is even a hint of a Homeric enjoyment of anger and that would be lost in later centuries. Certainly the idea of anger restraint as an obligation of civilized behavior, or a responsibility of social superiors as well as inferiors in the Confucian mode, had not yet taken hold. Even animals played a role in the indulgence of anger, as kicks at dogs and cats might express an emotion whose arousal triggered no particular warning signals save care in selecting targets. Anger, then, played a considerable role in what Johann Huizinga termed the "general facility of emotions" in premodern Western society.[36]

The Eighteenth-Century Transition: A New View of Anger

During the eighteenth century in Western society, a new emotionology took shape that attacked the vagueness of earlier anger standards. Anger began to be seen as a growing problem, and not only in demonically inspired others but in oneself, both in Western Europe and in North America. Attention focused particularly on controlling anger within the family, but it was assumed that the newly articulated civilized standards of anger restraint would become part of good character and so carry over into relations with others.

Diary evidence suggests that more and more eighteenth-century Americans committed themselves to a lifelong goal of restraining angry passions. Thus Jonathan Edwards resolved, as a young man: "When I am most conscious of provocations of ill-nature and anger, then I will strive most to feel and act good-naturedly." Or Hannah Heaton: "Ah I am ashamed to write what I said in anger, I am ashamed to have it brought into judgment at the great day."[37] These sentiments were not of course unprecedented, but their clear and frequent articulation was novel, flowing from a new emotionology that reproved anger in vigorous and sweeping terms. Diaries in the nineteenth century would build abundantly on the sense that anger must be struggled with and conquered.

More generally, eighteenth-century writings on the family evinced a new belief that anger was inappropriate in the domestic context. A new valuation of love for spouse and children carried with it the belief that anger must be controlled. Here was a central theme in what became the modern campaign to reduce anger in family life; the idea that love and anger cannot mix is not perhaps inevitable, though it has become so deeply ingrained in the Western mentality that its logic may seem unassailable. It was in the eighteenth century, building on some seventeenth-century precedents, that this thinking clearly took shape, Husbands and wives were urged to be affectionate with one another, and anger was seen as an intruder into this domestic harmony. Parents began to be concerned about their anger in dealing with children, as children became increasingly viewed as objects for loving tenderness. It is on the basis of the new ideals of romantic love in courtship and loving attachment between parents and children that some historians have claimed an unprecedented decline in familial hostilities, ultimately extending to more sentimental relations between adults and their older parents as well.[38] We need not go so far at this point, for the actual emotional content of eighteenth-century family life has not yet been thoroughly probed. What it clear is that the ideals shifted, producing the first statement of what became the modern emotionology of anger. With new ideals, the imagery of key family members shifted as well: babies began to evolve from greedy beasts into cuddly creatures against whom anger could not be legitimately directed; emphasis on the cantankerousness and avarice of the elderly began to yield to the rosy-cheeked warmth of the stereotypical modern grandparent.

A final sign of the new emotionology toward anger beginning to take shape in the eighteenth-century is in many ways the most interesting because it reflects an attempt to refine the cognitive approach to the emotion as well as to reprove it more explicitly that, in so doing, set the basis for further attempts to limit anger in the future. Quite simply, vocabulary began to change. A new word came into being, at the end of the eighteenth century, to designate and reprove bursts of anger. First in England, then at least by the early 1800s in the United States, "tantrums" entered the dialect. The word was initially used, always in the plural, to criticize adult outbursts and then in the nineteenth century evolved toward its present usage, marking a troubling phenomenon of childhood, one that had not needed a name before, and by extension an unacceptably childish display of emotion in later life. The word has no clear origin and was not picked up by dictionaries until after 1900. It may have derived from *tarantella,* the frenzied dance, or from a Welsh corruption of the word *anthem,* which was how it once appeared, fleetingly, in the seventeenth century. Use of *tantrum* in its present meaning dates to the decade after 1748, when it denoted scorn for anger in several British plays: "None of your fleers! Your tantrums! You are grown too headstrong and robust for me!" "Treating him with some contempt when he is in his tantrums." By the 1800s the word appears in Scottish, Welsh, and Irish as well as American usage. Darwinians used the word by the 1860s. But the main point is the timing of the neologism itself: a word was needed to increase precision in a new area of concern and to convey disapproval. It was during the later eighteenth century also that the word *temper* began to have unfavorable connotations, so that we now need the word *temperament* to describe the emotional pattern that the shorter word once designated.[39]

With new words or old, family manuals began to include specific injunctions against anger, as part of the larger emphasis on affection and on the mutuality of obligations among family members. Of course children still owed obedience to their parents, but parents also owed restraint. Likewise masters should guard their tempers with their servants and husbands with their wives.[40]

The transformation in the emotionology of anger had some limitations of course. It was focused heavily on family and household. Wider canons of civility did not change so sharply. There was no attempt specifically to discuss new emotional standards for work or politics, though without question the people most deeply concerned about anger tried to monitor its expression in any context. Lawrence Stone has argued for England that Romanticism's encouragement of emotional expression legitimized public outbursts of anger in the early nineteenth century. Southern culture, including a more indulgent child-rearing style at least in the upper classes, continued to cherish hot-tempered women and quick flashes of anger in men, particularly in defense of honor or authority.[41] Public-private and regional distinctions in anger control would continue well beyond the eighteenth century.

Even those concerned about anger were divided in approach. Philip Greven has described two key styles in New England and the Middle Atlantic colonies. Evangelical families attempted the difficult combination of will breaking and compassionate tenderness in dealing with children. They sought to deny anger, but undoubtedly provoked it in their charges; the resultant anxiety could be legitimately if unwittingly released more readily by passionate attacks on religious or political opponents. More moderate Protestants, such as moderate Quakers in the middle colonies, worried about anger with still greater thoroughness, for they forbade themselves even the luxury of wrath against evildoers. But their child-rearing style was more consistently restrained, and they may not have generated as much concealed anger through socialization.[42] Both evangelicals and moderates had broken with tradition; both groups thought more in terms of affection and of control of angry passions. But their approaches and results differed significantly. These differences would endure in American society. Even in the twentieth century, mainstream Protestants preached an ethic of moderate control: "It takes a truly big man to hold his tongue and master his temper when under severe provocation."[43] "We do not destroy our emotions. . . . But we must also not be carried away by them."[44] This mainstream tradition, in other words, saw anger control as imperfectly feasible, if highly desirable, and a lifelong process. The evangelical tradition, in contrast, continued to hold anger as a sin that would be and should be prevented completely in a Christian life; anger became part of an angry, sometimes guilt-ridden campaign, which could produce considerable anxiety: "Anger comes from within, and must be dispelled."[45] And the attack on anger can produce angry attack on surrounding evils, including the more easy going mainstream Protestants—a displacement effect similar to the evangelical patterns of the eighteenth century.

Even with its divisions, the anger-control effort constituted an important shift in emotional values, a new effort at emotional restraint. We cannot say with any certainty how widely this reevaluation spread, in any of its forms, before the nineteenth century. The emotional transformations of the eighteenth century, not only anger control but also the new quest for romantic love, seem clearest in the upper classes, who of course leave the most abundant records of their feelings. But there were some signs of emotional change among lower-class people as well, including a new search for sexual pleasure, and some generalized changes in child rearing such as the abandonment of swaddling in Western Europe. The new emotionology of anger, particularly in its moderate and ultimately mainstream version, was most widely preached by elements of the middle class, but even before 1800 it may have had some wider ramifications.

The potential scope of the emotionological transformation is revealed by one other eighteenth-century change: a new attitude toward animals. No longer were animals seen as such clear inferiors that they could legitimately be treated simply as servants to man's use or abuse. Animals were progressively removed—in the judgment of right-thinking people—as targets for human anger, a most unusual cultural development and one that severely constrained emotional expression in Western society from this point on. New laws and the formation of anticruelty societies in the early nineteenth century would carry this effort forward, with some gradual if incomplete effect on actual behavior. In this area as in others, the new emotionology began to create a new context for actual emotional experience.[46]

Did emotional experience itself change as early as the eighteenth century? Most claims by historians to date have focused more on new standards than on new experience, though Philip Greven, going beyond emotionology, has seen a real limitation of anger in the family lives and relations with outsiders of the moderate Protestant group. It is certainly possible to imagine that a revision of standards would not immediately take hold in actual experience, and indeed diary comments on the need for vigilance and struggle may suggest an initial reaction to change that nineteenth-century commentators, more accustomed to the standards, would downplay through assumptions that anger was essentially unnatural. But even in the eighteenth century the new emotionology was linked to the beginnings of new child-rearing practices that had important implications for the perception of anger and perhaps for its experience as well. Will breaking and physical discipline began to decline, and efforts to instill conscience and guilt began to replace the use of shame to reprove inappropriate child behavior. These changes involved greater parental efforts to supervise their children's emotional reactions and to restrain their own overt anger in discipline. The result may have been no less anger than before, at least on the part of children, but an anger more difficult to express even when not constrained by require-ments of obedience. Here is a theme of vital importance in dealing with the elaboration of the new emotionology and its ongoing effect in the nineteenth century.

Causes of the New Emotionology

The generation of tight standards of anger control was a major step in forming the criteria for the modern American personality. The novelty of the standards must again be stressed, for this was merely the first stage in what turned out to be a long and varied campaign. Well into the nineteenth century—and even in the twentieth, when the new emo-tionology was applied to work institutions as well as to family—the proponents of the modern emotionology displayed an acute sense that they were battling older standards, trying to free themselves and others from the hold of tradition.

A variety of factors fed the initial, eighteenth-century emotionologi-cal transformation. New emphases in religion and secular philosophy conjoined with new economic forms, including the strains of interact-ing with growing numbers of strangers in a context of rapidly rising levels of population.

At a basic ideological level, growing literacy may have played a role in shaping new emotional standards. Walter Ong sees oral societies as verbally aggressive, in part because of the many disasters that can af-flict people in an agricultural economy and in part because of the in-tense personal contacts needed for oral transmission. Literacy, gaining ground rapidly in the eighteenth century, produces a new sense of and desire for control, including a new interest in controlling anger and a new vocabulary to put this interest into effect.[47]

The new emotionology took shape amid rapid population growth and extensive migrations of people in Western Europe and North America. In a large sense, more rigorous rules of civility may have become necessary in the West to avoid unacceptable frictions among growing agglomerations of people, many of whom were strangers to each other. In this manner Western society began to catch up to the need for emotional rules that more populous Asian cultures had long before developed.

Without question, the disruption of many established patterns of au-thority called traditions of anger into question. Protestant views on the spiritual equality of women began to dent patriarchy. Servants, particu-larly male servants, began by the eighteenth century to display a new taste for dignity and independence. Anger control from the eighteenth century to the present day has been closely associated with shifts in social and political hierarchies and with uncertainties about the automatic legitimacy of established authority.

New religious and philosophical ideas played the most direct role in shaping the new concern about anger, and they focused some of the more general factors. By the seventeenth century Puritan writers were emphasizing the importance of affectionate family ties; some new currents in Catholicism worked to the same effect from 1700 on.[48] This revision of the religious view of the family helps explain the preeminently familial focus of the new emotionology; its stress on more equal as well as more affectionate relationships helps account for the effort to reduce familial anger. Supplementing this new religious impulse were the ideas of the Enlightenment: man is rational and therefore capable of emotional control; men are in principle equal, so anger against others should be restrained; humanitarian men should attack cruelty no matter how remote, and this attack might involve concern for angry emotions that motivated or expressed man's inhumanity to man (and animal).[49] A reaction to the religious wars of the seventeenth century, and in England, more particularly, to the religiously influenced civil wars, led to new notions that stressed the value of tolerance over zeal and poked fun at those too easily angered. The eighteenth century developed a new interest in taste, style, and aesthetics as opposed to simple moralism. It was not quite well bred to be enthusiastic, and anger was a most unattractive form of enthusiasm. Although these notions were certainly not those of Puritan Americans, they were influential in other parts of the colonies and, no doubt, by the eighteenth century had some general moderating effect even on Puritan ideas.[50]

Along with new ideas, new economic relationships prompted a redefinition of emotionology. Sheer (if uneven and relative) prosperity helped produce larger and more comfortable homes, and with this a reduction in household tension and competition for space, as well as a new desire to see the home as a blissful haven.[51] The new emphasis on household amenities had no inherent emotional overtones; but when families began to expect to share mealtime conversation and other civilities, they might strive to reduce bickering in their ranks. The rise of market relationships placed growing numbers of producers in interaction with strangers. This certainly spurred the attempt to improve familial bonds, as a refuge from competitive pressures. It may also have encouraged an attempt to reduce anger even in contacts outside the family, at least selectively: the growing legion of shopkeepers or of artisans newly competing for public patronage may have groped for the smiling personality that their capitalist descendants would attempt to inculcate more systematically. Along with the larger modifications of authority patterns and the new stress on family intensity, the new economic goals may have helped produce the sense that will breaking was no longer sufficient as a means of handling anger; a wider array of methods, greater subtlety, and more ongoing concern were essential.

Finally, one cannot ignore the often-debated question of the relationship between the growth of capitalism and the development of a new personality style. Whatever the cause, certainly most students of the subject have seen an association between investment capitalism, with its need to defer gratification, and the development of a modern personality that emphasizes impulse control and introspection. In the context of this aspect of modernization theory, then, anger control can be seen as a significant aspect of the development of the modern personality.[52]

Historians interested in the rise of love have legitimately emphasized the achievements of the emotionology generated during the eighteenth century. A new family style had been clearly delineated, and while it might have its drawbacks, its values are at least recognizably modern. Some other elements of the new emotionology of anger have also proved surprisingly durable. The major Protestant denominations, for example, maintained a high level of attention to the evils of anger and the need for control, in sermons and pamphlets throughout the nineteenth and twentieth centuries. Strategies changed slightly in the twentieth century, with the advent of formal training in pastoral counseling and the recognition that some anger was unavoidable, but the goals of anger control and a hope for loving charity were not significantly altered. Simultaneously, the concept of an angry or punitive God receded, another consequence of the new emotionology that has endured in mainstream Protestantism.[53]

But these persistent elements in the cultural environment do not describe a whole popular culture, even aside from America's religious divisions. The eighteenth century launched a new set of values toward anger; it did not spell them out fully. Hence it is probably best to see the century more as an emotionological revolution begun than as a revolution completed.

Certainly, the new anxiety about anger had just commenced its modern career. Traditional approaches to anger would easily persist through the nineteenth century, as we shall see. Much nineteenth-century advice literature, in fact, constitutes a long campaign to defeat persistent if increasingly outdated habits. Part of the larger tension in the American approach to anger must be seen as a durable process in which habits of anger visible in the seventeenth century jostle against the new values. Religious and social class divisions, apparent during the eighteenth-century transformation, would also produce persistent targets for the new campaign.

The campaign against anger would not of course be static. New values of Victorian and then of twentieth-century American society would alter its shape; the campaign would become progressively secularized, among other things. New conditions, particularly those generated by the Industrial Revolution, would alter its specifics, particularly calling into question the familial focus of anger restraint.

The idea of a long campaign, rather than some dramatic revolution, also usefully draws attention to the problems of the effect of the new values. The new approach toward anger was shaped by a variety of basic forces concerning religion and ideology, political authority, and economic life. It was not yet clear, in 1800, what results the new ideas about anger would have, in turn, in further shaping modern social forms and modern personalities. It remained, in other words, to translate the new concern about anger into the various social relationships that defined American life.

3 The Early Victorian Synthesis
Domestic Idealism

The long campaign to control anger, launched in the eighteenth century, grew to the proportions of a steady war in the Victorian era. It was not so much that the content of the message changed but rather that the degree of concern grew and that the emotional thrust behind that concern took on new tones.

Our detailed discussion of the campaign against anger in the Victorian family begins in the 1830s and 1840s and coincides with the burgeoning of a popular literature of family advice both in books and in periodicals.[1] It may be objected, certainly, that the degree of concern with domesticity had not changed and that the newness of this "cult" was really an artifact generated by the new assiduity of the press in dealing with an old subject. There is no way to counter such an objection definitively, but we would argue that the rise in the marketability of the ladies' magazines and family advice books surely spoke to a felt need of the readership, and if we cannot prove that the need was absent before, it certainly seems likely that it was less intense. At any rate, it is clear that the particular domestic matter that is of concern to us, the control of anger, was an issue earlier, as the introduction of such new terms as *tantrum* demonstrated. We now turn to the form this issue took as increasing numbers of middle-class families sought advice books or had such materials thrust on them in the popular magazines.

But there is another reason, aside from the proliferation of publications, for postulating a distinct early Victorian approach to family anger. The desire to encourage affection and to lessen anger within the family unit dates back certainly to Puritan reformers, but as that notion appeared to the Puritans and through much of the eighteenth century, the family was seen as a microcosm of a larger society. The growth of affection at home would nurture people who could use the same personality attributes in the larger society. Gentility was a desirable trait in all interpersonal relationships, not just those at home.

The literature of the cult of domesticity reveals a marked change in its view of the family's place in the world.[2] For the family, to the Victorians, was not so much a microcosm as it was an island of safety.

Between the lines of their paeans of praise to castle home we may read clearly of their distaste and fear of the changing world outside. With the rise of new market conditions and factory industry, home was less an exemplar than a sanctuary or, as Christopher Lasch has so aptly called it, "a haven in a heartless world." The Victorian consensus on anger in the home, then, follows from the desire expressed in the earlier century to muffle that emotion, but the reasons for concern, the intensity of concern, and the recommendations that ensued were characteristic of their specific era. Anger control became more specifically familial and vital if this cherished haven was to be preserved.

The concern that resulted from pondering the place of the family in a new kind of world is a thread running through marriage and family advice literature in America from the 1830s on. Themes that emerge as part of early Victorian family idealism, such as the anxious insistence on parental self-control, echo through later periods to our own day, as we will see in subsequent chapters, and spilled over from the family to the workplace in a more generalized insistence on repressing anger. In a new kind of world, a world in which home and work were for the first time clearly separate, how could a human being be developed who could successfully navigate both spheres? We suggest that one of the reasons that the Victorians and we, their successors, became so introspective, so concerned with feelings, is that they were, as we still are, searching anxiously for solutions to new emotional problems generated by the home/work dichotomy. Our specific concern, anger, is of interest in itself, to be sure, but we also argue that, in looking at the ways the Victorians dealt with that emotion, we can offer a new insight into their reactions to their entire experience and that this experience, generated by the central problem of the home/work dichotomy, has much in common with our own.

Emotionology

Victorian emotionology on anger in the family was unequivocal and insistent, even if its results, in terms of actual emotional experience, were less clear-cut. We will examine emotionology regarding marriage before turning to child rearing, for marriage was the first institution to attract the explicit attention of Victorians concerned with anger control. Standards here were clearer than in child rearing, in which greater variety prevailed, depending on religious persuasion, and in which attacks on old-fashioned authoritarian methods suggest a lingering debate in practice. The anger-control literature addressed to parents and children was, until about 1860, largely derivative of that addressed to husband and wife, and not surprisingly so. For it was the husband whose job it was to mediate between the dichotomous worlds of home and work, and it was in their discussion of how he would relate to his wife and to his home that the Victorians played out the tensions they felt about those two worlds. When later in this chapter we turn our attention to the child-rearing advice, we shall see that there too, although the explicit concern was to curb childhood anger, the implicit and perhaps more intensely felt goal was to state, again, a discomfort felt with the home/work tension.

As we will discuss in detail later, the child-rearing and marriage literatures began to depart from one another on the issue of anger control after about 1860. Thus what we describe as a Victorian synthesis really was relatively short-lived for child rearing, from about 1830 to 1860, and yet remained the mainstream in terms of thinking about anger in marriage until about 1900. The reasons for the change in attitudes toward children will be explored in our next chapter, as will the reasons for the persistence of Victorian emotionology for marriage. Suffice it for now to suggest that, as the Victorian synthesis on anger at home was to some extent an expression of feelings toward the larger world, so would the breakdown of that synthesis also be related to more general changes of feeling. For several decades, however, there was a synthesis, applied to all facets of family life, and this synthesis expressed the first approach to anger control in a society encountering the pressures of industrialization.

Emotionology of Marriage: 1830–1900

Marriage and home as a contrast or relief from work has been a common theme since the Industrial Revolution began, but the contrast has been subtly altered as views of work have altered. The home, after all, could be viewed as preferable to work for the reasons that were commonly adduced in the 1920s—because it was more fun, or, as in the 1950s, because there was more emotional sharing. But the Victorians were not looking for escape from monotony, as men were in the 1920s, or from loneliness, as in the 1950s. Their view of the work world was characterized by images of strife, chaos, and contention. The work world was seen, in contrast to images discussed in later eras, as too stimulating and too crowded.[3] For this reason, when the Victorians contrasted home with work, the emphasis was on home as a world of peace and quiet.

Home was "not simply a place to live in" but rather "a sacred enclosure—the hallowed retreat of the virtues and the affections; it belongs to innocence and Eden." A man could not reach perfection without such a home, for "the excitements of life and of business—the selfishness of daily existence'' were all to be corrected in the retreat of marriage.[4]

This theme of distaste for and discomfort with the outside world was a persistent one throughout nineteenth-century marriage literature, although less prominent by the last third of the century than it had been earlier. Women were over and over advised to cultivate good temper at home because ''men find so little sincere friendship abroad, so little true sympathy in the selfish world, that they gladly yield themselves to the influence of a gentle spirit at home.''[5] Wives were reminded repeatedly of their good fortune in inhabiting the ''serene region'' of the hearth, which was contrasted with that ''into which the head of a family is often driven,'' in which he must be subject to ''a thousand vexations for the stupidity, negligence or knavery of those with whom his business lies.''[6]

A typical marriage morality tale contrasted a bad marriage, one in which the wife, who knew nothing of domestic arts, was foolishly interested only in going out into the world, with one in which ''all was still happiness and peace.''[7] A typical writer on married life advised wives ''to make her husband's residence inviting and delightful to home . . . a sacred retreat . . . from the corroding cares and anxieties of life.'' These goals made it essential to ban anger. Thus the advice literature intoned: ''Cultivate a spirit of mutual and generous forbearance, carefully avoiding anything like angry contention or contradiction. Beware of the first dispute, and deprecate its occurrence.''[8] ''The reign of gentleness . . . is very much needed in this jarring, clashing, warring world,'' wrote William Alcott in an advice book for husbands. ''Quarrels of every sort are exceedingly destructive of human happiness; but no quarrels, save those among brethren in the church, are so bitter as family quarrels; and . . . should be so sedulously avoided.''[9]

T. S. Arthur, one of the major writers on domestic matters and widely popular, stressed the goal of complete avoidance of anger and quarrel in a story he published in *Godey's* in 1842 called ''I Will.'' The story begins with a young girl who is looking forward to her marriage but is troubled by the tales of her friends. ''Shocked'' to hear of one friend who has quarreled with her spouse, she tells her confidante, ''I tremble when the thought of opposition between us . . . crosses my mind. I would rather die . . . than ever have a misunderstanding with my husband.'' Her aunt warns her, if she would save her marriage, ''Avoid carefully, religiously avoid, setting yourself in opposition to your husband . . . nothing is to be gained by contention.''[10]

No quarrel was so small as to be judged insignificant according to most marital advisors. For instance, James Miller, writing in 1882, advised that even ''a sharp word may retard for months the process of soul blending'' and warned that ''the fatal estrangement that rent the home asunder and made scandal for the world [often] began in a little difference which a wise, patient word might have composed.''[11] Similarly, the phrenologist Orson Fowler advised, ''You cannot be too particular about little things . . . so exceedingly tender is the plant of connubial love, and so susceptible . . . that trifles impede its growth. . . . A single tart remark, or unkind tone of voice,'' may make a loving wife wretched.[12] To be sure, an occasional writer implied that one cross word might not spell disaster and advised spouses to forgive infrequent bad temper, but this was the exception rather than the prevalent view.[13]

The Victorians made something of a theme of ''The First Quarrel''; in fact, one writer went so far as to devote a whole chapter to its prevention: ''Let that be avoided, and that hateful demon, discord, will never find a place at the domestic hearth. Let it have its existence, no matter . . . how brief its duration, the demon will feel himself invited and will take his place, an odious, but an abiding guest, at the fireside.''[14] Even at the end of the century, couples were advised to avoid even a single fight. One minister, imploring wives, ''Never quarrel . . . it is death to happiness,'' warned husbands, ''If you become angry with her . . . she will never forget it.''[15]

When angry quarrels do take place in the pages of Victorian ladies' magazines, they are most often one-time occurrences, with consequences so awful that the hero or heroine vows to reform and the mistake is never repeated. Anger in marriage, in other words, is viewed as a lapse, a mistake, and certainly not as an emotion that might periodically but safely afflict any two people who happen to live together. As one author depicted a remorseful and reformed wife who regretted her first and only quarrel with her spouse, when later she was ''tempted to give utterance to impatient moods, fretful and angry words died away on her lips, rebuked by the remembrance of the terrible agony.''[16] For the authors of such tales, the single quarrel leading to total reform overnight was simply a dramatic way of stating the basic ideal: that no quarrelling was good, that all angry fights could be avoided.

In most Victorian stories, anger could lead easily to disaster. The angry quarrel that had led to the above-mentioned reform had caused the husband to become so ill that he almost died; but in that story at least, reform saved the marriage.[17] More extreme, but no less typical, was a tale called ''Only a Quick Temper,'' in which the habitual anger of the man of the family led not only to his wife's death but also to the ruin of most of his children.[18] The girl who had been shocked at her friend's quarrels in T. S. Arthur's ''I Will'' was advised by her aunt that her own marriage had ended because of her opposition to her husband. "I was self-willed; I was unyielding." They quarreled, and he left her. By the time she had repented, he had gone off to India to die, causing her to lose "a man with whom I might have been supremely happy."[19] In Erma Leland's story "The First Quarrel," published in *Peterson's Magazine* in 1875, a few intemperate words on a wife's part result in the husband walking out into the woods, being knocked out by a falling tree, and almost dying.[20] A three-year estrangement from her husband is the punishment for another wife who loses her temper. When he returns to her, close to death, and asks her for forgiveness for running off, she cries, "No, Tom, my cross word did it all . . . but for that we might have been happy together all these weary years," and she vows "never [to] speak cross words to him any more."[21]

A similar plight almost befell Isabel, the heroine of a story called "Clouds and Sunshine." In a fight with her husband "when her anger had lashed itself at that point at which truth, feeling and justice were forgotten, she took one unhappy step which coloured all her after life." She accused her husband of marrying her for money, and he too was off to India. Luckily for Isabel, they were reunited in the end after she had had ample opportunity to repent.[22]

Mary H. Parsons's story "The Adopted Daughter" was an archetypal example of the evil consequences of anger. In this tale, a reasonable husband is plagued by his unreasonable wife's hostility to the marriage plans of their adopted child. When she argued with him, "it was the demon of an ill regulated temper that possessed her; it blinded her reason. . . . To what fearful consequences does temper . . . often give rise." And the author goes on to describe the consequences: "Her face reddened to crimson and she exclaimed passionately . . . rage possessed her. . . . Terrible was the sight of that woman; she stood erect, her face and lips wearing the hue of death, every nerve quivering, and every muscle rigid with excitement, her brow knit, and her eyes literally glaring with intolerable light." Her husband threatens to leave her, and as he leaves the room "she raised her closed hands high in the air, the white foam gathered on her lip, the veins stood out rigid and swollen over her forehead . . . she stood erect . . . with eyes dilated . . . she strove to move forward, and fell headlong to the floor, the blood gushing from her nose and mouth." This antiheroine had burst a blood vessel because of her wicked anger. Her creator was lenient enough to allow her not to die but rather to repent, vow never to be angry again, and save the marriage.[23]

It was not simply the fiction writers who exaggerated the dangerous drama of quarreling. Ministers were no less certain than authors that even one quarrel could lead to lifelong consequences. James Miller, in fact, did sound more like a novelist than a minister in recounting several tales of spouses left surviving the death of a husband or wife after an angry dispute and the lifelong regret that ensued: "Suppose, then, that as you go out in the morning you have a little strife or quarrel with one of the household whom you truly love, and you part, perhaps in anger, with sharp, stinging words. . . . Do you not see how that parting may become a lifelong bitterness to you?"[24]

Anger, then, was one of the leading themes in Victorian accounts of bad character that would ruin marriage. It leads to disaster because an angry person is an unreasonable person. Anger means loss of self-control, and for the Victorians reason and control were equated. The Victorian man or woman was afraid of being swept away by passion. This certainly has been discussed many times in considerations of Victorian sexuality, but historians have overemphasized the uniqueness of sexual attitudes, which are, after all, but an aspect of attitudes toward the expression of all emotions.[25] A person of good character did not let himself get swept away by passion of any sort.

Victorians often chose metaphors for anger implying that the feeling came from an evil source outside the self. The essential self was the rational self, while the angry feelings were intrusions.[26] One husband was "a man in a rage . . . possessed of a devil . . . the innocent victim of his wrath."[27] When a young wife whose husband tried to cut off her girlhood friendships became angry, "an evil demon whispered a mad response to . . . injustice," causing her to speak harshly.[28] The sense here is that the evil spirits motif is metaphorical rather than theological. Interestingly enough, those with a more scientific than theological bent could use their methods to the same end. For example, the phrenologists felt that there was a section of the brain responsible for selfish sentiments. Spouses should remember this when provoked and calm themselves by thinking, "It is only [sic] the momentary workings, of excited combativeness," in other words, not the essential self.[29] They should control combativeness and avoid placing the self under "the tyrannical sway of . . . animal propensity."[30]

Indeed, the Victorians were projecting the angry feeling outside themselves, but the purpose of this projection on which bedfellows as strange as phrenologists and ministers could agree was not so much to make a statement about the origins of evil feelings in the world as to express the discomfort felt when assailed by such feelings. One writer described Marian, a young wife hurt by her husband's seeming inattention who brooded often on her wounds. "When we yield to evil thoughts, they gain upon the mind with fearful rapidity . . . her soul was shaken with fierce and angry struggles."[31] Better, it appeared, to give up anger, for anger could only make one uneasy.

If acknowledging anger could lead to loss of internal control, it also meant loss of external control. The Victorians felt that, in interpersonal relations, it was the calm and steady people who won the battles, whereas those dominated by emotion were invariably bested by their opponents.

"The First and Second Marriage" told the story of a bad-tempered husband who abused his first wife with his constant outbursts. He had his comeuppance though, with wife number two, a remote lady who controlled him by ignoring his temper until the point that he became afraid of her, for "the cold temper always masters the irritable one."[32] Husbands could gain control through the same devices, as did the spouse of a capricious and argumentative woman who was "forbearing and gentle—yet resolute when occasion demanded—the calm and even mildness of his disposition . . . preserved his own rights from being encroached upon . . . in their disagreements."[33]

One amusing story, "Sense and Insensibility," showed how an intelligent but hot-tempered husband came under the thumb of his less intelligent but more placid wife simply because she refused to be aroused by his constant scolding. Much to his chagrin, she laughed off his tempers and chatted about them with some amusement to their friends, thus further enraging him. "If he scolded now it was not so much to reform her as to relieve himself," for he dreaded her for fear of exposure to their acquaintances. "If I could only make her angry," he muses, then I could control her, and the author concurs, noting that it is usually the spouse with less feeling who is the boss in the family.[34]

Despite the consensus that existed on the necessity of restraining anger in marriage, a tension existed between the necessity for controlling feeling and the Victorian ideal of a companionate marriage. The cult of domesticity preached, after all, that husband and wife were to be the best of friends and that marriage, far from being a purely economic arrangement, was to be the main provider of emotional sustenance. It was clear that husband and wife must talk openly to each other in order to reap emotional benefits, and so the Victorians recommended that difficulties between spouses be explored rather than suppressed. A wealthy husband who became disgusted by his new bride's enthusiastic enjoyment of her freshly acquired riches was criticized for withholding his feelings from her and lapsing into "moody silence," eventually deserting their home.[35] T. S. Arthur laid major blame for dissension on an immature woman in his story "Sweethearts and Wives," but he did note that the husband bore some blame as well since "he should have been open and candid toward her, and explained to her rationally, calmly, and affectionately her duty; not shrunk from this for fear of wounding her, thus wounding her a thousand times more."[36] Mary H. Parsons preached against overlooking problems in "The Wife and Sister.'' '' 'Let it rest' has done fearful mischief in domestic life; rather 'clear it up'; sift it to the bottom, till every grain of discontent and mutual misapprehension, be scattered.''[37]

How, we might well ask, could one sift it to the bottom and yet totally avoid anger? There was an assumption here, foreign to us, that marital problems could be solved once and for all and that, if everyone only acted properly, there would be no conflict and hence no anger; discontent indeed would be "scattered." The Victorians wanted very much to believe that emotional openness was possible between spouses but preferred not to recognize that, when emotions are expressed, there will inevitably be more than sweetness and light. This kind of idealism, in talking about emotional openness while ignoring anger, does in fact recur in our own time; here is one of several places in which a Victorian contribution has proved amazingly durable.

Certainly, in Victorian emotionology itself the conflict between talking about one's feelings and ignoring feelings like anger was not explored. Readers were simply advised to do both, and we must speculate later on how they might have managed such a task. Occasionally, a Victorian author did advise a slight tempering of total honesty between spouses for the purposes of achieving harmony;[38] occasionally, also, there were hints of a more managerial approach to the problem of anger. For instance, one writer counseled practicing self-control by a technique of leaving the room when provoked,[39] and another suggested counting to one hundred, making sure to avoid drinking alcohol or stimulants, and reciting the Lord's Prayer.[40] But for the most part this kind of managerial approach to marriage was alien to nineteenth-century writers, who advised couples that they could have their cake and eat it too.

The contradiction might be "solved" by verbal sophistry; for instance, James Reed told couples to resist "every tendency to think that they are not suited to each other . . . as a snare" and that "separate wills should make themselves known by their voluntary blending and cooperation, not by any wish to override each other."[41] For couples who found it difficult to make their individuality known by "blending" themselves, there was the distinct if implicit message that they were somehow morally at fault: "Where you cannot attain perfect harmony of feeling, at least strive for peace; . . . at all events, *never*, on *any account* allow a harsh remark to pass between those whose relations are so sacred as those of man and wife. Nor will this be the case where *true* love exists . . . if those who are married do not possess this spirit . . . they do not really love each other."[42] It was unusual to find a writer as blunt as Daniel Wise was in admitting that avoiding quarrels might sometimes demand the "concealment of your dislikes" or require that the reader "crucify your feelings and tastes" to avoid a quarrel.[43] For the most part, marriage advisers insisted that one was supposed to be able to be perfectly forthright about feelings and yet banish contention.

Yet everyone knew all too well that angry couples existed. How did the Victorians account for this fact without having to acknowledge the universality of a fearful emotion? Again, projective mechanisms were employed, for readers of domestic tales were constantly advised that angry people were people of bad character and therefore could be viewed as alien or different from oneself. Here is a remnant of a premodern tendency to see anger as an outside force, though this tendency rested in the context of much greater overall concern about anger control. The "bad character" approach led to popular stories and even scientific accounts, well into the twentieth century, that stressed the distinctive physical features of angry people—red faced, with swollen veins, trembling—because these features denoted the destructiveness of angry behavior and its otherness, its location not in people in general but in bad people.[44] As we will see later in this chapter, the marriage literature was entirely consistent with the child-rearing literature on this point. Good parents would raise children with good characters so that when they grew up they would not feel or display anger. Angry husbands and wives, conversely, had clearly had inadequate upbringings.

This is one reason that Victorian marriage stories often seem alien to the modern reader. We have been repeatedly indoctrinated with the notion that, if a marriage is in trouble, both spouses bear some responsibility, but for the Victorian writers, there was usually one identifiably bad and one good spouse. These could be spotted early in the story, frequently before the marriage, for the bad spouse was one with a bad character who displayed his faults in every area of life. Anger in marriage was the fault not of a malfunctioning marital system, as we would put it in today's jargon, but of a person who could not control himself in any system, marital or otherwise. Typically in these stories, the angry spouse was described as having had an upbringing that left him "spoiled" or "capricious." One such, for example, was characterized as "arrogant and fond of having his own way," and he picked a spouse he thought he could control, precisely because of these faults.[45] An argumentative wife was described as a "woman whose errors were the result of a false education."[46] Another such wife had a good heart but ran into trouble because she had been perniciously educated. She suffered from "an ill-regulated mind."[47] Reading these descriptions, one could think about and acknowledge anger but ascribe it to other people. The dangerous emotion did not have to be incorporated into the self.

Since angry people were to be seen as the other and of bad character, an angry spouse probably represented a mistaken choice in a mate. Indeed, sizable portions of the marital advice literature were devoted to the selection of a "right" mate, and one of the qualities to be sought was a good temper.[48] The notion that anger was an expression of individual moral failure rather than of a malfunctioning marital system was stated clearly in one courtship story, "My Two Lovers," in which a young girl was advised to learn more about two suitors by observing their behavior with their own families. She overhears one of the men losing his temper and even swearing oaths at his relatives and is therefore not surprised to learn that he is after her only for money. Happily, now, she picks the other man.[49]

Thus far the reader may have been puzzled by the fact that we have not discussed separate standards for husbands and wives but rather have alluded to a single Victorian standard for anger in marriage. In this period, so often noted for its sharp separation of the spheres of the sexes and its almost axiomatic adherence to the differences between the basic characters of male and female, was there no difference in standards for emotional life? The answer is both yes and no, and perhaps it is only because we have been led to expect the sexes to have been treated differently that we are more struck by the sameness. For certainly, in terms of the expression of angry feelings, no more allowance was made for husband than for wife. Our expectation, in reading these stories, was that wives would be advised to overlook a spouse's irritability at home in acknowledgement of the difficulties he had encountered all day in the harsh and contentious world of work. Our expectation, in other words, was that a sharp dichotomy would be drawn between the male and the female sphere. But the reality is more complicated than this. For the real dichotomy was not so much between male and female as between work and home. At home, Victorian men no less than Victorian women were expected to control anger.

The story cited before, "Only a Bad Temper," presented the husband in a totally negative fashion because of his frequent outbursts. It was notable that he exploded at home and at work as well; in other words, he acted uniformly badly because he had a bad character. There was no feeling here that anger at home could be explained away as the result of anger that had been built up at work. In this story, the wife consistently advised her children "not to love him less for his harshness," explaining that "men could not be as gentle as women, they had so much to bear out of doors."[50] This excuse, however, clearly represented the wife's point of view and was not one whit acceptable to the author, who maintained throughout a totally unforgiving stance toward the husband in question. Good husbands, when angry, were supposed to remain "forbearing and gentle."[51] Even if they did work all day, they would remain "gentle" in discussions with their wives.[52] A husband who was clearly the "good" spouse in a story called "Mr. and Mrs. Woodbridge" treats his wife's lapses from decent behavior calmly and is rewarded: "A gentle remonstrance from Harvey always brought her to reason."[53]

A good man was a man who could control himself despite provocation; the stories are full of graphic descriptions of the Victorian husband's herculean efforts at this sort of self-control. One such was faced by a defiant wife, and "his face grew deadly pale. For a moment his whole frame trembled as if some fearful struggle were going on within. Then he quietly arose and without looking at [her] . . . left the room."[54] Harvey Woodbridge, mentioned above, struggled mightily to achieve the same calm. When his wife provoked him by refusing to serve their company, he asked about it "making an effort to throw as much mildness into his tone as possible." When she was similarly stingy on a later date, he was "annoyed, ashamed, and angry nearly the whole time" but never opened his mouth. When she finally aroused real wrath by begging him to go out and buy her some fabric, this Victorian paragon's only expression of anger was to leave the house with these fierce words, "Confound the worsted."[55]

One notices, of course, in these tales of magnificent self-control, that it is acknowledged that even good men sometimes feel anger. Many Victorians, in fact, believed that it would be a sign of a lack of manliness to be perfectly untroubled by angry feelings. William Alcott, for instance, made the point that "I should not envy those, who were so indifferent—so wanting in sensibility—as never to have a single feeling of displeasure," and took overt issue with those who felt the best temper was one "incapable" of being moved.[56] One young wife in a story in *Peterson's* overlooked her husband's anger by musing, "Tom was spirited and quick-tempered—great, loving-hearted men always are."[57] Thus men should not express their anger, but they could feel it.

And here we have the crucial difference between expectations for men and those for women, for Victorian wives were not even supposed to feel anger. Anger and femininity were antithetical. One author, in describing an angry wife, said that "every womanly emotion—generosity—delicacy—honour—yielded before the demon that held her in his iron fold" and that, at another point, temper "stifled the exercise of every womanly and gentle feeling."[58] A proper woman was described in "The First and Second Marriage" as one who tried to please her husband no matter how angry he became at her. The author at first seems to reveal some ambivalence about the wife's unquestioning acquiescence, even suggesting that, "had she known her own rights, and turned upon him with spirit, the effect would have been better." How far this was from a rejection of the Victorian ideal of suffering in silence we may see, however, in the author's musings at the end of the story as to whether this woman would have enjoyed seeing her husband bested by his less compliant second wife. "Yet we wrong you, Mary Harper, even in the supposition; your gentle, unoffending heart never roused to anger even here, when clogged with earth."[59]

Good wives were habitually described as bearing their suffering with a martyred air, as in the story "The Married Sisters," in which a wife put up "in silence" with a husband who squandered all their money, never feeling anger. (The author rescues her in the end by the husband's death.)[60] Another mistreated wife whose selfish husband married her only for her money did resort to tears but always remained "without complaint."[61] Plagued by her husband's terrible temper, a third wife would simply "tremble for him."[62]

On the whole, the advice literature was somewhat more lenient than the fiction was toward the notion that a woman might feel anger. For instance, one writer for women, recalling Alcott on men, remarked that "there is a noble and generous kind of anger . . . the person who feels not an injury must be incapable of being properly affected by benefits."[63] In their discussion of the brain, the phrenologists made no distinction between male and female and therefore allowed even good women to experience some "combative" sentiments.

The bottom line was, however, that angry women were worse than angry men. Men, to become angry, certainly must display the justification of a patently unreasonable wife, but at least there were some discussions of the anger felt by decent men, who must, of course, struggle with their anger and overcome it. No such struggle was allowed a woman, for even in feeling anger she proved her bad character. As William Thayer wrote, to have a scold for a spouse is the "bane of domestic bliss, and worst of all if it be the *wife*."[64] Alcott, who spent pages and pages in his advice book for husbands on the control of anger, simply glossed over the subject in his book for wives.[65] Anger in women made the Victorians more uncomfortable than did anger in men. If the advice books could mention the subject in passing, it was almost impossible to write a story with a good but angry woman, for the Victorians had a failure of imagination in actually conceiving of a woman who could be both. Mrs. Chapone probably typified her era in remarking that "an enraged woman is one of the most disgusting sights in nature." An exception, proving the rule, was Fanny Fern's *Ruth Hall,* which was more frank than usual in showing an angry heroine, and for this very reason was generally viewed as unfeminine and shocking. *Godey's,* in fact, refused to review the novel.[66]

The feeling/behavior dichotomy on anger in each sex should not totally surprise us, for it was not unlike Victorian ideals of sexuality. It was widely acknowledged that even good men had lustful feelings. This was less acceptable for women. Although recent historians have demonstrated that not all Victorians were as horrified by female sexual feelings as had once been thought, certainly even the revisionists would allow that there was much more conflict over the lust of the female than over the lust of the male.[67] The standards for the sexes were more similar in terms of behavior, however. Decent men did feel lust, but a man who could not keep it under control was departing fairly far from the Victorian ideal. Certainly, there was no question at all that women were expected to keep lustful behavior well controlled.

The function of the angel-in-the-house ideal in the larger Victorian culture has been discussed at length elsewhere and need not be rehearsed here. We wish only to insist on the importance of claiming the ability to feel no anger as a central angelic criterion. And this claim concealed an irony ultimately of importance to men as well as to women. Victorian women were regarded as quintessentially emotional, sometimes as proof of their inferiority but sometimes also—as when maternal emotions were emphasized—to their glory. But anger was entirely excluded from this emotionality, an entirely implicit pruning that has recurred in twentieth-century discussions of desirable emotionality in both sexes. Again, the Victorians took an important step in trying to dissociate, without discussion, anger from their vision of emotionality.

But while the distinctive approach to women deserves emphasis, it must not obscure the larger feature of Victorian emotionology: both sexes were held strictly accountable. The Victorians saw familial anger as dangerous, as antithetical to the notion of the home as a peaceful retreat. To admit that the angel who presided in that home might feel angry would have been to unloose a wild animal in that retreat. But it took two to banish anger. Perhaps because so much historical writing on the cult of domesticity has been written by women and has been part of a larger effort at "women's history," the curbs the Victorians placed on men at home have not been sufficiently appreciated. In terms of behavior, men were expected to adhere to standards as high as those established for their wives, for the sake of their homes and their marriages.

In truth, one is impressed, in considering Victorian emotionology, not so much by the inequality with which the sexes were treated as by the great burdens placed on each sex for the sake of dealing with the real dichotomy, that between home and the ugly contentiousness of the world of work. Peter Filene has discussed the almost impossible line Victorian men had to walk in defining their sexuality—if they denied all feeling they were unmanly, and if they expressed their feelings they were moral failures.[68] He well might have said the same of the man's plight concerning anger. What is one to make of a standard that counseled men that "there is no victory more glorious . . . than a complete victory over one's self" and that a good husband could always prevent a quarrel with his wife?[69] How indeed could this be reconciled with the notion that manly men did feel anger? What is one to think of the difficulties involved here for men who certainly had experienced somewhere, perhaps in childhood, anger taken for granted as the legitimate right of a patriarch?

On the other hand, the difficulties for women were also tremendous, for although an occasional writer might allow that women did have angry feelings, this was the exception. A woman would have to search far to find a role model for proper anger, and insofar as she dared to acknowledge that she recognized that emotion in herself, she would have had to be very strong-minded not to question immediately the essence of her femininity and desirability.

In sum, then, the Victorians had little tolerance for anger in marriage on the part of either sex and viewed that emotion as a threat to what they treasured most in the home. Angry people lost the ability to control themselves, and in a world perceived as already too much out of control, the Victorians could not forgive the introduction of chaos into the one retreat that remained. Angry people, both husbands and wives, existed, to be sure, but these were people of bad character. Good husbands and wives would raise good children, and in these children of proper character, anger would be almost excised. We now must consider how this first step was to be managed.

Emotionology of Childrearing, 1830–60

Concern about anger in child rearing was surely born of the same eighteenth-century emotional transition that produced the new desire to reduce anger between husband and wife. Explicit anger advice in the eighteenth century focused more directly on adults than on children, to be sure. Thus the neologism *tantrum* was originally applied to adult behavior and only gradually, during the nineteenth century, evolved to its present meaning, which describes a new level of anguish about a certain kind of childish behavior. But it was quickly realized that anger-free adult character depended on the proper rearing of the young. And the dominant view of childish character, expressed in mainstream Protestant family advice by the early nineteenth century, lent itself to this focus readily enough.[70] Picking up on Locke's idea of the child as a blank slate and on the elaborations of subsequent educational theorists who saw no demon to exorcise in their charges, family advisers urged that children's temperaments were neutral and indeed probably good at birth. From this it followed that parents need use no anger to root out evil—evil would be implanted in children only by bad training. The first stage of the modern emphasis in socialization for anger, in other words, leaned heavily on the environmental interpretation of human nature preached by the thinkers of the Enlightenment.

To be sure, there were those in the early nineteenth century, aside from religious traditionalists who still fussed at original sin, who noted some differences in innate temperament. Phrenologists located bad as well as good passions in various parts of the brain; there was a seat for "selfish sentiments," including anger.[71] Other authorities, less scientifically precise, admitted that some evil was inherent and that some people would have more troublesome passions—such as a quick temper—than others. But the key point was that anyone could (and should) reform the bad features of his natural endowment. In an implicit nature versus nurture discussion, nurture won hands down because of the possibility of human discipline.[72] "Human nature consists in disciplining and cultivating every good inclination, and in checking and subduing every propensity to evil."[73] The temper one is born with, whatever it is, should, in sum, make no difference in the management of anger. While the necessary discipline would be a lifelong project—character building in the early nineteenth century was not a matter for childhood alone—the need to form character in the first place naturally called attention to child rearing. From this a central preoccupation with informing child rearing with the values of anger control naturally stemmed.

From the late eighteenth century, the emotional values expressed in child-rearing literature and the most common stories directed toward children themselves began to manifest the newly explicit concern with preventing the development of anger in the formation of personality. The desire to prevent anger was fundamental to attacks on traditional parental methods of breaking the will; it also entered into early nineteenth-century debates over physical discipline in the schools. American society, in other words, was beginning a move that would carry it, by the twentieth century, toward the more repressive end of a comparative scale that measured various societies' tolerance of childish anger. This move was not fully realized, masked by, among other things, Americans' unusual tolerance for childish antics and high spirits (so often noted and bemoaned by European observers) and also by some ambiguities about children's anger that would develop after the repressive campaign began. But the development of a new and durable effort at repression had clear results, producing some central tensions over anger in middle-class child rearing by the twentieth century[74]—and perhaps, as we will consider later in this chapter, producing fewer angry personalities among adults.

Writing in 1914, Dorothy Canfield Fisher describes—and reproves—a classic episode of will breaking that she had witnessed a few months before. A mother forbids her son to play in water. The boy insists and falls into a tearful rage when the mother, now conscious of the greater goal of defending her authority, refuses to relent. The mother is relieved at the rage because it signals that direct, behavioral defiance of her edict is not being risked. As the emotion finally subsides, after much maternal clucking about how obstinate children are, the mother insists on apology and punishes anew when this is not forthcoming.[75] Here are all the ingredients of the traditional approach to anger in children: no concern with the emotional expression itself; discipline for behavior, which might prevent outburst in future but would not, and was not intended to, teach anything about anger itself; a strong possibility that greater anger was being built up for some future, if indirect, expression; and an insistence on obedience overriding any thought of emotional guidance.

Will breaking did not quickly or uniformly yield to the new currents of thought about child rearing that developed in the eighteenth century.[76] This is one reason that a passionately simple approach to anger control arose and long endured: the traditional enemy remained vigorous and elusive, so subtleties in dealing with childish temper could be ignored in favor of dealing with the larger ideal. Initial variations in the effort at anger control—between Evangelicals, who reduced physical discipline but increased the intensity of parental supervision, and more moderate Protestants, who attempted a more affectionate approach[77]—undoubtedly persisted among different religious groups in the United States; but the variations found decreasing echo in child-rearing advice, which increasingly plumped for the moderate approach that sought to avoid anger though consistent gentleness. Though they seldom placed parent-child relations in the same category as those between husband and wife, advice writers clearly sought to create an anger-free environment throughout the home—with husbands and wives, as parents, again primarily responsible for the necessary control.

For anger control was an important ingredient in a general effort by nineteenth-century middle-class spokesmen to spread the word that traditional views and treatment of children needed serious revision. As advice manuals began to impinge on American family life by the 1830s, they carried important messages about anger along with more elaborately worded concerns about proper styles of discipline, piety, and sexual behavior. The messages translted the eighteenth-century desire to restrain anger into recommended daily parental habits.

Family advice manuals and the popular "letters to young people" genre in the 1820s, highly religious in tone, directly preserved the tone of the eighteenth-century moderates. Temper control was handled in separately labeled chapters, but in addition the theme of emotional control and preservation of a cheerful attitude pervaded much of the general discussion. Family quarrels should be avoided at all costs, which extended the idea of temper control to servants as well as those in charge of servants. The high level of concern did not translate into very precise guidance for children themselves, however. The wise parent would try to prevent problems that gave rise to anger, avoiding frustration and needless nagging. But children would sometimes be irritable anyway, and while their sulky moods should not be humored, they should be met with patience. Primary emphasis remained on adult control. "I say to any father or mother, are you irritable, petulant? If so, begin this moment the work of subjugating your temper."[78]

As manuals became more secular, by the 1830s, somewhat greater attention shifted to children themselves. The goal, more explicit than in previous decades, was to shape children in such a way that anger could cease to be an adult anxiety. The original concern about adult behavior, with its somewhat diffuse implications for child rearing, was now focused increasingly on children themselves. Restraint of anger became part of good character training. At the same time, the level of explicit concern about anger declined somewhat. As optimism about human nature increased, and as hope developed that children could be so guided that adult anger would cease to be a problem, the need for extended discussions of this aspect of emotional control diminished.

One ingredient in the mid-nineteenth-century manuals went beyond translation of eighteenth-century concerns into the new expert advice for parents. This ingredient also helps explain the reduction of extensive, worried counseling on the subject. The manuals increasingly focused, in tandem with the marriage manuals, on the maternal role and on the distinction between family morals and emotions and the storm and stress of the outside world. In the process, the manuals emphasized the peculiarly anger-free character of the good mother and her responsibility for creating an atmosphere of affection and good cheer. The definition of women's character and the changes in roles induced by early industrialization thus completed the ingredients surrounding new concern about anger in child rearing.

The specific tone of the child-rearing manuals of the decades from 1830 to 1860 was short-lived, for it depended on a particular stress on children's basic goodness that went beyond most eighteenth-century belief and that would be contested later in the nineteenth century as well. For the most part, however, manuals in this period did not innovate, with regard to anger, so much as adapt earlier ideas to the new, secularized expertise, to new concepts of maternal responsibility, and to the new intensity of concern for the family retreat. Thus the mid-century decades were marked, overall, by an absence of a special sense of dispute or fundamental anguish. Key principles were already established: anger was bad, and children should be discouraged from the emotion. But precisely because these principles were accepted, even amid arguments about disciplinary tactics, there was no need to focus attention on anger as a moral issue among many others. Anger became one of several emotions to be mastered as part of building good character in a child.

Calvinist writers continued to see children as imbued with innate anger, which was part of their human depravity. But by mid-century the dominant tone of advice literature stressed childish innocence or at least the weakness of evil impulses. This led in turn to an emphasis on parental behavior, including avoidance of anger in dealing with children. Thus Horace Bushnell denounced the "heathenish ferocity" of parents who threatened and punished, extinguishing in children the very gentleness they should be fostering. "Fretfulness and ill temper in the parents are provocations." Maternal advice highlighted the need to provide cheerfulness and "good temper" for children as the environment in which children could in turn form a good character. Childish anger might be admitted, though it was not emphasized, but the focus was on the parental responsibility to turn anger away with soft answers.[79] The importance of adult gentleness was fused with an appropriate religious model, as Christ's goodness was meant to overshadow a thundering God.[80] "Light-touch Christianity" paralleled exceptionally self-conscious parenting.

There was an obvious logic in this approach. If mild parents could defuse by their own example what little anger inhered in children, these children in turn, grown to be adults, could readily provide the same anger-free example. Even Calvinist writers, though they disputed the innate goodness of infants, could agree on the importance of some gentleness in forming the conscience; hence the increasing pride taken in avoiding physical discipline in dealing with misbehavior. Both Calvinists and the adherents of childish innocence also agreed on the need for obedience and on the related need to teach children to govern their passions, all to be accomplished without anger on the parent's part. As in reform views of criminal punishment, discipline was to be free from any taint of revenge.[81]

Characteristic children's stories, similar to the marriage tales, emphasized the need for control of anger, though here it must be emphasized that this target was less popular than irresponsible or careless behavior. In Louise Chandler Morton's "Coals of Fire" (1868), a hot-tempered boy promises his mother never to fight. The mother lacks a husband's help in instilling self-control; hence her special insistence. The boy fears being labeled cowardly, but when he resuces a girl without a fight he demonstrates true self-mastery, illustrating the ideal of a Christian gentleman. Catherine Sedgwick drove home the same point in her best-seller *Home*. A child describes his mastery over temper in avoiding fights at school: "But I did not, father, I did not, I had to bite my lips though so that the blood ran." "God bless you, my son." To Cap the examples of control, moralists cited George Washington's dominance of his temper—his worst personal fault—as his greatest victory.[82]

One final bit of practical advice frequently accomplished the character-building approach: learn to avoid conflicts in the home whenever possible. Be sensitive to a child's mood, and while never yielding on the requirement of obedience, do not pick fights needlessly or inflict punishments that will rouse anger. For though children might be excitable, anger really comes from adults. A child "sees that his mother is irritated, and thus is he taught that it is proper for him to be angry." "A mother must have great control over her own feelings, a calmness and composure of spirit not easily disturbed."[83]

The mid-century effort to translate earlier anxieties about anger produced several durable themes in American child rearing that would survive some subsequent change. Anger is bad—"temporary insanity," "a bestial trait." Efforts to control anger now spread to attempts to block cruelty to animals, as a childish outlet, and to some new concern about children's quarrels.[84] Later interest in some more positive features of anger would not reverse the sense that highly personal anger, or anger toward animals and inferiors, was wrong. Still clearer was the message that parents have an immense responsibility to avoid anger in their own behavior. This theme alone, anchored of course in the concern about familial anger that had arisen earlier, was to persist as a central canon of child-rearing advice until the mid-twentieth century, a key element in the heroic approach to parenting and, particularly, in the assumptions about the virtues that mothers could bring to the process. Two subsets of this theme would recur well into our own time as well. The stress on parental control led to criticism of the older, will-breaking tradition, a convenient rhetorical foil but also, without question, an ongoing strand in actual child-rearing practices that all the experts deplored. Moral progress, and by 1900 scientific progress as well, in the art of parenting dictated vigilance against the bad old days. The assumption that women had a special contribution to make to the art of gentle parenting proved durable as well. As in the marriage literature, most authorities assumed that females were less angry by nature. (Even later, when some feminists contested this claim, they would still suggest a special maternal responsibility in learning to be calm and so governing annoyingly pugnacious males.)[85]

The mid-century approach did not produce elaborate recommendations about the tactics for controlling anger. The assumption of childhood innocence and the power of parental example militated against detail. The values were so sure, and the need for attention to other moral problems, plus the growing sense of responsibility for physical health, so pressing, that extensive discussion seemed superfluous. There is little of the intensity found in the marital literature. Furthermore, because control of anger was part of character building, which started but was far from completed in childhood, concern for this aspect of emotional control was shared by ethical literature for teenagers and adults. Indeed, the child-rearing focus on parental example, more than on children themselves, was part of the lifelong approach. The key problem, still, was parental self-government; a calm exterior on the part of adults, guarding against a "moody temper," was the key goal. T. S. Arthur put it this way: "As mother is, so will be children." Children could be granted moments of quarrelsomeness and disobedience—childish innocence was not so uniformly expected as has sometimes been claimed. And individual children, with bad tempers, needed specific guidance in the middle years of childhood. But no behavior problem could be cured by parental anger, and example was everything. With this approach, there was no need to examine children's behavior, or specific responses to it, in great detail. This first secular advice literature rarely offered detailed advice, as opposed to moral orientation, in any event.[86]

In this respect, again, the child-rearing literature was consonant with the marriage literature, which also tended to gloss over practical problems, to stress ideals, and to label all departures from ideals as failures. This tone is entirely understandable if we think of Victorian advice literature, both for parents and for spouses, less as a list of suggestions and more as a statement of a wish or a yearning. The yearning was to create an oasis of the home. The intensity behind that yearning sprang from the confusion and discomfort felt with the changing world outside the family. As people become more threatened by reality, their defense mechanisms tend to become more stereotyped and rigid. Undesirable phenomena are not just unpleasant if understandable—they are evil. They must be rejected, not understood. They must be projected outside the self. Thus angry spouses must be dismissed as people of bad character, and angry children lead, not to an exploration of psychology, but rather to condemnation of the parent or to another denial defense, the insistence on childhood innocence.

Thinking of the advice literature as an expression of a wish, rather than as a list of suggestions, also will help us to understand another aspect of the Victorian child-rearing literature on anger that may at first appear puzzling. How is it that, in an era so noted for stress on gender distinctions, the advice on anger made little important distinction between the treatment or even the goals for boys and for girls? Certainly, as we have noted, there were differences in beliefs about these grown children as husbands and wives, but yet if the child-rearing literature alone were examined, one would not know that such differences in spouses were expected to appear.

The child-rearing literature, in its attempt to postulate childhood innocence and to suggest that through proper rearing children of both sexes could grow up anger free, was implicitly stating that both sexes should grow up to be like women—that anger, in other words, should be removed from or, more properly, prevented from becoming part of the emotional arsenal.[87] Whereas the marriage literature allowed for the felt anger of men and placed its stress on control of the emotion, the child-rearing literature hoped to excise even the feeling and even in little boys. Where it was occasionally mentioned in the marriage literature that the ability to feel anger was a good thing in a man, even perhaps a sign of his essential manliness, the child-rearing literature, before 1860, saw no virtue in anger for either sex.

It was not, of course, the conscious wish of Victorian parents to emasculate their sons, but in their efforts to stamp out all anger, can we not read an unconscious wish to obliterate, in the home, all features of the outside world that were felt to be so distasteful? Chaos, strife, contention, noise, bustle—our subjects felt inundated with these. There was a grudging acknowledgment in contemplating adult men that their characters, including the disposition to feel anger, might suit the outer world, but the felt wish was to curb those sorts of feelings as tightly as possible at home. Therefore sons and daughters alike were to be modeled on mother. The problem, then, of how and whether innocent little boys might grow up to be contentious men was not a problem the Victorians wanted to discuss, for it would have been an unpleasant problem, a reminder that reality did not jibe so neatly with the wished-for haven by the hearth. It was, in fact, when the Victorians became more comfortable with the notion that strife, contention, and indeed the whole outside world had some more positive values that notions of childhood anger began to change significantly. This happened increasingly after 1860. Anger in children, from then on, began to be seen as having some positive as well as negative values, and this new view, coinciding with other significant changes, led to a reevaluation of anger in the home in general.

But early Victorian emotionology worked toward a simple idealism: child-rearing and marital literature were united in their attack on anger, and the intensity of that attack was generated, to a large extent, by the distaste and fear felt for the new world outside the home. If we think of emotional standards as the expression of a wish rather than as a program of advice, it becomes clear that the wish was to create an oasis of peace so secure that the world outside, when too threatening, could be shut out. In the process, a demanding new set of emotional standards was elaborated. We must ask, now, how well the emotionology worked as a program. How well did the Victorians really manage to excise anger from their homes?

Emotions and Their Expression

Without question, the new emotionology was accompanied by changes in behavior in the family. Outright physical abuse was on the decline. Physical punishment for childhood transgressions became increasingly infrequent, and even in the schools corporal punishment began to abate in frequency.[88]

Catherine Beecher reported that many of her contemporaries conscientiously tried to curb temper displays against their children and were aware that in so doing they were behaving differently from their own parents. In real life, of course, the anger of children could not be ignored so easily as in the emotionology of the time. Parents found other modes of discipline. For instance, when Francis Wayland's son refused his food in temper, the father shut the boy in a room alone without food or drink for twenty-four hours. Wayland visited his son, speaking "kindly" to him every few hours, until the boy was subdued. The father, proud of how had had handled the situation, published a report.[89] The tendency to turn from shaming as well as beating toward isolation of a misbehaving child was a key index of a desire to avoid the need to display active parental anger or to allow prolonged emotional display by children; isolation simulated calm.

Like Wayland, other parents found ways to rule firmly and yet to create the impression for their children, and for themselves, that they were not angered. Margaret Sangster recalled of her mother, "Her will was law. No child so much as thought of disputing it, though her voice was never raised and her manner was quiet and gentle." Parents sought to exact the same sorts of behavior from servants as they did when they were dealing with children.[90]

Many spouses, too, made some efforts to curb their anger. In letters, memoirs, and diaries, they occasionally mentioned their efforts to remain unruffled when provoked. Charlotte Howard Gilman, for example, recalled of her marriage, "I sacrificed my preference to a more sacred feeling; if any habit of his annoyed me, I spoke of it once or twice calmly, and then bore it quietly if unreformed."[91]

The marriage law was changing to reflect the new emotionology. States were revising divorce statutes so that excessive quarrelsomeness on the part of either spouse was viewed as adequate ground for dissolution of the marriage, even if there had been no outright physical abuse. While eighteenth-century law had held that "what merely wounds the mental feelings is in few cases to be admitted, where not accompanied with bodily injury," new standards held that "a husband may, by a course of humiliating insults and annoyances . . . eventually destroy the life or health of his wife . . . although . . . unaccompanied by violence," thus establishing new grounds for divorce. Legal changes, of course, represent changes in standards, and not necessarily in behavior, but in this case, at least, there is reason to believe that the alteration in emotionology was accompanied by altered behavior, for increasingly through the nineteenth century divorces were being sought and granted on the ground of mental cruelty.[92]

Certainly, the older methods of disciplining children through will breaking and beating did not disappear overnight, but a trend in that direction was evident.[93] While angry scenes between husbands and wives did continue, some couples, at least, were making efforts to tone them down. The absence in Victorian middle-class sources of discussions of public quarreling between spouses—the decline of the "scold," that angry wife who often asserts her presence in the early modern sources—indicates that more effort was being made to tone down marital squabbling or at least to do it in private.

What happened, then, when people felt angry at their families? We have considered the effect emotionology may have had on behavior, but how did it affect feelings? There is some evidence that, for many Victorian women who were not so perfectly socialized as to deny all angry feelings, guilt, remorse, and anxiety would follow on anger as surely as night follows day. "Irritable," noted Elizabeth Parsons Channing in an 1874 entry in her diary. "Ashamed of myself when I am so alive to the desirableness of a sweet temper." Rereading a notation in her journal, in which she had been critical of others' crossness, the young Lydia Sigourney rebuked herself the following day: "I hope

I did not write unkindly yesterday. When I read it over this morning, it seemed just like a slap of slander. I am afraid I did not feel pleasant myself. . . . I'll try to carry a sunbeam in my heart to school today."[94] Other women noted guilt at anger expressed toward children.

Many Victorian women, though, internalized the emotionology so completely as never consciously to feel anger. Diaries thus reveal a striking acceptance of emotionological standards in their assumptions of the ease and desirability of anger control and of guilt when this control—rarely—broke down; many diaries thus read no differently from the published manuals. Here is an interesting sign that emotionology was reshaping the cognitive structures through which anger was evaluated. What then happened to Victorian women's ability to express anger in real life? In response to unpleasantness and adversity, how would they have interpreted their biological responses? Let us assume that they, too, might feel the tension in the limbs, the flushed face, the rumble in the gut, that we have been taught to call anger. Without the cognitive equipment to label her response to a noxious situation in this way, what outs did the Victorian woman have?

Three popular possibilities were illness, martyrdom, and displacement. A great deal has been written about hysteria and neurasthenia in the nineteenth century in this context. Conversion of an unacceptable feeling into a physical symptom was a primitive defense mechanism that historians believe to have been widely used by Victorian women.[95] The emphasis in these discussions has been on repressed sexuality, but quite clearly, repressed anger was there as well. In her biography of Alice James, Jean Strouse has shown that Alice's rage against her father was the source of much of her early illness.[96] The Victorians, in fact, admitted that there was some connection between anger and physical illness, reversing, however, our causality. For instance, phrenologists advised that illness could excite the animal portion of the brain, "producing peevishness." In such cases, temper was to be forgiven instead of punished.[97] One may well imagine, then, why angry women found it safer to claim illness than to admit to simple rage; illness was both a justification for the feeling and an opportunity for ventilation of it.

Short of illness, there were also tears. Women's tears were hardly a Victorian invention, and they encompassed more than anger. But twentieth-century evidence that crying when angry constitutes one of the key differences between male and female experience of anger certainly recalls the Victorian setting, for if anger could not acceptably demonstrate feminine emotionality, tears most definitely did. Victorianism encouraged this outlet not only in allowing women to be the "weaker" emotional vessel but also in so firmly discouraging direct expressions of anger.[98] The fact that crying was widely resorted to, and that men had some sense of the antagonism beneath the tears, is reflected in one marriage manual's advice to husbands that, when the wife sobs, the tactful husband "does not get up and rage about and kick footstools out of the way and say 'Oh, for Heaven's sake! stop crying, or you'll drive me to drink!' "[99] How many husbands, recognizing the hostility behind the tears, must have done exactly that!

Some women carried the tears further, into the posture of martyrdom. The culture embraced the notion of female moral superiority, and one may imagine with what zest some angry women used this device to get back at their spouses. Helen Papashvily sees this as the central theme of nineteenth-century domestic literature.[100] She is struck by the fury in these strong women heroines and the sympathetic fires that must have been aroused in women readers who consumed quantities of books in which inadequate husbands were punished repeatedly by becoming physically maimed. The Victorians themselves were not unconscious of this mechanism. It was a common theme in marriage manuals to advise women to get their way through sweetness, as with the writer who made it explicit in his caveat, "You cannot gain true ascendancy over a man by ill-temper, but by gentleness you may."[101] F. L. Benedict's story "Taming a Husband" was the tale of one wronged wife who gained control when she "did the martyr." The husband "tried to quarrel with her . . . it was useless." The author notes with relish that he had "met his match."[102]

Mrs. Abigail Bailey was a real woman who used martyrdom with flare. Her memoirs, written earlier than the period under discussion, nonetheless capture the essence of the Victorian woman's victory through suffering. Major Bailey flaunted his sexual affairs, physically and sexually abused his chileren, and raged repeatedly at his wife. Throughout this, Mrs. Bailey cast herself in religious terms as a Job and did not complain, mentioning his transgressions to her spouse only for his sake. "I felt obligated to bear my faithful testimony to him against his wickedness; which I repeatedly did." Her victory over him is entirely consistent with the stories in *Godey's* that suggest that it is the calm spouse who triumphs. Asked about one of his transgressions, "He was so overcome with anger that he was unable to sit up. He took his bed. . . . Just before evening he said to me, 'I never saw such a woman as you. You can be so calm; while I feel so disturbed.' . . . I was blessed with a sweet composure." Later he begged her forgiveness, and she suffered him for a while, "willing to forgive all that was past, if he might but behave well in future."[103]

Women who had no taste for illness or martyrdom may have found some relief in expressing anger outside the home. How much of the

impetus behind the increasing entrance of women into social movements, abolitionism, temperance, and feminism was a displacement of
unacceptable family anger? Obviously, we are on speculative ground
here, but we would doubt that it was simply historical accident that this
new era of women's activism coincided with the new effort to stifle
their familial rage. Fanny Kemble's journal admits to no outright fury
with her spouse except insofar as he mistreats his slaves. A modern
reader, however, cannot help wondering whether she was angry at him
simply because of the slaves or whether, indeed, her zest in that cause
was, in part, the result of her antagonism toward their owner.[104]

This raises the problem of how we know another person's real feelings. Seen in modern terms, illness, tears, and political action would
appear to be defense mechanisms against anger. Illness may be
described as a conversion; martyrdom, the assumption of moral superiority, may be seen as a reaction formation in which the person, suspect-
ing that he is very bad, strives instead to show that he is very good
indeed. It also clearly contains projection, in which the evil anger,
suspected in oneself, is attributed to the other. Displacement of the
anger into political causes may legitimately be described as a form of
sublimation. However, defense mechanisms represent unconscious
processes, and we have no way to be certain of the unconscious processes of our ancestors. We may guess that what they really felt was
anger, but it is essential to remind ourselves that we can do no more
than guess. And then it is essential to stress that what we are describing
was unconscious. The Victorians did not know that they were angry
and then try to become sick or tearful or active. They were most likely
often unaware that they were angry. Without the cognitive equipment
to label their feelings as we might, their responses must have differed
from ours. It would be misleading, then, to say that they were angry
and did not admit it since, in some sense, they did not feel angry in the
way we do when we label ourselves *angry*. If this problem is a difficult
one in evaluating Victorian women, it is even more so in evaluating
men, who have left even sparser evidence regarding their anger in the
family, except toward children. It is hoped that more historical research
will produce more answers on this issue, but at this point it is almost
impossible to say to what extent Victorian men felt and how they evaluated their own familial anger. Their relative silence on the subject in the
sources may be a result of the fact that they had less difficulty; the
emotionology, after all, granted them freer right to feel, if not to express, anger. But the silence may also represent denial, a defense
mechanism certainly not foreign to contemporary men in their efforts to
deal with anger.

In the meantime, though, it does seem fair to say that there was some sense of struggle and discomfort on the part of many Victorians, and particularly women, regarding their own anger. For those who acknowledged the emotion, there was guilt. Other alternatives, such as illness and suffering, were clearly not happy ones. An occasional glimmer of the struggle appears, as in this passage by Charlotte Brontë, printed in *Godey's*. Speaking of the fury of a woman who is disappointed in love, the author confronts her rage at not being able to express her disappointment: "If she did the result would be shame and anguish, inward remorse for self-treachery . . . [it would lead to a] thunderbolt of self-contempt smiting suddenly in secret. Take the matter as you find it; ask no questions; break your teeth on it, and don't shriek because the nerves are martyred. . . . Never mind: in time, after your hand and arm have swelled and quivered long with torture . . . you will have learned the great lesson how to endure without a sob . . . [you will learn] . . . a placid dissimulation."[105] Or Charlotte Howard Gilman: "The task of self-government was not easy. To repress a harsh answer, to confess a fault, and to stop [right or wrong] in the midst of self-defence, in gentle submission, sometimes requires a struggle like life and death."[106]

Again, a sense of the alienation from self required to master anger emerges from this description by Margaret Sangster, who described her technique in her autobiography.

> Another subtle experience might be chronicled as a dual personality. When I was a tiny child it strangely consoled me in transient troubles to think of a tall and beautiful girl who lived in our neighborhood. . . . I used to say to myself, if I had a childish trial, "Emily is not unhappy, Emily has everything she wants . . . Emily is not disappointed," and in a subtle, unexplainable way the cloudless joy of the triumphant Emily made up for my misfortune. I could bear to be hurt or scolded or misunderstood, so long as Emily was the admired and beloved of all.

The little girl, who grew up to write popular advice books for her sex, used the same device to keep irritability under control when she was older: "As I grew up I learned to keep intact a second self . . . who walked in tranquil beauty, serene and undisturbed no matter what agitations might be shaking me. This second unsuspected double maintained her place unruffled when the other self was annoyed, dismayed or . . . remorseful."[107]

In considering just what the Victorians did to cope with anger and how frequently they felt that emotion, it is difficult to avoid asking ourselves a question that we know we cannot finally answer. What was the degree of Victorian anger? Were they less angry than we are? Were they less angry than their own predecessors? Did all the effort to change treatment of children indeed produce the desired effect of a less angry cohort in the younger generation? Current authorities would rate the early nineteenth-century emotionological approach toward childish anger as the one most likely to reduce this anger in fact—a point suggestive of the real continuity in emotional values between generations of experts but one suggestive also of some potential inroads on more traditional styles of parenting. Recent inquiry cites a firmly nonpermissive stance toward anger, one enforced, however, by positive models rather than punishments, as most likely to produce mastery of anger during childhood.[108] As advice was followed by actual parents, it might then have had visible benefits in reduction of parent-child tensions, even as children grew older.

Actual change in personality from one generation to another, however, comes slowly at best, and one may hazard a guess that parental anxiety over new standards increased more quickly than actual childhood anger declined. Surely, parental guilt was on the rise in this period, a feature of American parenting readily visible from that point to the present.[109] And guilt, a kind of anger against the self, is hardly conducive to the creation of an unangry person. We see here a kind of vicious circle generated by the Victorian emotionology and still with us today: I should feel less angry with my kids; I will act as though I feel no anger; they misbehave; I lose my temper; I have failed: I am irritable, and perhaps resentful, all ready to explode at them once more. While direct evidence from the Victorian decades is almost entirely absent, children themselves might face new confusions when told that their childish state and the sanctity of the home were incompatible with angry feelings. Here was a potentially tougher regimen, in terms of emotional control, than the insistence on obedient behavior characteristic of more traditional child rearing. The little Wayland son, hungry, thirsty, and confined for twenty-four hours by a stern but ever kindly father, surely felt as much rage as if he had been whipped. Elizabeth Cady Stanton admitted that her parents were "kind, indulgent and considerate" but also felt that "fear rather than love, of God and parents alike, predominated" in keeping her in line and recalls a sense of the "tyranny of those in authority."[110]

If anger in children probably did not decline notably, though becoming much harder to express openly or to admit, then what of Victorian marriages? We would speculate that this was in fact a period when marital anger was on the upswing. Three reasons for this will be discussed: the increased expectations that people placed on marriage, the closely related phenomenon of the decline of nonmarital or community supports to the individual, and the tension generated by changes in the "outside world" that could not be expressed outside the home.

Almost all discussions of the cult of domesticity have stressed that it represented a bid to increase the importance of marriage. Several historians have gone on to speculate that such increasing expectations must have led to increased anxiety and disappointment. Robert L. Griswold, in his book on divorce in Victorian California, argues that increasing expectations were a crucial phenomenon behind the increasing divorce rate. People who might a century previously have tolerated a poor relationship with a spouse now felt robbed of something that was their due and sought remedy in divorce.[111]

This phenomenon was closely related to declining expectations of emotional support from church and community. Marriage was expected to be the prime emotional solace. It is certainly possible to exaggerate this notion, and much good revisionist work has been done in the past decade or so arguing that women, particularly, also found support in the extended family and in friendships with other women. Still, that marriage was the prime job of a woman and that her relationship with her husband was central in a way it had not been before has not been denied even by these historians.[112]

We become angry when we are disappointed and particularly when we view the disappointment as unjust or unexpected.[113] This is one reason, perhaps, that recent research has shown that we become angry most often at those to whom we feel emotionally close—in fact, at our loved ones.[114] Considering this, then, one must doubt that the formula love up, anger down, suggested by several historians of eighteenth-century emotionality really makes much sense. Love up, or at least expectations of love up, may well have meant anger up as well. Jill Conway has noted that by the late nineteenth century Victorian marriage advisers viewed their subject as problematic. Our perception is that, even before the divorce rate became a commonly discussed phenomenon, there was a sense among marriage writers that things were not working as well as they might and that their books were meant to address a problem.[115]

The third phenomenon that may have led to increased anger in Victorian marriages was the sense of frustration with the world outside the home combined with a notion that it was unacceptable to express such frustration in public. Although without exception the writers of manuals told husbands they were wrong to vent their work frustrations on their wives, it is striking how many of them mention such phenomena as frequent ones in the marriages they had observed. For instance, Daniel Wise noted that "some husbands, after being vexed and tired in their business go home with a sour temper, and breathe out their anger in surly complaints."[116] Similarly, Michael Ryan noted how "every imperfection, capricious temper, vanity, folly . . . appear in the married state. The demeanour toward the world is agreeable and obliging; but in domestic life, the mask is thrown off."[117]

James R. Miller gave an elaborate discussion of how men who exercised control in the outside world lost all care at home: "In society . . . they pride themselves on their thoughtfulness. They are careful not even by tone or look to hurt a sensitive spirit. But at home too often they are rude . . . they blurt out in their own houses the ill humor they have suppressed all day on the street. They answer proper questions in an irritated tone . . . a man thinks that because a woman is his wife she should understand him . . . even if he is rude to her."[118]

Now one may well ask if these observations were generated by an attempt to set new and more rigid standards to control conflict at home or whether the attempt to impose standards was rather an effort to maintain harmony in the face of some actual increase in conflict. In other words, we are asking if in this case the emotionology of Victorian marriage was the cause or the effect of changes in the emotion. And though we posit the question as having provocative value, we feel that it would be futile to be forced into making a single choice for one side or the other and seek here merely to demonstrate that there was an association and that the causality probably worked in both directions.

Certainly, we have ample evidence from the writers of the manuals that there was a felt tension in the world of work and society in the nineteenth century—one that had not existed previously. It is also clear in reading what these writers say that many men had internalized general standards about emotional control that have been discussed in the previous chapter. It was not all right, for middle-class people at least, to express emotion freely among relative strangers. Since so many writers throughout the century observed that they felt outside tensions were being ventilated at home, one is inclined to expect that this may, indeed, have been a real phenomenon and not just an artifact of changing expectations. In other words, as home and work were separated, home became more and more the only place to express negative emotion safely. The world was growing more complicated and frustrating. People expected more from their marriages. Other sources of emotional support were declining, as were acceptable reasons for the expression of anger. Here, then, were the several factors that may have produced an actual increase of anger in nineteenth-century marriages.

At the same time, and in part precisely because anger at home was increasing, the home was being elevated into a kind of moral panacea for Victorian problems. The new family emotionology, responding to a growing problem without resolving it, did succeed in heightening sensitivity. Theoretical expectations for harmony in the relationship between man and wife were rising. The home must be a haven from frustration and conflict. Anger, more than ever before, must be banned from the home. Spouses who might once have been satisfied with a contentious relationship were now taught to see themselves and their marriages as failures.

A kind of vicious circle had been generated. The more people looked to their marriages for solace, the more disappointed and perhaps angry they were doomed to be with those marriages, and the less solace they would find. It was difficult for the Victorians to see any way out of this circle except to keep trying harder. Thus *Peterson's* magazine took to editorializing against temper and for cheerfulness at home repeatedly, as if simply reiterating the message might finally do the trick.[119] We know, however, that such remonstrating did little to change feelings, and the growing trickle of divorces showed the limitations of the Victorian solution. In fact, it was the recognition of that rising divorce rate, perhaps more than any other factor, that ultimately forced some reconsideration of the Victorian orthodoxy on marriage.

The orthodoxy on marriage fell hard, however, perhaps because it was so central to the Victorian synthesis. Views on child rearing, less essential to the cult of domesticity, were the first to change when the Victorians began to alter their views on anger. How and why these changes occurred, and how, eventually, new ideas on marriage were also accommodated, is the subject of our next chapter.

The Victorian contribution to emotionology and emotion concerning anger was predictably complex; this is why, as we have indicated, the emotionology itself was so insistent. In marriage, the emotionology did not work and could even be counterproductive in raising expectations and so disappointments; with actual anger if anything increasing, the new emotionology was doomed to fail from the start. But its effect was real, even aside from the durable public culture of which it was part. It helped to create new anxieties, and, more generally, it called attention to the family as an emotionally charged institution. Unintentionally, in translating the new home/work dichotomy it helped install the family not only as an affectionate haven but also as a safe house for other, officially less desirable emotions and particularly for anger. Simultaneous efforts to limit the expression of anger against children could also serve to concentrate anger toward the spouse, who at least was not a helpless innocent. To be sure, some of the changes in child rearing might have had a minor effect in limiting the amount of anger in the personality; lacking a tested theory of personality formation as well as the necessary historical evidence, we can only suggest this possibility.

More surely, the new child-rearing standards, insofar as they were adopted, helped limit men's and women's ability to recognize their own anger as legitimate, which would feed marital idealism while complicating the marriage itself. In their domestic ardor the Victorians unquestionably advanced the effort to repress anger, as they intended, but they complicated the actual emotional experience of the family in the process. Certainly there must have been some Victorians who ignored the emotionology entirely and many more who took it with a large grain of salt. The evidence proves, however, that the new standards did affect both the behavior and the feelings of many real people.[120] And although no longer Victorian, Americans still grapple with the legacy of these Victorian standards. As we turn now to a distinct new period in the modern approach to familial anger, it will be clear that the Victorian legacy, while seriously modified, in part because of its own internal contradictions, was not to be reversed.

4 A New Approach to Anger Control
1860–1940, The American Ambivalence

The early Victorian synthesis on anger depended on a more general synthesis of beliefs about the relationship between home and work and on a style that handled unpleasant subjects by pressing for more effort, more self-discipline, and more control. That home/work dichotomy began to undergo some modification in the second half of the century, and at the same time a new style emerged that encouraged dealing with unpleasantness through understanding rather than conquest. Not surprisingly, then, ideas about anger also began to change. These changes became evident, at first, in the child-rearing literature and only later began to be accommodated in thought on marriage. We will describe these changes and then attempt to explore in some detail the reasons for change. After this discussion of emotionology, we will then consider what form the actual expression of anger took during this period and offer some speculations about the relationship between the emotionology and the reality of anger in the American home.

Family emotionology at the turn of the century became more complex, which may ironically have made it more realistic. Two new ingredients entered the picture, altering the earlier Victorian stance: a recognition that anger existed as a natural personality trait and a belief that anger could be put to some good uses. These novelties were combined with continued insistence on avoiding anger in the home, which made for some careful statements about child-rearing strategies and new discussions of marital tactics as well.

During the decades between about 1860 and 1940, as Victorian idealism confronted new realities about the human personality and marriage, basic anger-control goals persisted. No one emerged directly to praise anger or to urge that restraint was less important than the Victorians had believed. Indeed, on the subjects of both child rearing and marriage statements of almost literal Victorianism continued to be made or could be revived when external reality seemed to turn particularly sour. But strategies did change, as it was realized, for various reasons, that literal avoidance of anger was more difficult than had previously been thought. Furthermore, particularly in child rearing, the definition of desirable personality shifted somewhat, so that a person devoid of anger's zest was now seen as unduly flaccid. The shift in tactics and the partial alteration of goals combined to create a new period in the American approach to anger, one still modern in its attack on anger itself but far more complicated than the Victorian decades had been.

Perhaps no character exemplifies this complexity so well as Melville's Billy Budd, whose demise may fairly be viewed as the result of his unsuccessful attempt to handle conflicts about anger. Melville, introducing his hero, tells us that his slowness to anger was viewed as unmanly by some peers. One man thought "such a 'sweet and pleasant fellow' as he mockingly designated him . . . could hardly have the spirit of a game-cock." He tried unsuccessfully to provoke the hero, but finally, when he struck Billy, the hero "quick as lightening . . . let fly his arm." Melville commented on this through another character: " 'Well, blessed are the peacemakers, especially the fighting peacemakers!' "[1] Anger, when justifiable, was manly and admirable. Billy's and Melville's confusion about how to express the anger, however, was the central problem of the tragedy.

This newly complex approach to anger that was epitomized by Billy Budd must be explored in detail for two reasons. First, several aspects of it seem quintessentially American, constituting a clearer national variant on a general modern-Western approach to emotionality than Victorian idealism had done. In child rearing, the characteristic ambivalence about goals generated during this period corresponded to some measurable and unusual features of American parenting. The approach in marriage advice was less clearly distinctive, on a comparative basis, but here too ambivalence corresponded to some unusual empirical aspects of the American scene, notably the rising national divorce rate. The American approach to anger during the turn-of-the-century decades sought still to discipline the emotion, but a confusing sense that the discipline could not or should not be complete was also present.

The second reason to attend to this period is that it provides a crucial baseline for evaluating subsequent developments. For Americans did not stick to an ambivalent approach to familial anger, despite its linkage to some important facets of national character. Recent alterations in approach must inevitably be measured against the turn-of-the-century style. And the existence of this style, coming after the more straightforward Victorian attempt to attack anger without qualification, might lend some encouragement to those who find contemporary Americans again too thoroughly repressive. For while it is clear that an effort to identify and discipline anger forms an important part of modern social norms from the late eighteenth century, the new twists that emerged after about 1860 demonstrated that this effort was compatible with some subtle usage of the emotion as well: it may be tempting to appeal in future to the turn-of-the-century willingness to draw benefit from anger.

Child Rearing: A New Emotionology

The emergence of a new ambivalence toward anger in child-rearing advice was particularly striking in the decades after 1860, for it represented an attempt to preserve an anger-free home while developing a new kind of vigor in economic and public life. American child-rearing emotionology had already gone through two phases, and in each the approach to anger was quite clear-cut. In the first period, child-rearing advice ignored anger in favor of selective concern over its behavioral consequences. In the second, ultimately Victorian stage, anger had been thoroughly reproved, though the reproval was surrounded by idealistic assumptions of childish innocence that might mute its effects in practice. Now, while reproval continued, particularly within the family circle, properly controlled anger was seen as a useful goad to constructive behavior in the wider world. This was the pattern of advice that corresponded to measurable behavior on the part of many parents, producing the distinctive American approach to the handling of anger in children, indeed, a distinctive American approach to the definition of an emotionally appropriate personality.

Some portion of the new ambivalence may have resulted from a partial merger of expert advice with parental reality. We will see a similar realism enter, more hesitantly, into marital advice as well. Victorian advice had, after all, paid little attention to the actual personality traits of children, assuming that proper parental example was everything. It is very unlikely that many parents attempted to alter traditional disciplinary behavior to meet this ideal fully. Thus while there is some evidence that the strictest will-breaking behavior declined and evidence also of new anxiety on the part of parents about their own anger, it is clear that many parents did indeed encounter anger in children and that they often attempted to punish expressions of angry emotion. Certain child-rearing experts toward the end of the nineteenth century explicitly recognized childish anger; they also recognized, with the larger goal of anger control in mind, the need to do something about it, and were therefore sending more realistic signals and also picking up on actual parental experience. This is one reason, in turn, that the new pattern of advice had a wider demonstrable effect than Victorian idealism had won, even though this idealism had served an important stage in the development of anger-control goals.

The new approach toward anger in child-rearing unquestionably related to another trend in actual parenting, particularly for males, that took shape toward the end of the nineteenth century. Moral discipline, as part of character building, declined in favor. Fathers who advised and wrote to their sons increasingly pulled away from this Protestant-Victorian approach, replacing it in part with growing concern about physical health and athletic development.[2] This shift did not eliminate anger control as a purpose, but it required a new sense of tactics; moral restraint and parental example would no longer suffice.

Two new themes predominated in child-rearing emotionology concerning anger from the late nineteenth century through the interwar years. First, there was greater recognition that children did naturally get angry, as against Victorian assumptions of innocence, and that childish anger required some firm disciplinary approach. Anger remained unacceptable, but the mechanisms through which to achieve anger control inevitably became more complex and explicit. This was the area in which the new tone in advice corresponded most obviously with parental realities. The second change related in part to the new strategies sought, but it also reflected an alteration in personality goals. Anger, while unacceptable, was now seen as a desirable emotional spur that could be channeled into useful endeavor. The concept of channeling, into competitive drive or moral indignation, was the most significant innovation of turn-of-the-century emotionology.

Fairly literal Victorian statements did continue, particularly, of course, in the 1870s and 1880s but even into the 1920s. At first an ideal of the Christian gentleman maintained the Victorian approach toward anger in children, with an emphasis on complete anger avoidance through proper moral guidance and parental restraint. Evangelical pamphlets espoused this approach into the twentieth century. Thus, for example, the Christian gentleman school maintained that parents have a "sacred duty" to instill anger control by forming habits early through their own examples; and the Evangelical approach held, with an interesting increase in concern about violence, that "the same temper that smashes a toy in anger may, when the child is grown, kill a man."[3] Such continuity of idealistic concern means of course that diversity continued in the American approach to anger. This is no great surprise, but it is important because it underlines the fact that key Victorian goals persisted in this area, not only in the genteel Christian literature, but also in the more innovative materials. The changes that must be discussed were not reversals. Older goals were to a great extent retained, and this is why literal Victorianism could still be maintained without seeming hopelessly anachronistic. We will see a similar pattern in marital advice, in which real changes did not obscure an intense desire to keep the family largely free from anger.

But the most popular child-rearing advice manuals, soon joined by magazines for up-to-date parents, shifted away from literal Victorianism. Darwinian findings about the animal bases of human behavior, including elaborate inquiries into the evolutionary role of anger, helped alter the view of childish innocence in the mainstream literature from the 1860s on. The fact had to be recognized: many children, even when well treated, did grow angry and have tantrums. Indeed, it was during these decades, and initially through Darwinian usage, that the word *tantrum* finally settled into its contemporary form, designating an objectionable pattern of emotional outburst among young children and therefore a genuine problem for parents.[4]

The new empirical view of childish anger produced a growing concern about the issue of parental emotional control from the 1880s until about 1910. G. Stanley Hall inquired into anger in an elaborate research project, and he incorporated some of this concern in his discussion of adolescence. Partly under Hall's influence, several child-rearing manuals took up the problem of anger between 1900 and 1910, and the National Institute of Child Life issued a special pamphlet on the subject. After about 1910 attention grew less detailed because an acceptable range of approaches had been agreed on, at least among the advice givers; but any manual that went beyond physical health advice now regularly included a section on tantrums, a pattern that continues to the present day.[5]

For childish anger was a problem precisely because the new empirical view of children was combined with a basic desire to maintain older goals of anger control. The flurry of attention to the subject produced a general consensus that childish anger was an appropriate subject for discipline and that it required as well more elaborate strategies than the Victorians had suggested in order to avoid angry confrontations in the first place. Hall and his followers criticized parents who were too indulgent of anger in young children and urged physical punishment for its expression. They also saw anger control as part of a childhood-long process of parental guidance, one that would extend to advice on proper behavior for adolescents. During the 1920s and 1930s, concern about very young children increased, in advance of real acceptance of Freudianism.[6] John B. Watson and other behaviorists found childish anger easy enough to control, through elimination of unnecessary restraint and also of undue coddling; calm, nonangry discipline remained a key. Other experts handled growing parental concern about tantrums differently. Some urged neglect pure and simple; others favored careful inquiry into the causes of anger; others, including several authors in *Parents' Magazine,* urged outright punishment lest tantrums reveal a child unduly spoiled.[7] The increasing concern with childish anger, while it did not produce a single enduring recommended parental response, did show a new, or newly articulate, belief. Childish anger control was not only important, as earlier in the nineteenth century, but also somewhat difficult. Parents needed more than their own self-restraint if the child was to grow into a "self-controlled and useful adult."[8]

As part of this new concern, the need for patience and control of anger in relationships among brothers and sisters received growing emphasis, for, along with positive affection, the absence of sibling conflict was vital to family harmony. Authorities called to mind evil fraternal conflicts in the Bible. Louisa May Alcott, in *Little Women,* painted the problems of quick tempers among sisters: Jo lamented her "dreadful temper," and her mother assured her that this was a temptation that would require lifelong control. "You think your temper is the worst in the world, but mine used to be just like it. I've been trying to cure it for forty years, and have only succeeded in controlling it. I am angry nearly everyday of my life, but I have learned not to show it; and I still hope to learn not to feel it, though it may take me another forty years to do so."[9] Clearly, the later nineteenth century did not abandon the arduous goal of emotional control.

Growing recognition of childish anger as a problem did not produce a single strategy for coping. Child-rearing authorities got a good bit of mileage from arguments about whether ignoring anger was better than outright punishment of it, with advocates of the former approach (combined of course with greatest possible avoidance of childish fatigue and other irritants) gradually winning majority support in the advice manuals. This tactical disagreement was significant, for, as we will see, it corresponded to considerable diversity in parental approach. But the authorities did agree on key goals: childish anger should never be rewarded; childish anger, including sibling rivalry, should be excised as fully and as early as possible to preserve the proper emotional tone of the home and to start the process of building a civilized personality; and parents must see this aspect of the emotional life of their charges as a problem area.

Concern about childish anger spilled over, more clearly than in early Victorianism, into perceptions of social class. Experts, using the dominant emotionology, widely criticized the way working-class parents handled anger, from the late nineteenth to the mid-twentieth century. Worker or immigrant parents were judged likely to respond to childish tantrums with anger and physical punishments of their own. Some even encouraged and enjoyed their children's aggression against others as an outlet for their own feelings. The net result was inconsistency (so the experts held)—the generation of anger in reaction to parental anger, without firm and uniform rules against its expression. Here, the experts argued, was a major source of disproportionate delinquency, another theme that reveals growing recognition that childish anger could turn into a problem unless handled with care.[10]

In some ways the second new theme of child-rearing emotionology complicated the first, for it recognized that anger could mutate into useful drives. But the complication was not intentional, for the goal of anger control, particularly within the family, was not explicitly altered. And channeling anger—the strategy that resulted from the new theme—formed a widely agreed on technique for handling part of the problem now so widely perceived.

This second new theme, addressed particularly toward men, did, however, pull away from Victorian idealism quite decisively. For there was a growing belief that anger could be good as well as bad. Not in raw form: no one pulled back from disapproval of literal displays of personal temper. But, properly channeled, anger was a useful spur; indeed, its absence was to be lamented. Here indeed was another new parental worry by the late nineteenth century: children incapable of anger lacked individuality and independence and were truly "pathetic."[11] The notion that anger reflected a kind of admirable spunk, at least in males, had not been totally foreign to the earlier period, but now it became a central strain of the emotionology rather than an insignificant aside. Child-rearing experts, in the eighty years after 1860, produced the emotionological base for the American ambivalence about anger—the ambivalence that Lloyd Warner still discerned in middle-class families in the 1950s.

Some of the new tensions about anger emerged in outright disagreement, particularly during the 1860s and 1870s, when the transition to new beliefs was in progress. Thus handbooks on the Christian gentleman stressed control of anger at the same time as literature in the Horatio Alger school urged the importance of aggressive, competitive behavior, in which values such as anger were instrumental in personal advancement. Anger, in this literature, was by itself of no concern, for it could easily shift to spur achievement. Children's literature similarly provided examples of pacificity cheek by jowl with the more sensational stories of the post–Civil War era, which praised brawling and manly strength.[12]

By the end of the nineteenth century, and recurrently thereafter, the new tensions emerged in individual discussions, producing many near contradictions. G. Stanley Hall blasts anger as destructive and damaging to health, the sign of a weak will and of decaying intellectual power. But he also held that "a certain choleric vein gives zest and force to all acts" and, in an effort to reconcile, that "the best work of the world is done" in the tension between anger and control. According to the American Institute of Child Life: "Anger is not lovely"; children's rages, though inevitable to a point because of the fighting instinct, create such ugly physical symptoms that the person seems "a child no longer, but a creature under demoniacal possession." But while childish anger warrants some "counsel and punishment, an atmosphere of grief and disapproval," and efforts to prevent or distract, and while the aggression that leads to "wars, rapine and misery" is unquestionably bad, anger cannot and should not be entirely eliminated; it has many good qualities and should be "a great and diffused power in life, making it strenuous, giving zest to the struggle for power and rising to righteous indignation."[13]

The key to this new perception, the ultimate reconciler, was channeling, as part of character building. Thus a turn-of-the-century manual urged a balance between encouraging and discouraging anger as the fighting instinct. Too much combativeness is obviously bad, but a boy with no tendency to fight would be an unnatural nonentity. So fighting should never be promoted, but no parent should ever say never fight. Similarly for adults, competition "is a form of fighting that is very prominent all through life." In a similar vein, according to the founder of the National Congress of Mothers, while girls should be trained to prepare a tranquil home and face problems "cheerfully," boys should simply be tained in righteous indignation. The process was to be highly rational. Children could be taught to look at the results of ungoverned temper and then urged on to proper targets. Here, for example, is an uplifting conversation between mother and son on a dirty street: " 'I'm sure, my little son, when you are a man, and serve in the City Council, you will see that the laws are enforced and that we have a clean town.' See the flash of righteous indignation in the boyish eyes. . . . the active brain has received an indelible impression, the emotional nature has found a legitimate vent." Even a violent temper, with such training, can be a "splendid force," providing "royal service."[14]

Thus the tension about the uses of anger, though it did produce some contradictory or confusing statements, was not fundamentally illogical. It did pull away from the simpler disapproval of anger that had developed by the mid-nineteenth century without returning to the lack of explicit concern characteristic of will breaking. To this extent the tension was more complex. Even when not illogical in theory, it could add new worries to the process of parenting. The decline of belief in the innocence of young children justified new admissions that some children had ungovernable tempers while other children might frighten by their passivity, their lack of anger.[15] Furthermore, the new, limited value found in anger did not remove the parental obligation of self-control. Children must be allowed some anger, but adults should have learned that anger was inappropriate in the home. Both competition and righteous indignation were for external use only. Thus the translation of the new tension into practice may have been constructive, but it raised several potential difficulties as well. It is also obvious that authorities who saw channeling as the solution to parental problems disagreed somewhat about direction. Advice produced by men, and also many stories for boys, tended to emphasize the competitive joys of channeled anger and suggested various specific devices, such as boxing, to begin the channeling process during boyhood. Other literature, particularly that produced by women and directed toward the mothers of boys, focused more explicitly, Progressive fashion, on the moral utility of indignation. Their strategies rested more on sage maternal advice than on competitive sports, like the ideal mother who strolled down the streets with her son pointing out targets for reformist zeal.

Contradictions and complexities in the new approach to anger should not be overdrawn. Experts did disagree over precise methods of disciplining anger, just as they more implicitly argued about whether anger should be channeled into business or into reformist activities. But a sense that anger in children, though a problem, was a manageable problem developed widely. Children's stories could toss off glib, moralistic pronouncements about anger with a firm belief that the values of control were undoubted—they often focused on anger in boys since girls were not angry anyway. Thus Uncle Wiggily (the rabbit gentleman popular between the wars) disdained an angry boy: "And I think he stamped his foot on the floor, the least little bit. It may have been that he saw a tack sticking up, and wanted to hammer it down with his shoe. But I am afraid it was a stamp of the foot; and afterward that boy was sorry." Note that the angry gesture itself was wrong, even in private; this involved more than the traditional insistence on obedience and readily continued the Victorian emphasis on avoiding a nasty emotion.[16] Other stories, of course, showed teenagers, who had presumably mastered personal anger, displaying commendable emotional drive in pursuit of business success or in attacking social evils. No shadow of a psychological or philosophical dilemma entered these lessons.

Child-rearing literature also usually handled the complexity of the emotionology of anger with admirable brevity. Particularly after about 1910, when the Darwinian findings about children had been assimilated and the channeling approach widely accepted, the space devoted to anger problems was typically limited. This helps account for the confusing signals that resulted in some treatments, but it also expresses the real confidence that a satisfactory synthesis had been achieved. If anything, after the initial discussion, the new sense that anger could be channeled reduced the need to talk about it, in contrast to the more thorough uprooting projected in the mid-nineteenth-century approach, though, as we have seen, a subject such as sibling relations, involving family harmony, roused great interest still. Character building, of which Victorian anger control was a part, required repeated lessons and examples, for parents and children alike. The new approach, for all the disagreements over specifics, tended to assume that childish anger could be handled early, with channeling developed through a series of physically as well as mentally uplifting exercises until adulthood was achieved. Hence, again particularly after 1910, other issues easily predominated: sheer physical care (for infants), the treatment of sexuality, and even the handling of fear. Some manuals focused only on physical health; this was the official stance of the early editions of *Infant Care,* which viewed the emotional area as beyond really scientific judgment to date. Even manuals that did take up emotions tended to favor inculcation of temperance, chastity, honesty, and courage, though anger received its due formulas.[17] Most typical was the brief, confident comment. Children could usually learn to handle anger naturally, through interaction with peers under parental guidance. Wild anger had to be discouraged, though remedies varied somewhat. But parents should not exaggerate even a modest tantrum problem since anger was valuable when channeled and even tantrums might be channeled through vigorous exercise or competitive games.[18]

This general approach, including the central ambivalence about anger's value depending on private or public expression, survived several generational swings in other aspects of child-rearing advice. Historians have identified the cycles 1840–60, 1860–80, 1880–1910, and 1910–30 as marking shifts and sometimes outright reversals in such basic practices as toilet training and feeding schedules and in parental emotional tone.[19] These shifts, if carried through by actual parents, might have had a major effect on actual childish anger, the effect varying, of course, according to the school of experts listened to. Thus Watsonian benign neglect, intended among other things to limit anger, would be seen by later experts to be productive of anger in adults because of its strictness and coldness toward young children. The shifts in child-rearing fads unquestionably revealed the ingenuity of experts in seeking an audience, for each succeeding generation had the awesome task of undoing its predecessor's work. And each of the shorter cycles undoubtedly had some real effect on the actual behavior of some real parents and, even more, on their professed goals and anxieties. However, with respect to anger, at least, the somewhat longer periodization 1860–1940 must also be emphasized, for a fairly consistent stance, calling for control but not repression, underlay the shorter cycles. The fact that such consistency can be discerned may possibly point to a more realistic connection between child-rearing advice and actual parental behavior. The assumptions of 1860–1940 did represent change from the previously dominant approach, and they were to change again. But as they were not quite as volatile as the cycles expertise in other areas went through, actual parents and children were exposed to them longer.[20]

The theme of controlling private anger while channeling it to good purpose continues from the Darwinians through the muscular Christians to the various child-rearing schools of the first third of our own century, creating vigorous appeals for less or for more anger, depending on the context. G. Stanley Hall cites the attitude of one of his teachers in the mid-1890s: "I plead for more anger in schools. There is a point where patience ceases to be a moral of pedagogical virtue, but is mere flabbiness."[21] Dorothy Canfield Fischer, a tireless writer of manuals for parents, felt that a child should never be permitted to gain anything by showing anger, for children must learn to solve problems by other means. *But* anger can spur useful energy. A recent manual for black parents regards anger as typically destructive; it should certainly never dominate action, for too often it leads to crime and violence. Mothers should prevent anger in children by large doses of affection. *But* anger energizes the fight for legitimate rights. According to a Watsonian of the 1930s, parents can easily teach children not to throw tantrums by ignoring them, and while some anger is indeed unavoidable since children must be restrained, it is a learned emotion and can largely be omitted from a child's emotional lexicon. *But* anger is valuable to individuals and to society: "If he is stirred, if he reacts powerfully, out of that very stirring may come achievements and performance of a high level." A more permissive approach, from the 1940s, stresses that civilization depends on rational control of anger and that a well-adjusted person is not angry. *But*, some pages later, anger is a great thing, from childhood on, in calling attention to individual rights.[22] Even specific aspects of anger elicit contradictions. After noting how tantrums can best be avoided and how they can signal problems with parent or child, a manual subsequently lauds the normalcy of tantrums as the root of a baby's individuality, self-respect, and strength of character.[23] *But* tantrums after two years of age show physiological and serious behavioral disturbance (though later in the same book the age is confusingly pushed back to three and a half). And, elsewhere, children's anger "serves an excellent purpose."[24]

The durability of the tensions in the new child-rearing emotionology suggests again that they served an important cultural function and represented a satisfactory amalgam to several generations of writers. We will turn later to the equally important and durable correspondence to actual parental styles. Clearly, many people found the turn-of-the-century complications in the anger-control effort a valid addendum, one that addressed real-world needs without sacrificing a proper definition of personality or the ongoing desire for an anger-free family environment. The channeling concept was of course the key reconciler of diverse purposes. Supplementing this was the implied division between the socialization of boys and that of girls. Early Victorian child-rearing ideals had merged the treatment of gender largely on a feminized base. The new approach to anger, which in part reacted to growing fears of feminization as women took on novel roles and gained predominance in the teaching corps, stipulated the importance of aggressive behavior for males.[25] A few child-rearing experts, such as representatives of the National Congress of Mothers who stood against the feminism of the day in the name of domestic authority, explicitly differentiated between the channeling needs of boys and the continued anger-free qualities of girls. Without question, as we will see, many parents adopted this dual approach, continuing to stress Victorian restraint on girlish anger. Such a division did help reconcile the channeling impulse with domestic idealism. Both boys and girls should shed literal anger, but girls, as future promoters of domestic bliss, should do their shedding without qualifications. Only boys, with business and public roles in mind, should work toward anger control through channeling.

It is important to note, however, as a final complication in this new emotionology, that most child-rearing authorities only implied this clear gender division; they did not state it outright. Examples of channeled anger used boys as subjects. Worries about angerless children were, mainly, worries about boys. Sports used as channeling mechanisms were boys' sports. Save for the few exceptions noted, few authorities actually stated that girls should not undergo a channeling experience or that they might not find the vigor of sublimated anger useful, as men would, in later life. In a period when many women, as feminists or temperance advocates, were in fact demonstrating high levels of moral indignation, this common omission is significant—as if child-rearing experts, like many women themselves, had not decided on an appropriate emotional definition for womanhood. This implicit hesitancy about gender divisions (or their absence) in emotionology carried over into some of the obliqueness of the treatment of anger in marriage, as we shall see. It may also have suggested that, in practice, some girls as well as boys were exposed to the new esteem for channeled anger, if with some confusion because of the lack of overt comment on this emotional outlet for women. This exposure, too, could bear on marriage.

Marriage: A More Tentative Shift in Emotionology

Changes in child-rearing standards might have led to some frank discussion of how to reconcile an aggressive personality with successful marriage, but in fact this issue was largely avoided. Comments on the problems of bringing work irritants home were no more frequent than they were in the previous period. For the chief innovations in child-rearing emotionology in essence maintained or even heightened the division in standards between home and work. Boys and girls were to learn discipline of anger in their home activities; but while girls, as homebodies, might need to learn nothing more, boys should have to learn a distinctive emotional style, through channeling, for their lives outside the home. This approach suggested considerable tension in practice between conflicting emotional impulses, most obviously for men, but also potentially for women who might have to deal with male outbursts when the home/work dualism broke down. But in theory the approach was compatible with continued insistence on Victorian idealism for the home itself, for the child-rearing complexity consisted precisely in this unusual effort to create two approaches to anger, depending on private or public context.

Some of the same ambivalence about anger expressed in the child-rearing literature did, however, emerge in discussions of marriage, though the Victorian consensus on the marriage question lasted longer and was not to be thoroughly displaced until after 1945. The new ambivalence that did appear resulted not from rigorous application of child-rearing tensions to discussions of marriage—in part because different sets of experts were involved in the two fields—but rather from a new recognition of the divorce problem and its implication for a discussion of anger. Here was the central new reality for marriage advisers; it produced, however, not a full reevaluation of anger in marriage but a new set of shadings, a wider range of pragmatic tolerance, that were in some ways more complex than the tensions in child-rearing values. For the new socialization standards did form a logical whole, however difficult it was to achieve; the innovations in marital advice did not produce a new overall pattern.

One key to the tentativeness with which the topic of marital standards was reopened lies in the general effort to avoid a focus on anger as part of the rising discussion of the problem of divorce. A huge and contentious literature emerged in the American press after the Bureau of Labor's 1890 publication of its report *Marriage and Divorce,* which revealed how increasingly common the dissolution of marriage had become.[26] But none of the parties in the ensuing debate viewed anger as a central part of the divorce issue. Explicit discussion of anger in marriage in most of the manuals written between 1890 and 1930 was also absent, although a careful reading between the lines of various comments on marriage does produce some sense of change. It was as if, despite the growing centrality of divorce as an issue, there was an intense desire to preserve Victorian emotional standards in those marriages that remained; this in turn required that anger control be assumed rather than opened to widespread scrutiny.

Three factors encouraged the treatment of anger as a nonissue in discussions of divorce itself: a concentration, strange to modern readers, on the legal issues involved in divorce; a concentration, somewhat less strange to us, on the centrality of sex in marriage; and a growing attention on the part of social scientists to divorce in the context of social trends rather than of psychological concerns.

As William O'Neill has argued, many writers on the divorce issue zeroed in not on the causes of divorce but rather on the solution, which in turn led them to discussions of law and, particularly, to arguments about whether divorce should be made easier or harder to obtain. Conservatives who argued for tighter laws indirectly operated from Victorian assumptions, believing that bad people opted for divorce and should be legally impeded from acting on their badness. Radicals argued for more liberal laws in the name of individual freedom but also in the belief that partners might simply be missuited—not bad—and might therefore be able to find a happy, loving marriage if released from their present situations. Neither radicals nor conservatives had a view of individual psychology or the emotional dynamics of marriage. Both would have agreed that anger has no place inside a good family.[27]

Today we think of most marriages as neither all good nor all bad and as presenting a set of problems that we should try to resolve. We are also taught that all parties may bear responsibility in a poor marriage and thus that trading for a new spouse may not solve any of the problems involved. This sort of psychological complexity had not yet been invented in 1900, so the liberal-conservative debate was free to focus on issues of social control versus freedom. It was as though each individual was a black box to be observed only from the outside, as good or bad, free or controlled, with no consideration for internal emotional complexities such as anger. At most, advice on marriage should include greater attention to the right choice of mate, now seen as an obvious problem. There was no need for new layers of advice once the marriage was formed, for anger should still be prevented either through social controls or through legal freedoms to form a proper, anger-free marriage if a mistake had been made.[28] In any case, the Victorian consensus on anger needed no restatement.

Where an internal dynamic was addressed, it involved sex, not anger.[29] Just as the child-rearing literature placed a new emphasis on the importance of physical well-being, so the marriage literature grew increasingly concerned with the physical side of matrimony. Sex became the crucial, and for some writers the only, determinant of the husband-wife relationship, and many so-called marriage manuals consisted of sexual advice pure and simple. It was argued frequently that quarrels or anger must be understood as the symptoms of a bad sexual adjustment: "You will find strife, bickering, quarreling among the highest and the lowest; and all this perversion, all this misery . . . is made possible . . . by simple and avoidable causes . . . all largely physical."[30] Insofar as Freud was read, and he was cited increasingly during the period under discussion, he was understood to be a proponent of a new view of sexuality. Americans managed to ignore his other great drive, aggression, until after World War II. Anger, then, was not of great interest because it was simply a symptom of bad sex, not a problem in itself. For intellectuals at least, anger in marriage was of less interest than anger in childhood. This, of course, was in accord with the channeling notion, for, again, it preserved the ideal of an anger-free home.

The third reason that anger in marriage was largely ignored as an issue was that the subject of marriage was increasingly taken over by professional social scientists, for whom, in the first decades of our century, psychology seemed irrelevant. For these theorists, the problem of divorce was seen as a subset of the problem of modernization. Marital difficulties were a result of conditions such as the pace of modern life, overcrowding in cities, inadequate housing, poverty, and immigration. An example may be seen in a feature published in the *Ladies Home Journal* telling the story of a marriage in crisis: "Modern conditions have made a machine of the man, and the high pressure under which he lives, the money he spends, and the money he is obliged to earn . . . sends him home to his wife worn out and exhausted. . . . she has waited all day for his homecoming . . . and she finds him, nine times out of ten, asleep in his chair as soon as he has finished his cigar . . . [so she spends more and more time out of the house]. . . . I do not criticize her, nor for that matter . . . her husband. I sympathize with them both. They have merely been caught in the whirl of modern conditions."[31] Differences among families, those who coped more and less well, were not explored, nor was the family seen as a force that might affect its environment rather than simply being a passive victim of it. This was a social science without a psychology, and therefore one relatively uninterested in emotions such as anger. For these writers, as for the pro-divorce radicals and for the sexologists, anger was a symptom, not a fundamental. And they were in accord with the conservatives in thinking that reform must come through social measures, not through addressing the individual.[32]

It is striking, considering the huge literature on the divorce question generated after 1890, how few marriage manuals were actually written, but in view of what has been said the reasons are understandable. Moralists, both conservative and liberal, saw the central issue as a social problem, not one to be addressed by individual families. Social scientists felt the same way. Sexologists did write marriage manuals, but of the narrowest sort. We have been able to locate very few manuals that deal with the general interpersonal difficulties between husband and wife in the same way that the Victorian tracts did or in the same way that those written after World War II do. Marriage as seen by the *Ladies Home Journal* reflected the same approach. The divorce question received a great deal of attention, but in the context of a debate on the legal issues. Otherwise marriage was seen as a matter of furnishing the house, selecting the right clothes, and picking the right recipes. When the *Journal* published a special "Marriage Number" in October 1910, the only feature that even touched on the question of the relationship between the spouses was an article on why wives needed their own allowances. Although the *Journal* featured regular columns on cooking, fashion, home design, and child care, there was no regular feature on the marriage relationship until after World War II.

We see, then, that interpersonal relationships between spouses were not considered to be of significant interest during this period and that, insofar as they were, anger was far down on the list of subjects of interest. There was no flurry of concern comparable to that in child-rearing discussions around 1900 or even routinized brief treatments as there were in parental advice literature once the channeling approach was assimilated. This does not mean, however, that there was no emotionology of anger in marriage; it was simply more implicit than explicit and more ambiguous than the more overtly stated emotionology of the earlier era.

The first new ambiguity, based on implication rather than frank assessment, involved some modification of the Victorians' idealized rejection of all taint of anger in a proper marriage. As in the child-rearing literature, in which there was increased recognition during this period that little ones did get angry, there was some nod in acknowledgment that anger in a marriage might surface without wrecking it. Usually, this was seen in the context of an increasingly feminist view. The idea was that women had rights as well as obligations, including the right to get mad if their rights were denied.

Even the *Ladies Home Journal*, which catered to traditional middle-class women and self-consciously avoided appealing to "intellectuals," offered some place in its pages to the new view that anger in marriage was to be expected and was not necessarily a bad thing.[33] The argument was made that a couple was really the sum of two individuals and that, if the individuals were to remain true to themselves, some conflict was inevitable. "The Fly in the Ointment," a story published in 1915, made the case that it was perfectly reasonable for a dissatisfied wife to nag her husband and even to leave him. "To harness two animals together doesn't necessarily make a team of them," spoke the author through one protagonist. Defending the individual and rejecting the notion that a spouse should repress her own wishes for the sake of the relationship, he goes on to say that "when it comes to the point that a woman has to 'get around' a man to make him keep his teeth clean it's high time she quit the job altogether in my opinion." The story had one mother explain the modern view to her bewildered and old-fashioned son: "We want just about what men want . . . why not?"[34]

The sort of conflict in which anger was depicted favorably in the *Journal* was, most often, one about money. A story called "The Purple Hat," published in 1915, was the most forthright example we encountered of an author's defense of anger on the part of a deprived wife. The heroine spends years suffering in public, always dressed in last year's frumpy styles, because her husband will not give her an allowance for clothing. The turning point comes when she hears some other women mocking her attire and is overcome with hate for her husband, "crazed with anger and shame." When she confronts him, he blames her at first for not taking enough pains with her apparel, but her response is hardly acquiescent. "I always recall with something like pride that scene of violence that followed, pride that I dared speak out at last. I remember how I sprang up fiercely, and turned loose upon Hartley the pent-up slow forming wrath of these five years."

Had this been a Victorian story, the husband would probably have died from shock and the wife immediately repented her display of feeling, but this was not the case here. The husband mildly agreed to give his wife a regular allowance. In looking back on it, the wife allows that she had been a fool to try Victorian methods in the first place. "If I had been a sensible person I would have marched boldly downstairs, laid my case clearly before my husband, and shown him it would be necessary for me to have a reasonable allowance. But I was not sensible. I felt it would kill me to 'have it out' with Hartley about money.''

Having it out, now, seems quite the right thing to do. At the end of the tale, the wife throws the purple hat that has caused her humiliation into the fire and in a very patent metaphor for her own anger tells her husband, ''a little blaze—oh, a little blaze is pleasant Hartley.''[35]

In a similar vein, a notice the *Journal* ran for Girl's Club, a service through which women could earn money at home, was subtitled ''Do You Hate to Ask for Money?'' and quoted a letter from a reader, Emily R. S. of Indiana, who frankly admitted anger with her spouse. ''When I ask him for anything for myself he requires a detailed explanation which is particularly trying to me.''[36]

Beyond the specific money conflicts, some tentative hints began appearing in the literature that too much suppression of feeling might harm a marriage. In the story of one relationship that had become stale and boring, the wife mused, ''We do not quarrel; and I am not sure but that is the worst sign of all.''[37] ''The Wedding Film,'' another tale of a marriage gone stale, contrasted the impulsive emotional bride with her undemonstrative and matter-of-fact husband, and in opposition to the Victorian view that would have blamed her, faulted him instead for his lack of emotionality.[38] Ella W. Wilcox advised in 1894 that ''a man prefers temper to sulks. . . . an occasional thunder-storm clears the air.'' The Reverend E. J. Hardy, who had published a classical Victorian manual in 1886 complete with dire warnings against the first quarrel, revised himself in 1914, suggesting that ''five minutes of rage, even though a simulated one, may do more to reclaim a man than a whole year of nagging and weeping. . . . The woman who has learned how to get angry knows also how not to do so, and is always ready to sympathize and encourage.''[39] The idea, then, was that a little display of anger might be the price required if more positive emotions were to be expected as well.

We may note in all these examples, however, that the permission to be angry was rather muted. Certainly there was a tacit admission that even good people became angry, but it was just as clear that anger was to be fairly circumscribed and had better be provoked by some clearly identifiable flaw in the spouse. Discomfort with anger was still prevalent.

One way in which people often mask such discomfort with feelings, and reassure themselves, is to joke about it, and much of the fiction that dealt with marital conflict in this period did take on a jokey, almost cute tone. The *Journal* ran a series in 1910 called ''The Little Woman and the Busy Man'' in which there was usually a conflict of interest and even, at times, an admission of anger but in which unfailingly the dispute was mediated mainly by teasing and kidding and in which things always ended happily, with the sense that each partner had been silly to be mad at the other.[40] In George Hibbard's story "The Chaperon" the wife supposes "that every young married woman has known periods of impatience" but manages to end her quarrel with her husband on an upbeat note and then to state that she was silly to be angry at him for anything."[41]

In some of the stories, there was a kind of playing with the idea of the quarrel, reminiscent of a child's playacting out of a conflict when he is not quite ready to experience the emotions aroused by the real situation. A short piece called "When I Love Him," published in 1915, is a good example: "I love him when I say, 'Oh, I don't need rubbers today!' His face is adorable when he says; 'what do I care what a little chit like you thinks? You put those rubbers on!' [The joke is she had them all along.] . . . 'I poke out my feet and laugh. I love to have him pretend to beat me.'"[42]

This "cute" argument was sometimes a defense for a husband as well. In a poem called "Any Husband to His Wife," the author begins, "You ask me why I only call you 'Dear,'" and going on to enumerate all the wife's demands for money, explains that "Dear" refers to her costliness as much as to her emotional value—a useful pun to cover the annoyance that may have been aroused by a wife's acquisitiveness.[43] It might prove very revealing to examine, in detail, the transformation of the Victorian angel in the house, certainly an idealized mother figure, into the "cute" flapper of the twenties, dressed to minimize womanly attributes, often called "girlie" by her husband, and clearly a daughter figure to many men. When we think of someone else as diminutive or cute, it certainly minimizes that person's potential to hurt us, and the rise of the cute woman in the early part of our century was probably a useful mechanism by which to dilute the threat of the increased demands actually being made by women. For our purposes, suffice it to say that humor and cuteness constituted a useful vehicle with which to cushion the acknowledgment of conflict and anger.

In the same years that people were beginning to whisper that anger in marriages did exist and might in some limited cases be acceptable, devices for managing that anger began to be explored. A kind of management approach to emotions, which was to cohere into the undisputed consensus and assault readers in article after article after World War II, began to emerge in tentative form as early as 1910. We will discuss this approach in detail later but for now just note it as one strand of thought among many on anger in this middle period. The managerial approach, consisting of a focus on strategies to reduce one's own anger or to avoid

provocative situations, constituted the final innovation in marital emotionology during the latter decades of the turn-of-the-century period. It
followed from the desire to maintain a goal of nonanger between spouses
added to the recognition that some anger would in fact arise, and it was a
more important reconciling device in the long run than was patronizing
humor. But the approach could develop only hesitantly and incompletely
because of the partial unwillingness to recognize that a new view of
marital anger was developing. The managerial approach was thus not yet
fully explored or fully adopted, and it added to the atmosphere of ambiguity in marital advice.

A management approach was suggested as early as 1910. An episode of "The Little Woman and the Busy Man" described an ongoing
dispute in which the husband criticized his wife for not handling their
servants more effectively. The wife consciously decides not to argue
but rather to force herself to be agreeable by thinking of something
else. She sets things up so that he must handle the servant for a while
and thus come to appreciate her situation, offering her money to raise
the girl's wages. The wife vows to ask him no "embarrassing questions" about his experience, thus allowing him to save face.[44] Edi-
torials in the same year advised spouses to arrange their lives so as to
minimize conflict, suggesting that what was needed was a deliberate
effort, on the one hand, to maximize "chumminess" and, on the other,
to learn how the other spouse spends his day and therefore to enhance
appreciation of his difficulties.[45] E. J. Hardy suggested avoiding quarrels by "stepping out of the room in the nick of time; by endeavoring to
divert attention . . . from the burning question, above all, by [pray-
ing] . . . for calmness before making reply."[46]

An advertisement subtitled "But Her Husband Didn't Get a Divorce" described a wife who had become "nervous, impatient, incapable of enthusiasm," and whose constant whining was causing her
husband to become dissatisfied. The couple handled the problem, we
are told, by buying her a pair of arch-preserver shoes, thus saving their
marriage.[47] While it is unfair, certainly, to reduce the management
position to the absurdity of this sales pitch, the advertisement did state
the germ of the notion that conflicts and negative emotions did exist
between spouses but that they could be managed or handled. The same
notion was at the heart of Dr. Abraham Myerson's advice to *Journal*
readers in his column on the "Nervous Housewife" in 1920. Acknowledging that a husband may well become "exasperated" by the wife
who uses sickness to get her way in any domestic conflict, the doctor
advises men to deal with the difficulty by consciously trying to be more
sympathetic.[48]

There is, in most of these managerial pieces of advice, a tacit admission that the spouses have differing points of view and differing interests, an admission that would have been difficult for the Victorians, who preferred to believe that perfect harmony could be achieved. The managerial point of view, while hardly embracing the idea that individuals, although married, might not want the same thing, did allow for such differences. Husbands and wives who thought of themselves as "handling" difficult mates were acknowledging individual consciousnesses even though they might decide to put aside their individualism for the sake of marital harmony. It is notable, however, that the marriage managers acknowledged, but preferred not to dwell on, angry feelings. Anger was an emotion that should be handled by correcting the situation that provoked it. Difficulties must be patched up by the end of the story. Anger should not be a consistent and recurring feeling.

There were limits to the acknowledgment of anger among spouses, even as the Victorian consensus began to crumble. And it must be stressed that during the entire period, before World War II, while tentative explorations of marital anger began to emerge, the older view continued to be expressed forcibly. E. J. Hardy, who has been noted for arguing in his 1914 book that women who got angry were also the ones most capable of sympathy, argued in the very same book that temper was the worst ruiner of domestic felicity, leading often to rebellious wives and drunken husbands. Lillian Bell's 1906 book *Why Men Remain Bachelors* had a chapter on "management" of spouses but also emphasized the Victorian virtues of self-control and suppressing the self.[49]

In 1915, the very same year that "The Purple Hat" was published, a story called "The Uttermost Farthing" appeared that ended a tale of marital conflict by having the wife repent, agreeing totally to renounce all her own wishes as she nurses her husband through an illness. She is rewarded for this renunciation with continuing marital happiness.[50] This same story might have appeared in *Godey's* fifty years earlier, with only superficial changes. In a similarly traditional piece in 1920, a woman wrote of her difficulty in persuading her husband that she should quit her job in order to stay at home and have children. Although she is upset at having to continue to work because he wishes it and even admits to some feelings of "hate" for him, she forces herself to laugh and smile when they discuss it and utterly rejects the notion of an overt argument.[51] It is interesting that maintaining the traditional emotional relationship takes precedence over maintaining traditional work roles in this piece.

The Victorian point of view, unashamed, appeared in "Her Last Affair" published in 1920, complete with a wife of bad character used to having her own way. She attempts to coax, wheedle, and manage her husband in their various conflicts, but the author was clearly unsympathetic to the managerial approach. The husband, who makes multitudes of patronizing speeches to this wrongheaded wife, is presented entirely sympathetically. Her anger is presented as the result of her flaws in character. In the end she capitulates, clearly the right thing to do from the author's point of view. As late as 1928, Arthur W. Spalding wrote a manual arguing that hot tempers led to grossness of body and mind and that Jesus' model of self-control should be recalled by an act of will, by those guilty of "flaring anger."[52]

In the first decades of the twentieth century, there simply was no single point of view on anger in marriage to compare with the Victorian view. On the other hand, this was not a situation in which several clearly reasoned positions coexisted in mutual antipathy. Rather marital anger was just beginning to be acknowledged, and people were very rarely thinking about it in a focused, coherent fashion. Anger was not an issue, a problem, in the way that divorce was. For this reason, the main impression one gets is of a kind of confusion on the subject. Although we have discussed different approaches for the sake of historical clarification, perhaps the most common approach in these years was a hodgepodge in which elements of individualism, Victorianism, and managerial advice coexisted, happily oblivious to contradictions that seem apparent to us.

A survey of one hundred readers on "How to Make Marriage a Success" expressed a managerial point of view, for the most part, in 1905. Participants had been asked, "How will she manage him . . . keep him contented and even-tempered, while meeting the daily problems of life in the home, and secure her own way where she honestly believes it the best?" However, a more Victorian approach was evident in the writer's conclusion that "the average American girl believes the womanly, domestic methods are the most effective" and in her approving quote of one participant who wrote "I think married happiness must mean harmony . . . no matter how reached . . . even though we may have to put away the deepest seated qualities of our character-self to reach it."[53]

In the regular column "The Ideas of a Plain Country Woman," the author was forward looking in her acknowledgment that even good wives become angry yet Victorian in her recommendations: "Most of the bickerings between husband and wife are the merest froth, never touching their real love for each other. Couples go on living together . . . in a sort of dull warfare. I believe it to be the woman's fault. She adopts a sort of abused air." But then the writer goes on to say that, if a husband is a "real scamp," she does not think a wife should put up with it because "we are looking questions squarely in the face these days. . . . women are gaining courage."[54] Yet the same columnist had written only a few months earlier of the "warfare between husband and wife which exists in so many households," advising that the woman "nearly always is the keynote to the matrimonial situation. . . . she must stoop to conquer him in nine cases out of ten . . . putting away . . . false dignity and pride. . . . if you are engaged in a warfare of diverse opinions . . . with the person you married . . . examine yourself. . . . Try the experiment of throwing this pride away."[55] Here we have the acknowledgment that anger exists, advice to manage the problem, advice to employ a repressive stance, and pride in a modern point of view, all within one column within one year. Five years later the same column had moved no closer to a single stance. In 1915, the author wrote that housewives, if dissatisfied with their mates, should simply "make a glory of it. . . . If there isn't one person in the house who simply shoulders more than his share and goes on quietly saying nothing about it, there are going to be friction and unhappiness. . . . If you succeed in making the household share burdens equally it is only by assuming a greater mental responsibility and saying nothing about it."[56] A final example will suffice—an editorial entitled "Temper" published in 1930. "A good rule for every married couple is that by which some friends have lived for many years—never to put out the lights at night while any anger or resentment lies between them. They have occasionally sharp words and disagreements, as every couple has when equal minds are spoken in true comradely manner; but never do they harbor resentments from one day to the next, never do they let petty arguments develop into cancerous rancors. Truly, they will live together in happiness till the end of life."[57]

Here, certainly, we have an acknowledgment that anger between spouses exists even in people of good character. Here, too, we find some managerial advice—notably, to settle the quarrel by the end of the day. And here, too, we have that Victorian assumption that no real discord will exist if everyone tries hard enough, the Victorian refusal to admit that there might be some tensions between individuals speaking their minds and marital harmony, and the Victorian insistence on the happy ending in which good people put anger aside permanently in order to live happily ever after.

Emotionology: Summary and Causation

The new ideas expressed about anger from the later nineteenth century were in many ways contradictory and confusing, but they gain partial coherence through the three major themes of the period's emotionology. First, most clearly in marital advice but also in the familial aspects of disciplining childish emotion, there was substantial continuity in goals: most authorities still wanted largely anger free families, and no one saw real virtue in anger per se. Continuity was, however, modified by the two other leading themes: increasing accommodation to reality and the concept of channeling. The child-rearing literature of the period, though not for the most part viewing anger as a central issue, did begin to deal with the emotion in more realistic terms than the earlier period had done. Slightly later, in the context of the generally acknowledged divorce problem, those who considered marriage also began to recognize that anger could exist and might, in some cases, be a good thing. There was still a heavy Victorian undercurrent of idealism about marriage and home, however. Childhood anger had to be channeled into the world outside the family, as the home/public distinction received explicit emotionological recognition. Anger between spouses remained an uncomfortable subject. Those who acknowledged its reality and its value were at the same time hedging their bets by joking about the subject, inventing new managerial devices to keep the emotion controlled and, not infrequently, retreating to the earlier exhortations for willpower and self-control.

But there were new ideas afloat, ideas that set a distinctive tone particularly in child rearing; and these ideas stemmed from some larger shifts in American society. Three clusters of factors, intellectual, economic, and cultural, caused this new emotionology. Cultural change was preeminent at this point, embracing formal intellectual factors and also perceptions of the economy. More strictly economic causes would reenter the picture a bit later when emotionology was not just modified, as it was around 1900, but more fully transformed.

Changes in formal ideas played a leading role in the introduction of greater ambivalence to Victorian strictures. Most obvious was the changing view of human nature, derived from the work of Darwin and his many scientific and social scientific successors. It became increasingly difficult to insist on childish innocence (though the insistence continued de facto for girls). Children again had some animal impulses that must be recognized, anger or a fighting instinct among them. The realization helps explain the groping for more explicit measures of anger control to deal with childish tantrums. While anger remained bad, it was also viewed as inevitable; therefore different strategies, apart from the best parental example, had to be contemplated.

The rise of social science during this period supplemented Darwinism in teaching that man could not become anything he wished, simply through the exertion of will; rather he was to a greater or lesser extent controlled by forces larger than himself. If will was mitigated from inside by animal impulses, so was it mitigated from outside, by the complex forces of modern urban life. It appeared increasingly useless to seek change through exhortation and willpower. Understanding was what was required. In this atmosphere, then, there was a decreased emphasis on the responsibility of the individual and some new allowance to look at the individual realistically, warts and all. Insofar as anger was considered in child rearing and marriage, there was an enhanced effort to examine the problem as it appeared rather than to bury it: thus the genesis of the managerial approach to emotions that was to become so important in the mid-twentieth century. The idea of a recalcitrant social reality also undergirded the new belief in the utility of anger-derived zeal, which had to be vigorous to fuel business or reform success—just what social Darwinists were urging in adapting the idea of the survival of the fittest.[58]

Intellectual change was supplemented by changing factors in the economy. From the late nineteenth century, it became increasingly functional to encourage consumerism. A self-denying personality might have suited the economy of the early nineteenth century, when there was no chance that production could meet potential demand, but a hundred years later the demand side definitely needed attention, as the rise of emotion-laden advertisements attested. Thus it was functional to encourage the development of men and women who wanted more things for themselves, who thought more about their own desires, and who might even get angry if they did not get the things they wanted. It becomes understandable, in considering the economic needs of the nation, that anger in marriage was first seen as justified in disputes over allocation of finances and that divorces could be seen as legitimate in the context of disappointed consumerism. Disappointed consumerism, in fact, was probably increasing since during this period the expectations were rising faster than middle-class incomes were. It was becoming increasingly difficult for middle-class families to afford servants, and thus it may well be that economic hardship caused increased familial anger and that the emotionology that consented to the expression of such anger followed from a newly perceived problem. This emotionology, then, allowed for some ventilation of feeling and was also functional in encouraging personalities that might fuel the economy.[59]

The consumerist component of emotionological change was indirect and gradual in its effect on personality style. This was not a sharp and clearly recognizable shift in economic context, comparable to the period of early industrialization or the later dominance of corporate structures. The connection between increasing emphasis on self-gratification and an economy now dependent on ever-growing demand was surely not an accident. However, this is not to say that it was a planned connection or even that it was consciously acknowledged or understood by most Americans.

Advocates of the new emotionology were conscious of the connection between their beliefs and economic need, but in the context of a different perception of the economy. They saw the economic situation, somewhat anachronistically, as one that required competitive entrepreneurs. It was not yet widely acknowledged that those entrepreneurs of the early nineteenth century were being increasingly replaced by the managerial types of the Gilded Age and beyond. A lag of this sort in child-rearing standards is not unusual,[60] but it means that the actual goad to the idea of channeling was a perception of the economy rather than the economy itself. In other words, cultural rather than economic factors were of prime importance in explaining the new emotionology.

Changes in the cultural context were varied and complex. Increasingly, at the end of the nineteenth century, there seemed to be some acceptance of the new industrial world and some ability to embrace that world on its own terms rather than to retreat from it. The first decades of American industrialization had not spurred an effort to develop competitive children, but by the 1860s the interest was in full swing. The Horatio Alger literature revealed the limitations of stressing only anger control, lest valuable drives be thwarted. The new advice on anger was closely linked to values of competitiveness and righteous indignation held by the new captains of industry and many reform-minded critics alike.[61] Social Darwinism, which gained unusual popular attention in the United States, also glorified channeled anger. Anger had evolutionary utility in animals; it was a basic ingredient of the notion of the survival of the fittest. Properly directed, anger had obvious utility in the competitive industrial world as well.

The early Victorian home/work dichotomy had acknowledged the existence of a new industrial society but had looked on it with some distaste. Progress certainly was desirable, but it came at a high price. Thus the seat of morality was still entrenched in the home. The Horatio Alger myth and social Darwinism did not reject the home, but they did allow that another moral world existed outside and that it, too, had positive features. It was possible, then, to allow greater flexibility on the subject of anger: thus the idea of channeling.

The increasing comfort that Americans felt about the new industrial society also allowed some loosening up of the Victorian insistence on the fortress home. If the world outside appeared less frightening, it became possible to be less anxious about the walls of the fortress. This was one factor—though only one—in the rise of feminism in these years, for it explains how feminist ideas became increasingly acceptable to the middle-class public.

It is true that the realities of the divorce problem were thrust on the nation and would have been difficult to ignore, but we would surmise that the eagerness with which the question was considered in even the popular magazines reflects a new relaxation about the question of the family. Henry May has discussed in detail the many new radical ideas that challenged Victorianism in this period.[62] For us, it is essential to point out that these ideas were not simply the preserve of a narrow section of the intelligentsia but were considered by a larger reading public.

The *Ladies Home Journal* was far from a feminist organ, but unlike its Victorian predecessors it was, in the early twentieth century, open to discussions of working women and career marriages, the legitimacy of divorce, and even the legitimacy of anger. The outside world was no longer so threatening that questions about the home must be buried. The necessity of preserving the angel-in-the-house myth was no longer so acute as to prohibit the possibility of considering an angry woman. It is of note here that in the 1930s and early 1940s, when the world outside again appeared more threatening, torn as it was by the successive horrors of depression and war, the *Journal* did retreat from its most feminist stance. Stories of domestic conflict were rarer in these years, with increased attention paid to larger "world problems" and more frequent publication of a type of story that, in its treatment of male-female relations, was romantically escapist. Feminism was no longer a possibility in a threatened world. Although it was no longer intellectually possible to retreat to Victorian exhortations, the unstated message of the 1930s and early 1940s was that men had enough difficulties without angry women, and there was a temporary revival of the notion of separate spheres for the sexes.[63] To be sure, the formal marriage manuals of the 1930s and early 1940s increasingly took a managerial stance. The fact that the *Journal* in this period, unlike the decades earlier and later, departed from the manuals can be seen as the exception that proves the rule. The rule was that anger at home could be confronted as the world appeared less frightening. Temporarily, in the 1930s and early 1940s, the fright had returned.

The overall trends, though, do indicate that a changing intellectual climate, changing economic needs, and an increasing accommodation to the new industrial world all combined to allow greater relaxation in the consideration of anger during this period than had been possible for the early Victorians. The emotion was clearly allowed to have some value in the world outside the home, and if not embraced inside the family, it was no longer adjudged quite so demonic.

Yet the explanations of the new emotionology, including the accommodation to parental complexity in combining new concern about anger with some older disciplinary traditions, should not disguise the central tensions involved. Expert confidence in the idea of channeling would not necessarily translate to actual parents confronted with an angry child. Hence growing signs of concern about angry young children parallel the more obvious shift to strategies of channeling. Even among experts themselves, important tensions were not fully resolved because of the hold of earlier beliefs in anger control and continuing hopes for harmonious family life. An advice manual could therefore simultaneously condemn tantrums not just as small problems but as serious behavioral disturbances while urging the equal importance of encouraging righteous anger. Parents, certainly, had a complex message to deliver, though possibly a fruitful one, in trying to discourage direct emotional display without destroying an essential base: "Big boys do not get angry about that"; but "every big boy should be angry when smaller children are fought by bigger ones."[64]

The tensions in the marriage literature were even more obvious. Certainly, the forces that allowed for discussion of anger between spouses had by no means obliterated the Victorian point of view, even during the 1920s, which is why the 1930s and early 1940s returned to greater Victorianism than had characterized the decades immediately previous. In considering the actual experience and expression of emotion, then, we will be looking at the question of what it was like to be angry when no clear-cut emotionological guides existed—when ambivalence ruled. More than the Victorians and more than their children and grandchildren of the post–World War II generations, the Americans of this transitional period had to handle their anger in the absence of crystal-clear rules.

Emotion and Emotional Expression

There is strong evidence that many parents stepped up their attempts to control their own anger from the later nineteenth century on, continuing the trend from the earlier period. Worries about angry children became more articulate, but channeling was also attempted and produced results that many parents found satisfactory. A striking correspondence between actual parental tactics and the new channeling idea was a fundamental aspect of emotional experience in this period. Results for children were less clear, as anger became a tantalizing emotion not always easy to express when it was felt. Anger in marriage may have been slightly less guilt ridden in practice than in emotionological theory, and some of the new control tactics were utilized. But marital anger remained a difficult and confused topic, as experience mirrored emotionological ambiguities. As before, we will deal first with anger-related expression and then with evidence of feeling.

Expression

The extent to which the relaxing of the emotionology of anger was translated into actual changes in marriage styles is difficult to evaluate. Although by the turn of the century sociologists studied and recorded child-rearing behavior, there were no equivalent examinations of marital conflict until much later; in view of the lack of interest in interpersonal psychodynamics during this period, this is hardly surprising. A systematic and extensive study of diaries and letters of the era may at some time tell us more about the outlets for marital anger in this period. For now, however, some speculation may be in order.

It certainly appears likely that women reaped some benefit from the new, albeit guarded, sanction to express anger at home. Certainly, the rate of female invalidism declined, as did the prominence of the stereotype of the tearful wife. The widespread recognition that there was a "New Woman" who liked to have fun was surely related to the new permission granted to women to get in touch with their true selves, with anger as well as sexuality, just at it was linked to the new consumerism. One may ask, indeed, if the decline of interest in female "causes" such as temperance and feminism after the 1920s had something to do with a relaxation of the rules for anger expression and therefore a declining need for sublimation.

Certainly, not all divorces represent an expression of anger, but insofar as they do, the rising American divorce rate did reflect an increasing willingness on the part of both sexes to reveal anger to a spouse. And the divorce rate continued to rise, with both men and women initiating proceedings. The temporary drop in the early 1930s was almost certainly a result of economic limitations. All the evidence is that, if anything, marital conflict rose during the depression. The popular emotionological retreat from discussions of anger in the early 1930s was almost certainly a psychological defense against facing one's frustrations with one's spouse. All the studies argue that that brief retreat into the fantasy of the anger-free home did nothing to lessen real anger. As soon as the leanest years had passed, the divorce rate began to rise again.[65]

We know more about changes in expression of anger in child rearing than we do about trends in marriage, though the social scientific evidence about child rearing accumulates particularly from the 1920s on. The bows to greater realism in the turn-of-the-century emotionology by definition increased the correspondence between anger standards and the actual experience of anger. Insofar as experts were coming a bit closer to actual children, they inevitably picked up substantial echoes of real life. In child rearing, the link between emotionology and child-rearing behavior went beyond heightened realism. Parents, particularly in the middle class, adopted many of the precise cues of the channeling approach. Whether their stance was new, whether it partly resulted from the emotionology, or whether it merely corresponded to it cannot be ascertained. But there is no question that emotionology at this point suggested a distinctive American parenting style, despite some clashes on specific tactics.

Concern about unusually angry children prompted many parents to consult outside experts in this period, as we will see; and while this trend reflects the new secular expertise available, it may also have translated parents' growing anxiety about how to handle intense child-ish anger without using anger themselves. Even middle-class parents without problem children tried to translate the pervasive emotionology into their own styles. They did try to restrain their own anger. They did seek to channel childish aggression into socially or individually useful achievement. In contrast to what experts saw as the working-class model, middle-class parents by the twentieth century were more con-cerned about the intent behind a child's loss of temper than about man-ifestations in behavior; in this sense, workers more traditionally tended to stress obedience in deed. Even when middle-class parents diverged on tactics, they often shared emotionological goals with the advice lit-erature. Thus parents who punished tantrums were expressing the kind of concern about anger that the experts urged in the decades around 1900, and they may have helped provoke responding anger in children that would permit subsequent channeling.[66] Certainly, many parents agreed that they themselves should set a good example by not punish-ing in anger, though intent may often have differed from fact. Sixty percent of all parents urged this strategy in one survey, 12 percent admitting that they fell short. Overall, behavior did change in the direc-tion of less overt anger being expressed against children. This was consistent with a gradual, measurable decline in physical abuse.[67]

Thus parental behavior in the late nineteenth and early twentieth centuries revealed divisions that could be evaluated, and were evalu-ated by researchers and therapists, in terms of anger-control values, creating groups of "good" and "bad" parents, in part according to class. In the middle class, but also among some workers and Ameri-canizing immigrants, a fairly high concern about anger control was manifest—a sign that the campaign launched in the eighteenth century was bearing ever greater fruit.

At some point, indeed, between the late eighteenth and the early twentieth century a generation or more of parents had broken with the disciplinary styles of their own parents, with distinctive mechanisms for handling anger a central element in this shift. The break was sometimes fragile. In the economic hard times of the 1930s (and, again, of the 1970s), job loss and other pressures would produce rising rates of physical anger, mainly by fathers, taken out against children. But these oscillations were not total reversals, and they occurred in the working class almost exclusively; middle-class fathers would not react to job loss with the same kind of overt anger. The impression of a distinct, if incomplete and sometimes inconsistent, transformation in parental style is inescapable,[68] a shift compatible with both the early nineteenth-century and the turn-of-the-century emotionological emphases, but one that for most families probably occurred after 1870, though it built on some modification of literal will breaking introduced earlier. Here the rather detailed attention to handling anger in advice literature written between 1890 and 1910 may well reflect not only intellectual currents but also real parental demand for information about a problem translated from behavioral into emotional terms. The transformation completed, it was small wonder that studies of actual middle-class parents from the 1920s to the 1950s would find substantial acceptance of the emotionology of anger control embodied in common child-rearing strategies.

Along with this general evolution, the particular twists of turn-of-the-century emotionology also showed up in actual parental attitude and behavior. The ambivalent emotionology produced or reflected ambivalence in real emotional guidance. This is where American parenting seemed uniquely complex, in comparative perspective. American parents translated the emotionological precepts quite precisely, in the following manner. A number of comparative studies conducted between the world wars or shortly after World War II rated Americans severe in punishments of anger directed against parents but unusually tolerant of angry behavior, particularly of retaliation directed against peers, a situation in which a child's ability to stand up for himself—the talisman of later competitiveness—could safely be tested. The absence of overall rules on anger was unusual: researchers found societies just as strict as Americans were as far as anger directed against parents was concerned or as permissive as Americans were as far as anger directed against a child's peers was concerned, but in no case, other than that of America, did they find both at once. American parents, then, really did seek to channel anger toward approved outlets, from quite an early age, instead of trying to excise it completely. Their approach contrasts not only with those of several non-Western cultures (some more permissive overall, some less) but also with that of Western Europe. Thus the American prompting to do battle with peers, at least when provoked, finds no counterpart in French or German child-rearing culture. There children were encouraged to turn to adults to right the wrongs done to them. It was an adult supervisor who would step in when a child's toy was taken away, and the child himself was punished if he took direct action.[69]

Typically American was the fascination with contact sports, picked up and encouraged by channeling enthusiasts such as G. Stanley Hall around 1900. Boxing was a particular favorite. The physical energy it required made mastery of temper in daily life easier, while the sport also taught how channeled anger could generate competitive excellence. This interest in turn helped produce unusually high levels of American middle-class interest in boxing, not only as spectator sport, but also as a participant activity; it produced an almost obligatory gift of boxing gloves to middle-class boys, from early in the century through the 1940s (an obligation that revealingly has since died off, the victim of a newer emotional code).[70] Emotionology, in other words, nourished some distinctive American male sports interests, perhaps even helping to explain why some national sports gained in popularity over less violent West-European analogues, as both societies experienced the cresting modern interest in sports of some sort. For not only boxing but also football provided the expression of intense but channeled anger that sports like soccer or even the earlier American staple of baseball could not; and so what has become a rather parochial American sports interest might feed and be fed by a distinctive set of emotional values in child rearing.

Thus the late nineteenth-century/early twentieth-century American child-rearing culture moved partially away from otherwise general Western patterns, despite the common evolution toward anger control in Western society in the eighteenth and early nineteenth centuries. Elements of the American duality may go back to the colonial period, in the separation that Demos has noted between anger against neighbors and harmony within the all-important nuclear family. Protecting the family against childish anger may simply have been more important in a land of comparative strangers and protection of neighbors less so. But the duality was unquestionably deepened and legitimized by the child-rearing approach that took shape in the later nineteenth century. The particular appeal of social Darwinism in the United States was an element in the unique American approach to childish anger. More basically, the American middle class, free from concern about irrational effects of aristocratic temper (a concern evident in Western Europe in the ongoing debates over dueling), may also have been freer to shape a child-rearing style that seemed molded to the emotional context of business competitiveness. American indulgence of children, noted by travelers much earlier, may also have encouraged an approach that allowed legitimate outlets for childish emotion, rather than a stricter discipline, when it turned out that children were not angelic. Whatever the combination of causes, American experts, while sharing in interests such as competitive sports that developed more widely in Western middle-class culture, helped forge an ambivalence about anger whose effects would be visible for many decades.

The American child-rearing style was not the only one compatible with turn-of-the-century capitalism or high rates of indignant social protest. Though Europeans raised their children differently, with regard to anger, they produced their share of aggressive capitalists and certainly their share of protesters. Obviously, factors other than child rearing enter into adult emotional styles. The tendency of European parents to intercede, sometimes angrily, on behalf of their children—rather than encouraging angry response to slights by children themselves—suggests a high valuation of anger differently expressed. But the American style could relate, if not to protest or competitive levels, at least to specific forms. That social Darwinism spread more widely in the United States than in Europe, as a gloss for capitalist competition, owes something to the emotionology of child rearing. The tendency to righteous indignation in middle-class reform movements in the Progressive era also picked up elements of what children were being taught.

Emotionology and actual emotional standards applied in child rearing thus flowed together in the decades around 1900, particularly in the middle class. Expert advice was not taken literally, to be sure, even by parents who approved of it in principle. Thus twentieth-century studies showed that parents were not as willing to ignore childish tantrums as the advice literature urged they should be (though the literature was not unanimous on the point): in one study, 27 percent of all parents responded to tantrums with excited talk and 25 percent with spankings. On other occasions parents were surely less careful of restraining their own anger than the advice literature continued to urge.[71] However, on the whole there was a correspondence between the emotionology and the practice of child rearing. The correspondence was not perfect, and there is of course no way to demonstrate which came first; probably the interaction was mutual, as parents and children picked up cues from the literature and affected this literature in turn. The combination produced an important ingredient in the American character.

Before considering what effect this new child-rearing style may have had on the children, however, it must be noted that the new emotionology posed some hardships for the schools, which embraced the new emotionology less readily than did parents. Prior to the late eighteenth century, teachers had no difficulty supplementing the standard style of child rearing with stringent discipline and an often angry insistence on obedience to authority, Dutch schoolmasters in New York, though less severe than their Puritan counterparts in New England, were warned against discipline that was "too easy." Teachers, like parents, easily permitted themselves the right to grow angry at inferiors.[72]

Changing views of children and of education began to affect the emotional climate of some schools by the 1790s. Parents as well as educational theorists increasingly insisted on teachers of good character, and this in turn was to include mastery of temper.[73] Even earlier, Cotton Mather urged the translation of the new emotional style of the home into the schools: "I try to form in the children a temper of benignity. I caution them exquisitely against all revenges of injuries. . . . I would never come to give a child a blow, except in case of obstinacy or some gross enormity. . . . The slavish way of education, carried on with raving, kicking and scouring (in schools as well as families), 'tis abominable."[74]

But while the new concern about anger gained ground in pedagogical theory, practice lagged somewhat. Corporal punishment, for example, became more moderate in the early nineteenth century; it did not disappear.[75] Given the complexity of making a transition from will breaking to anger control in parenting, some parents were not loath to see others—such as teachers—administer discipline they could no longer countenance on their own part. And teachers, faced with large numbers of children and a setting unalleviated by the affection now encouraged in the family, understandably found it hard to make as complete a shift as some middle-class parents contemplated.[76] They continued to value obedience and had less compunction than parents did about using anger to elicit it. Thus the emotional atmosphere of schools differed from that of many families, just as actual classroom discipline often differed from official administrative recommendations.[77]

Ideas of anger control did spread gradually, however. Well into the twentieth century they worked in tandem with the obvious temptation to insist on a tranquil student body. Girls therefore so often seemed more desirable students because the docility urged at home blended nicely with teachers' expectations.[78] Teachers, for their part, were increasingly urged to keep an even temper. Educational theory that stressed greater equality between student and teacher and greater freedom from rigid constraint found some translation in teacher training manuals.[79] By the twentieth century, the idea of teacher responsibility for emotional guidance spread more explicitly: "Schools must be watchful that they do not contain the exciting causes of such emotion in their own inflexible or unreasonable program or treatment of children. . . . If the educator fails to deal with . . . the control of passion, he may properly be charged with . . . negligence."[80]

School programs certainly picked up the idea of channeling anger. Many a school athletic program was justified largely in these terms, as part of character building. George Creel, in 1916, urged that schools help immigrant children channel their "ferocity" to their own benefit and that of society.[81] It was in this context that some teachers could write authorities like G. Stanley Hall, bemoaning too-passive students and urging more, rather than less, anger in their charges. This current particularly attracted those educators concerned about the effects of women teachers on the character of boys.

But there were limitations to the correspondence between teachers' attitudes and those of parents and child-rearing experts. Many women teachers found aggressive male students hard to channel and certainly hard to ignore. Here was a practical problem in classroom order but also a clash between gender styles that could be quite vivid in the decades after 1900. More than one such teacher unwittingly stimulated angry behavior by the attention they paid to it; more than one, in fact, responded by righteous anger of their own.[82] Certainly teachers found less value in childish anger than parents did, during the period in which the dominant emotionology stressed channeling. Regularly, from the early twentieth century through the 1950s, teachers reported far lower tolerance for acts of temper than did parents (particularly fathers) and child experts. Teachers correspondingly failed to share parental concern about the insufficiently aggressive child. Thus problems of temper produced three of the top fifteen behavior problems in teachers' ratings in the 1920s, whereas none made the parental top twenty; predictably, the disparity was particularly marked for boys and helped explain boys' ten to one lead in teacher-rated behavior problems. A lack of fit between home and school reactions may explain an important aspect of the experience of childhood, especially boyhood, just when school became a common requirement.[83]

Clearly, then, schools and teachers followed the dominant emotionology selectively, though they were touched by it. They preferred portions that stressed student anger control and therefore girls' ideal standards over boys'. They were wary of the complexity of translating channeling ideas into classroom practice, and while they increasingly adhered to temper-control standards—"freedom from over-aggressiveness," as one teacher personnel form put it[84]—as part of their emotional responsibility, they did not in fact abandon angry tones and punishments in response to what they saw as angry or disorderly acts in their charges. The problems of coping with large groups of children, some from families in which anger control seemed problematic in a period of working-class and immigrant exposure to mass education, easily explain the disparity.

If children received different messages from teachers and from parents, there is also some evidence of a disparity between mother and father. A number of studies, from the 1920s on, showed greater tolerance by fathers than by mothers of aggressive children. Mothers adhered to expert opinion more closely than fathers did in disciplining childish anger, but also they reported themselves as stricter than fathers and therefore may well have appeared angrier to their children. Fathers were more interested in channeling, more concerned about children (particularly sons) who lacked spunk.[85]

In sum, the new emotionology did have an effect on child-rearing behaviors, but not a simple one. Schools were slower to change than were families; fathers and mothers did not always behave consistently. This complexity served to translate much of the ambivalence of the dominant emotionology into the behaviors to which children were exposed.

Feelings

How and to what extent did the new approach to anger control affect the way people felt about their own anger? We have looked at new trends in the expression of anger in the family, but this does not tell us what it felt like for those who actually experienced anger. The predominant note in family memoirs remained indicative of an effort to minimize or ignore marital conflict; in this area there was less shift from Victorianism than the emotionology suggested. Certainly, though, some people may have felt a little more comfortable about displaying vexation. One man, for instance, wrote his local newspaper that he thought marriage was a kind of safety valve, one that "provides a man and a woman with somebody to quarrel with at times when they feel like it, without any loss of self respect. . . . whenever my wife or I have had any ill-humor to vent, we have immediately vented it upon one another. . . . in a little while we are perfectly happy and comfortable with one another. . . . That is what marriage is for."[86]

Some people also clearly took advantage of the new style, often seen in the normative material, of cute or humorous anger. "You're lovely when you're mad" was a strategy that was used in real life and not just in romance novels. Winifred Babcock, recalling a protracted love affair, remembered that her boyfriend thought she was cute and pretty when she got angry. At one point, the couple vowed to stop quarreling, and the man jokingly said that from then on, she should be a "reasonable child," at which point, the author recalls, "I had to laugh." Babcock admitted to more fury than most Victorian women would have but always temporized it with self-deprecating humor. It is certainly striking that, at the end of her memoirs, she skips as quickly as possible over the destruction of the relationship on her discovery of his affair with another woman and her unabated wrath: "But rage! What has it ever done to heal even the slightest hurt or wound. Oh I could tramp up and down . . . and wring my hands . . . but alas! would that bring me any comfort?"[87] The book quickly ends as she puts this experience behind her and embarks on a career.

For both sexes there were still severe limits to permissable anger. Little girls were still treated differently from little boys in this respect, and their teachers' differing responses to them were often based on the girls' greater ability to repress temper. One doubts that the girls so repressed grew up to be women who accepted their own anger without discomfort. That men were ambivalent if not downright hostile toward the "New Woman" also was a factor that probably limited comfort with expression of anger.[88] Women who read articles telling them it was all right to get angry may well have backed down when faced with their husbands' discomfort. Conversely, husbands faced with wives who seemed angry in ways their own mothers would not have dreamed of revealing may have bitten their tongues but experienced more internal anger.

The continuing discussion of divorce, in itself, may have frightened some spouses and discouraged them from overt recognition of conflict. The research that has been done on divorce today shows that people seldom take it as lightly as some of the liberal theorists may have wished in the early part of our century. One may well doubt that it seemed innocuous to most Americans at that time any more than it does now. We would guess, then, that, if they were frightened by the specter of divorce, they were frightened also at anger within their marriages. They were not as frightened perhaps as their parents had been, for no one any longer told them that even one fight could spell disaster. It was possible to survive a few storms and still believe one was a good person in a viable relationship. Still, there were limits.

Since there was no clear consensus on the management of anger in this period, most couples must have experimented on their own with solutions. Whether this was experienced as liberating and pleasurable and gave people the opportunity to be more fully themselves is not clear. It is indeed possible that more people felt instead confused, adrift, and helpless. Certainly, when new advice literature began to flood the bookstands after World War II, the public bought it eagerly. Although some recent authors have criticized professional interference in family life,[89] the demand for expert advice, after decades of vague treatment of the emotional aspects of marital conflict, showed a genuine popular demand for firmer guidelines.

As in marriage, there was clearly some confusion in the experience of anger in parent-child interactions. There is some evidence of a new relaxation with anger on the part of both parent and child. Although a growing trickle of parents from both working- and middle-class families took their concerns about particularly angry offspring to child guidance experts after 1918,[90] there was general agreement from the 1920s to the 1950s that behavior problems resulting from anger fell in the middle-to-low range of significance in the eyes of parents (though not, as we have seen, of teachers). They did not loom as large as sexual problems or even excessive shyness. Two factors explain this parental belief. Most parents were successful in stressing anger control in the home, even though their tactics did not always measure up to recommended standards. And they saw some value as well as nuisance in children's tempers, so long as this could be largely channeled. A child with high and familial anger was unquestionably a problem, and the rolls of child-guidance therapists attest to parental concern about such cases. But in the main American ambivalence seemed to work to substantial parental satisfaction.[91]

Relaxation of concern about anger is striking in one woman's recollection of her grandfather from her girlhood. "It was during the same visit, I think, when I was spluttering about something with characteristic fury and demanding my rights that he began to address me as John Doe. I didn't understand why he called me by this name and from the twinkle in his very blue eyes, I knew he was laughing at me, but somehow his amusement never hurt my usually tender feelings."[92] Here we see a relative lack of shame on the part of the angry child and a lack of concern on the part of her grandfather. The same woman recorded a punishment by her mother that again reflects a certain diminution of early Victorian intensity. Her sister, in the midst of being spanked, shouts to her friend that she will join her in a minute. "Mother, outraged by such indifference to punishment, said sternly, 'Elizabeth Spencer, don't you know that I'm spanking you?' Whereupon, tears obligingly flowed. This memory suggests that Mother's spankings did not hurt very much." The author notes that there were also few such spankings.[93]

This is hardly to suggest, however, that anger between parent and child had become conflict free. Many parents were clearly far more upset than the Spencers were by childish anger and described their offsprings' tantrums as "terrifying."[94] Certainly, the effort parents felt they should make to control their own tempers could not always be successful and thus, in turn, produced guilt. "Every time I yell at my kids, I have the feeling I'm being reported to some psychiatric police force," one parent complained. Guilt was to remain a pervasive theme in American parenting, fueling a heavy demand for child-rearing advice that was not abated. Insofar as people resent feeling guilty and as that resentment leads to anger, American parents, and especially mothers, may have experienced some growing internal anger as the price of their efforts to stifle their sharp responses to their children. This could, of course, color family life more generally.[95]

Children, too, by no means felt unconflicted about their own anger. This may be one reason that there is some evidence that they felt a kind of thrill, or joy, when the emotion occasionally surfaced. Was it this joy, as well as the intent to channel, that fueled the rage for boxing? At any rate, Ethel Spencer recalls loving a game called "Ten Steps," which was "always both a favorite game and the cause of tears and conflict." "I don't know why we liked this game," she muses, "for it always ended in a fight." We may speculate that she liked it precisely because it offered one avenue to express anger, which was usually forbidden. Similarly, we may suggest that this is the reason that she recalled so vividly another scene from her school days. She was waiting on line to sharpen her pencil, and "a big girl said, 'Oh, the dickens!' when her point broke. I was filled with admiration and yearned to imitate her, but since even the mildest oaths were discouraged at home, I never dared to use such a vigorous expletive."[96] Anger for parents and children in this period, then, was a less frightening experience than it had been earlier, but channeling did not eliminate conflicts around anger, nor had it been intended to do so.

In sum, it is clear that the period between 1860 and 1940 represented a new approach to anger control and that the new approach reflected more than a change in emotionology. There is a great deal of evidence that in child rearing, at least, the new standards were affecting behavior. There is some evidence too that new standards enabled some people to feel a little more relaxed about their own anger but that this relaxation was, as the emotionology designed, very circumscribed.

Channeling produced some sense of overall satisfaction with the treatment of anger in actual child rearing, as related to the emotionological standard setting of the various experts. Diversity continued between social classes and among variant Protestant groups. But the idea of disciplining anger while using it did produce, for many parents, a happy response to the continued tension of home versus public atmospheres. Indeed, as we shall see in a later chapter, it is tempting to look back on this particular approach to anger with more than a bit of nostalgia, precisely because it did serve varied functions while maintaining a modern distaste for the raw emotion itself. The approach in practice produced some flexibility, as between home and school authorities and even between mothers and fathers, who could emphasize the repressive or expressive elements according to taste. The result, for parents at least, was an important if—from our contemporary vantage point— precarious moment in the American treatment of anger in child rearing. Of course, one doubts that the channeling solution to the home/work problem, satisfactory as it may have seemed to intellectually mature adults, ever made sense to children. In their more direct and less intellectualized experience, the major conclusion may well have been that, however they dealt with their anger, they could not predict the response of key adults and that it was difficult or even impossible to know how to please mother, father, and teacher with any consistency.

New ambiguities in the approach to anger in marriage reflected, and may have encouraged, a new restiveness among women. Bombarded on all fronts by statistics on the rise of divorce, the individual wife no longer had to fret that she was the only woman who ever became angry with her mate. Middle-class magazines offered enough advice sanctioning some feelings of anger that it was no longer necessary entirely to deny that emotion—or, as had been a common possibility in the Victorian period, to collapse in anxiety at the slightest conflict. Even the more conservative writers advised their female readers not so much to ignore anger as to keep their behavior controlled. In this way, then, the advice for women was becoming more similar to what it had been for men in the previous period. One may guess that giving women some tentative permission to feel anger may have been tremendously liberating.

However, while the ambiguities that resulted from loosening Victorian standards may have been useful to some spouses in reducing anxiety, they hardly constituted the happy synthesis that child rearing seemed to have achieved. There is certainly sparse evidence, in turn-of-the-century sources, of any real ease with marital anger. Indeed the lack of full connection between child-rearing and marital experience was the final ingredient in a series of unresolved dilemmas. For males, restraint and channeling might provide, in theory, a valid formula for adult behavior, though in practice the ability to turn off work anger, or reactions to others' anger, on returning home was no easy matter. Men in fact, from their childhood on, received contradictory messages about anger as about other standards, in a period of real confusion about how a good man was supposed to behave.[97] For women the dilemma was less acute on paper if they could carry childhood repression of anger into an adulthood of wifely sweetness. But in fact the childhood personality of females was becoming a bad predictor of adult emotional styles. Girls did display less anger than boys, as school authorities (often female) so happily noted. But whereas a boy's anger style predicted his adult style, girls often shifted as they matured.[98] As women they had cause for anger, and some of them, in the first part of this turn-of-the-century period, duplicated much of the moral indignation that was more explicitly recommended for men, as temperance advocates, feminists, or Progressive reformers. One of the reasons that some mothers delighted in urging channeled anger on their sons may have been as an indirect expression of emotions they felt strongly in themselves. Yet if channeling and restraint raised confusions for men, confusion might be doubled for women, who had fewer public outlets in which to exercise their channeling desire. Even many of their public causes, such as temperance, continued to smack of domestic grievance.[99] The angry woman, than, was defying childhood standards, often an uncomfortable experience, while lacking a full range of expression outside the home. One may speculate at this point that the decline in women's causes after 1920 may have had something to do with an increased ease with expressing anger at home, though the evidence available thus far is at best suggestive. Overall for this period, the divorce rate shows that the halfhearted tolerance of anger within the family did not seem to keep pace with actual conflict.

The simple fact was that, while the ambivalence in child-rearing values and practice concerning anger were in many ways satisfactory, the vaguer ambiguities in marital emotionology were not. Suggestions, particularly by experts, of new familial management techniques already sketched a new approach, which, however, was not fully fleshed out or consistently translated into popular advice before 1940. A new consensus on dealing with marital anger would emerge; it may have been in the cards already, despite lingering Victorian idealism. But it was not from family life itself that a consensus first developed but rather from unprecedented efforts to control anger in the workplace. Techniques and goals developed on the job were brought back to the family. The resultant message produced a spate of marital advice, which is not surprising, given the lack of clear guidelines during the early decades of the twentieth century. Less predictably (and, some would argue, more frighteningly, in undoing what might seem a quintessentially American compromise), the new approach attacked the ambivalence in child rearing as well. In fact, the new anger-control movement at work was to change the context in which family anger of all sorts could be discussed and, quite possibly, the way in which it was experienced as well.

5 Anger at Work

A Contemporary Approach

Good and bad employers in late nineteenth-century literature. In *Billy Budd,* Captain Vere: "At the presentation to him of some minor matter interrupting the current of his thoughts, he would show more or less irascibility, but instantly he would control it"; and the villain Claggart: colliding with an inferior, Claggart "impulsively [gave] him a sharp cut with the rattan, vehemently exclaimed 'Look where you go.'"[1]

Both emotionology and actual child-rearing emphases in the nineteenth and early twentieth centuries had some obvious relationship to the work experience. The early Victorian sense that the outside world was filled with dangerous emotional currents suggested that there was an experience of anger, as well as risk and fatigue, on the job and that the home should provide a contrast. There were also suggestions that certain jobs required considerable emotional control, so much control that the home in fact became an outlet for anger—a theme that would continue in the mid-twentieth century. Changes in child-rearing in the later nineteenth century attempted to come to terms with a home/work division, trying to preserve the home but to allow for channeled anger on the job (whether directed to competitive zeal or the righting of wrongs). Without question, the problem of differentiating home and work emotional styles continued to be a vexing one.

What the nineteenth century did not produce, however, was a clear set of emotional standards for work itself. It might be assumed that good character would extend, as *Billy Budd* suggested, to work, but given the belief in a public world separate from the home, this assumption remained rather vague. There was no more attempt to formulate an anger-control emotionology for work during the first decades of industrialization than there had been in the eighteenth century, when work and home had normally been associated and when a presumption of a single emotional standard had some plausibility. The one nineteenth-century exception was domestic service, and here the home-work division obviously did not prevail.

Beginning in the 1920s a new approach to management began to apply the modern emotionology toward anger to the workplace, undercutting the turn-of-the-century compromise that had allowed more scope for channeled emotion. A variety of forces prompted this shift, and a host of institutional devices arose to enforce it. This was a major extension of modern emotionology, but it led also to a new set of tactics, stressing the management or manipulation of anger, that would ultimately spill back into family and child-rearing standards. The campaign against anger at work, which reached a high point from the 1930s to the 1960s, thus serves as a major bridge between the nineteenth-century approach to the emotion and its more contemporary version.

The Effect of Industrialization

Anger felt at work certainly may have increased during the nineteenth century, though the opportunities for anger expression in the personalized work hierarchy before industrialization have already been noted. Rapid (and often nervously taxing) technological change, a more rigid work hierarchy armed with demanding work rules, and the experience of dealing with strangers as bosses and colleagues certainly could have heightened emotion. Evidence drawn from worker behavior, particularly frequent absenteeism and job changing, during the first decades of industrialization suggests many an angry clash with superiors or fellow workers, as does the rising rate of more formal protest from the 1870s on.[2] Here, certainly, was one source of the middle-class sense that work could generate irritations that the home should escape, for which, indeed, the home should compensate. There is abundant evidence that work-based anger came not only from the labor force but also from the management side.

A foreman in a Chicago clothing sweatshop cuts the piece rate. Workers are angry and threaten to quit. The foreman, angry in his turn, says, "Quit if you want to. You are welcome to quit." Five of them do, moving to other jobs. From an employer vantage point, in 1864, many young workers are too quarrelsome and belligerent—with "too much mouth." They often quit "just because they get their back up."[3] But many workers knew the lashings of anger from manager or foreman. Many a strike started because of a foreman's temper, in the pattern of personal clashes that heavily influenced the strike movement around the turn of the century. And the same increase in protest brought management anger into greater visibility, when employers responded to even the most sedate of protests with true wrath—"raging like a tiger," as one worker put it.[4]

This is not to argue that workplace anger definitely increased during the nineteenth century and certainly not to argue that it was uniform. The Industrial Revolution did gradually promote a more extensive work hierarchy in which anger could be used to enforce distance and in which protest might be greeted with more than instrumental anger in defense of cherished prerogatives. Hierarchy cushioned many managers from the need to express anger directly, for irascible foremen could do the job on a day-to-day basis—a practical compromise between good character and a discipline encouraged by anger. Yet the emotional tone of the work experience cannot be charted with full precision for the nineteenth century. It undoubtedly varied with the temperament of those involved and may have changed over time as labor relations became more acrimonious.[5]

What is demonstrable is the absence of any serious discussion of emotional standards. Managers did not introduce the subject into their endless manuals for foremen, in which technical subjects held pride of place. They did not talk of anger as a problem at work, relying instead on the ideal of home as emotional haven. Still more revealing, nineteenth-century management did not discuss anger control explicitly for the labor force. Rather they relied on an earlier ideal of obedience, in place of the more subtle concept of emotional restraint. Factory rules specified behaviors—punctuality, diligence, cleanliness—not emotions. While female docility was valued, it was phrased in terms of reluctance to protest, not of the domestic ideal of the angerless women; and in fact female docility did not win a large place for women in the new manufacturing labor force. Nor did workers evince particular emotional expectations; even the frequent clashes with foremen were treated matter-of-factly, as incidents rather than emotional landmarks.[6]

The lack of explicit emotionology, essentially a continuity from the preindustrial period made more vivid by the separation of work from home, was not entirely surprising. During the first century of industrialization, most people involved had more pressing concerns than discussions of emotional style. Anger control was not the only area in which tradition was utilized to shape labor relations in a new setting.[7] While management might criticize belligerent workers, they also valued some emotional spark as part of a proper work drive. Only with regard to domestic service were employers forced to confront a new problem of anger and work in the nineteenth century because here the home was not protected from the emotional issues that changing labor conditions tossed up.

Domestic service was highly productive of anger—another reminder that personalized employment generates important tensions of its own. Middle-class employers were attempting to impose new standards of cleanliness and household care on a labor force of predominantly rural and/or immigrant origins, livened by an active sense of independence.[8] Many middle-class women treated servants with angry disdain, and there is some impression of an increase in anger from the employer side, though much depended on personal whim.[9] Yet in this case, because of the home involvement, whatever the actual emotional experience, a new set of standards had to be established. Anger must, at least in principle, be controlled. Catherine Beecher lamented the lack of deference of American servants but emphasized the need for restraint: "There is nothing, which has a more abiding influence on the happiness of a family, than the preservation of equable and cheerful temper and tones in the housekeeper."[10] Even when a servant misbehaves, the mistress must "refrain from angry tones." Anger is not necessary to win obedience; often it just produces anger in response; calm reproof is more effective; and servants have feelings too. Thus hierarchy, in this important case, did not justify anger, and an important emotionological effort was launched.[11] It is more than conceivable that the difficulty in fact of living up to acceptable emotionology, on the part of servants and mistresses alike, contributed to the decline of the institution of live-in domestics from the late nineteenth century on.[12]

But this was, again, an exceptional case, one based on the domestic environment and the unusual involvement of women as active employers. Work-based emotions more generally did begin to receive comment late in the nineteenth century, and the subject began to win its ongoing appeal for middle-class readers. But it was emotional tension and nervous strain, not anger, that first roused interest. Popular comment on this subject raised the idea that work forced too much repression of emotions, to the detriment of health, though the great problem was rapid pace and, for the middle class, overwork of the "thinking organs." The only link between this widely popular discussion and anger was the admission that nervousness might manifest itself in an undesirable irritability over trifles, but this was merely a symptom, not an insight into real issues of anger at work.[13]

Several factors prompted a change in the benign neglect of work-based anger in the early decades of the twentieth century. Rising rates of unionization and strikes, and also high labor turnover, prompted new concern about how to manage workers: trying to instill obedience was not enough. At the same time the growth of corporate structures, with their more remote management and large white-collar staffs, logically prompted a concern with smooth emotional relations.[14] Indeed the overall rise of a white-collar labor force, in sales work as well as corporate management, encouraged attention to superficially friendly demeanors. Mass retail outlets needed smooth relations with consumers who were not personally familiar. The basic factors that caused the extension of anger-control emotionology to work were, then, economic and organizational, as the first effects of industrialization passed and more sophisticated approaches to management and marketing could be, perhaps had to be, undertaken. The original factor, which prompted attention to anger-control techniques even in the depression-ridden 1930s, was supplemented by changes in social science, notably, the decline in Darwinian interests and the rise of psychology, though the clearest social science concern with aggression resulted in part from the changes in workplace emotionology sponsored by industrial psychologists rather than causing these changes initially. Organizational imperatives predominated over ideology in this instance.

Yet there was also a more personal factor involved in causing a new interest in anger control at work or, at least, serving as mediator between the general organizational factors and the actual definition of the new emotionology. In a climate of growing labor hostility, many middle-class managers felt emotionally uncomfortable. Here was a direct link between nineteenth-century domestic and child-rearing emotionology and the attempt at standard setting on the job. Frederick Taylor, the pioneering efficiency engineer, wrote readily of the unease he felt, as a middle-class boy serving a working-class apprenticeship, at the anger he saw among his workmates. His response, to be sure, was toward more impersonal efficiency, though he believed that the scientific management he espoused would smooth emotional relations on the job.[15] More important was the emotionological baggage that Elton Mayo and his followers brought to their inquiries into labor-relations in the 1920s. They did not expect to focus significantly on work-based anger, but they found themselves compelled to do so because of the contradictions they experienced between anger on the job and their own parent-induced sense of the inappropriateness of the emotion. The idea of channeling anger, appealing to some of the efficiency engineers,[16] was simply unacceptable. Growing contact with women workers also taught management a need to control temper, for these operatives tended to cry when exposed to the verbal abuse routinely directed at their male counterparts; here was a direct contrast, particularly in sales and office work, in which women were playing a greater role, between traditional work habits and gender socialization.[17] Hence Mayo and his crew, and hosts of followers, were led to attempt direct changes in the emotional tone of work, comparable in many ways in goal, though not precisely in method, to those undertaken by Victorian family writers a century before.

This personal element in the introduction of a new emotionology at work is vital in explaining portions of the campaign that were never assessed in terms of cost effectiveness. While the anger-control campaign was clearly a function of corporate capitalism, it answered personal as well as economic needs because of previous changes in domestic anger standards. The personal element also explains why so much of the campaign turned out to focus not on blue-collar workers but on managers themselves, as they attempted to create an immediate work environment linked at last to their personal emotional ideals.

A New Crusade: Emotionology at Work

The explicit discussion of anger at work, beyond occasional asides about "mouthy" or surly workers—"troublemakers"—or somewhat abstract invocations of the importance of channeling anger into competitive zeal, opened, tentatively, on several fronts after World War I. During the war itself, governmental concern about labor harmony spurred some new measures to cut workplace tensions, among other things encouraging the development of new personnel specialists who would supplement foremen in the direction of workers and who would consider factors other than production alone. Private companies, led by Ford, also began to install personnel programs, toward reducing chronic problems of labor unrest and turnover.[18]

Simultaneously, industrial psychology began its professional existence with the publication of Hugo Münsterberg's treatise on the subject in 1913. Initial concern focused on problems of fatigue and testing for physical and mental aptitudes. But this led to some consideration of emotional factors; fatigue, for example, might manifest itself in irritability, while in addressing problems of absenteeism or even illness emotional reactions could not be excluded. Münsterberg himself noted the importance of "secondary personal traits," including belligerence, that could render a worker unfit for a job. His simultaneous proclamation that "experimentation could secure the selection of the fit workman"—while again primarily directed at appropriate physical and mental characteristics, including those that would lead to predictable toleration of monotony—opened the way for some emotional selectivity as well.[19]

From this point on the outline of institutional arrangements to improve the supervision of workers is relatively familiar.[20] It depended heavily on the proliferation of personnel experts and personnel departments in the larger concerns in sales and in industry, in some contact with industrial psychology. Personnel experts were not always highly trained. Much of their attention went to basic record keeping and company benefit programs. And in Ford and other concerns that initially pioneered in new personnel work, the emphasis on highly directive controls of worker behavior, toward "Americanization," long took precedence over explicit concern about emotionality. Cleanliness and good family habits had pride of place, in what essentially involved a concentration on nineteenth-century middle-class behavioral goals with a substantial new supervisory apparatus.[21] But additional facets were not slow to emerge. Metropolitan Life began an employee counseling service in 1922, initially for outright psychiatric illness but ultimately to aid in any adjustment problem. Some personnel experts took further comfort from the New Deal's emphasis on improved worker-employer relations, citing the Wagner Act as a spur to more sophisticated treatment of job disputes.[22]

By the 1930s, 31 percent of all large American companies had an industrial relations department. World War II definitely stimulated the personnel movement still further, under the sponsorship of the War Industries Board. Particular concern about the integration of women workers, unfamiliar with conditions of employment in large organizations and, apparently, in particular need of a friendlier supervisory approach, led to redoubled efforts at counseling and guidance. According to some accounts, the war also initiated the use of personality testing in employment and job assignment. Without question, previous testing had emphasized aptitudes. But even in the later 1920s, tests for introversion and extroversion involved attention to emotional characteristics, including temper control. The use of the Humm-Wadsworth Personality test, first in Lockheed aircraft in the early 1940s as a means of screening out troublemakers, merely applied earlier testing interests on a larger scale and with more explicit attention to docility. Doncaster Humm, one of the authors of the test, proclaimed that 80 percent of all problem workers had testable deficiencies in temperament, with the remaining 20 percent accounted for by poor job assignments in relation to aptitudes. Certainly, the 1940s and 1950s saw a heightened interest, as far as testing and other personnel activities were concerned, in human relations issues and leadership. New training programs for supervisors and widespread attitude surveys, in which workers were asked to rate their employers' characteristics, date from this period. By 1947, 250 companies were regularly using attitude surveys, particularly in service areas and in defense-related industries like aircraft and shipbuilding. But even in the 1930s companies like Proctor and Gamble, Kimberly-Clark, Sears, and Armstrong Cork had been using attitude surveys to test worker satisfaction.[23]

Within this institutional framework, the new attitude toward anger at work took shape. Early stages of concern, in the late 1920s, came after a decade of concentration on other personnel issues. It was in the 1920s that personnel divisions in department stores began to emphasize personality factors in the recruitment and handling of the sales force. Skill in complex social interactions, including the manipulation of people in the "art" of selling, became a sought-after attribute. At the same time handbooks—forerunners of Dale Carnegie, who published first in 1936—began to urge that salesmen learn to avoid the provocation of anger, for irritation was the emotion "most to be feared" in a sales situation, and efforts to beat down the customer's temper, to respond to anger with anger, would be counterproductive.[24] The emphasis on aggressive, go-getter traits among salesmen tended to yield, after the 1920s, to the greater insistence on a need for courtesy and extrovert friendliness. For female sales personnel, again from the 1920s on, the cheerful smile in the face of the most aggravating upper-class customer became a standard badge. Department store supervisors, concerned with imparting to their sales force a veneer of middle-class culture, included anger control in their goals.[25]

In the 1920s, the tenor of secretarial manuals changed in similar way, in partial correlation with the feminization of this occupation.[26] Manuals in the nineteenth century had urged trustworthiness and other virtues of character focused on reliability. Now the stress shifted toward the emotional qualities desirable for a smoothly functioning bureaucratic office, in which the importance of individual responsibility declined. The man with a naturally agreeable personality could count himself lucky. He who was cursed with a bad temper or irritability was "faced with the problem of remedying these defects"—otherwise he could rarely keep a job. While certain innate problems might impede improvement, habit training was possible, so that the secretary could remain patient in dealing with the employer or with a disagreeable client. "The secretary should never forget that *in order to please people, he needs to exert himself.*"[27] Personnel experts claimed that clerical workers were more often fired for lack of emotional control than for lack of skill. Employers frequently insisted that their secretaries learn to bear their own tempers without retaliation. More than one woman was fired or not hired for protesting these ground rules, as when a candidate frankly said, "Well, if you are snappy without cause, I'll certainly say something back."[28] While some employers commented favorably on the sweetness of the growing army of women secretaries, others claimed that women brought more office quarrels and a greater tendency to backbite. At the same time, employers saw new responsibilities of their own in setting an anger-free office mood. Office supervisors were urged to avoid irritating criticisms and nagging and, in general, to cajole and manipulate rather than berate.[29]

Finally, even on the shop floor emotions received new attention. The famous experiments in the Hawthorne works of General Electric, launched by Elton Mayo and his associates in 1927, quickly involved an emotional component after an initial plan to focus on more purely physical arrangements relating to job fatigue and monotony. Mayo found that attitudes as well as conditions that gave rise to "irritability" could not be ignored and that study of them involved careful attention to workers' subjective reactions and to the emotional implications of different supervisory methods. Interviewing, counseling, and informal retraining of "hard-boiled" foremen—a general concern for "morale"—became a dominant focus of the Hawthorne effort. Here was an important addition to the work arrangements and wage motivation emphasis of industrial engineering. The concern became a commonplace in industrial psychology from that point on.[30]

From its start in the late 1920s through the 1940s, intense interest in reducing and indeed avoiding anger in the workplace constituted a major ingredient of personnel discussion and operations. These were the decades in which the variety of mechanisms to develop new emotional control in work reached a high point, with the special emphasis required because the goal, in the job setting, was so novel. Thereafter, as we will see, explicit concern about work-based anger diminished, not because goals changed, but also because an appropriate temperament was increasingly assumed.[31]

Anger control played a central role in the unprecedented effort to shape a distinctive emotional environment at work because the emotion, or at least variants labeled "irritation" or "bad temper," seemed to loom large in unacceptable worker behaviors. In the late 1920s and the 1930s, the new concern for anger obviously stemmed from an emotional control approach toward quite traditional problems in the industrial labor force, most notably, worker turnover and collective protest. These were problems that industrial psychologists set about to master or to moderate, using tools of emotional management. Their first statement of work-related emotionality had a traditional ring as well, in that it exculpated employers or objective work conditions from significant responsibility. But even in this cautious framework, the old effort to identify a "handful of troublemakers" was jettisoned. As earlier in family life, anger was not just a function of others' bad character but a personality issue for everyone. Wider emotional patterns, not just a few hotheads, now seized center stage, and the response could not be simply dismissal or avoidance—it had to involve some form of emotional treatment.

Elton Mayo and his 1930s successors in personnel counseling confronted the angry worker. They were vitally preoccupied with the question of harmony in the workplace—not a new concern, but novel in its intensity and in its involvement with emotions. For Mayo, a work dispute was the collective equivalent of a nervous breakdown, a severe and ideally avoidable malfunction. Mayo's preoccupation was particularly great, deriving perhaps from his small-town middle-class belief in social harmony; other industrial psychologists could grant that some conflict was not only inevitable but potentially beneficial. Dispute always should be minimized, however; the personnel professional increasingly staked a good bit of prestige on the pursuit of this goal.[32]

In the quest for harmony, with its pragmatic advantages in terms of reduced labor turnover and time lost in strikes, Mayo and his associates made three important claims that centered on the understanding and treatment of anger at work. First, much worker anger had nothing to do with the job itself. This idea struck a conventional chord—surely our workers cannot really be mad at us—and was a clear crowd pleaser for the manufacturers who employed both workers and industrial psychologists. Thus a human relations expert in 1938 claimed that critics of capitalism are "projecting their own maladjustments upon a conjured monster, the capitalists."[33] But the basic notion was somewhat more subtle. Workers brought anger to the job from other sources, often from home situations. By the 1940s, the same idea sometimes conveyed Freudian implications: poor early relations with parents might carry over into angry belligerence at a supervisor. In this idea was a genuine pride in the amiable rationality of objective work arrangements in modern industry and an effort to explain why worker anger might persist despite the best efforts of engineers and other experts in the work environment.

But in addition to its self-serving qualities, the new idea had a number of interesting implications. First, it reversed the nineteenth-century commonplace that anger was often generated at work and then brought home, to be soothed by the ever-cheerful family. The idea maintained the larger motif of this nineteenth-century approach, that anger was unacceptable but somehow nonetheless present and therefore to be explained by pointing to a source outside the expert's particular domain. But the transfer of focus to family causes may have interesting implications for the subject of anger in the home, reflecting among other things a possibility that domestic tensions, or at least perceptions of them, were genuinely changing by the 1920s and 1930s.[34]

For work itself, the temptation to point the finger elsewhere involved more than the exculpation of job conditions and their sponsors. It inclined some industrial experts to a patronizing view of many workers, one that also revived elements of the nineteenth-century view. Workers were less rational than other folks, less able to control their emotions. "It is known that complaints, very often, have nothing to do with the matter complained about."[35] Responsibility to arrange for proper work zeal despite the distracting impulses of the labor force lay with those who have superior control. Worker anger, in this view, was unacceptable but possibly manipulable. No industrial psychologist stated the case so baldly, though some who commented on the particular emotional volatility of women came close. But the idea echoed beliefs current in earlier industrial decades that pointed to the different—and inferior—emotional and familial characteristics of the working class.

These implications of the new approach to anger at work did not prove to be the most important element in the industrial psychologist's view of anger. More durable significance rested with the further discovery of the methods available to treat and to prevent anger at work. For the second discovery of the Mayo group, zealously repeated by later authorities, was that anger in the workplace could be talked out. "Sometimes a worker just bursting with rage at the 'unfairness' of his foreman is able to proceed normally with her work after expressing her feelings . . . and receiving a few words of sympathy or explanation."[36] Some anger did of course arise from objective conditions, and some might indeed be justified, so that dealing with a grievance involved changing something in the work setting. But personnel workers, from Mayo on, were impressed with how often merely talking about anger reduced its intensity. With talk, a worker progressively became embarrassed about expressing so much emotion and often ended with a sheepish apology for coming on so strong; the cause of the emotion might be forgotten or pushed aside in the process. Anger, in this approach, was not only unacceptable but also almost unreal; hence mere venting was sufficient to restore the desirable calm to work relations.[37]

But the third ingredient of what by the 1930s was conventional wisdom among personnel experts qualifies any impression of sheer Machiavellianism toward angry workers. The desire to create harmony in the workplace required restraint from supervisors as well as from employees. After all, if a supervisor really could understand that workers were angry not because of the job but because of home life or even personality, he or she could also realize that an angry response to a worker outburst was inappropriate. Rarely were workers really attacking a supervisor—as opposed to expressing emotions caused by a nasty mother-in-law or a sick child—so why should their anger be met with anything but sympathy and a willingness to explore real causes? If, relatedly, the managerial corps was to enjoy a superior rationality over emotion-driven employees, it was essential that the manager display consistent restraint. Otherwise, as a few personnel experts ventured even in the 1930s, it might seem that executives, too, were driven by irritants stemming from nonwork conditions.[38]

So the experts began to urge a uniformly benign emotional style among those who managed or supervised others. This was perhaps the greatest specific novelty in the recommendations that emerged between the wars. Attempts to deal with angry workers were not unprecedented, though the explanatory apparatus and the methodology involved in these attempts now began to change. But the insistence on a specific managerial emotional style was a new ingredient, and it received steadily greater attention. Indeed, there is more than a slight similarity between this new approach to work atmosphere and the approach urged a century or more earlier in child rearing. For the reformers were not interested in abstract recommendations alone: they knew that there was a traditional, angry style to be attacked. The gruff, authoritarian employer or foreman now took his place alongside the angry, punitive parent in what amounted to a major enlargement of the campaign against anger.[39]

In fact, although Mayo's initial efforts focused on production workers, the new emotionology soon shifted its primary attention to middle managers and supervisors. Some belief continued that occasional worker outbursts and individual feistiness were inevitable, given lower-class character and conditions. This was the thinking behind insistence that supervisors learn to open themselves to worker grievances, "even when they are silly."[40] For supervisors, however, anger became one of the leading justifiable causes for dismissal.[41] The standards for good foremanship changed accordingly. Once a man who met production quotas and took charge of technical innovations on the shop floor, the ideal foreman by the 1940s was a human relations expert who blocked grievances and reduced turnover by managing his own emotions as well as defanging the anger of his workers. Foremen were urged to recognize that "the day of the 'bully' and the 'slave-driver' had gone, and the day of the 'gentleman' and 'leader' had arrived."[42] Snarls were out, a cheery demeanor no matter what the mood or provocation installed in their stead. Even workers, long interested in the fair-minded foreman in any event, picked up the new message, augmenting the standards of courtesy and anger control they cited in discussing ideals with factory observers.[43] Foremen themselves were urged to restrain their own irritations,[44] even in dealing with hostile union representatives: "Control your emotions—control your remarks—control your behavior."[45] The foreman's checklist: "Do I correct the mistakes of my workers considerately, and in a manner to indicate that I am more interested in helping them to avoid future mistakes than I am in the opportunity merely to 'bawl them out?' "[46]

Anger control at work thus became a two-way process. It involved downplaying the seriousness of worker emotions and frankly trying to talk workers out of their wrath. It was freely stated that a majority of workers were childish and immature and needed to be patronized. But anger control also involved managerial reform, toward preventing needless conflict. The hard-boiled approach was out. The aggressive executive remained desirable—possibly—but not if he could not moderate his drive with tact. For anger directed against workers was unwarranted and ineffective (just as the mistresses of servants had been told several decades before): "Bullying begets bullying."[47] Shouting, arbitrary and angry orders, the whole effort to win production through "driving" the worker, were unacceptable according to this approach. In their stead, the experts urged a cooperative stance that would carefully avoid irritating the worker—a stance that admittedly required more self-control than traditional managerial methods and, particularly, control over temper. The tolerant, patient, indeed cheerful supervisor was meant to be responsible for a new emotional climate at work, just as the tolerant parent had been assigned the task of anger prevention in the middle-class household.[48]

Anger, in the new emotionology, had lost any legitimate place at work. "The angry man may himself be the chief victim of his own emotion. It incapacitates him from dealing with his problems in a corrective way."[49] Along with the basic statement came a new style, talking out any anger that did arise, that placed great responsibility for tolerance and self-control on management.[50] Personnel offices directed more attention toward controlling middle amangement than they did toward blue-collar labor, though a manipulative intent cannot be denied.[51] Indeed, the ideal manager not only could turn the other cheek but also could gain skill in probing often inarticulate workers to determine potential causes of anger in advance. If this were not possible, the nearly ideal manager should at least have the wit to employ personnel departments that could accomplish the same end. Not only overt anger but also unvoiced emotion became targets in the new managerial approach.[52]

Early versions of these counsels received mixed reception in the managerial audience. Many supervisors judged that an attempt to see the workers' point of view and the development of a pattern of emotional restraint were simply irrelevant to their job. "I would like to know how some of the other group chiefs would handle the bunch of crabs that I have to deal with."[53] And of course the actual effect of this new advice on managerial behavior remains to be discussed. But the personnel people stuck to their guns, and they were not entirely ignored, which suggests that their recommendations, like their goals of less workplace anger, struck a responsive chord. Indeed, the belief that supervisors were responsible for determining the workplace tone became steadily more explicit and elaborate. By 1941 some of the Hawthorne experimenters, while still insisting that many worker complaints were not "real" and could be treated, not "as facts in themselves, but as symptoms or indicators of personal or social situations which needed to be explored," were also placing on supervisors the task of preventing any work-based anger that could spoil other aspects of an employee's life. Employers, by dealing sympathetically with worker anger regardless of cause, must relieve anxiety so that no worker would go home "carrying with him a mind full of worries and bitterness." The workplace became the center of an attack on all manifestations of serious anger.[54]

With time, indeed, the emphasis on the childishness of angry workers and the nonwork origins of their emotions began to recede. If workers grew angry, they had emotional needs, and it was the job of management to attend to them. Even apparently objective grievances, over pay and benefits, might mask other complaints—"some disturbance in the equilibrium of the individual"—and the good supervisor would learn to fathom what was "eating" the worker involved.[55] Personnel experts in the 1950s urged not just a reduction in traditional authoritarianism but positive efforts to create open communication and rank-and-file participation, in part to reduce the incidence of anger at work. While personnel departments were vital in this task, the good executive would have many of the necessary talents himself. Scientific management demanded fairness in the treatment of other human beings, but a personal element was essential beyond the dictates of science.[56]

This general approach carried with it a host of recommendations for implementation. To avoid causing or expressing anger, a good supervisor would sedulously shun argument: no one ever wins an argument at work. He would cushion the feelings of his workers by avoiding harsh words or ridicule. When criticism was unavoidable, he would offer it in a cool, dispassionate tone, surrounding it if possible with praise for other aspects of the worker's effort, and he would never criticize the worker in front of others. He would smile a lot. Even when a worker quit in anger, the employer should seek a final, courteous interview, in which he would try to instill, by his own restraint, a more favorable attitude. After all, the worker might want to come back some day. And even if not, there was every reason to avoid an angry souvenir. In all this there was the belief that anger control would reduce worker grievance and so promote greater labor force stability and fewer production errors. But pragmatic reasoning was not the only issue. The new goals simply called for avoidance of anger for its own sake; harmony was its own purpose. Of course the self-interest of personnel experts helps explain this preoccupation with anger reduction, for the creation of smoother work relations was their self-assigned mission.

But the effort to apply to the workplace values preached earlier as personal virtues in the middle class had its own appeal, to personnel experts and also to those who employed them.

For the burdens of anger control on the managerial corps were immense, and even if the control was imperfectly applied, as was surely the case, could not have been tolerated in theory if they had not appealed to a more consistent emotional style. For quite simply, all outlets for legitimate anger were being denied to the supervisors of labor on the job. They could not even vent range on worker errors or on angry workers escaping their control. Here was the clearest sign of a revolution in the preferred emotional environment of work, a marked departure from preindustrial as well as earlier industrial norms.

Revealingly, at the same time that the body of industrial expertise was taking shape, new manuals for the personal development of businessmen picked up many of the same themes. The anger-control motif was a basic part of the Dale Carnegie approach to winning friends and influencing people, delivered in multiple editions of his famous book, from the mid-1930s through the 1950s, and in countless lectures to aspiring salesmen and entrepreneurs throughout the United States. Skills in business, to Carnegie and similar secular preachers, meant skill in human relationships and the ability to avoid provoking irritation under all circumstances.[57] The skilled human relater will recognize that people are not rational. Therefore even justifiable criticisms or rebuttals can draw fire. The positive approach is essential: praise people, and smile a lot even when dealing with complaints. Carnegie specifically noted that his business style was precisely the emotional formula desirable in the home, with restraint against all ugly passion. In both domestic and business settings, criticism might sometimes be essential, but it should always be indirect, prefaced by self-criticism and lathered with praise. Never should a heated word or an argument be ventured. Rather not only courtesy but also apology—even when one's course of action had been correct—should be used to turn away wrath. All this was not only tactically wise but also morally satisfying. Carnegie confronts an insulting customer: "By apologizing and sympathizing with her point of view . . . I had the satisfaction of controlling my temper, the satisfaction of returning kindness for an insult. I got infinitely more real fun out of making her like me than I ever could have gotten out of letting her go and take a jump."[58] So if someone else is angry, sympathize, defuse—never be lured into a hostile expression. And—inevitably— let the anger be talked out. Almost anyone can be softened, even when in a raving temper. One's own mood becomes irrelevant: smile whether you feel like it or not. An effort of will is all that it takes. The businessman turns a happy face not just to customers but even to strikers and—it might be guessed—government officials.

The rise of personnel psychology, with its goals in dealing with anger at work, and the concomitant surge of manuals of emotional control in business represent significant changes in twentieth-century work culture. They might, of course, have been cultural artifacts alone, a new public relations window dressing. And so in part they doubtless were. The climate of work had not been consistently angry before, and it did not suddenly become consistently benign. But the new approach to anger at work was followed up by a number of institutional developments, designed simultaneously to reduce the element of personal whimsy in work or sales relationships and to impose a greater degree of emotional control. These institutions constituted the practical implementation of the new business advice, for neither managers nor workers could be trusted to convert their temperaments through exhortation and personal tactics alone.

One key ambivalence did remain in the otherwise sweeping twentieth-century emotionology of work. While anger control was to be arranged for workers and internalized by the various white-collar employees, it was not, even in theory, consistently applied to the summit of the corporate hierarchy. Executives urged restraint on secretaries without promising reciprocity; they sent, as we will see, subordinates to emotion-training sessions without going themselves. Hierarchy, at the top, continued to condition anger control.

Thus while executives were touched by the new emotional standards, seeing increasing importance in a pleasant demeanor and avoidance of petty irritability, they did not look to the kind of emotional reformation that they were sponsoring for many other job levels. A 1950s survey of management traits revealed the distinction within the ranks of management itself: top managers prided themselves on pleasant personalities but in a fairly generalized way, whereas middle managers made a particular point of their patience, avoidance of aggression, and ability to control their tempers under provocation.[59]

In the heyday of the personnel movement, some experts unquestionably hoped to include top executives fully within their standards of temper control. Various studies and tests worked toward selection according to tolerance and ability to restrain anger; in one interview schedule, anger-control goals constituted three of a total of seven desired personality traits. Even aside from the experts, the spread of new emotional criteria among lower management levels may have reduced the tolerance for arbitrary, angry behavior from the boss; this was the implication, for example, of a study of changes in morale factors among country farm agents.[60] It was certainly easy to believe that top executives, like other supervisors, should learn new patience with subordinates, a new sensitivity to the sources of emotional disturbance in themselves and others. In dealing with grievances or disciplinary cases, standards of restraint urged on foremen might equally be urged on top management ranks. While this disagreement may merely have masked the emotional perquisites of power—the right to be angry when on the top—it touched base with traditional thinking and had real force in its own right. For the top ranks of American business had long been associated with the traits of aggressiveness and drive, which at least in terms of popular belief were not totally compatible with total restraint of temper or other powerful emotions. Thus while a few personnel experts tried to downplay the value of aggression in all job categories, a more common stance was to argue that tact and diplomacy were desirable but not essential in a chief executive and should not be allowed to dim the necessary aggressiveness. Similarly, the same authority who urged the need for strict control of initiative in an organization—"otherwise it is not a social asset"—commented on the importance of managerial willingness to "bump heads" when needed to get action taken within a bureaucracy. Implicitly the reconciliation of these ideas came through different hierarchies within management, with the restraint of the middle level not allowed to ensnare the upper officials.[61] Somewhat more ruefully, another human relations expert, while bemoaning the childishness of executive displays of temper, had to admit that superior organizing ability might bypass the need for humane contact with subordinates; ruthlessness could still win success.[62]

The bifurcated approach to emotional control within management created some undeniable dilemmas for the middle layer. Realistic advice had to urge restraint on the part of middling bureaucrats against not only the irrationality of workers but also the moodiness of the boss. The executive temper had to be tolerated, though the clever subordinate would learn how to time bad news and to put a favorable gloss on problems in order to minimize conflict.[63] For their part, the absence of consistent pressure for restraint might excuse chief executives from any commitment to share personally in emotional reform; it was easy to believe that their participation need not go farther than the cosmetic level.

There were of course some unresolved issues in this messy managerial division, though they were not brand new in the history of work. A hierarchy of management styles is hardly surprising; nor is the result that many top executives falsely exaggerated their commitment to human relations skills, claiming more attention to "consideration" than they in fact put into practice. School superintendants in the 1950s, for example, while claiming emotional control, in fact exercised it selectively, showing a far pleasanter side to school boards than to managerial subordinates.[64] But most chief executives passed through middle management on their way up and thus experienced some need for emotional restraint that might color later behavior. And if some managers gleefully shucked off their restraint when they had it made, in fact using anger as a weapon to spur subordinates, some of whom had internalized norms of control that might increase their vulnerability to displays of temper, others managers maintained at least a veneer of the impersonal friendliness that, all authorities agreed, was preferable even at the top of the work hierarchy.[65]

It remains true that the exceptions granted to top executives posed some interesting tensions for the anger-control movement at other levels and created some painful encounters in offices and meeting rooms among people held to different standards of emotional accountability. It is clear that a part of the anger-control effort involved the translation to a corporate environment of older inequalities of emotional freedom at work.

Yet the anger-control currents were not simply a reassertion of traditional hierarchy, even aside from the extent to which they touched executive behavior itself. Various kinds of workers, particularly in the white-collar categories, were being subjected to new emotional standards that were designed to produce more than grudging or fatalistic docility in behavior and intended, most revealingly, to affect their own behavior toward customers or subordinates.

Between Emotionology and Emotion: Implementing the New Standards at Work

The same decades that produced the new insistence on anger control and its endless reiteration in personnel manuals of various sorts saw an important series of institutional devices designed to enforce the new standards. In this pattern the history of work differs from that of family, where there were relatively few intermediaries between emotionology and actual behavior. Counseling services, testing procedures, foremen retraining, and Sensitivity-Training groups (T groups), which developed somewhat consecutively from the 1930s into the 1960s, are not evidence of the actual emotional experience of work, but they did serve to translate emotionology actively onto the job site.

The development of counseling services was the earliest and most obvious practical result of the findings of industrial psychologists. Counseling increasingly preoccupied the Hawthorne experimenters, and it spread still further during and after World War II. Western Electric,

Hawthorne's parent company, had but a single counseling officer in 1936; by 1941 it had twenty-nine, for 10,000 workers; and by 1954 it had sixty-four. And the counselors became steadily more professional, after an initial tendency simply to select well-liked workers. The Federal Social Security Board, which set up its counseling staff in 1938, found the actual usage steadily increasing: 215 employees availed themselves of the services in its first eight months, but 1,995 used it in the second half of 1941.[66]

Counseling services handled a variety of matters, of course, including discussions of benefits and retirement options. But their principal justification lay in the area of defusing emotional tensions—ideally, defusing them through discussion before they reached the stage of requiring action. Counseling activities thus mirrored the new beliefs about anger in the workplace: that anger was unacceptable; that it derived usually from nonwork causes; and that its unreality, or at least its irrelevance to objective problems, opened the way to talking out as a remedy. Through patient listening, counselors could aid workers in adjusting to the industrial structure—without doing anything about the structure itself, without doing more, normally, than providing an audience for often vigorous emotion. As one authority put it, counselors mainly allowed workers to gain some understanding of their own problems, which lay at the root of expressions of anger.[67]

Counseling services also served, however, to revise or supplement supervisory bluntness. Personnel authorities urged that workers should be able to see the counseling staff without foreman disapproval, for what was needed was a distinct orientation to the human relations aspect of work. Counselors had the time and ability to get at deep-seated emotional issues, including those that led to conflict between worker and supervisor. Supervisors, for their part, were urged to use counseling services freely for troubled workers, without a sense of failure—for anger so often had nonwork roots that defense of turf would be meaningless. Obviously, many foremen resented the intrusion of the counseling services, and many doubtless let workers use them only grudgingly if at all—though personnel experts tended to look on the bright side, claiming that most supervisors welcomed what counseling could offer. Without question, the intent of counseling—and managerial support for it—involved a modification of the traditional possibilities for arbitrary, angry supervisory behavior.[68]

The counseling staff itself was urged to preserve a uniform emotional style that would maximize its chances of drawing wrathful venom from its clients. The purpose was to spread calm, not to take objective conditions in hand. A woman janitorial worker in Chicago was frequently caught sleeping on her job but so abused the supervisor who challenged her—swearing, showing great anger—that he became afraid to direct her at all. Enter counseling. The worker poured out her dislike for her present job, her belief that she deserved a better position. The counselor listened patiently, waiting for her tirade to subside. More tranquil, the custodian agreed to work better and decided that her job was not so bad. For his part, the counselor urged the foreman to be a bit more tactful, remembering that workers, too, are human beings with feelings. So, apparently, the issue was resolved—with nothing of substance altered. The caseworker noted with self-satisfaction that workers who were blocked by their anger from dealing with foremen opened up easily in the congenial atmosphere of the counseling office.[69] Another case, again involving women (the favorite counseling target in the 1940s), involved arguments between two workers, one of whom, when teased, burst into tantrums. The counselor's task here was easy. The angry worker needed greater maturity: "You look silly having a temper tantrum at your age." With anger controlled, the worker could hope to gain greater popularity, and smooth shop relations could be restored.[70]

The key to good counseling rested, then, in patience, noninvolvement, and a tranquil mood that could set the tone for what was desirable on the job site. Despite temptation, the staff person was to talk to angry workers "without getting excited."[71] A vague sympathy was desirable in that the counselor should "communicate to the speaker that he appreciates how he feels." But there should be no commitment to sympathy, for the good counselor would listen, not judge or advise.[72] In what might have served as a motto for the new emotional style at work overall, the counselor was to be "impersonal, but friendly."

Counseling activities could of course involve efforts to reassign workers or otherwise alter objective conditions as well as urging greater control of anger on workers and supervisors alike. But the emotional function remained central. And counseling services amplified their contributions by conducting interviews of new and existing workers even apart from problem cases, to try to identify potential sources of emotional trouble and, on occasion, to prevent a bad appointment. Interviewing skills involved the same friendly but uninvolved calm that other personnel functions demanded. Interestingly, an initial temptation to use interviews to promote additional anxiety among job candidates, as a means of character testing, gave way to a desire to create the calmest possible atmosphere. No one, in an interview situation, should encourage vigorous emotion. The same style applied to the exit interview, also conducted by the personnel staff. Here, the defusing of anger was even more salient, for exit interviews were designed not only to determine on-the-job problems that might be remedied in the future but also to alter the level of grievance of the departing worker. If possible, no one should go away mad.[73]

The logic of the new desire to control anger on the job also informed the personality testing movement, which grew up simultaneously with counseling services from the late 1920s on. It would be tempting to try to paint a picture of control-hungry managers seizing on personality tests as a means of screening out emotionally undesirable—among other things, choleric—workers, thus building a monochromatic emotional blandness in the workplace. Without question, tests provided important new means of control, less in weeding out undesirable workers than in regulating characteristics necessary for promotions and encouraging at least superficial adherence to certain emotional goals. But the assessment of the effect of personality testing, at least given the present state of research, must be somewhat more qualified. Personality testing spread rapidly and did, as will be discussed shortly, conduce to the control of anger at work. But this testing was largely an adjunct of other testing programs that were taken more seriously. Experts and employers both disagreed internally on the significance and usability of personality tests. Even managers who used tests often preferred to rely on their own ''feel'' for a worker's traits, determined in interviews. Furthermore, personality testing had a shotgun element, designed to elicit so many potentially undesirable features that no single goal, such as anger control, might be pursued through the tests' use. Testers took aim not only at anger but also at sexual habits, cultural interests, and a host of other personal proclivities. Overall, however, personality testing, particularly for white-collar workers and aspiring managers, provided an additional ingredient in the campaign to control anger at work; it did not prove, independently, to be the weapon that some critics envisaged.

There is no question that personnel experts and managers alike saw the initial promise in tests as an improved means of spotting troublemakers and more generally as aids in smooth human relations at work. As early as 1928, tests were developed to measure introversion and extroversion, with the latter immensely preferred as a work personality. Included in the drawbacks of introversion was lack of temper control, whereas extroversion, with its superior adjustment to reality, offered unusual control. A personality test used by a Los Angeles utility company, in the 1930s, to screen initial hirees toward producing minimal emotional interference with work deliberately sought to identify the desired low-level emotionality associated with extroversion. Test developers argued that self-control was a trait that could readily be measured, warning against the untested worker who might demonstrate ''explosive temper and readiness to take offense.''[74] No supervisor would wish to work with argumentative employees, so why not remove them in advance? Early personality tests, for example, the Humm-Wadsworth Temperament Scale, thus asked questions such as, "Is a disappointment more likely to make you angry than sad?"[75] as a means of determining whether a job candidate tended toward "hysterical" reactions. A variety of test questions probed whether reactions to various job or domestic situations would involve anger.[76]

Other tests focused also on supervisors, attempting to measure their sociability and human relations abilities, with restraint of anger one ingredient of these larger skills. Other tests, including the Bernreuter, aimed somewhat more diffusely at "aggressive" characteristics, with questions like, "Are you bothered by shyness?" The Bernreuter battery was particularly recommended because of its measurement of tact and the emotional stability needed to handle grievances sensibly. And of course other questions, common during the 1940s, that aimed at political "deviance" would have been viewed by some managers as relevant to the anger control theme as well. Small wonder that, during and after World War II, test proponents had some success in arguing that their efforts could improve work relations immensely, reducing turnover and expensive grievance procedures alike.[77]

Certainly personality tests won wide usage, though of course emotional control interests account for only part of their popularity. A 1960s critic claimed that ten million Americans had been subjected to tests, either at work or in school, with an additional million being added to the list each year. The Bernreuter test alone—the most popular—was selling at an annual rate of 350,000 during the 1950s. Unquestionably, all the widely used tests worked, among other things, toward job tranquility, with angry, abrasive personalities identified and eliminated if possible. Thus sociability and related skills loomed large. Finally, the overall effect of the tests contributed to, or at least reflected, an alteration in the definition of the desirable work personality, an alteration particularly noticeable in the ranks of managers and supervisors themselves. Undue aggressiveness and striving for dominance became targets for criticism, as denoting a potential lack of the amiability and permissiveness now sought in those whose task it was to work with people. Anger and hostility were taken as the opposites of the desired cooperativeness, and friendliness rather than angry chastisement was sought among those who were to be responsible for motivating subordinates. Thus Pillbury Mills, in the 1950s, directly tested foremen otherwise eligible for promotion with a series of questions designed to make sure that anger would be excluded in their basic approach to personnel problems.[78]

By the 1960s, test questions related to anger were becoming less direct, more generalized in tone. A central polarity now, replacing the older preoccupation with introversion versus extroversion, was "consideration" versus "initiating structure." The latter proclivity denoted a manager whose main attention would go to organizational matters as the basis for intense drive toward greater productivity. The characteristic of "consideration," far more beloved by personnel experts, marked social skills—an interest in the problems of subordinates as fellow workers and a real desire to get along well with everyone. Angry temperaments were not directly envisaged. But the theme was not entirely absent, for irritability and an insensitivity toward provoking anger in others were traits held common among supervisors with the initiating structure temperament. Such men would "needle" their workers as a means of motivating greater effort, among other things criticizing them in front of their fellows. Here was an interesting modification of the older idea of the "driving" supervisor, now presumably laid to rest, but one that suggests that measuring variations in sensitivity to anger remained significant in personality testing. One important supervisory test, the Leadership Behavior Description Questionnaire, first developed in the late 1940s and then revised in the 1960s to focus on "consideration" more explicitly, reflected this measurement attempt. Consideration consumed about 10 percent of all questions on the 1970s Supervisory and Peer Leadership test, with some additional questions directed at an anger-related "hostility."[79]

While testing reflected the growing desire to limit anger in the workplace, it did not in fact become the central instrument some initial proponents had envisaged. The multiple uses of tests, concern about reliability, and some continued sense that aggression might still have its uses at the high executive level all limited test use. Furthermore, the new approach to workplace anger, focusing on the malleability of the labor force, stressed the possibility of reform more than the exclusion of temperamentally undesirable employees. Firing or even failing to hire might after all promote anger; now that "impersonal friendliness" reigned, the focus shifted to modifying unacceptable emotional expressions. And this meant, along with counseling, specific efforts at retraining.

As one personnel expert put it, commenting on retraining programs for foremen at General Electric and Hotpoint, supervisors can be schooled toward a reduction in self-righteous anger. This belief served as the core of the enthusiasm for education programs, particularly for production-line foremen, that lasted for the better part of two decades, beginning with the programs developed under the War Manpower Commission during World War II. Even earlier, in fact, some conference groups in military production areas had begun the task of training foremen in better methods of handling "surly" workers.[80]

The basis for the training interest was the belief that foremen and related supervisory personnel were the core group in changing emotional relations on the job. If their personalities would improve, toward greater friendliness and courtesy, other emotional tensions would fall away. The emphasis on desirable traits did not differ markedly from that offered to salesmen in the Dale Carnegie courses. Indeed, foremen and salesmen occasionally took the same program, as in the Schenley Distillers course in the 1950s. Training courses stressed the irrelevance of most worker anger. They told foremen what employers had long been telling them, that the company was right, but with the added twist now that worker complaints and even union campaigns were based on anger generated off the job. But foremen nevertheless had to deal with workers' grievances, and the focus of training was to permit the control of anger in this process. Foremen were told to stop pressing so much, to get closer to their workers, and to aid them with any problems. Detente was the key—the word itself was used—in what it was hoped would be the conversion to a workplace low on grievance and high on harmony. What the foreman needed was not technical expertise, which the company's engineers could provide, but human relations skills and an ability to communicate and to listen. Some companies, of course, attempted to select a new breed of foremen through personality testing, but the interest in retraining usually won out as the key to humanizing relations with labor.[81]

But the preference for training programs did not suggest, in principle at least, a retreat from the idea that the traditional work personality of the foreman had to be reshaped. Leadership-training teachers bombarded foremen with examples of the bad old days—foremen who shouted, put down worker grievances, and ridiculed employees in front of others. They used teaching questionnaires, before and after lessons, so that supervisors would learn how to respond correctly to issues of personnel procedure. How should a worker be told of a mistake on the job? Should a foreman be friendly with subordinates? Role playing was introduced. Foremen were put in the role of an angry worker so that they would understand the emotions involved and learn that anger should not be answered in kind.[82] Worker anger might or might not be legitimate, but it was periodically inevitable. Anger on the part of supervisors was never legitimate, and its avoidance would in fact reduce the incidence of worker complaints. The foreman should be, like the personnel counselors, friendly but impersonal. He should maintain some sense of hierarchy but also an openness and amiable countenance that would convey some sympathy. The foreman should learn to repeat some counseling ploys directly. Faced with an aggrieved worker, he should insist on a private discussion, and he should maintain calm. "Any discussion of the grievance should be made with a great deal of light and with as little heat as possible." Get the worker to repeat his complaint three or four times, to cool him off. Frequently the worker will see the silliness of his own emotion and drop the whole affair. But even if the grievance demands action, the foreman should make it his responsibility to defuse the emotion involved, by his own self-control. "It is of the utmost importance that the foreman remain cool."[83]

Many actual training programs were quite cursory, with little actual effect even when they were informed by the anger-control principles. Nevertheless, it was clear that the conception of the foreman was changing and that the idea of some remolding of his personality was an important part of the process. Training programs implicitly emphasized the belief that foremen should guide the emotional context of work as they once had been asked to guide production techniques and work pace. They should either reduce workplace anger or prevent its consequences from reaching higher levels: thus they should prevent grievance or at least handle most grievances that did arise, in part through control of their own and their workers' emotions; and, relatedly, they should minimize turnover. These responsibilities were novel and considerable, which explains the commitment to hundreds of retraining programs involving thousands of supervisors in manufacturing firms, insurance companies, and banks. Foremen themselves were apparently eager to learn more about the new approach. One survey in 1944 claimed that 80 percent of them wanted some new human relations training.[84]

After the 1950s the emphasis on supervisory training cooled somewhat if only because many courses became routine parts of the preparation of foremen and related personnel. Fashions within the courses shifted somewhat. In the 1960s the new fascination with consideration entered into the preparation of foremen and managers, providing a new term and possibly some new substance for the kind of sympathy and friendliness foremen were meant to convey to their subordinates. But the motif of attitude change continued and, along with it, the stress on anger control, although this was less singled out because of the apparently successful assault on traditional practices.[85]

Furthermore, shading off from the supervisory training programs, a new fad in the 1960s took up some of the same themes but for a higher level of management personnel. T groups continued the effort to open managers to a greater concern for worker needs, including emotional needs, urging attention to people in addition to levels of production. Like the earlier training groups, the new sensitivity movement hoped to alter attitudes and emotional styles at work. But the T group enterprise focused more on executive relations within a corporate bureaucracy, and it developed a more elaborate approach to emotional control while retaining basic goals of anger restraint from earlier efforts. The distinct focus of the movement and, even more, the more amply documented and argued emotional stance warrant a brief separate comment.[86]

T group sessions began in the 1950s and reached a peak of popularity in the 1960s; some momentum carried on into yet a third decade. The groups, often fashionably and tax deductibly housed in vacation settings, involved small numbers of executives—often younger middle managers with promotion potential—from a given corporation. The groups were designed to improve on earlier socialization in dealing with people. They offered a vague commitment to more democratic and open management styles, but above all they stressed the need for emotion-free communication and for compromise rather than conflict when values or policies were in dispute. Groups met for several days or weeks, alternating discussion of reactions to problems encountered in the past or new situations presented by group leaders with role playing designed to simulate stressful exchanges within the management hierarchy. Considerable attention was devoted to the reduction of prejudice. Advocates of the movement claimed—as their counterparts had urged in discussing the retraining of foremen—that human relations skills, not aptitudes, were the key to success in the modern corporation.[87]

T group participants, particularly as leaders of the movement, were often self-selected, so that hostile or angry personalities, unable to exercise restraint in frank exchanges, would not disrupt proceedings. Executives who defended an authoritarian management style often found themselves hurt or aggrieved—or angry—in discussions that attacked such traditions in favor of more open discussion and interchange. No traditional image emerged as clear as that of the driving foreman, for in dealing with executives the T group leaders had to exercise more subtlety; but the overall direction was clear. Executives who bossed others about, showed no sensitivity to feelings, and used anger as a weapon were counterproductive. They should be altered or bypassed. To promote the desired style, T groups operated through confrontations that juxtaposed executives, normally in a hierarchical relationship, with each other as equals, to teach participants both to give and to accept criticism. A central lesson involved learning not to retaliate against hostility but rather to stress the development of more "tender" emotions. Since the confrontations in T groups were contrived, not real-world conflicts, they permitted participants to experience tension without being carried over into outright hostility.[88] The overriding goal was better management of one's own feelings, which in turn would promote rational reactions in others. "Effectiveness decreases as emotionality increases."[89]

These goals obviously overlapped substantially with the earlier purposes of the supervisory training movement. They were phrased somewhat less abruptly, as befitted the august station of the intended participants. Foremen could be ordered to change emotions—at least in theory; executives had to be coaxed. Greater diffuseness also resulted from the need to encompass a greater range of job behavior. Foreman retraining had often focused simply on handling grievances or other relatively specific tasks in anger control. T groups urged executives to develop a more generalized sensitivity to themselves and others, a process that could justify the greater intensity, and the obfuscating verbiage, of the T group movement.

For while the goals of T groups show a clear affiliation with the anger-control effort and spread this effort from the lowest management level to higher echelons, the methods involved some interesting conflicts over precise emotional style. Thus a given T group leader could simultaneously advocate full emotional control on the job, in the interests of rationality, and claim that sensitivity training would open the executive to greater understanding of feelings and would allow him or her to use feelings as the basis for administrative innovation. Rationality thus warred with a desire to let employees express their true sentiments, as a means of encouraging loyalty and a willingness to take risks. At the least, this moved to a higher level the 1930s attempt to postulate an emotional division between worker and supervisor, with the latter responsible for rationality. Now a T grouped executive might sense that his own rationality should be exercised in the manipulation of his colleagues' emotions. But this division may be oversimple, in that the emotions discussed were preselected to exclude anger. Rationality might confront "real feelings," but these latter could not legitimately include hostility.[90]

Chris Argyris, one of the most prominent T group students and the leader of several pilot groups, put the case as follows. Organizational rationality too often ignored the emotional impulses of corporate executives. Yet emotions were not removed merely because corporate rules sought to ignore them. Hence an effective executive must gain skill in dealing with irrationality, for the sake of genuine interpersonal relations. Too much repression was bad for all concerned. Too many meetings produced an artificial harmony through the careful exclusion of passion in any disagreement—and the result was a needless sacrifice of potential creativity, the production of mindless yes-men who mechanically implemented decisions in which they felt no personal stake. Emotions too often enter the corporate world only in crisis situations, when executives use an emotional tone to "needle" staff members and to impress on them the seriousness of the problem at hand. But this introduction of emotion is unilateral; it ignores the feelings of subordinates and so becomes frankly manipulative. Save in crisis situations, management dismisses feelings as immature or childish.[91]

To this point, the argument is consistent enough. Argyris seems to propose a more integrated executive style, which will include the emotions of participants on a mutual basis. This approach was a necessary concomitant to the organizational decentralization Argyris simultaneously urged, wherein the impulses of a larger number of executives must be given some free play. The only lacuna in this thesis is a clear discussion of emotions themselves. Argyris and others in the T group movement discuss freeing up emotions, but with a careful if implicit list of what emotions they envisage. Anger is simply not on the list.[92]

The contribution of T groups to emotionality was thus twofold. In the first place, by setting up artificial conflict situations, group leaders were expected to expose the hollowness of anger. They might tolerate brief exchanges of tension, but participants were not supposed seriously or durably to engage in the angry emotion. After all, they had to go home friends—indeed, friendlier than before. Second, T groups hoped to promote greater warmth, at least a surface affection, in management relations. Argyris talked of "more authentic" relationships, by which he meant "more affectionate." The ultimate reconciliation of the T group principles lay in the fact that a full emotional release was *not* intended, despite some confusing rhetoric about the reduction of stiffness and repression. Rather emotions were to be seen as falling under the same controls as other attitudes: they were conscious, discussable, and controllable. "The rationality of feelings and attitudes is as crucial as that of the mind."[93] T group leaders like Argyris in fact rarely mentioned anger directly. They talked of reducing hostility, but they assumed a prior socialization that would have taken care of the rawest expression of anger. Thus the T group movement explored warmth or coldness in interpersonal relations but left out the factor of temper altogether. Openness of feelings, often urged, was predicated on this previous emotional control. The emotions to be released were only "positive." At most a brief bow was made to resentments engendered by the repression of feelings. But the possibility of realistic or deeply felt anger, that might surface in a climate of emotional release after the therapeutically positive emphasis of the T group, was simply ignored.[94]

T group training was intended to improve specific aspects of executive performance, along with modifying overall styles. The accuracy of reports would improve. When subordinates no longer feared a superior's anger—since the superior would have learned to control himself—and when chief executives stopped encouraging destructive competition among subordinates, with the hostility and anxiety this could engender, subordinates would more willingly report problems and mistakes. They would increasingly feel responsibility for their own acts, rather than regarding themselves as creatures of the boss and his decisions. Tension would decline and "brotherly love" increase. Bosses would learn to play down the table pounding in crisis meetings, and this reduction in the use of anger for manipulation would encourage subordinates to reduce their own inner anger. Even a willingness to admit a mistake to a subordinate could convert the latter from a hostile, uninvolved competitor for advancement into a loyal participant on the executive team.[95]

Under the guise of emotional liberation, then, the T group movement sought, in its own way, to reduce, indeed if possible to eliminate, anger in executive relationships. It sought to move further than earlier efforts had done, by going beyond restraint of angry behavior and advocacy of a cool demeanor, to a reduction even of inner anger and repressed hostility. The result would be a loving rationality, a realistic approach to problem solving bolstered by the warmth of fraternal fellow feeling. These goals, clearly, reached farther and deeper, toward revision of job emotions, than most earlier attempts had done, though they maintained the same aversion to anger. The intentions are interesting, even if they seem naive and unrealistic, because they parallel efforts at anger control in other aspects of life, such as child rearing, during the same decades. Whether the results of the T group movement at all paralleled the intentions is more difficult to determine. Many programs were undermined by the failure of the older, top executives to participate at all. Some T group experiences left trainees tense as a result of the conflicts experienced in the sessions themselves or as a result of finding that the brave new world painted by the session leaders bore no relationship to the same old world of the actual office when encountered on return. One assessment of the movement, certainly plausible, suggested that the main effect was to alter surface emotions in executive interaction, reducing expressions of overt hostility and encouraging a superficial bonhomie, without changing deeper sentiments or affections. These effects would dovetail with the effect of other anger-control devices, such as counseling and supervisory training, in limiting the permissibility of open expressions of annoyance or anger.[96]

Beyond Anger: Emotionology and Implementation
from the 1960s On

The widespread attempt to alter the emotional context of work crested, as we have seen, between the late 1920s and the late 1950s. It then slacked off somewhat, which means that before venturing an assessment of the practical effect of the implicit campaign—indeed, as part of this assessment—we must discuss what followed in the personnel approach. The greatest enthusiasm for using testing, counseling, and training to restrain anger, the most open discussion of the need for temper control, began to fade after the 1950s. Other issues, including equal employment rights pressures and a renewed interest in organizational reforms, began to dominate personnel literature. The T group movement, it is true, received primary attention during the 1960s, but we have seen that it took a more amorphous, less direct approach to anger, bathing control efforts in a rhetoric of fraternal affection and emotional release.

Yet as the T group theories demonstrate, the goals of limiting anger at work did not yield. Rather they were taken increasingly for granted. It was no longer necessary, or at least so the experts believed, to talk about retraining foremen; the war against more traditional styles was over, with the victory going to greater calm. Increasingly, it was simply assumed that telephone operators would put a smile in their voice, that salesmen would know that the angry customer was right.

Thus many of the institutions established in the mid-century decades continued after 1960, with less fanfare. Foreman training maintained a substantial human relations element, and indeed occasional laments about unduly bossy and insensitive foremen continued on the part of personnel experts. But the specific emphasis on temper control was largely absent because assumed; training-group leaders emphasized more complex skills of empathy with worker problems and an ability to listen. This greater sophistication also allowed increasing admission that many worker grievances were real and demanded constructive attention, though the importance of off-the-job irritants was still mentioned.[97] The insistence on humane attitudes on the part of middle-level managers was maintained as well, though again it was couched more in positive terms—the need for consideration and empathy—than in stark recommendations of temper control.[98] The idea of temper control also spread increasingly to union ranks. A United Auto Workers booklet urged members not to bully foremen or to respond to supervisory anger with displays of temper: "A lost temper usually means a lost argument."[99] This dissemination, like the greater sophistication in discussions of managerial skills, reflects the assimilation of the earlier anger-control goals, at least at the level of advice and theory.

Personality testing for supervisors, salesmen, and managers—like the Leadership Behavior Descriptive Questionnaire revised in 1963—continued to include items relevant to anger, but the shift to a more positive emphasis on consideration and openness to workers' personal problems was evident here as well. Thus questions rarely asked directly about anger, focusing instead on the friendliness and approachability of the candidate. Selection of airline stewardesses, for example, relied heavily on the outgoing friendliness of applicants. Similarly, questionnaires on job satisfaction, though they included a few questions on reactions to supervisors, moved more toward explorations of frustration with potentially meaningless work. Interviews also maintained an interest in temper as part of temperament, and the earlier trend to reduce the temptation to put candidates on the spot, as a means of testing under fire, reflected a continued concern with gentle emotional management. But interview lists now stressed the more general skills in interpersonal relations, not emotionality per se. Interviewers wanted to check on excessive potential bossiness and skill in handling grievances and avoiding favoritism—they saw no further reason to worry about explicit outbursts of anger.[100]

Growing concern with organizational arrangements, rather than temperament training, diverted attention from anger control, but not to the extent of creating a different emotional model for work. Indeed, consideration and personnel skills remained essential even when reorganization problems took pride of place. Better communication, for example, continued to involve human as well as organizational elements, and the human elements included proper personal control over hostility. Thus a dry article on rational problem solving, while manifesting far less attention to anger than the personnel literature of the 1950s, noted its assumption that conflict and aggression would interfere with problem solving. Managers should think, not in terms of emotional confrontations, but in terms of resolution of a specific issue through calm compromise and through careful attention to relations with subordinates. Self-understanding remained vital to this process, even though it required less attention than before from personnel experts.[101]

Attitudes toward ordinary workers and employees showed a similar elaboration on the basis of presumably established principles of anger control. Concern for the seriously troubled worker, rather than the run-of-the-mill troublemaker, increased—not because troublemakers were more tolerable, but because they were perceived as a lessened problem. Mentally healthy workers were viewed in terms broader than the management of anger, as experts increased their emphasis on positive needs for esteem and recognition. But these amplifications assumed a calm supervisory tone and outlets for grievances; they did not suggest a new emotional style.[102] The burgeoning fascination with techniques Japanese, in the mid-1970s, included concern for emotional context and the need to discuss emotions on the job. Here too, however, anger played no direct role, for its inappropriateness to the work setting was assumed—this was not one of the job emotions to explore. The closest approach to control of temper came in a vague reference, in dealing with aggrieved customers, to "inoffensive communications techniques."[103] More formal studies of working life, though they included concern for "affective" problems such as anxiety and depression, similarly avoided direct discussion of anger. At most the possibility that workers might turn aggression against themselves, as manifested in mental or physical health problems, evoked notice. Anger and work did not mix, and while this assumed continuation of older personnel programs, it rested on a deeply rooted model of the emotional context of work. Save from some "problem" symptoms, often self-directed, anger had receded from the forefront of inquiry into the psychological qualities of work.[104]

The only suggestion of an alternative emotional model might have been the new interest in assertiveness training for managers, which burgeoned in the 1970s. But assertiveness was not anger; indeed, the properly assertive manager was skilled in calm conflict resolution. Assertiveness training in fact often presumed a desire to improve in other skills, including openness to worker problems. Assertiveness concerns do not, then, demonstrate a new approach to anger at work. Rather, the assertiveness interest rested on the assumption of anger control and may have reflected the success of earlier lessons of conflict avoidance and surface friendliness on the job, particularly in middle-management ranks. Some middle managers, in other words, needed to relearn some decisiveness; there was no implication that they also sought to relearn anger. In fact, assertiveness programs characteristically insist on a careful distinction between their goals and aggressive behavior or attitudes.[105]

And in some particularly sensitive service jobs, an emphasis on anger control if anything increased. A recent description of the training and regulation of stewardesses on Delta Airlines notes that management essentially joins the techniques of deep acting with social engineering, in teaching employees to suppress anger. Initial training emphasizes empathy with the passengers, so that the employee learns that any outburst can be understood and managed without an angry response: "If you think about the other person and why they're upset, you've taken attention off of yourself and your own frustration. And you won't feel so angry." Twice yearly "recurrent" training emphasizes management of employee anger more directly and tries to make this a personal good: "I'd like to talk to you about being angry. I'm not saying you should do it for the passengers. I'm saying do it for *your-selves.*" Anger, in this presentation, is part of stress, its control vital to health and self-satisfaction. In this case, at least, anger control goes beyond insistence on proper emotional control at work, toward a deeper integration of anger avoidance; quite apart from the incompatibility of anger with proper behavior, anger and true health do not mix. [106]

Thus a change in tone and in the explicitness of concern about work-place anger during the past two decades has not involved a redirection of the basic emotionology or the implementation devices that it sired. The sense of combating older, inappropriate standards yielded to assumptions of indisputable emotional goals. Training implied less unlearning. But there were signs that the basic interest in anger control extended, if anything, more deeply than ever before.

Emotions and Emotional Expression on the Job

The emotionology of work, developed in the decades around mid-century and implemented through a variety of new personnel arrangements, affected actual emotional behavior and expression on the job. Feelings of anger may have remained or even have been increased precisely by the new attempts to manipulate; this basic emotional experience remains beyond measurement. But behavior stemming from anger and, to an extent, an ability to identify one's own anger did change, and in the direction the new emotionology urged.

In this sense the emotionology of work had a more clear-cut effect than earlier family emotionology. Revealingly, there was far less articulation of anguish at goals unfulfilled at work than in the family. The new work emotionology itself responded, to be sure, to perceptions of growing anger on the job, expressed in strikes and labor turnover. But here the response was successful, though of course not perfectly or uniformly so. For emotionology at work, particularly directed at white-collar workers, could and did build on earlier family and child-rearing assumptions that had already conditioned the belief that anger was wrong. It built also on a long-standing assumption that work behavior should be rational, simply extending rationality to anger control. And, as already demonstrated, anger-control emotionology at work was enforced by a variety of intermediary devices unavailable in American family life that bridged the gap between emotionological advice and actual behavior and expression. Thus the development of new standards for anger on the job, which ended a century of separation between domestic and work-based emotionology, produced an important shift in the actual history of emotional expression as well. Indeed, the effect of anger-control efforts was sufficiently great to have the usual consequences of significant change in human affairs: to wit, major disadvantages and important advantages.

To be sure, some workers and factory observers, aware of the new personnel literature and its claims, professed to see no change in job emotions in the decades after World War II. Thus Harvey Swados, in his perceptive novel on factory life, specifically claims that foremen have not really changed from the days when they were called "drivers" or "pushers." His foremen often rage at worker errors, shout, curse, and gesture in anger, and his workers, for their part, often labor in "fury." Supervisors become hysterical when the line stops, impelled as they still are by production quotas, and they curse the "frivolity" of younger workers. In his only concession to a possible effect of the new personnel norms, Swados notes that the contemporary factory system encourages workers to get angry at themselves for errors rather than at what happened—but even this tension is not demonstrably novel.[107]

Without question, anger remains in the workplace and perhaps particularly in manufacturing. Various studies indicate continued variety among foremen in styles, with some angry supervisors still provoking more than their share of grievances. Many foremen during the decades when the new emotionology was being installed simply rebelled. One supervisor in the Hawthorne group, after listening to a gaggle of experts explaining how fear of fathers could lead workers to hate their bosses, as a prelude to a plea for sensitive understanding, observed: "Well, even if it is true, what of it? I've got to do something with such birds."[108] This attitude has not vanished. Up to 30 percent of all worker grievances, according to a 1976 study, derive from harsh, arbitrary supervision, and while it is conceivable that this figure is down from what a comparable survey would have revealed in the past, it is still noteworthy. Many foremen, and particularly those on the line as opposed to assignment supervisors, still react to worker problems by attempting to fire or to transfer, ignoring decades of personnel directives to take a more empathic interest.[109]

Articulate anger remains among workers as well. Personal characteristics are still cited as the main cause of dismissal (save for outright lack of work), surpassing problems with skills. Some airline stewardesses rebel against anger control, finding ways to vent irritation on passengers; others conceal, but find personal outlets to express, an emotion they know they feel. At various points in recent decades, workers have found new targets for anger with the advent of new racial groups. Workers still value union leaders as "fighting men," and union meetings can serve as important outlets for vigorous anger. In certain years, disciplinary actions relating to worker anger have risen, most typically with the advent of a new generation of employees. Thus in one Chicago steel plant disciplinary actions over swearing and arguing rose from 100 cases in 1965 to 3,400 in 1970. Finally, some workers believe that older suprvisory styles were less provoking than the bossiness and over-the-shoulder supervision of younger foremen, who leave less to worker initiative than was once the case.[110]

But a number of observers, including some of a radical persuasion who judge that overall worker satisfaction has declined in recent decades, believe that human relations efforts have restrained the use of temper in factories and shops. A few deplore this development, holding that workers are being emotionally manipulated so that they have lost some ability to react to real causes of distress.[111] Older workers sometimes note a change, though obviously memories are not uniform on this subject: "You want to know somethin', the younger workers don't even know how to take the crap we took."[112] While the new emotionology has not been pushed as hard as public relations releases suggested, it has won some enforcement. Thus into the 1960s employers continued to rate job knowledge and organizing ability above sensitivity to workers in traits they expected from foremen—though, interestingly, personal compliance to superiors was rated most highly of all. But "consideration" was on the list, and it would not have been a few decades before. Furthermore, personnel departments and complex labor relations rules hemmed foremen in, enforcing some control of angry behavior.[113] Traditional manifestations of angry clashes with supervisors, such as voluntary job changing and absenteeism, have definitely and steadily declined since the decades from 1920 to 1940, by over 300 percent by the 1970s. This may of course be the result of other factors, such as more settled working-class family lives and simply an older work force, but it certainly suggests that, if anger has not declined, its unrestrained expression probably has. Institutionally, older systems of personalized handling of grievances have given way to formal procedures in which calm treatment can be more uniformly stressed.[114]

Without question, some of the most sweeping claims of improvements in anger control have been hollow. The personnel movement exuded undue optimism, particularly in the late 1940s. Some employers would claim breakthroughs in human relations on the basis of the friendly tone and amiable title ("The Friendly Forum") of the company newspaper and the fact that few workers ventured an outburst in its carefully supervised pages. Surveys of worker morale, including their contentment with management styles, were often self-selected, as angry employees did not respond.[115] Furthermore, it must be recalled that work situations were by no means uniformly angry before the new emotionology; many company settings have been described in which paternalistic traditions and factors of personality prevented abrasiveness, even in the absence of a generalized set of emotional standards.[116] New language in describing work emotions may reflect awareness of the current emotionology more than some measurable use of it.

But the probability of some change in tone remains. Even where foremen still expressed anger readily, they might now be supervised in turn by department chiefs who, because their contacts with workers were less frequent and their exposure to the anger-control principles more ample, took a friendly (if more aloof) tone with workers.[117] Workers themselves definitely reflected the new ideas about job emotionality in their own expectations of supervisory behavior. This claim, too, must be phrased with care. Workers had always wanted humane treatment and respect, a foreman who would not bully. The point is that there is evidence that their traditional wishes now became more prominent, more expressable, and phrased more directly in terms of self-restraint on the part of supervisors. "Cool headed" thus became a phrase used in ratings of foremen, along with older demands for fair and tactful treatment. Women workers added increased concern for the quality of interpersonal relations on the job. Characteristically high ratings of foremen (72 percent of all workers claiming to get along well or pretty well with foremen in one study) were based more directly on the foremen's personality and temperament, including their knowledge of "psychology." While there is no way fully to prove that high ratings were above those that might have been derived in the past, the impression that personal tensions with supervisors have declined as a job problem is hard to escape. Thus less than 10 percent of all workers, in several studies, now list problems with their supervisors as a significant work concern.[118] Those who do rate the problem as serious encounter foremen who bawl them out readily—"he should use some psychology"[119]—in a style that was probably more current before anger-control efforts began. If this impression of reduced—not nonexistent—anger in worker-supervisor relations is correct, it reflects some increase in attempts at self-restraint by both parties.

The probability of real change—not necessarily in levels of anger but in willingness and ability to express it—derives thus both from some measurable behaviors and from comments by workers and supervisors themselves about their own emotional effort at work. Behavioral evidence, including declining rates of worker-foremen clashes and job changing, is highly suggestive, though flawed to the extent that it derives from several factors, of which new emotional styles are only one. It is noteworthy, nevertheless, that U.S. strike rates have declined rapidly on a per capita basis since the 1950s, despite, initially, a growing demand for labor. Sheer numbers of strikes rose each decade from the late nineteenth century to the early 1950s; they then declined until a new crest between 1965 and 1974, after which they fell again rather rapidly. Total number of strikers reached peaks during and after World War I and after World War II. Here the late 1960s surge in strikes was only modestly mirrored in the number of strikers, which rose just to early 1950s levels despite a significant increase in the labor force. Equally revealing, insofar as government statistical categories allow, are strike rates over issues particularly likely to arouse or express intense anger. Bitter strikes over union organization problems have never matched late 1930s and early 1940s levels. Conflict over shop conditions did rise in the early 1960s and again from 1969 to 1977, and while this reflected new safety standards, it could generate or express anger. But strikes specifically over the most personal aspects of employment—supervision, discipline, and grievances—have stagnated or declined in recent decades (and, again, have fallen markedly on a per capita basis). The decline of strikes over grievances, though briefly interrupted between 1966 and 1969, has been particularly noteworthy, and strikes over discipline, though somewhat more prominent, have followed a similar trend. Strikes remain; even seemingly banal wage strikes can express anger; and stagnation in strikes certainly results from a host of factors besides mutual anger control. Yet the rapidly declining strike rate, and its correlation with the increased numbers of white-collar and female workers, who have been most heavily affected by anger-control efforts, remains suggestive and, in combination with personal statements, highly persuasive. Open anger on the job has declined.[120]

Certainly there is evidence that many groups have partially accepted and perhaps internalized the new norms of emotional control at work. Employers as well as personnel interviewers cite traits such as "would maintain self-control when provoked" as important for all categories of employees, though particularly for managerial, sales, and white-collar groups.[121] Even more interesting is the fact that supervisory personnel themselves rate self-control high and aggression and initiative low in the traits they value and believe are valued by their employers.[122] Of course there is some delusion in this. Control of anger is one of the traits in which the largest gap exists, among managers of all levels, between self-appraisals and the ratings of others. Anger-control goals thus affect professed intent more than actual behavior. The unresolved tension, even in the theories about job anger, between emotional desiderata for top managers and those for middle managers inevitably leaves its mark. Thus high-level managers who emphasize social skills do best in polls of workers, but more assertive and temperamental managers win the plaudits of owners. As one result, executives frequently vacillate in style, opting for temper control as a norm but yielding to outbursts when the going gets rough.[123]

Still, there are a number of signs that there has been some managerial change. Tensions about work style had spread to union leadership ranks by the 1960s, with a gap opening between top leadership, still bent on an aggressive style, and middle-level managers, who put a greater premium on tact. In business, even aggressive managers began to back off from a confrontational style with subordinates, hoping to avoid direct comment on subordinate performance because of a desire to escape emotionally charged sessions. Revealingly, some subordinates began to complain, by the 1960s and 1970s, that their employers seemed too tolerant, so worried about doing psychological damage to others and maintaining a friendly reputation that they failed to push through clear policy directives; this was a problem cited particularly on the part of graduates of T group experiences. Thus a survey of California state agency employees suggested that employers had become so reluctant to criticize that they no longer were able to guide subordinates to improved performance.[124]

Studs Terkel's celebrated interviews demonstrate the new concern, among various worker grades, with controlling anger. Through the early twentieth century, work interviews and worker autobiographies reflect little explicit concern about anger. The one exception, and it is significant, is a frequent tendency to bemoan the need to bring job-caused irritation home because it cannot be safely expressed at its source, given the need for docility and obedience. This theme, suggesting considerable if implicit emotional control, recurs in recent interview data such as Terkel's. But now there is more. Service workers cite the special requirements of emotional control that their jobs impose. A phone operator discusses the need for "a nice sounding voice. You can't be angry. . . . You always have to be pleasant—no matter how bad you feel." A salesman admits frequent anger, indeed a desire to hit the customers, but also his awareness of the need to conceal. A gas-station operator cannot help losing his temper once in a while (he would not be a "red-blooded American" if he did not), but he has learned that customers want a pleasant demeanor, so usually he manages to keep cool. A bank teller, also aggravated by the customers, has to bottle up: "You can't say anything back. The customer is always right." Perhaps most revealing are the foremen who claim responsibility not only for temper control but for creating an atmosphere of positive cheer on the job.[125] While interviewed workers may note the impersonality of upper management or the inflation-induced tensions of customers as new emotional problems—again, actual anger is not necessarily on the wane—their uniform and explicit awareness of control needs vividly illustrates the effect of the new emotionology in conditioning expression.

Certainly, signs of emotional constraint, revolving around the repression of anger, have won increasing comment, particularly among white-collar and middle-management personnel. C. Wright Mills described some of these workers, forced into emotional conformity, as self-alienated. A bureaucrat described his own emotional dilemma when he noted how "frazzled" he felt going home after a day of keeping peace with people "at all levels."[126] The anger-control efforts thus effected some real change in behavior, expression, and emotional self-perception. They increased a desire for self-restraint among many categories of workers and managers. They heightened an expectation of restraint when dealing with others on the job from superiors and subordinates alike. The norms of the personnel movement were not entirely met, and though more formal than before, the norms themselves—as in hopes for a friendly foreman—were not entirely new. But there was a change, a change that can be interpreted variously as creating a more humane job atmosphere or as putting new and heavy pressures of emotional conformity on many kinds of workers.

The change, finally, was rather quick. Whereas the campaign to control parental anger in child rearing took many decades even to reach partial fruition, with the result that traditional lack of restraint could still be a theme over a century after the effort began, the roughest edges at work seemed under some control within a few decades, even if this control was less complete than some optimists liked to believe.[127] This is why attention could veer from the strictest anger control after the mid-1950s and why traditional targets, like the driving foreman, disappeared from the hortatory literature. The behavioral conversion, involving greater restraint of temper at least on the surface, owed its rapidity to two factors. It built on the conversion previously introduced into family life and socialization. People were being asked to handle anger at work as many of them had been taught, long since, to handle it at home. But rapidity was also due to the power of corporate-backed personnel leaders, who threw immense resources into selection and training and sponsored extensive dissemination of the new standards. As a result, more than ever before, anger could no longer legitimately be indulged, as weapon, reaction, or simple release of tension, on the job.

Conclusion

The modern history of anger at work demonstrates that, not surprisingly, organizational rather than technological change is the key to establishing emotional context—though organizational change was itself shaped by culturally induced perceptions of human relations. Within this framework, and therefore particularly in the twentieth century, the evolution of attitudes toward anger picks up many of the major themes in the larger evaluation of work history. Work hierarchies, their growing complexity with the rise of corporate forms, and white- and blue-collar divisions are mirrored clearly. Problems of assessing work satisfaction recur in the attempt to determine the effect of anger-control efforts.

Several critics have already seized on elements of the new personnel movements of the twentieth century to blast the growing psychological manipulations of the labor force. Those who attend primarily to the blue-collar working class frequently see the efforts of Elton Mayo and his successors as a crass attempt to elicit labor's cooperation with the speed-up programs earlier imposed by the engineers.[128] So in part they were, though we have seen that they also stemmed from autonomous emotional standards. It would not be implausible to use the history of anger-control efforts as simply another chapter in the growing imposition of capitalist power over hapless workers. The first century of industrialization saw the installation of physical conditions new to the mass of workers, along with the raw assertion of industrialists' domination; the second century, beginning in the 1920s, sees the more subtle effort to co-opt workers' emotions. This picture would be deepened by inclusion of the white-collar layer, where recent attempts to set emotional standards unquestionably embellish the earlier attempt to set this group apart from blue-collar workers and to instill a "false consciousness" of membership in the middle class. The attempt to control anger at work also fleshes out the often-evoked concept of depersonalization on the job; depersonalization means, among other things, that deep emotions such as anger need not apply. The goal becomes the reduction of emotionality, and a surface friendliness masks any intense involvement.

At an extreme, the efforts to dilute anger may be seen as a final ignominy of capitalist labor. Having suffered massive deterioration in work satisfaction, workers are progressively denied the ability to percieve or express their own plight. Anger control on the job certainly contrasts with new potential sources for the emotion itself, given growing management impersonality, the new strains of technological displacement and inflation, white-collar mobility frustrations, and the growing isolation of many unskilled workers. Felt anger may well have risen even as its outlets on the job and indeed the standards that would allow its explicit perception have diminished. New anger control itself can cause frustration, as was the case earlier in marital relations. Some observers have also seen the emotional controls at work spilling over into other aspects of life. Thus the emotional shallowness instilled on the job, for white-collar employees, merges with the plastic friendliness of the suburbs, equally devoid of real or intense feeling. Certainly the attempt to control emotions among blue-collar workers might bear some relationship to the privatization trends widely noted since World War II: the tendency of blue-collar workers to abandon more traditional contacts among workmates in favor of a solitary retreat to the home and family as soon as the workday ends. Other factors are involved, of course, including the compelling lure of home-based television. But the notion of a work-based emotional control impinging on other social contacts and helping to explain patterns that do differentiate contemporary workers from their nineteenth-century counterparts has real merit. [129]

Yet it would be inaccurate to claim that the history of anger definitely confirms a thesis of deteriorating work conditions. In the first place, anger control bore incompletely on blue-collar workers, embracing as it did a real ambiguity about the possibility of internalizing emotional restraint. Arguments about subtle "self-alienation" ring much truer for the white-collar category. Even here, however, controls did not necessarily become complete. And for blue- and white-collar workers alike, the emotional control movement brought gains along with potential losses. Even radical observers have noted the improvements in workplace atmosphere that the new directives in labor management produced. [130] Just as a case can be made for anger control as a new stage in the manipulation of modern workers, so can one be made for a growing democratization of management styles in the workplace. To be sure, such democratization is incomplete; and insofar as surface friendliness masks an ever-greater separation between the real sources of power and the ordinary worker, it rather fits a deterioration thesis. But in the actual, daily contacts between workers and their middle-management supervisors—and it is these contacts that produce much of the quality of working life, even though they do not express the ultimate power relationships—a greater equality of tone does now prevail. Much of the history of work before the twentieth century involved the possible use of anger, depending on personality factors, in a work hierarchy, with those on top lashing out at those below. This personal meanness now became more difficult. It does not take a blind apologist for modern capitalism to see some gains in this change.

Mugwumpery of this sort—an effort to balance gains and losses—admittedly lacks panache. Labor history is more commonly punctuated by ringing denunciations of change or, less commonly, equally strident defenses. Examination of anger at work suggests change, though not necessarily complete for all workers, but it also produces some problems in slotting that change into simple categories of good or bad.

A similar hesitancy must mark any effort to link the recent efforts at anger control to the history of twentieth-century labor protest. Attempts to control anger were definitely designed to limit protest. They did not entirely succeed. Movements of worker anger have surfaced repeatedly since the anger-control current began to affect labor relations; the outbursts of young workers in the late 1960s are an obvious case in point. Furthermore, emotionality is not the only ingredient in labor protest, and it probably must rank well behind structural features (the organizing potential on both sides) and the evolution of central objective issues such as real wages or technological change. As noted earlier, a leading student of labor protest has even argued that anger plays no role whatsoever in the incidence or conduct of protest.[131]

Yet an element of anger in the early decades of the modern labor movement seems undeniable. It surfaced most noticeably in the numerous small strikes that burst out against individuals—foremen or other workers—who were perceived as behaving improperly (including foremen who behaved too angrily). But similar motives often informed other strikes, which moved on to larger issues when the personal offense proved inadequate to mobilize large numbers of workers.[132] Thus without pretending that emotional change can describe the whole history of protest, it is essential to note the relationship between changing emotionology and the signs of changing behavior and expression, on the one hand, and the historic decline of labor protest since the 1950s, on the other. Even the waning of the union movement, though due in part to changing occupational structure and the geographic migration of jobs, may owe something to changing emotions, as the characteristic union style of angry rhetorical outburst becomes increasingly dated. Unusually low levels of unionization and protest by American white-collar workers since World War II, compared to patterns in other advanced industrial countries,[133] certainly suggest the effectiveness of the efforts to promote a friendly, anger-restrained work style in this large and growing group in the United States.

This linkage between anger control and larger themes in recent labor history suggests the importance of changes in the emotional context at work. The linkage also evokes the now-familiar problem of interpretation. Is the decline in work-based protest the sign of waning felt anger, a genuine increase in the pleasantness of human relations on the job, or does it suggest heightened manipulation, through which management persuades many workers to conceal their own legitimate emotional reactions?

Whatever the evaluation, and it is decidedly complex, it is clear that the anger-control movement at work constituted a significant new phase not only in job life but in American emotional life more generally. Potentially, at least, the movement gave promise of reconciling emotional standards—at least concerning anger—between private and public life. This indeed, as we have seen, was among the first spurs that directed the attention of industrial psychologists to emotional issues in the workplace. Managers were being urged to become increasingly like parents, in avoiding situations that might needlessly provoke anger and in seeking to divert anger once it was aroused. To be sure, some work authorities continued to vaunt an emotionless rationality that would seem out of place in family life. But most authorities did recognize that work, like the family, had an inevitable emotional component that should be channeled toward institutional loyalty and good performance and away from disruptive behavior. Many a parent, both before and after the anger-control movement began in the workplace, could have agreed with the personnel experts who argued that their charges—children or employees—should be so managed that resentments, if not prevented, would be dissipated "before they add up and trouble results."[134]

But the new approach to anger at work was not simply the extension of Victorian family values to the job. It also picked up more recent currents that would soon spill over to the family itself. Anger control at work thus stemmed in part from the rise of psychology and related theories of emotionality, which by the 1920s had only begun to touch child rearing and family advice. It expressed a current of at least surface democratization that would also extend to family relationships toward the middle of the twentieth century. Above all, the new emotional goals at work were the first results of a felt need to produce a new personality suitable for the complex human interactions of the corporate world and, subsequently, a service economy. This, too, would soon spill over into family and, particularly, child-rearing styles. The fact that new anger goals and strategies first took shape in the work world, rather than the familial orbit, suggests a primacy in advanced industrial society for the goals of dominant economic organizations, as filtered through the litmus of middle-class distaste for anger.

Suggesting primacy is admittedly not the same as proving it. Firm proof of causation is rarely possible for large historical changes, and in this case several factors, including the rise of psychology and its intellectual bent, were involved. But the basic process entailed a belated transmission of middle-class personal values—the distaste for anger—to the definition of suitable organizational norms once the managerial direction of the economy was well and truly established. This definition of organizational need, in turn, then supported not only the alteration of emotional norms in the workplace but also other attempts to set stricter emotional standards as well. In arguing that shifts in economic organization bolstered the ongoing anger-control effort, we do not intend to maintain that these shifts were entirely economically rational—again, this is economic causation not in the starkest sense but as shaped by the cultural context. Special factors such as the unusual ethnic diversity of the American labor force may also have prompted an emphasis on harmony as a managerial goal. In fact, elaborate attention to, and expenditure on, emotional context may have been a diversion from optimal use of funds and from the personality emphases most conducive to organizational drive. American productivity problems may owe something to the fact that too many managers took the injunctions against productive, competitive zeal too literally. This is an issue to which we will return in the concluding chapter. For now it is important to recall that the organizational goals that caused the anger-control movement were themselves caused in part by earlier middle-class family emotionology; they did not necessarily spring inevitably from complex bureaucracies, although the record of other bureaucratic societies, like China, in trying to limit impulse suggests that some strong probabilities may be involved. In any event, in explaining why the anger-control movement had such a substantial effect, culturally conditioned organizational goals loom largest among several factors.

This conclusion, also, is hardly surprising. But it deserves emphasis for two reasons. First, it logically guides a search for the causes of earlier emotional changes, particularly those that took shape in the eighteenth century. Here factors of economic organization are much less obvious, and indeed causation may simply be different from that which has emerged in the twentieth century. But the possibility of a need for emotional change as a basis for the new economic interactions of a market economy, and as underlying the more directly relevant ideological factors expressed in new religious and Enlightenment ideas, at least merits further exploration.

The second reason to note the organizational substructure for changes in emotional context is to provide a more credible anchor for ideas about changes in the American personality in recent decades. The examination of criteria for anger and their probable effect on actual emotional experience does not demonstrate the kind of sweeping personality change asserted by scholars such as David Riesman and Christopher Lasch, though it may be partially compatible with some of their conclusions. Much previous analysis has been largely descriptive, seeking sophisticated categories by which to generalize about the forms of change. Causation has been relegated to somewhat vague invocations of change in family authority, undergirded in Lasch's case by contestable psychoanalytic theory, or to a critique of meddling experts whose motivations and effect are not fully explained. Evidence that at least one major emotional change, in the valuation of anger, stems from a concomitant change in organizational and occupational structure seems to be a firmer basis for analysis. It provides no more hope, to be sure, that recent changes can be reversed. But it may make more sense of these changes, as being compatible with and perhaps essential to a transformation of economic activity.

It is of course important to recall that changes in the emotional standards of work, though uniformly pointed toward greater anger control, displayed continued complexity, which must modify invocation of work as the source of a single dominant modern personality. Work criteria clearly reflected class differentiation, with the most extreme standards of control applying mainly to the growing white-collar sector. Distinctions between blue- and white-collar workers echoed traditional divisions. Distinctions between top and middle management were potentially more significant. For the tolerance still displayed for anger or related drives at the top constituted an important loophole in anger control, and this loophole in turn confirmed that American values still had not converted to an all-out effort to constrain anger even in theory. Distinctions in anger control made obvious sense in terms of the new economic hierarchy. Two kinds of managers were being created, with distinct emotional styles: one trained to command, presumably with some finesse but without the strictest constraints on anger; one trained to get along smoothly with peers and superiors and to manipulate subordinates through impersonal friendliness. But these distinctions, along with remembered traditions of previous decades of greater emotional autonomy for middle-level supervisors, inevitably created some tensions. A young executive could be pardoned for some uncertainty about how fully the anger criteria had to be internalized, for if he reached the top, the rules might change somewhat. This diversity reinforces the contention that contemporary American society seeks new controls over anger somewhat selectively rather than across the board, with potential confusion resulting for those who accept the new constraints while recognizing that others—sometimes, more successful others—do not.[135] Ambivalence in work standards may of course prove transitional, and even by the 1950s a host of personnel experts were urging anger control on top executives. But the ambivalence may also prove more durably useful to a modern economic hierarchy, despite or even because of the confusions in emotional style that result.

The new efforts at anger control at work raised obvious issues for family life and for other potential outlets for the anger that survived the genteel assault of the modern experts. New work standards posed a challenge for child-rearing authorities because they obviously moved away—save for those destined for the summits of the executive hierarchy—from the dominant model of channeling. In fact, as we will see, child-rearing authorities quickly moved to integrate these new and more rigorous goals and to imitate some of the strategies for defusing anger first suggested in the workplace. But family life in general might not be so readily assimilated, for if work increasingly denied anger, even for those in middle-management positions, might the family not become, more than before, a receptacle for irritations felt but not expressed on the job? The new dominance of the workplace in emotional standard setting could easily restate older questions about work/family relationships, with work now under orders to become the tranquil sea in human life. To be sure, if children could be newly trained to fit an emotionally disciplined workplace, as was suggested even in the mid-1950s in the corporate-bureaucratic families of Detroit,[136] older disparities might erode, as the principles of family and work merged after two centuries of complex separation. This improvement in integration might in the long run prove to be extremely important, whether its results are judged a regrettable enhancement of human manipulability or a welcome increase in civilized restraint over unworthy emotions.

In the short run, at least, the integration is hardly so smooth. Even white-collar personnel are not yet so thoroughly socialized against anger as not to chafe against some of the new constraints at work. Possibly, of course, they never can be; and possibly it is desirable that they not be. During the past few decades, the reduction of outlets for anger at work—the clear result not only of new theoretical standards but also of new institutions and a new set of experts in the workplace—has produced noticeable needs for surrogate targets, at least for some workers; or they have produced noticeable tensions. The failure of strike activity to keep pace with labor force growth has only exacerbated these problems.

Thus many workers, perhaps particularly in the blue-collar ranks, continue to echo the old theme of a need of domestic outlets for anger that cannot be expressed at work. One worker, frequently unemployed and without targets on the job for the anger he feels, fights often with his wife and children: "The slightest little thing would set me off."[137] Middle-management executives, more circumspect, also speak of the tensions they would bring home after day-long efforts to be pleasant to all comers on the job. Even a few personnel experts, at least into the early 1940s, admitted the need for "healthy" outlets for aggression off the job in order to face the emotional rigors of work itself.[138] The idea of some distinction between emotional styles at home and at work, though much changed since its original formulation in the nineteenth century, survived, and with it some opening for release of anger disapproved in the workplace itself. New constraints certainly created new possibilities for the use of marital outlets, even apart from the convolutions of theories about anger. Of course many people found emotional restraint at work congenial; many had been bothered by the more rough-and-tumble atmosphere of earlier decades, including the fiery tone of many union meetings. But the fact remained that one potential outlet for anger was being closed, or at least reduced, and the effect on other facets of life might be considerable.

And a theme of sheer emotional confusion arose as well, especially in white-collar ranks, where the management of anger was farthest reaching. C. Wright Mills's concept of self-alienation, long more dramatically asserted than explored, is now receiving serious attention, as a category of "emotional workers" can be identified in a variety of service industries, including the airlines and some branches of social work.[139] The argument is that "managed friendliness" goes beyond the strains imposed by more traditional injunctions of obedience and docility by positing stricter and more artificial emotional controls affecting a larger percentage of workers on a lifetime basis and that the necessity of masking emotion and producing a false front can take a serious emotional toll. According to one estimate, approximately a third of all American men and half of all employed women hold jobs that demand this sort of emotional labor, guided by rules that govern how they ought to feel.

Cases of stress and new needs for outlets for anger in a society that decreasingly tolerates even mild expressions of annoyance in major facets of life add up to significant emotional change and, possibly, to new kinds of personal and social problems as well. With new emotional criteria for work as a fulcrum, American society has been engaged in a significant effort to change the rules of emotionality—an effort not always explicit and often masked by injunctions of emotional permissiveness designed in fact to increase controls. The effort at anger control may be necessary; its roots in new organizational complexity certainly suggest a serious rationale and not the idle whimsy of a random crop of psychological experts. The effects of the effort, in altering the work experience and in touching other social institutions, even other expressions of emotionality, may be as far-reaching as the organizational changes that provoked it.

6 The Managerial Style
Raising Cool Kids

The new approach toward anger at work was caused in part by an extension of the nineteenth century emotionology of the family; it now, in turn, caused new development in family styles from the 1940s on. Both in child rearing and in marital relations, the emotionology at work encouraged a new tactical style, in which anger, rather than being denied, would be quickly dissipated, even trivialized. But while the anger standards sought in work were rather directly translated into child rearing, creating a major shift away from the idea of channeling, the same work standards had more complex implications for marriage. For if work now explicitly compelled anger control, might marriage have to serve as release? The abandonment of the nineteenth-century emotional dichotomy between home and work raised different questions for marital relations than for child rearing, despite some shared tactics, and these questions require distinct explorations.

The idea of rigid anger control at work had striking echoes in child-rearing emotionology, starting in the 1940s, and in at least aspects of parental behavior by the following decades. At the emotionological level, the new approach to anger was a major part of a shift in personality goals, toward a style more suitable for corporate and service-sector behavior. The earlier emotionology, complex but seemingly successful, simply did not fit the growing emphasis on an anger-free workplace. The effort to channel anger had been predicated on the idea that a rigorous control of the emotion in the family context could conjoin with a use of anger, as goad rather than direct expression, in work and public life. The effort to dissipate anger at work, however, made this channeling concept increasingly irrelevant, even risky. Consistency suggested a return to a more thoroughgoing attack on anger in the socialization of children.

There was no need, of course, for a complete shifting of gears. Parents did not have to be taught, at least in theory, to control their own anger in dealing with children, as employers and supervisors were learning now at work; for advice had never swerved, since the eighteenth century, from insistence on parental self-control. But the channeling addendum did have to be dropped if the change suggested in the emotionology of work was to carry over into child-rearing standards.

This is precisely what happened, beginning around 1940 and carrying forward to our own day. Having passed from an idealization of childish innocence, in which anger had no place, to a more tough-minded attempt to channel anger, modern American child rearing entered its third phase: an attempt to manage anger out of effective existence.

This third phase was not a return to Victorian notions, save that the basic goals, of anger removal, were the same. The contemporary approach did not assume childish innocence. Anger was there, indeed was natural, and had to be dealt with. A host of tactical suggestions accompanied this new phase, in contrast to the blissful neglect of practical suggestions in early Victorian literature. The point was that anger could be defanged, as children were carefully taught that the emotion led neither to action nor to practical result. In essence, the long-standing familial concern with anger, beyond the idealistic aspirations of the early Victorians, now changed the terms of the American ambivalence about anger. Ambivalence remained, in the difficulty and unevenness of translating the new advice into practice and in a real problem in extending the new approach to other agents of socialization, particularly in the schools. But this was different from the internal ambivalence of the turn-of-the-century style. And the difference lends further credence to the idea of a significant change in American character, or at least in the official goals for American character, from the mid-twentieth century on.

Emotionology: The Anger Management Approach

The big change in child rearing that started around 1940 conventionally comes under the heading of a new permissiveness. In dealing with a new emotionology of anger in child rearing, we are arguing for something rather more than, and different from, the familiar evocation of a permissive generation. Rather more, in that the new goals of anger control easily outlived the permissive style and entered into the reaction to permissiveness that began in the late 1950s. Again, we describe a change in anger strategies that is more durable than the customary generational fads in modern child rearing. This change even at the outset was different from permissiveness in other respects, in that the concern for emotional damage resulting from repression did not lead to pleas for an untrammeling of anger. Rather, permissiveness encouraged in this case a new strategy, which only barely masked what was in fact a more rigorous goal—to teach children the valuelessness and nastiness of anger.

During the Victorian period, women had implicitly been asked to see themselves as intensely emotional—part of their charm, part of their weakness—while carefully not acknowledging anger in their emotional repertoire. Now this combination was written larger, as a period proud of its encouragement of emotional freedom quietly sought to bury anger.

Without question, of course, the Victorian period had sought to impose new controls on anger as part of the more general attempt to discipline or repress impulse. For sexuality, it remains largely correct to see Victorianism as a time of repression in socialization, including more detailed tactical suggestions than concern about anger inspired; followed by several decades of gradual but incomplete easing, as in parental anxieties about childhood masturbation; followed by a much more concerted attack on repressive shibboleths from the 1940s on. For anger, the pattern was different. Victorian interest in repression was in some ways lightened by the channeling approach. One sign of this easing—which came more readily than the easing of sexual restraints—was the relatively low level of parental, particularly paternal, concern about anger as a problem among their own children, in the early decades of this century. But in contrast to changing attitudes toward sexuality, this period was not followed by further liberation with the rise of permissiveness, for in fact child-rearing experts and many parents began to insist on greater controls. This is why the new interest in subtle repression easily survived the replacement of permissiveness with greater strictness from the later 1950s on. Like the frank ambivalence about anger that it replaced, then, the contemporary approach shows signs of significant durability.[1]

Two points must be stressed before detailing the contemporary change. First, elements of the earlier tension continued to be expressed in some child-rearing manuals after the 1940s. Dr. Spock's first edition (in the mid-1940s) showed little contact with the shift that other, less popular experts were spelling out. Even later, some manuals continued to praise anger when channeled into competition or righteous indignation; this was particularly true in advice directed toward subgroups such as women or blacks, though even here the idea of channeling anger against injustice was hedged with far more warnings against anger itself than had been characteristic around 1900.[2] Second, some "mental hygienists" in the 1940s did write as if the problem were removal of restraints on anger—a literal permissiveness in this area too—rather than the imposition of new controls. Translating elements of Freudianism, they worried much more about withdrawal and resentfulness than about aggression, which some ranked well down the list of behavior problems. These hygienists differed notably from teachers and parents in this ranking. Some also read Freudianism as saying that anger was inevitable and therefore had to be taken out somehwere; this in turn, among optimists, could lead to a restatement of the older view, that anger could be channeled into sports, art, or competition.[3] Here anger among young children was viewed as natural, no matter for concern: "Comfort yourself by remembering that all this behavior is a normal part of the child's growing up and learning to adjust to the requirements of living in a world with other people."[4]

While sharing some features with the manuals produced by advocates of tolerant permissiveness, most manuals from the 1940s on shifted gears in two important respects. First, the experts began to devote more space to anger and its management. This followed logically from the general increase in attention to emotional well-being as a basic goal in child rearing. Second, the experts began to seek tactics that would minimize anger at virtually all stages of life. Permissiveness in this area was tactical, only barely masking the new goal of anger avoidance. It differed from the more straightforward shifts in sexuality, where permissive strategies were genuinely designed to produce more tolerant adult behavior. To revert to Lloyd Warner's set of basic child-rearing tensions, child-rearing experts began, though perhaps more slowly and with more qualification than the experts themselves imagined, to reduce traditional middle-class ambivalence about sexuality, with important behavioral results by the 1950s and 1960s, as adolescent sexual behavior measurably altered. Here literal Victorianism steadily declined. But the experts did not undertake a similar simplification in the area of anger or, if a simplification, at least not in the direction of greater ultimate expressiveness.

It is true, that, even aside from the literally permissive school, the new approach had some confusing elements. Explicit moralism, as in urging temper control, largely disappeared. The new approach recognized that some anger was unavoidable; it was concerned to avoid overt repression or making children feel bad about emotions they experienced. Hence children's television programming might refer to getting angry without any judgment at all, as in Mr. Rogers's bland "this makes you feel angry, doesn't it?" "Sesame Street" issued a catchy song about being "mad . . . very, very angry," describing anger at hurting a knee or at friends' scorn or at parental discipline, complete with physical symptoms of hair standing on end and a desire to scream—and there is no resolution. Being angry is simply something children should know about and have words for. But even in these nonjudgmental, "factual" approaches, the old channeling idea is missing. Some anger may be inevitable, but it is not good, cannot be turned to good. Most of the presentations aimed at children bore some implication that being angry was not very pleasant—an unfortunate necessity at best. The Mr. Rogers approach conveyed a strong sense that anger was a disagreeable feeling that did occur but that should be purged as quickly as possible and without result—a problem to be handled by the child himself until it went away because attempts to express anger against those who provoked it would clearly be inappropriate. The more tough-minded "Sesame Street" largely followed suit, certainly in urging that anger should be dissipated without action against its cause. This approach contrasted with similar attempts to teach about emotions such as fear, where recognition of inevitability was conjoined with considerable sympathy.[5]

For parents, the same nonrepressive style might admit that anger could occur without wounding the family. Here, too, an initial impression might hold that older prohibitions were easing up. Siblings, for example, inevitably came into conflict; there was no way to urge complete emotional control here. But while control was downplayed, avoidance and cajolery loomed large.[6] Keep the siblings apart. Bribe them a bit to minimize tension; hence the practice of giving older siblings presents on a younger one's birthday. The growing attention accorded to sibling relations from mid-century on, though it owed something to the belated popularization of Freud and something to the increased birthrate coupled with close child spacing, revealed a parental sense of discomfort even when the inevitability of some anger was admitted. A sophisticated tolerance of childish anger is not, then, the main point: it barely masked the new level of concern and a search for new managerial tactics along with the disappearance of the idea of channeling.

Increased concern about anger showed in the postwar editions of *Infant Care*, where for the first time tantrums and the anger expressed in sibling rivalry received attention, with recommendations of calm, distraction, and understanding affection as preventatives or antidotes. Various manuals also increased the stress on beginning the control of anger early in infancy, warning against a parental tendency to approve early displays of tempers that might demonstrate "spirit" in a child.[7] Here is clear reaction against the channeling ideas of the previous period: anger is too dangerous to confuse with "spirit." And here in fact is the suggestion of an ambitious enterprise in the standards of child rearing more generally. Even many anger-repressive cultures, such as the Utku Eskimo, readily accept anger in infants up to two years of age as simply unavoidable. The new American advice, building on the growing concern about the formative aspects of infancy that had started in the 1920s, tended to cut into this normal tolerance; infant anger became not only annoying (even the Utku grant this in allowing expressions of parental anger against babies) but also worrisome.

The tactical shift that accompanied increased concern involved allowing children to express anger that was inevitable anyway, even in a loving, permissive environment, but only in order to prevent a festering that would lead to deeper anger later in life. Advocates of loving permissiveness hoped, of course, that greater affection and the removal of artificial restrictions and discipline would reduce the need for anger. One authority even explicitly argued that, with the new enlightenment, the number of childish tantrums had gone down (unfortunately providing no evidence to document this achievement). And the insistence that parents avoid role-model displays of anger for their part was maintained with most of the traditional force. Still, admittedly, children would sometimes be angry. The enlightened parent would not attempt to punish or even disapprove of this anger, for openness was the new key. But the goal was *not* acceptance of anger as a permanent ingredient of personality or even channeling anger to acceptable usage; it was rather the maximum possible avoidance in later life. A loving, understanding, open response to childish anger was designed to "prevent emotional sores from bursting." Children who learned to drain anger at home would not, in later life, need to blow up at school or in the office. "The more [the child] releases the anger, the less of it will remain, *provided* it has been handled in an acceptant way, that doesn't make new anger take the place of what has drained off." Parents should in fact cheat a bit, even in their tolerance. They should talk through anger, to divert it from physical expression; and they should encourage its expression through drawing or acting out. Emotional openness, in the matter of anger, was equated with cautious, sometimes indirect manifestation.[8]

This new approach recalled the goals of anger control that had marked child-rearing advice in the mid-nineteenth century, before the shift to the concept of channeling. In part the approach was a return to this earlier concern for restraining anger, which had been partially diverted by changes in culture and economy in the later nineteenth century. But the new style was much more explicit in its attention to anger than nineteenth-century authorities had been; anger demanded more care and loomed larger as a priority than it had before. Furthermore, the image of children had changed. Innocence had vanished. Anger was an inherent drive, with a fearsome propensity to build up if improperly treated. From this new view, plus the recognition that proper adult behavior in work and family should not include anger, came the final divergence from the Victorian approach, the development of managerial tactics. Proper role models were not enough. Outright punishment was wrong, not because it taught bad examples of anger, but because it was futile; indeed, it was counterproductive, for it fueled inner rages that would burst out later, possibly in adult life. The new strategy involved accepting some limited anger among children much as one would drain a boil, to prevent worse trouble later. The Victorian and even late nineteenth-century emphasis on character building had more directly sought to prevent angry behavior in children, on the assumption that this would form appropriate qualities for later life. There were important emotional goals here, but concern for proper behavioral habits prevailed, so much so that a child who did not act angry was taken at face value. The movement that opened in the 1940s had quite different views of character formation, views that involved less attention to the inculcation of proper habits in children and were more tolerant of mild outbursts as a means of achieving the overriding goal, which was making sure that child rearing did not produce an angry person. Some childish anger could be permitted as a means of preventing angry adulthood, now that the sanctions for angry behavior in normal adult life were so severe. Anger had come to be viewed as a potentially volcanic force that could build to explosive proportions if not manipulated early on.

Here, then, was a new-model parent. Their own past repression was responsible for the upset parents felt at children's expressions of anger; parents should loosen up. They should also apologize carefully when they did show anger to children. But the goal was manipulative: "Feelings *can* be changed, with changed behavior intelligently following." Anger should be replaced with other feelings "more socially useful and personally comfortable." Interestingly, humor was recommended increasingly as a good way to dissolve anger even in the very young. Still more commonly parents were urged to assure their angry children that they knew how they felt, ostensibly to avoid repression but in fact to teach that anger should never be deep: after all, if the most common target of childish anger—the parents—constantly assured of their sympathy, it is clear that the real message was that anger should never lead to conflict.[9]

For the new approach quite explicitly moved away from the acceptance of legitimate anger that was characteristic of the previous model. Angry people did not behave well, period. They were expressing repressions dating from early childhood, so that they were "only dimly aware of this underlying passion." But the fact remained that, with anger, "they are possessed of a devil"—tyrants in office and in the home.[10] Advocates of permissiveness were trying to break a cycle in which repressed childhood anger led to angry parental behavior and to serious anger in children in the next generation. Anger was a sign of trouble, not a healthy emotion. Even childish temper tantrums signaled an unhealthy relationship between parents and children, though of course they should not be directly repressed. Significantly, experts' tolerance of fighting among children declined; fights should be stopped if they could not be prevented. Comments on the importance of righteous indignation, on anger as preparation for competition or reform, disappeared by the later 1940s, except in the rare holdovers from the earlier approach. Specific warnings addressed earlier channeling strategies. Experts condemned such tactics as encouraging children to vent anger on inanimate objects—"hit that nasty old floor, Johnny," now became a reprehensible diversion. For since all anger was bad, even childish displacement of the emotion could produce poor habits in adulthood. It was exactly this sanctioned displacement, one manual urged, that taught adults how to bring suppressed rage home from the office and vent it on hapless family members. Even the recommendation of humor as a means to curb childish wrath declined by the 1950s; temper was serious business. At most, experts in the permissive school might express some sympathy for occasionally angry children, who were expressing their helplessness. But the idea of channeling anger, much less building it as a weapon against injustice or a spur to achievement, almost completely vanished.

New attention to emotions led to some recognition that parents might sometimes be angry and an admission that children might be able to tolerate infrequent, mild outbursts when the basic environment was affectionate. Parental efforts at self-repression might after all lead to more damaging behavior on their part in the long run. But this tolerance, like the sympathy for childish helplessness, was merely grudging recognition of the inevitable; it bore no relationship to the earlier idea of selective utility in anger. Anger, whether in children or in parents, could not be fully prevented, but its expression served no purpose save in preventing deeper anger later on.[11]

With this outlook, the shift away from permissiveness, beginning in the later 1950s, involved little change in the basic estimation of anger. The emotion was bad; the postpermissive advice involved only a new belief that more direct measures against it were necessary. In this important sense the reaction against permissiveness did not represent a partial return to the tone of the 1920s, as in other respects it seemed to do.[12]

In the third edition of his *Baby and Child Care,* Dr. Spock moved toward the new position against anger. Initially, as we have seen, his echoing of the older tolerance of anger as preparation for a competitive life was out of step with other advocates of permissiveness in the late 1940s and out of step as well with his own predominant emphasis on the importance of friendship and smooth peer relations.[13] By the 1970s he moved toward greater consistency, influenced of course by his own reaction to the violence of the 1960s and his general concern about war. Parents should not feel guilty about some angry reactions to childish misbehavior because children might exploit this guilt. One of the key targets for careful discipline should now be unacceptable displays of childish temper. Children should not be completely thwarted; they should learn that mild, occasional anger is natural. But they should also learn that anger must be controlled at all times, and they should be carefully led away from indulgence in symbolic expressions of anger, ranging from play with toy guns to television representations. Spock, commonsensical as ever, does not envisage an anger-free environment, but he wants to minimize the emotion and places no positive value on it. Mature behavior consists of solving problems without anger. And American society is too immature; it needs more control.[14]

Other authorities had moved to this position earlier.[15] Anger should be avoided, for it complicates adult behavior, and its repression is either ineffective or personally damaging (concern about the somatic effects of repressed anger entered some commentary by the 1950s). Anger was not effective in righting social wrongs, for only calm and compromise could have any effect. A central belief was that child rearing should be sufficiently subtle that children would grow up without any expectation of injustice from authority and thus without any belief that anger is an appropriate response. These views were common both to the decade and a half of permissiveness and to the reactions to permissiveness. The only shift came in tactics, with an increasing assertion that openness and tolerance were not enough and that parents had to take some active measures to teach children that expressions of anger were wrong.[16] The new generation of experts wanted rules; they feared that permissiveness, whatever its intent, had created rebellious adults. Children must be made more obedient, but always without anger. Rules, like society's laws, might not always be right, "but we cannot break them or have temper tantrums because they do not suit us personally."[17]

To be sure, some manuals in the 1970s paralleled marriage advice and assertiveness training in seeming to open new doors to positive uses of anger.[18] A "fair-fighting" school had less effect in child rearing than in marital matters if only because it implied more equality than parents were willing to grant. But the argument did receive some attention, and it serves as an interesting summary of the essential continuity in the later twentieth-century approach. Fair-fighting advocates opened with ringing assertions of the inevitability and need for anger and the desirability of its expression: no repression here. But even in this introit, the anger was somehow to be released without damage or even hostility—a neat trick. ("You don't want to worry or irritate anyone else when you use your Rage Release.") The bulk of the specific recommendations involved elaborate strategies to avoid anger by improving behavior on all sides and opening new channels of communication. Conflicts should turn into passionless discussions, surrounded by constitutional rules limiting duration, providing equal rights, and avoiding anything that might resemble a real outburst. The rare venting of anything like genuine anger should be circumscribed by all the same limits and should always end with kisses and hugs. Advocates reached back to older channeling ideas to suggest mock fights, exercise, and painless paddlings with styrofoam equipment, though revealingly some of these exercises were designed to prevent anger rather than to let off steam. Above all, there should be no residue of anger or resentment, for where the emotion cannot be avoided, it should be dissipated. Not only parents but also siblings should largely be content with calm statements, to the tune of "do you know that makes me mad?" The mere suggestion should avoid any normal need to experience or express the emotion itself.[19]

Overall, the main tactics recommended for the management of childish anger were maximum possible avoidance of situations that might provoke anger—an old idea that now received more fervent and detailed attention; ignoring childish tantrums to prevent repression and to teach that anger brought no results—certainly no rewards but, equally important, no denting of parental calm; a loving environment and maximum possible parental avoidance of anger; and a willingness to talk anger out, so that its inevitability should be recognized as against potential buildup, but at the same time its results would be nil as children were subtly made to feel embarrassed by their emotion and uncomfortable in experiencing more than mild irritations. Postpermissive advice added mainly clearer injunctions against tolerance of outright aggressive behavior.

In the importance attributed to managing anger and the anxiety expressed about results, the mid-twentieth century compared in fact with the eighteenth century, when the whole issue of controlling anger first found elaborate expression. Then changes in ideology and alterations in the valuation of family life and in the definition of proper family relationships led to new concern that in turn produced new child-rearing norms. Changes of comparable magnitude, though less easily defined, spurred the mid-twentieth-century shift, which in turn underlay two quickly succeeding child-rearing fads.

The importance of the new concern, and its contrast to both major approaches of the nineteenth century, showed in ancillary recommendations about the treatment of children, recommendations that may indeed have contributed to important alterations of the environment in which children lived. Permissive experts of course urged teachers to share with parents a willingness to explore the sources of any childish anger rather than to respond with repressive prohibitions. The attempt to imbue schooling with an emotionally friendly atmosphere was not new among experts, but it received greater emphasis. More significant were recommendations that the school structure change, toward reduction of anger-producing frustration. Thus teachers should abet children's desire to fit in with their friends. They should cut grade skipping and flunking, lest these disrupt peer relations and cause damaging anger with its consequences in aggressive behavior. In a sense, and again in contrast to the mid-nineteenth-century disapproval of anger, childish anger was now seen as sufficiently difficult, and its consequences sufficiently harmful, that it must be circumvented wherever possible. Character building was not enough.[20]

There were other signs, admittedly hard to weigh with precision, that the idea of restraining anger with new thoroughness, away from the ambivalence of channeling, was catching on. A new current of criticism of older standards of masculinity developed, mainly from individuals in the "generation of the '60s,"[21] and while formal movements of "male liberation" remained small, some of the concerns expressed were more widely shared. Among the several targets of this new criticism was what was seen as a traditional male readiness to anger and to anger-based aggressions against other men as well as against women. A conscious effort seemed to be taking shape, in behavior as well as the critical literature, to break from older paternal patterns of angry discipline and from paternal expectations of a belligerent spirit in properly masculine boys.

More widely still, the media presentations offered to, and by all appearances preferred by, teenagers shifted away from much of the imagery associated with the channeling approach. The Western virtually died, no doubt partly because the frontier was long dead but also partly because the gunslinger image—the man moved slowly to righteous anger but then ready to act quickly once aroused—no longer fit the youth culture. Rather young people were increasingly offered space-age heroes who might often be quite violent, but with careful passionlessness. At an extreme, it was as if the preindustrial message had been reversed: traditionally, excessively violent behavior had been repudiated, not anger itself. Now behavior sometimes seemed less important than preserving a cool emotional base. What one did, up to a point, mattered less than what one felt; and anger was a proscribed feeling save for some clearly marked, and often older, villains.

In many ways, later twentieth-century child-rearing emotionology seems designed to ease the parental task. Compared to earlier literature, concerns about physical health have lessened. Goals remain the same, but as the fact of improved childhood health has been assimilated, the level of concern has been allowed to drop. The responsibility of regulating sexuality or even regulating childish reading matter and media contacts has lessened as well, though not without considerable anguish, as the image of childish innocence has faded.[22] Some of the anger advice might be interpreted in a similar vein, as parents were authorized to ignore certain outbursts and to strive for surface friendliness through avoiding serious conflict. Such interpretations could contribute to a more superficial parenting, as some critics have charged.[23] But the intent of the new emotionology of anger was quite different. It was in fact far more demanding than Victorian idealism or even channeling had been with regard to this basic emotion, and there are signs that some parents picked up on the new seriousness, not content with misinterpreting toward greater superficiality. Parents were now being told, albeit somewhat indirectly because of the desire to avoid the language and explicit tactics of repression, that they had an awesome responsibility in curbing a basic human impulse toward aggression that could only do harm in later life. The child who did not learn that serious anger was futile and dangerous, that anger when sensed should be talked away, would be fit for neither job nor home, and he might contribute to wider acts of aggression, often mentioned in child-rearing manuals, such as war, crime, or, in the most recent manuals, brutality against women. Since children were not innocents—the contrast to Victorianism in this area—and since the wider world had no place for anger or anger-driven behavior—the contrast to the channeling approach—a major burden rested on proper adult management. In this sense, late twentieth-century child-rearing advice did not so much lessen responsibilities as reshuffle priorities so that more attention could be paid to anger avoidance. Several traditional norms yielded in the interest of greater emotional control.

Causation

The growing anxiety about anger from the 1940s on stemmed from several concomitant changes. Indeed, the complexity of the causation easily matched the importance of the shift in approach.

The most obvious causes, as in the previous shifts in the familial approach toward anger, were intellectual. The belated popularization of Freudianism in child-rearing literature led to a new definition of children's emotional life and contributed to the new attention to emotional well-being as part of successful upbringing. Popularized Freudianism certainly increased the importance attributed to childhood, as opposed to later life stages, in emotional control, thus furthering a trend that had begun in the 1920s and 1930s. The new concern with emotional well-being was accompanied by a shift in family sociology more generally, away from social reform to personal interaction, and in social psychology toward a new interest in discouraging aggression. Social psychologists, awed by the events of World War II and the Nazi Holocaust and spurred by evidence of crime and prejudice in the United States, increasingly emphasized proper emotional guidance, including control of anger. Reaction to later events, particularly 1960s student unrest and the Vietnam War, continued to fuel this strand. Here was the intellectual background to the rising concern about anger, a background that used reactions to mid-twentieth-century violence as one reason to utilize—somewhat belatedly—Freud's insights about basic human drives.[24]

It is vital to note, as against some recent criticism of the role of Freudianism in facilitating expressions of anger,[25] that the overall intellectual package did not lead to the most literally permissive stance. If a few mental hygienists did, as noted above, downplay aggression, using Freud to justify a freedom-for-impulse definition of mental health, most interpreters of Freud among the child-rearing experts hoped to use permissiveness to dampen anger, not to sanction its expression. Freudianism here dictated new tactics because of the understanding of primal drives, but it accompanied a declining tolerance for actual aggression. The shift in social-psychological usage, from the term "anger" to the term "aggression," correctly denotes new concern about the social effects of the emotion. Most child-rearing experts interpreted Freud as arguing, not for unlimited expression of anger, but for careful control in the name of civilized social behavior. And the experts' reaction to the violence of Nazism and World War II, as evidence of the destructive force of human aggression, certainly led them to seek maximum restraint of this emotional drive.[26]

The shift in psychology meant more than a change in index listings, in the child-rearing manuals, from discussions of anger to disquisitions on children's aggression, though the terminological change, duly popularized, was interesting. Social psychologists also discovered that some traditional beliefs about anger, including reliance on the cathartic effects of military play and of sports, were erroneous, in that such exercises increased anger rather than the reverse. These messages, as well as the more general concern among experts about guiding children's emotions away from intolerance and war, gradually affected child-rearing advice. Expert findings were reflected in the new advice not to encourage children to transfer anger to toys or other objects. The idea of using exercise to reduce anger also declined in the advice literature. And of course the new findings helped push expert opinion away from full permissiveness as the means of reducing anger.[27]

Intellectual causation doubtless moved some manual writers to the new concern about reducing anger. But on the whole new ideas help explain particular strategies; they do not provide the motivation for the basic shift. Here the interaction with events and real or apparent behavioral trends was crucial. Reactions to war and the Nazi crimes, reflected in psychology itself, provided part of the motivation. These were joined by rising concern, in the 1940s, about adolescent behavior and about crime. Not novel in any event, this concern fit neatly with the new stress on childish emotionality to read that control of anger must be imposed early. By the teenage years, control would be too late, both in the sense that earlier repressions would now begin to reemerge, more dangerously than before—the contribution of popularized Freudianism—and in the sense that teenagers could behave so destructively. Childish anger, improperly controlled, would now produce adolescent monsters. The new emphasis on personality, over social reform, led easily to the view that delinquents were simply overgrown children "choking with anger" who had not been properly treated before.[28] Delinquency, with explicit references, increasingly hovered over the manuals for care of younger children. On the positive side, the literature directed toward teenagers increasingly stressed the importance of popularity and friendliness. In contrast to Hall's turn-of-the-century concern with adolescence as a central period of character building, experts now downplayed the significance of anger among normal teenagers. Here was both the symptom and the cause of the new concern about anger in younger children. Properly raised, teenagers would have scant need to deal with anger; improperly raised, they were nearly hopeless delinquents. Growing parental concern about their children's success with peers and about juvenile crime, partly caused by this expert advice, facilitated some acceptance of the new approach to anger overall.[29]

Intellectual changes, themselves related to political and social shifts among experts from the 1930s on, were thus linked to some broader parental anxieties. Changes in economic structure, perceived by parents and child authorities alike, were even more important. These changes, which helped alter the definition of a successful teenager, explain, more than any other factor, the timing of the shift toward anger, in the 1940s and 1950s, and also the intensity and durability of the shift. Americans were waking up to the implications of a managerial and, increasingly, a service-sector economy, and child rearing quickly reflected the shift.

Here was a main basis, indeed, for the popularization of Freudian ideas, though these unquestionably had independent intellectual appeal. The search was for new methods to shape new, pleasing personalities, and anger control was a vital ingredient of the quest. Earlier changes regarding anger had touched base with economic developments. We have seen that new anxiety in the eighteenth century may have had some relationship to the burdens of increased economic transactions with neighbors and strangers. Still more clearly, the American ambivalence about anger, in the later nineteenth century, reflected the desire to build a competitive spirit. Without question, the shift away from this ambivalence, in turn, was fed by a new set of personal criteria for job performance.

Both experts and ordinary parents testified to a redefinition of the personal characteristics that would be most conducive to business success. Evidence of this shift within the child-rearing manuals, although predictably less rich than where Freudianism or social psychology was involved, appears surprisingly frequently. Several manuals directly mentioned the need to control emotions on the job and the related need to learn such control when young: rebels and troublemakers need not apply. Advice writers like Dorothy Canfield Fisher moved to this concern by the 1940s, after having ignored it in previous works. Advocates of the permissive approach specifically mentioned the importance of home control of anger in preventing unacceptable behavior in the world of work. In some cases this approach accompanied warnings against excessive competitiveness and pleas for greater cooperation: examples of occupations such as that of the salesman were used to illustrate the need for temper-controlled friendliness on the job. Anger, which prepared for combat, had lost its economic relevance.[30]

This is the point that Dr. Spock ultimately conveyed after his initial repetition of the conventional wisdom about competitiveness. In 1943, when Spock echoed the channeling concept in urging that some childish anger was a good thing, he pointed to later careers as farmers and businessmen. When he shifted toward a concern for minimizing anger, he specifically noted future occupations as managers or salesmen, in which of course the standards of anger control were different. This is the point that actual parents in managerial rather than entrepreneurial environments themselves picked up, in working to restrain their own anger in child rearing and in attempting to limit aggression in their children. Thus it is not farfetched to suggest that the rise of a corporate and service economy placed new demands on control of anger, demands that were conveyed in child-rearing literature and, for some parents, caused by this literature's influence. Shifts in what was considered a desirable work personality dovetailed with the acceptance of a particular brand of Freudianism, leading to an emphasis on anger control from a very early age.[31]

One other concomitant ingredient deserves mention, though in this case it appears not at all in the actual advice literature: changes in women's lives may have affected reactions to childish temper. Increased suburbanization after World War II put ever-greater child-rearing responsibility on mothers, who had long been urged to take particular care in aggression control. The baby-boom upsurge, primarily in middle-class households, certainly encouraged new attention to anger among siblings, and this was indeed picked up by the manual writers. Freud's thoughts on sibling rivalry undoubtedly help explain the popularization of his ideas during the 1940s. More generally, behavioral studies demonstrated that households with often-absent fathers produced less aggressive boys on the average, reflecting maternal concerns. Comparative studies suggest that mothers who are discontented with their roles—and female discontent loomed large in polls in the late 1940s—are more likely to be intolerant of children's expression of anger than are more satisfied mothers. Most important, comparisons also suggest that mothers who work move toward the same intolerance, either because of new burdens on their time or because their work gives them the kind of confidence that allows them to dismiss childish temper more readily. Since the 1940s and 1950s saw the beginnings of fundamental changes in women's outlook and work behavior, the possibility of a related decrease in tolerance of children's anger deserves some attention. This shift would have been particularly compatible with the more restrictive child-rearing advice that arose in the later 1950s.[32] Along with an ideological shift and the basic alteration in economic structure, it points to the new approach to anger as a considerable break with earlier American tradition.

The sum total of new factors, particularly of course the new ideas about personality and aggression as mediated through the various branches of psychiatry and psychology and the shift in economic structure toward service occupations and managerial hierarchies, produced an important correspondence between the emotionology of child rearing and that of work. In both spheres, for the first time since the anger-control movement began in the eighteenth century only to be disrupted by the separation of home and work, goals and tactics overlapped. In both, anger was to be treated as illegitimate and, carefully, was to yield no result. Neither children nor workers could be allowed to learn that anger was a positive drive. In both fields also, the attempt to excise serious anger led increasingly to a flurry of new attention to the emotion, followed by gradual internalization of the new standards such that strategies became more routine. In both fields, overt repression yielded to growing emphasis on friendliness—the parent as pal and confidant, the T group graduate as supervisor—in an atmosphere of greater surface democracy and less hierarchical use of anger. Both child-rearing and personnel behavior, finally, became permeated with a rhetoric of emotional release. Thus in both fields authorities tended to claim greater emotional freedom (though this current was modified, in child rearing, after the 1950s), but in both the claim was an embellishment on what was in fact a program of selective emotional manipulation, toward the reduction of anger and the attempt to divert the emotion's expression from behavior and toward talking out. Parents and supervisors alike must listen to verbal annoyance patiently, punctuating with sympathetic murmurs, so that no serious emotional buildup could occur. The result would be a child or worker capable of the most friction-free interaction possible with others, at home or on the job.

Emotions and Emotional Expression:
A Changing American Personality?

The dominant child-rearing emotionology of the previous period had, as we have seen, a demonstrable effect, at least in shaping parental behavior, particularly in the middle classes. The new emotionology was intended to alter this behavior and to create a more thoroughly anger free child. What was its effect?

As before, dealing with actual emotional experience is far more difficult than tracing significant emotionological change is, even for parental behavior and certainly for the more obscure emotional world of children. The recency of change and the probability that new emotionologies have an effect only gradually complicate appraisal of actual child-rearing styles, as does the lack of any comparative sociological study of the sort popular through the 1950s.[33] Assessment is complicated by several additional factors. The new emotionology did not require quite such severe parental repression of anger as had both Victorian and turn-of-the-century standards. It was admitted that parents might become angry and that, so long as the anger was mild and apologies forthcoming, the results would not be catastrophic. This new though limited permissiveness for parents, along with the probable new strains of child rearing in a society in which growing numbers of mothers worked and control over older children, at least, became more tenuous, produced some signs of increasingly overt anger in parent-child relations. Certainly there are fewer examples of parents exercising heroic control over their own emotions than occur in the diary and recollection literature of the nineteenth and early twentieth centuries, though the anguish at lapses might be just as great as before.

For despite some important change in tone, the basic modern desire for parental control of anger, certainly maintained in the new emotionology, does seem to have persisted. A variety of studies suggested that angry conflict continued to be seen as symptomic of family malfunction. Thus while perceptions about occasional irritation may have changed somewhat, and while changing circumstances may have produced new frictions between parents and children, the basic standards applied by parents themselves, which bridged the gap between emotionology and behavior, continued to correspond to the modern emotionological emphasis: parents did not feel easy with deep anger in themselves, much less in their children.[34]

A major sign of continuity comes from the anxieties of feminist mothers in practice, as opposed to their rhetoric. Evidence suggests that many feminist mothers, though interested in developing new assertiveness for themselves and their daughters, clung to the old standards of anger avoidance; as in work personalities, assertiveness and anger were held apart. The result could produce some of the familiar kinds of guilt about expressing anger: "J. had to be assertive with the children and at times angry with them. These experiences added to her problems. They caused her to become upset and self-critical, since she held the common belief that a good mother has virtually no anger."[35]

The fact that this new emotionology is so recent certainly complicates assessments of its effect. Parental behavior does not shift as rapidly as child-rearing standards change; brief fads in child rearing, indeed, while they may color what parents say they do, may have little behavioral effect at all.[36] We have argued that basic emotionological changes in child rearing run deeper than the generational fads, as is demonstrated by the fundamental continuity between the permissive and stricter generations of advice between the 1940s and the present. But it is still logical to assume that it takes some time for parental behavior to catch up with the new standards. We have seen that studies of American child rearing into the 1950s revealed strong correspondence with earlier channeling behavior, maintaining the distinctive national ambivalence noted in a number of comparative analyses.

Yet it was in the 1950s also that the first attempts by parents to change were noted. A few parents, indeed, experimented with a more permissive approach to childish temper, accepting any childish outburst rather than risking its repression. More generally, the growing popularity of Dr. Spock's manual and other literature reflecting the new standards suggests a felt need for new advice and a potential openness thereto. A number of younger parents, by the 1960s, began to depart from the approach their own parents had taken, for example, increasing their willingness to ignore rather than to discipline tantrums; the growing residential separation between grandparents and parents aided this development. Here was a measurable change in tactics, reflecting the concern with emotional rather than behavioral discipline. Spanking almost disappeared as a response to tantrums, according to one survey, and even the effort to talk the tantrum out declined. For a time, at least, partial adherence to advice literature opened further gaps between middle-class and working-class child-rearing styles, as middle-class parents, particularly mothers, worked harder to avoid punishment when angry and to understand the basis for childish temper instead of reacting to its expression.[37] The middle class became still less tolerant of mild, verbal expressions of anger against parents and much less supportive of children's efforts to fight back against peers.[38] Here was the clearest shift away from the bifurcation encouraged by the channeling approach.

Even aside from the obvious fact that great variety remained in parental styles, there can be no assurance that parental goals changed as much as tactics did in the decades after 1950. Some mothers, as feminism crested, tried to reduce repression of anger among their daughters in order to encourage more effective anger in later life. Even parents who shared the experts' desire to reduce anger might find their efforts hopelessly complicated by the violence available in television programming or even by the models of useful anger visible in school sports. In this sense, again, considerable ambivalence remained in the American approach.[39] Even parents who did intend to reduce anger through more permissive tactics may not have won the desired results. Some experts did claim improvement, noting that greater permissiveness reduced the number of occasions for parental irritability by reducing the number of petty standards that required enforcement; in the heyday of permissiveness, some believed that childish temper itself declined. One theory maintained that increased physical cosseting of infants produced lifelong improvements in emotional control.[40]

On a far more measurable level, there were signs of an interesting shift in parental concerns about "problem" children, as revealed in referrals to child guidance agencies from the 1940s on. In Pittsburgh, for example, the balance of parentally defined symptoms definitely changed. School problems and habit-training problems dropped notably, beginning in the 1940s. But problems of family conflict, disobedience, and other symptoms of unacceptable childish aggression rose markedly among parent referrals. Some of the initial shift may have resulted from wartime situations in which mothers had to cope alone. But the durability of the shift suggests either more difficult children—always a possibility—or, more probably, a change in parental standards such that behavior indicating anger more easily triggered concerns.[41]

Reasonably solid evidence certainly suggests that many middle-class parents adopted anger-reducing goals along with shifting their tactics away from repression and channeling. The most extensive studies predate feminism and so do not preclude the possibility of more recent encouragement of anger among daughters. But they suggest that changes in the goals for boys are likely to have predominated, which is consistent with the turn away from channeling that had been viewed primarily as a male path.

In their path-breaking 1958 survey of parental behavior in the Detroit area, Miller and Swanson found a distinct trend, spearheaded by parents in managerial rather than entrepreneurial positions, to reduce rigid training in the hopes of reducing children's anger, with the larger goal of preparing personalities that would fit smoothly into a corporate environment. Entrepreneurial families remained more likely to discipline manifestations of childish anger outright, with full recognition that concealed anger might remain; the latter possibility was accepted in part because of a continued belief that properly channeled anger could be useful. Managerial families, and also white-collar families, were much more explicitly concerned with emotional smoothness and were willing to step around limited behavioral problems for the sake of this goal.

Interestingly also, surveys among teenagers revealed a marked intolerance for expressions of anger among their peers, as the popularity of "cool" suggests. Hostility to anger and a decline in the belief in justified indignation became part of the peer culture—just as the experts, bent on smooth peer relations, had hoped.[42]

In sum, the change in the dominant advice about anger in child rearing struck responsive chords in at least portions of the intended audience. Both experts and their parental followers were moved by new concern about social violence and by changes in the personality desired in work, away from aggressive individualism and toward smoothness in interpersonal relations. Shared goals made the shift in tactics from the late 1950s on easily assimilable: youth violence demonstrated that sheer permissiveness was not effective, so a modified strategy could be introduced without alteration in purpose. Young people themselves seemed to pick up some of the anger-control cues.

Inevitably, particularly in a situation of impressionistic evidence, objections and qualifications spring to mind. There is no reason to assume uniformity of parental strategies across ethnic or class lines. The probability of ethnic variations even entered the child-rearing literature targeted for specific groups, as noted above. Class variation undoubtedly persisted, though the rapid growth of the middle class after World War II, based on the expansion of the service sector, surely helped generalize middle-class norms, and class variations in standards measurably declined. Thus Miller and Swanson found white-collar families of working-class origin pursuing anger-management strategies rather similar to those of managerial groups, even in the 1950s. Adverse conditions could still prompt countercurrents, even against the professed intentions of parents themselves. We have no clear record yet of the actual emotional behavior and norms of hard-pressed single parents, whose numbers continue to grow. Economic setbacks definitely increased angry parental behavior, though most notably in the working class.[43] Similar strains in middle-class families did not generate an increase in physical discipline or abuse. Still, there can be no claim of some homogeneous or undeflectable movement to the new child-rearing standards.

Nor can one show a uniform effect on children's personalities, even within the middle class. The angry movements of the 1960s unquestionably revealed that, at least under the provocation of events, young people could manifest serious anger and genuine moral outrage. Some observers found youth protest a sign of anger against remote or materialistic parents; the protest might also have expressed anger developed previously but incapable of articulation within the home itself, a sign that new parental approaches had some, but incomplete, success. It was noteworthy, of course, that even student protesters during this decade put a premium on "cool" behavior among themselves and seemed somewhat uncomfortable with their own anger outside the heat of the moment. It may be significant that the succeeding generation of students, after collective action subsided in 1973, recovered a pervasive quiescence, professing among other things feelings of warmth toward their own parents.[44]

There is no reason to claim that children became less angry than they were before as a result of new parental strategies. Even aside from doubts about the efficacy of any strategies, children had some new sources for anger as a result of rising divorce rates, changes in maternal behavior as work participation grew, and other anxieties. Where attempts to reduce anger in the home won some success, they may often, as we will see, simply have diverted anger to other settings, such as schools, though this shift would itself be significant. It does seem probable that the new parental tactics, building on earlier anger-control efforts, taught many children a new discomfort with their own anger, making it difficult to find appropriate targets and tempting, perhaps, to turn anger inward, blaming themselves for an emotion that their parents and the media had urged should never be serious or durable. Middle-class youth protesters, even when enraged, revealed some of this discomfort in stressing the power of loving comradeship to damp down the fires of wrath.

Certainly the ramifications of the changing valuation of anger since mid-century deserve attention, all the more since we have been only barely aware of our engagement in it—indeed, deliberately distracted by misleading rhetoric of emotional openness and letting it all hang out. If, as our earlier chapter confirmed, Lloyd Warner was right three decades ago about the importance of tension over anger along with sexuality in middle-class child rearing (a tension then, too, largely unnoted in the greater enthusiasm for agonizing over sex), so do the changing standards of anger have considerable implications for personal and social behavior. The popularity, in 1983, of newspaper columns on anger, though doubtless the result in part of the media's relentless quest for new issues, belatedly signaled the effect of change, though they rather misconstrued its direction in arguing against a literal permisiveness that had never been widely held in child-rearing ideals or behavior. Interesting assessments of recent American culture that omit the shift on anger are almost certainly wanting, as they miss an emotional component of real importance in the national tradition.[45] Many American parents have changed the way they view and treat childish anger, compared to the habits of their own parents and grandparents in the period of channeling; and their new strategies, combined with the anger-control movement in the workplace, have had genuine effect on youth culture and on personality formation.

Anger in the Schools: A New Ambivalence

The parental approach to childish anger is not of course the only factor in socialization. Indeed, most authorities would argue that its role has declined somewhat in the twentieth century. From much of peer culture and some, at least, of the media available to children, the signals about anger have partially paralleled the changes in parental attitude. Children's television programming has sought to aid children in identifying anger, but on the whole with the implication that the emotion could and should be worked out without serious effect on others (and of course without guilt for the child). It is true, of course, that parental monitoring of books, films, and television, for the sake of preserving a childish innocence, has declined. As a result, children are more freely exposed to tales of violence (and other human woes) than was the case before. While some of the rising media violence stresses cool emotion, particularly in science-fiction products, a motif of righteous anger continues to permeate many police shows, the efforts of Clint Eastwood, and other creations directed in part toward youths. Thus the media continue to promote an ambivalence about anger that is not fully in keeping with the new emotionology or, as we have argued, the trends of parental tactics.

A more serious and direct ambivalence, however, stems from the emotional context of the schools. Even before mid-century, teachers tended to diverge from parents in their estimation of anger, more commonly seeing childish anger as a problem. But the difference was one of degree: school programs in general meshed with the channeling approach, trying to prevent angry outbursts against authority but using sports programs and other outlets to guide anger toward appropriate behaviors and targets.

Schools unquestionably implemented some of the new managerial strategies that developed after 1940. Individual suburban schools developed and still maintain a cheery, no-problems no-intense-emotions atmosphere. Permissive parenting was mirrored in some small but interesting preschool and school programs, such as the spreading Montessori movement, that sought to deflect childish anger by careful, loving teacher attention and avoidance of constraint. In some part, then, American schools, particularly those designed for upper-middle-class children, made some of the same transitions that parents began to make.

More widely still, the guidance-counselor movement, which began after World War II, was designed to provide authorities who could duplicate the parent or the retrained foreman in listening anger out and preventing it from taking root. Guidance counselors were increasingly advised to take their emotional problem solving task seriously—a clear response to the new emotionology. Angry children formed one of the "adjustment problems" that the newly trained guidance specialists were supposed to handle.[46] Interestingly, schools in the late 1940s began to refer aggressive students less often to outside agencies, such as child guidance centers, on the assumption that they could mediate such problems on their own. Furthermore, important and widespread institutional changes, most notably, the reduction of the expulsion or flunking of students and, from the 1960s on, the escalation of average grades, clearly reflected a desire to avoid the provocation of anger and to escape angry confrontations between teacher and student in the name of smooth interpersonal relations and the teacher as pal. This was an important response to the new emotional values, related to the rise of egalitarian attitudes, and a response with real social effect.

Finally, the training of teachers themselves sedulously stressed anger control, not a new motif, but one that in the new emotionological climate received growing emphasis: teachers "should demonstrate control over their own temper if they expect students to control theirs."[47]

Yet, in the main, American schools did not make a massive shift to a new emotional climate. In their traditionalism, they stood out from new home values and the anger-control movement in the workplace. For schools remained hierarchical. They were less touched than the home or the workplace were by the new currents of surface democratization. Furthermore, schools in the postwar era faced important new pressures that could generate new kinds of anger. The pressures began with classroom crowding and the resultant disciplinary problems presented by the baby boom. Since the 1960s, school anger has resulted from new teacher frustration at lagging rates of pay and prestige, from the new tensions generated by the widespread unionization movement, and from the emotional repercussions of school integration movements, which could mark teachers and students alike and which forced many teachers once again to deal with wide variations in the cultures of anger within the student body.[48]

As a result of new tensions and old hierarchies, many teacher training manuals, even in the 1980s, continued to have an old-fashioned ring to them, compared to recommended parental styles—which means not that they were wrong headed but only that they were increasingly distinctive. Thus secondary school teachers are told to treat any sign of angry student behavior very seriously, even when students merely seem to be horsing around, and to impose the appropriate penalty after at most a single warning. Only the smallest bows are made to letting an offending student cool off, to trying to ascertain the reasons for anger, or to using counseling specialists for troubled youngsters. As in the old days, if with different disciplinary means, anger is to be met with punishment, for the goal is to control behavior, not to worry directly about emotional manipulation. The teacher should be objective but unbending: "Point out that the behavior was not acceptable and state the penalty clearly." The approach clearly recalls the school traditions of the past.[49]

More important, considerable evidence suggests that teacher anger, and the expression of that anger, has risen in recent decades, one manifestation of what several authorities see as a steady increase in teacher strain from the 1940s on.[50] Despite continuing evidence that angry punishment merely made children angry in turn, angry discipline remained in 1982 the most common form of reaction to behavior problems in the classroom.[51] A 1972 survey revealed that 500 teachers (the entire sample) got angry at least once a day: "The realities of teaching—overloaded classes, endless demands, sudden crises—make anger inevitable."[52]

Clearly, many teachers were not just lagging in emotional style but moving in opposite directions from the standards being suggested for parents. In part, without question, the real gap was modified by the fact that parents also were frequently angry; they too did not manage to appropriate the most stringent anger-control advice. Yet the evidence of real parental effort to meet the new emotional management standards of the late twentieth century is simply not matched by the indications from the schools. The question is, Why and to what effect?

Two factors, visible previously in the partial gap between parental and school standards, continue to apply. Teachers, because of a necessary concern for order among large groups of children and because of ongoing traditions of expecting obedience, do not quickly participate fully in the nuances of each modern anger-control configuration. Like traditionalist parents, they stress behavior control over emotional guidance, and they balance innovations against the customs of their profession. Second, changes in emotionology raise certain problems in the school that do not appear so vividly in the home. Many parents after the 1940s thus tolerated some mild childish outbursts in the interests of talking problems through and preventing deep resentments. This pattern carried over into schools could seem unduly bothersome, even disrespectful. Certainly many teachers did believe and still believe that parents impose insufficient discipline, leaving the entire job of instilling obedience to be done in the classroom. Small wonder that the earlier gap between teacher and parental concern about childish anger grew: teacher concern about angry behavior was higher in 1952 than it had been in 1928, whereas parental confidence in the boundaries of anger among their children had grown.[53] In a distinctive way, teachers were reflecting the same growing concern about anger that entered the general emotionology of child rearing—certainly, educational literature from the 1950s on is dotted with explicit discussions of the emotion; but their response differed from the anger-management style, despite expert recommendations to attempt more ''psychological'' techniques.[54]

But we have noted novel factors in the equation as well. Increased curricular demands and bureaucratic rigidity in the schools, which add up to loss of teacher autonomy and a sense of recurrent disruption and crisis, almost surely increased teacher stress, heightening the probability of angry reactions from another angle. Unionization movements gave some legitimacy to expressions of grievance and certainly complicated the teacher image of benign selflessness. Some teachers also resented the loss of individual disciplinary authority, which could augment daily outbursts of verbal anger against student targets.

Many teachers would argue that student expressions of anger, and not just their sensitivity to such expressions, were rising. Rates of student unrest, from the 1960s to 1973, and more individual violence and vandalism after that point gave credence to the claim. Again, larger social changes, including the tensions of growing racial integration, played a role in this development. But so, perhaps, did growing permissiveness in home discipline. There were experts to argue that parental styles of anger control so repressed children, particularly adolescents, that they needed school outlets in order to let off steam. Anger-control tactics, in other words, had an effect but an incomplete one, leaving the schools increasingly vulnerable. Children felt inhibited in outbursts in the home or against the anxiously friendly parent but still felt an anger that required an adult target, and the teacher, as a more obvious disciplinarian, easily filled the bill. Unremarked but also possible for some students was the effect of the gap between school and home models for anger in creating its own confusion as they confronted teachers periodically angrier than family had taught them that adults were supposed to be. Anger-control tactics here could create heightened sensitivity to teachers' use of anger for discipline, even when this remained at traditional levels; and while many students would be intimidated as a result, others might finally respond with some anger of their own. Certainly student polls have indicated teacher anger as a major complaint for several decades.[55] Small wonder that, in their turn, educators routinely refer to anger as "the emotion that creates the most trouble, especially in schools."[56]

Clearly, a characteristic modern gap between recommended home and school standards in handling anger, and in the adult expression of anger, has widened greatly in recent decades, in part as a result of the major, and still fairly recent, modification of child-rearing emotionology. The gap shows that the new emotionology, with its emphasis on avoiding or talking out anger, has not uniformly triumphed and certainly has not produced all the desired modifications of anger in children themselves.

The gap maintains, in new form, the older American theme of ambivalence in the control of anger. Eighty years ago, the ambivalence nestled within the emotionology itself. Now it affects children in the difference they can perceive between anger-control strategies at home—even when incompletely adapted to the emotionological standards—and those often visible in the classroom. In time, of course, the gap may close somewhat; and certain features of schooling already reflect the desire to reduce anger and frustration. Many parents express discomfort about the emotional treatment particular children receive in school, and this may have some effect. For the moment, however, children are simultaneously taught that serious anger is wrong and that certain important adults get angry routinely. The result is continued diversity over the role anger may legitimately play.

At the least, the distinctive emotional context of many schools demonstrates that in fact the new American style toward anger has not produced the consistent, thorough effort to use socialization to attack this emotion that is visible in some primitive cultures. For children themselves, tensions between school and home ideals pose some of the same problems that adults faced, earlier, between home and work emotional codes. The resulting confusions deserve further exploration. For some children, the school atmosphere unwittingly may contribute to a tolerance for angry behavior that will serve poorly, or have to be unlearned, in the workplace. The maintenance of a distinctive school approach to anger also suggests a serious lingering ambivalence about anger among middle-class adults. For the outcry against teachers' use of anger has not, as yet, been massive, though restrictions on disciplinary measures have been considerable. Many parents undoubtedly see schools as providing a useful dose of emotional reality, even as they alter their own stance toward childish anger. The rise, in the 1980s, of school reform movements that urged tougher curricula in part as a punishment for real or imagined childish laxness evoke this attitude strongly: parents may want teachers to use anger to force children to toe the line precisely because they no longer find the approach appropriate in the home. So a real ambivalence remains, though it finds different outlets than in the heydey of channeling.

Child Rearing and the Valuation of Anger: The Wider Culture

The fact that continued complexity exists, in part the obvious result of the varied institutions of socialization, in part perhaps the inevitable confusion of a transition in child-rearing styles, should not obscure the significance of the substantial shift in values that has occurred. The shift has indeed touched the schools, albeit incompletely, and it has more substantially altered parental tactics toward anger and some of the attitudes about anger held by children themselves. The overall direction of the new emotionology is clear, even if divisions remain among the agents of socialization. While it is important that ambivalence remains in the American child-rearing culture, though less in emotionology than in practice, it is vital to realize that ambivalence is now more muted in favor of an interest in nipping anger in the bud, quickly dissipating it by talking it out not with its target but with a sympathetic audience, parent or peer, eager to help remove the unpleasant emotion. This constitutes a considerable reduction of ambivalence or at least an embarrassment at its lingering symptoms, leading among other things to a desire for more strictly symbolic expressions of anger, as in sports, more removed from daily life.

The new direction of anger control is brought into more vivid relief when one final facet of child-rearing goals is briefly evoked. Anthropologists argue, persuasively, that the child-rearing goals of a society, as ideals and as cues for actual parental behavior, have an evidential importance even apart from their effect on children. They translate some larger characteristics of a society that can be measured in ways that go beyond (though ideally include) close monitoring of parent-child interaction.[57] A change in child-rearing values, such as that which has occurred concerning anger since the 1940s, thus mirrors a shift in the wider culture.

Here the evidence in contemporary American culture is strong and varied. It was no accident, for example, that since the 1940s one strain among Americans psychiatric and psychological therapists has been a concern about the difficulty some troubled adults might have in expressing anger, as the idea of justified anger began to dwindle in child rearing.[58] More recently, feminist attacks on the macho stereotype— often, admittedly, angry attacks—and male liberationist echoes of a desire to encourage a new, less aggressive masculine personality fit into the wider changes in emotional context. The advocates of male gentleness are attacking an ideal of channeled anger that is more dated than they realize, but in swimming with the trends in child rearing they contribute to a new emotional climate—a new hostility to anger—in various facets of adult life.[59]

Further, the new effort to manage anger may relate to the perception of a general, if incompletely admitted, decline in competitiveness in American life; the increasing interest in avoiding angry frustration through bad grades in school suggests indeed one direct relationship. There is striking correspondence between the recent trends of child rearing and what Barrington Moore has termed the decline of moral indignation in Western, particularly American, society since World War II.[60] Moore attributes the change to the bureaucratization of protest, which managed to absorb and deflect even the gut reactions of the 1960s. When moral outrage converts to mail-targeted solicitation of funds, its emotional component undoubtedly declines. But we can see also that the decline of moral indigation accompanies a much larger change in social values and their conveyance through child rearing. For in child rearing, quite literally, the justifiability of using anger toward some larger goal has measurably declined. We have moved away from the concept of channeling anger, and wider protest movements may well reflect this change. To be sure, some recent comments on anger have still tried to distinguish between personal anger (bad) and the good effects of (past) anger by blacks, women, and youths. This preserves a remnant of the older idea of channeling. In fact, however, we may have turned so fully against anger in child rearing (in part because of its apparently disorderly consequences in social movements) that we have limited the emotional basis for moral indignation.[61] The idea of a decline in moral indignation needs further assessment, of course. If it seems somewhat confirmed by the quick quiescence of 1960s revolt—and particularly in the United States—it must also take feminism, environmentalism, and other movements into account. Yet the impression of a decline on balance, confirmed as it is by the more definite shift in child-rearing ideals, merits consideration as part of the assessment of the effects of the changing valuation of anger on American society and its place in a changing American character.

Similarly, the widespread increase in tolerance in American society, imperfect as it still is, reflects a shift in willingness to express and to tolerate anger. Greater tolerance was one of the goals of the permissive child experts of the 1940s, who saw the reduction of anger and disapproval of any effort to redirect anger to other targets as central to their effort.[62] They may have succeeded. And their success may account for some of the troublesome side effects political observers note in the rise of toleration, notably, the reluctance to venture emotional commitments to large political causes.[63] A change in emotional climate, though surely far more complex and qualified than the alteration in child-rearing advice is, may have far-reaching implications in the evolution of contemporary American society.

The evidence of changing standards for the treatment of anger, despite ambivalence between home and school, relates to other evidence of changes in the modal American personality. Assessments even in the 1950s, which emphasized a turn away from individualism toward peer-group signals (e.g., David Riesman's other-directed personality),[64] were certainly consistent with the attempt to reduce and to talk away anger in favor of smooth interpersonal relations. The shift in the valuation of anger, toward avoidance rather than selective guidance, may have come a bit harder than other aspects of the new peer-group orientation. At the level of emotionology, we have seen that Dr. Spock moved clearly toward a new emphasis on peer relations in the first edition of *Baby and Child Care,* well before he modified the traditional ambivalence about anger, for the idea of channeling anger into useful competitiveness was deeply embedded in American ideals.[65] But the shift did come, not only in ideals, but also in some aspects of parental behavior and internalized perception. The addition of a serious change in the stance toward anger enriches the frequently asserted claim that some basic changes in American personality have been in the works since mid-century. The change has been gradual and, of course, uneven; but it is rooted in a number of new factors in the social environment, headed by the rise of managerial structures and a service economy. If the past is any guide—for Americans have undertaken basic reevaluations of anger relatively rarely—the change may prove persistent, with increasing effect on actual parenting and on personality.

The shift concerning anger does depart somewhat from one of the most powerful recent statements of personality change, that by Christopher Lasch. Lasch sees a rise of narcissism involving inadequate working through of primal, infantile rage, the result of confused and superficial parenting. His theory rests on Freudian assumptions of a constant and inherent level of anger in the personality and on rather scattered empirical grounds.[66] The new approach to anger does not prove such a sweeping or fundamental personality change as Lasch posits (though it would be compatible with substantial change). And it casts some doubt on the idea of primal rages somehow more adequately handled by older middle-class parental styles, though again it is not entirely incompatible with such a claim. The approach does stress that changes in parental values toward handling anger, and not merely a weak-willed abdication of responsibility, are involved in the new emotional style. Although the subject must be assessed more thoroughly in our concluding chapter, a focus on anger suggests less the rise of unfocused rage than a newly far-reaching discomfort with anger as a key to the emerging American personality. Still, the new anger style overlaps with many of Lasch's claims and in general supports, embellishes, and explains the numerous signs of a shift in some basic personal characteristics.

Finally, the new concern about anger corresponds with society-wide fascination with diseases of the choleric personality. Anthropologists have suggested that prohibitions most emphasized in child rearing crop up also in a society's favored disease patterns. Surely it is no accident that a major shift in the outlook toward anger is accompanied by a concomitant emphasis on heart attacks and the hard-driving "A-type" personalities that presumably contribute toward them. Anger did not loom large in the first popularizations of ideas about the health effects of emotional tension in the late nineteenth century. Confidence in character building and in channeling helped to limit the vision of anger's physical effects to a few strikingly uncontrolled individuals. Thus the angry person reddened, swelled, and throbbed, but the angry person was part of an unfortunate minority; he did not live in everyone. By the 1960s, however, anger's physical effects were seen in all of us—silent, undramatic, but deadly. Angry emotions in anyone produced changes in blood vessels, heart rate, and glands, and all these in turn contributed to the leading killer disease. Health warnings, however legitimate, thus reflected warnings against anger accumulations in child rearing and continued the enforcement of childhood messages.[67] This linkage adds to the accumulation of evidence that the emotionological shift toward anger management, like the earlier fascination with channeling, had wide ramifications not only in parental behavior but in the larger American culture.

Conclusion

The Hutterite religious sect in Canada, known for its abundant fertility, carefully discourages aggression by providing no rewards for angry acts and no examples of adult anger. So despite a severe discipline and many frustrations, it avoids virtually any kind of interpersonal aggression.

In the American Southwest, the Zuni Indians carefully preach a way of peace. Preparation for major religious ceremonies involves avoidance not only of outward signs of anger but of any inner feeling of the emotion as well. Children learn and internalize these goals by their early teens as part of their initiation into religious adulthood.[68]

It is hard for Americans, confronted with examples of this sort of careful anger control in socialization, to imagine that they participate in any comparable system. Of course they do not participate fully: the diversity of subcultures in the United States by class, gender, and ethnic group produces many styles toward anger, and even mainstream values continue to harbor ambiguities and inconsistencies. But American child rearing has engaged in a considerable movement toward goals of anger control, with significant consequences within the family and without. We have described the beginnings of the attack on anger in child rearing, with its explicit renunciation of traditional will breaking; the development of an undoubtedly comfortable American amalgam of anger control with efforts to channel—an attempt to have one's anger and vent it too; and the more recent reversion to fuller control through management and manipulation. Modern American society has experimented with several styles of anger repression, with major shifts adding to a complex emotional legacy. But there is little question about an overall interest in limiting anger, little question about some resulting effectiveness in limiting the expression of anger at least toward certain key targets.

The most recent version of the attack on anger commands the greatest interest, and not only because it describes a significant part of our own emotional context. The transition is relatively recent, and it moves against a previous pattern that seemed particularly expressive of an American character. The combination of recency and the hold of strong remnants of earlier values, may be particularly productive of emotional misdirection, of confusions about anger's place and legitimacy. And the transition is complicated also by its veiled quality. A society that touts its war against Victorian repression, that hails the emergence of "real," unfettered human nature, has, in one major respect, become subtly more repressive. Urging emotional expressiveness and the importance of feelings, its emotional guides in fact intended a new selectivity: love, sadness, even fear, might legitimately hang out with new freedom, but serious anger may not. Recent attacks on anger, which mistakenly claim that Americans are far more tolerant of the emotion than they actually are, continue to express the silent campaign. The effort may be worthy, indeed essential, to the conduct of a civilized society in a crowded world. But its assessment surely depends on a greater awareness of the repressive effort than Americans have thus far been granted.

Earlier American efforts to limit anger through child rearing were central pieces in the growing reproval of the emotion. They formed a basic part of a putatively anger-free familial environment that stood against the harsher outer world, though of course they were also supposed to generate personal character that would serve the larger world of business and reform as well as the family. But the earlier efforts were marked by some complexity in the family–wider world relationship, which the idea of channeling—hold back personal anger but put it to work in the world—rather uncomfortably attempted to manage. Jerome Kagan has noted that Americans could not attempt the repression of anger that is possible in some other societies because family goals would run afoul of expectations of aggression in other contexts.[69] Elements of this tension persist, as in the gap between school and parental emotional models. There may indeed be danger in an approach that downgrades the legitimacy of anger, as one of the goals of child rearing, while failing in fact to excise the emotion; the result could be a lack of restraint and unsuitable or unproductive targeting when the emotion bursts forth. We must remain unsure about the actual extent of the parental effort to translate emotionological goals, particularly when the precise goals are novel and depend for their translation on parents, including overburdened working mothers, whose patience with demanding counsels of talking through and avoiding frustration may easily flag.[70]

But with all the complications and incompleteness of the most recent attempt to limit anger through child rearing, the novel outreach adds to its importance. Contemporary child rearing goals and even methods now join wider efforts to limit anger in American life. They no longer assume familial isolation, even familial primacy, in emotional control. For Americans in the later twentieth century, guided against serious anger in much of their upbringing, now find these messages echoed and enforced in the world of work. The anger-control movement, still not entirely consistent, is at last armed with new tactics to bridge the home/work dichotomy through the attempt to create a harmonious, rather than a basically ambivalent, approach toward anger that explicitly links child-rearing goals with expectations on the job. It remains to trace the other major aspect of the home/work relationship, the approach toward anger between spouses. Here consistency might in theory have prevailed as well, urging anger control in all settings; but it was complicated by old ambiguities about marital emotional style and new pressures resulting in part from the more intense manipulation of anger in the workplace.

7 The Managerial Style
Fighting Fair in Marriage

New approaches toward anger developing in the workplace and in the socialization of children posed an obvious challenge to the purveyors of marital advice. On the one hand, the effort to reduce anger at work risked adding to the burdens of family emotionality: would people— women as well as men increasingly holding jobs outside the home— need the family as an outlet for angry emotions they could no longer express so freely in office or factory? But at the same time, the effort to extend anger repression might ease some of the burdens on the family, by uniting its emotional standards with broader goals, rather than seeking to preserve the family as a refuge from external reality. And the increasing interest in managing anger, rather than trying to master the emotion as part of rigorous character development, suggested the expansion of tactics that had been hinted at in marital emotionology before the 1930s. Through mangement, older goals of anger minimization might be more readily achieved.

Marital emotionology did respond to the new climate of anger discussion, ultimately by producing a new synthesis of goals and tactics. As we have seen, no single consensus on the issue of anger between spouses had been generated to replace the early Victorian view, despite great concern about the problem of marriage during the turn-of-the-century decades. Synthesis was further retarded by a decline of interest in the emotional side of marriage, in response to the Great Depression and, later, World War II.

But after the war, several factors combined to spur new attention to marriage: the public was aware of the sharp rise in divorce that took place with the return of the soldiers, and both experts and popularizers attempted to stem the flood. There was an increased emphasis on the pleasures of domesticity seen as a retreat from the distasteful world of war. For the first time in many years, prosperity was on the rise, and the nation was at peace; Americans were delighted to turn their attention to their personal lives. Debbie Reynolds, the film star, writing with regret of her own divorce, epitomized the new retreat to the family in her advice to couples to minimize arguments by thinking, "in terms of

190

the atomic bomb, how big is this argument. Most anger doesn't last. . . . When Mr. Khrushchev was here, I became even more aware of this, of the need to put the emphasis on your personal life. In a world threatened by As and Hs [bombs] what is important except to live for those you love.''[1]

With the nation ready, the new professionals were only too glad to spew out reams of advice. Their position had been formulated much earlier, and with the end of the war, public interest coincided with the professional point of view. The reading public consumed vast quantities of their wisdom.

The New Emotionology

The essence of the new thinking, from the expert point of view, was to grant couples permission to acknowledge conflict. The new writers viewed themselves as liberating husbands and wives because for the first time they were telling them that it was natural to have aggressive feelings and even, perhaps, to act on them. Many such arguments would start with an attack on the "myth" that happy couples had no quarrels, sympathize with the spouses who "needlessly" worried every time they bickered, and go on with the reassurance that "a couple need not give up their marriage as lost the first time there is conflict, tension, or a difference between them."[2] All this was very much in line with the new approach at work, which acknowledged that conflicts, even angers, would arise, and with the new literature of child rearing, which claimed to reverse old orthodoxies by facing squarely the fact that all children had angry feelings. A graphic case in point of the new willingness to attend to anger involves the series of advice books by Paul Popenoe, the founder of the American Institute of Family Relations, written between the 1920s and the 1940s. While the earlier books devote only a few lines to quarreling, those appearing in the 1940s devote whole chapters to the subject of conflict between spouses.[3]

Marriage manuals of the earlier part of the century had been prone to explain all conflicts as the result of poor sexual adjustment. Freud, in fact, had been seen by most Americans in the early decades of the century as an advocate of expressive sexuality. It was only in the 1940s that Americans became conscious that Freud had had something to say about aggression as well as about sex. The marriage manuals switched gears so that, increasingly, bad sex became a symptom of a disturbed relationship rather than the other way around. Illness, which also had often been seen as the result of sexual repression, was increasingly viewed in the 1950s and after as the result of repressed anger. This represented a significant change in views of interpersonal relations.[4]

As with the orthodoxy on work and child rearing, however, there were strict limitations on the permission to be angry. Anger was acceptable, but only if it was managed. Most postwar marriage manuals had chapters on handling conflict, but after the initial few paragraphs that defended the idea that conflict, perhaps even outright anger, was all right, the major part of the discussion was usually devoted to how to keep the conflict within stringent boundaries.

Groves and Groves had advised back in the 1920s that, if couples made a habit of quarreling, family peace was in danger. Robert Blood stressed this in a book of advice for the engaged in 1955. He made the distinction between arguing, which was acceptable but not very good, and quarreling, which was downright threatening. Arguing always puts the couple in "mortal danger of slipping over the brink into quarreling," he warned, and quarrels will do more harm than good.[5]

Smart spouses would swallow their anger. If an issue could not be discussed calmly it was better to "write it out."[6] People should tolerate the defects of their partners: "Look at the doughnut not the hole."[7] If one could not repress anger, one could "vent it." Angry people were advised to chop wood, make a cake, or shout into closets to "vent hostility."[8]

A slightly different point of view, which found quarreling better than such methods as shouting into closets, existed from the early postwar years and became more prominent in the late 1960s. It argued that, insofar as conflicts existed, they must be faced and negotiated; but here too the emphasis was on the importance of maintaining limits. Readers were advised to preserve tact at all times and to avoid verbal abuse or shouting matches. Fights should be postponed until times when the couple could be "calm" and keep things under "control." It must always be remembered that the purpose was to come to a resolution of the understanding, not simply to express emotion.[9]

At the same time that they spoke glibly of the universality of aggression, the experts cheerfully advised that anger was the result of problems that had not been worked out in childhood and that in day-to-day life there was really nothing to be angry about. Here was a clear analogy to the approach taken toward anger at work, particularly in the 1930s: anger was the result of something outside the context being analyzed and therefore was not really integral to that context. Hence it should be managed, even though it could not fully be avoided; it had no useful role.

The wonderfully successful "Can This Marriage Be Saved" column, which started in the *Ladies Home Journal* in the 1950s and ran with continually greater frequency, employed this reductionism as the standard line on anger. The format was always to have each spouse speak for himself on his troubled marriage and then to have the answer given by the counselor. The cases were based on real records of the American Institute on Family Relations, founded by Popenoe. Through the early 1970s, anger was always explained as a displacement of tension from childhood, as indeed were all marital problems. The counselor usually got the couple to see this and then patched things up, for in "mature" people there was really nothing to be angry about. The marriage counselor thus did for marriage what the personnel specialist did for work or the sensitive parent for children. The *Journal*'s advice was, "Try not to take personally everything a spouse says in anger. His anger is often based on his own insecurity."[10] Ted, an angry husband discussed in the column, was advised that, since his anger at work and at home was simply the result of his being an angry person from childhood, he should learn to hit inanimate objects when he became angry.[11]

Those who were often angry simply revealed themselves as inadequate people. The Victorians had been forthright about this same point, and the basic judgment had not changed greatly despite new terminology. Angry people were bad people. For the marriage counselors, the key word was "immature": frequent anger resulted, not from a real reason, but from immaturity. A quiz in the *Journal*, "Am I a Disgruntled Wife," concluded that those with too many yes answers could be "expecting too much" and that "your husband is impossible to get along with—or . . . you are."[12] It was all right to quarrel occasionally, but grown-up people put the emphasis on "occasionally." Blood advised that most disputes should be settled in the early years of marriage but that, "once husband and wife have gotten together on how to throw a party, how to make decisions, and how to handle Junior, they can play from memory."[13] Popenoe felt that "most bickering in marriage would stop if husbands and wives would just be polite and 'behave like adults.' "[14] While the writers of the 1960s and 1970s were more likely to acknowledge that quarrels might last beyond the honeymoon years, they too felt that quarrels were about issues that should be "resolved."

Influenced by Freud though they may have been, the emphasis of the marriage counselors was not on feelings but on proper behavior. Feelings were contrasted with rationality, to the disparagement of the former. For instance, Popenoe asked his reader, Is your voice one for peace or war in the home? You can be sure you are on the side of peace if you recognize yourself in the following situations. When you are stopped by a traffic cop, you "wait calmly until he finishes and then state your case without any show of feeling." When your mother-in-law peers into your cupboards, you regard this as a friendly show of interest. But if, when another driver cuts in front of you, "you are irritated," this is a bad sign.[15] Blood, who had made the distinction between arguing and quarreling, advised that, "as long as two people are able to cope with their problems objectively, rational methods work. . . . As long as emotions are still under control, the term 'arguing' can be used. When the emotions run wild, the couple are beginning to 'quarrel.' "[16]

The *Journal*, in its "Making Marriage Work" column, which began in 1947, advised couples to explore their differences. If disagreements arose, a spouse was advised to tell the partner "calmly and reasonably" how he or she felt.[17] As Popenoe so pithily put it, "Stop 'merely expressing yourself' . . . the impulsive person is often too intent on asserting himself. Forget it."[18]

The books published in the 1960s and 1970s were more likely to emphasize that no true intimacy could exist without a sharing of feelings, even angry feelings. But even these books emphasized the importance of rules for behavior at all times, stressing that shouting be avoided, that issues be limited, and that quarrels be made up quickly. The bottom line was that it was all right to fight, but only if the fight led to greater intimacy: "Every marital quarrel is, in a sense, an emotional separation. Every fight is a declaration, both to yourself and to your spouse, 'I am an individual . . .' No matter what the argument is about, it fills one with a heady freedom and a frightening loneliness. But once ended, the quarrel makes the following point: 'No matter how awful I think you may be sometimes . . . it is better to be with you than to be separated.' "[19]

The underlying Victorian distinction between emotion and reason had not been abandoned, and especially in the postwar years, the expression of emotion was seen as potentially threatening to civilized life. The metaphor of the marital quarrel as a war pervaded the literature. One book of advice to brides emphasized calm in conversation: harsh words, these authors counseled, had no place at home. "They belong in the commands of an army perhaps, but home talk is not army talk . . . [and later] make your home a place of emotional security, not an armed camp or battlefield."[20] Popenoe advised against the danger that aggressiveness presented to romance. The prime example of unbridled aggression he cited was Hitler, but all people were aggressive. "Man is one of the few [animals] which systematically makes war on his own species." It was important when fighting with a spouse not to use "weapons" you might regret.[21] For the *Ladies Home Journal* editors, in 1947, "ill-considered divorce may be as threatening as a third world war. . . . irresponsible men and women are as dangerous as atomic bombs."[22] One should remember that "criticism should not be performed like a flank attack with all guns blazing."[23] Quarreling spouses should always be willing to give an "armistice" on demand.[24] Even for George Bach and Peter Wyden, who wrote with the ostensible purpose of encouraging couples to fight more, the repeatedly used metaphor for going too far was creating a "nuclear explosion" or risking a "Pearl Harbor" or "dropping the bomb on Luxembourg."[25] This widespread use of the war metaphor is interesting, not simply because it tells us something of the source of the new interest in the subject of aggression, but because it reveals quite plainly just how dangerous marital quarreling was seen to be, even by those counselors who ostensibly encouraged readers to let it all hang out.

One is certainly reminded of the Victorian stress on controlling feeling in reading this advice. How, indeed, were these counselors, with their stress on the danger of emotion, different from the Victorians? From our point of view, there may not have been a great deal of difference. It is only fair, however, to point out that the counselors claimed at least to be scientific. If we find their science more facade than substance, this is not how they saw themselves.

The counselors felt that they based their recommendations on the science of sociology, just as the child-rearing experts claimed the science of psychology. They were, from the beginning, enamored of surveys, which they used to make statements about what did and did not work in marriage. The thrust of this approach changed somewhat after the war. The prewar surveys, most heavily influenced by Freudian notions, concentrated on analyzing the personality characteristics that could be correlated with spouses who claimed to be happily married. From this, recommendations were made on the choice of a good spouse. In fact, the earlier marriage manuals often spent more time on choosing the right spouse than on what to do with him once chosen. To readers more sophisticated than these early samplers were, this approach, relying heavily on the individual's own assessment of some nebulously defined "happiness," appears far from scientific. Not surprisingly, the conclusions for the most part were that if one were to be happily married one should pick a kind of conservative, conforming, and phlegmatic mate and attempt to become such a person oneself.[26] Happy people made happy marriages. One wonders just how different this is from the Victorian belief that virtue was rewarded. Nonetheless, if the surveys were not quite scientific, at least they tried to be.

The notion that science should be applied to making the right choice faded from view after the war. Perhaps American democracy could not long tolerate a science that after all distinguished between the saved (or happy) and the damned (or unhappy) so irrevocably. Perhaps the marriage counselors felt that they could be kept busier giving advice for the entire duration of the marriage than simply for the initial choice. At any rate, after the war the surveys shifted to emphasize the study of what sort of techniques or methods could be used to keep husbands and wives happy. Now the claim was that everyone could enter the land of the saved—that is, with a little professional guidance.

The popular marriage advice books made an effort to look scientific. Some had glossaries. Almost all of them liked to make general statements and then to offer, in different print or indented to look important, a list of numbered "rules." These writers grasped at anything that seemed to have the veneer of quantification. Thus couples were advised that things would go well if they followed certain rules for "six months" or that there "cannot be much happiness in marriage until adjustment is achieved within at least four of these areas."[27] "Making Marriage Work" always had a narrative section on a particular problem and then featured a quiz by which the reader could "test" himself for this or some other difficulty by toting up his "score." Our readers may be curious as to what, after all, these scientists advised. Let us offer one example from a 1950 "Making Marriage Work." To prevent quarrels, mates were told to (1) get enough sleep, (2) get up early enough to get a leisurely start, (3) don't try to do too much, (4) don't retort if your spouse is angry, (5) time discussions of problems carefully, and (6) avoid blame.[28] It is possible, certainly, that the content of this commonsensical advice may have been useful to some readers. What seems overblown, however, is the claim to science. For this was merely prosaic wisdom enumerated.

Perhaps one reason it was difficult to be scientific is that the purveyors and consumers of the advice literature insisted that the conclusion of all the research be cheerful. Freud's pessimism would not sell books or magazines. Anger might be discussed so long as the reader could be promised that, if he minded the techniques or, at worst, consulted a professional, all would end well. Popenoe's blurb in one of the early columns of "Can This Marriage Be Saved" assured readers that "fortunately human nature is inherently so well adapted to marriage that we are able to aid 80% of these people to straighten out their difficulties." Indeed, in our perusal of some forty of these columns, we came across only one in which the counsellor did not stave off divorce. The message was that anger was a kind of mistake that arose because of lack of communication. If only couples spoke freely and honestly, no differences need remain. "The Nileses *communicate*," explained one author in describing a marital success. The wife continued, " 'We've agreed that if something bothers us, we get it off our chests, and then it's over.' . . . For a time they had a heart to heart conversation every Sunday night about the minor annoyances bound to crop up in a week of a new marriage. . . . Now they communicate so constantly and so well that the Sunday night conferences have been abandoned.''[29]

Annoyances were bound to be minor and even these expected only in a new marriage. Communication was in itself to be healing. A quiz in "Making Marriage Work," "What Are Your Grievances," advised readers that, if the score was too high, this was "a sure sign that you and your husband are not talking things over freely and frankly."[30] Couples who talked frankly only to discover that they disliked each other more than ever were not considered.

We have not yet discussed whether the new consensus on anger made the same distinction between the sexes that the Victorians did. For the most part, the nineteenth-century line between men who felt but could control anger and women who did not even feel it was dropped by the modern writers. Although there were distinctions made in advice to the two sexes, for the most part these distinctions did not rest on the view that their natures were intrinsically distinctive.

Insofar as different advice was offered, it was based more on the notion of separation of spheres; the stress was on the woman's primary responsibility for maintaining the marriage, and the man was given some latitude at home because of his difficulties outside. This sort of distinction peaked in the years immediately after the war and was consonant with the general mood in America to thrust women back into the home. The *Journal,* which had been receptive to career women up until this point, printed articles stressing the dangers of two-career marriages.[31] There was a resurgence of the Victorian theme of the difficulty of dealing with the world outside the home. Wives were advised to put up with the irritability of returning soldiers in consideration of the terrible hardships they had experienced.[32] This theme, however, did not long predominate. By 1950, a rough equality of expectations for the sexes in the matter of anger control prevailed.

This new consensus was remarkable, certainly, for its similarity to the Victorian synthesis. With a brief nod to the universality of anger in marriage, the new writers shifted their emphasis immediately to the importance of controlling that anger. As the Victorians had predicted disaster for those who could not control dangerous feelings, so did the new writers—the major disaster being, quite clearly, divorce. If the Victorians used the concept of moral virtue to separate those who could and those who could not keep the lid on, the new writers substituted the notion of "maturity"; but the message was not vastly different.

In some areas, though, there was a change. Certainly, it was not unimportant to acknowledge that everyone got angry and, further, to extend that privilege to females, to whom it had once been denied. Some of the implications of this change will be explored shortly. Certainly, also, the dominant theme of managerial optimism was new. The message now was that there were always some techniques to try, some professional to consult, if things were not going well. If the science offered was spurious, nonetheless the message was a new one: people who got angry were not irrevocably damned but, rather, could do something for themselves.

What of the Victorian tensions between the belief that full and open communication was possible and the necessity for eschewing feelings that might come between the couple? Although the 1950s certainly touted "communication" between spouses, we are struck by a slight shift in the tension toward the other pole. There was an increase in the superficial jokiness in the new treatment of conflict that had not existed before. For instance, while the domestic fiction in *Godey's* had often depicted strong and passionate men and women and is capable of eliciting, even today, a serious response from the reader, the fiction that appeared in the *Journal* after the war was almost entirely escapist in nature. Conflicts were usually joked about, and things almost always ended up happily, the couple amazed that they could ever fight in the first place. The husbands and wives are passionless to the point of being unbelievable. Quite apart from an arguable decrease in the literary quality of this fiction, what shines through is the reflection of the general effort to trivialize angry passion. Whereas Victorians tried to isolate anger by designating powerfully angry people, contemporaries, forced to grant the universality of anger, worked to demonstrate that the emotion, though a potential nuisance, was never deeply felt. Anger in marriage here united with anger at work and in childhood. The same insistence on making light of conflict emerged in the *Journal*'s regular feature "If I Were," an advice column in which each sex could contribute suggestions, on a theme, as to how they would run things better if they had the other sex's tasks. The humor was useful in that it allowed the sexes to express a consciousness that their interests were not quite coincident at the same time that the significance of the divergence was minimized or laughed away. It is as if, once the universality of anger was acknowledged, a consistently serious approach could not be maintained, for this would force readers to look the demon in the eye more clearly than anyone was ready to do. So the demon was acknowledged and then winked at. A brief nod was made to anger, and then the reader was assured that it could be conquered and dismissed, preferably as quickly and as permanently as possible.

Causation

The causes of the development of the new consensus on anger in marriage were much the same as in the new consensus on children, for the message on marriage and child rearing was one and the same: anger was acknowledged more plainly than it had been and then was to be managed into oblivion. The marriage counselors, like the child experts, were familiar with Freud and increasingly familiar with his thought on aggression as well as on sexuality. The war had certainly spawned a new interest in the general subject of aggression as well as a pervasive belief that emotions, when not well controlled, could be extremely dangerous.

It is noteworthy, though, that as with the child-rearing literature the new consensus on anger had begun to emerge among professionals well before the war. The fact that the war metaphor was used for marital conflict so widely means not simply that war directed attention to conflict but rather that critics were unconsciously prepared to see even the most minimal conflict as a potential war. The most basic assumption in the marriage literature was that all conflict was essentially undesirable and all anger dangerous, and this assumption predated the war. Where did it come from?

Although the child-rearing literature speaks explicitly of a need to form personalities suited to participate in a new sort of work environment, there is no such conscious avowal in the marriage literature. Reading between the lines, however, it is clear that the requirements of the new work world had been so thoroughly accepted that there was no reason to state goals explicitly. Whether conflict-free interpersonal relationships were ideal was not asked but rather assumed. With this came the again unquestioned assumption that those who frequently found themselves in conflict must have something wrong with them; that is, they were immature. Just as, in the world of work, keeping the machine functioning smoothly was the number one goal, so in marriage staving off the ultimate rupture, divorce, came first. The expression of feeling was repeatedly disparaged as unimportant compared to maintaining the right behaviors. And there was the pervasive sense that feelings, unmonitored, were more dangerous than helpful—which means that, implicitly, a great deal of attention had to be paid to repressive manipulation.

The new family sociology that developed in the 1920s and 1930s and formed the intellectual foundation of marriage counseling was starkly different from the family sociology of the Progressive era. That sociology had seen the family as an institution buffeted by and created by a larger society and as essentially passive. The family unit and the individuals within it were so dependent on the complex world around them that they had almost no potential or responsibility to alter themselves. The new view isolated the family from the larger world and emphasized the interpersonal, psychological relationships within this small unit. Although this radical about-face has been commented on, it has never been entirely explained. To say that the interactionists were influenced by psychology describes the phenomenon but hardly accounts for it.[33]

Certainly, it would be absurd to argue that family sociologists deliberately set out to justify a new economic system, but it is remarkable that, whatever their motives, the new family sociology did work harmoniously with new standards for the work world. Emphasis was placed increasingly on the individual's and family's responsibility for its own well-being. Those who could not maintain proper behavior were dismissed as "immature." The brief Progressive flirtation with the notion that society had an overwhelming responsibility to the family and the individual had been abandoned. Victorian phraseology, referring to good and evil people, had been altered, but the message that if things did not work out it was your own fault was essentially Victorian. The new orthodoxy, then, whether conscious or not, was well designed to suppress the desire to question authority or to stir up dissension. The personality styles and goals of the new work world were so widely accepted that they were unquestioningly adopted, with little change, in the home environment. People who were taught to be embarrassed by raising their voices in anger or by finding themselves bickering with colleagues would not have been able totally to reorient themselves at home. Standards for child rearing and marriage were, not surprisingly, similar to standards at work. The fact that more and more women, especially after World War II, joined the work force encouraged an emotionology that treated the sexes as essentially the same. It is perhaps no surprise that one sociologist of marriage has found that middle-class couples, who, we would argue, were more prototypical of the new work world than blue-collar workers were, are also far more embarrassed and distressed by their quarrels than are working-class couples.[34]

Variations on the Theme

As with child rearing, the new consensus on marriage has not changed drastically since it was created around mid-century. There have been two periods of alteration, however, that merit some discussion. The period from the late 1920s until the end of the war differed in a few respects from the postwar period. First, as has been mentioned before, there was less interest in marriage before the war, as reflected both in the numbers of manuals and in the attention to the topic in popular literature such as the *Ladies Home Journal,* than there was to be later. Insofar as a consensus about managing anger was being developed among professionals, it was not of widespread interest to the general public. We have argued above that this disparity probably resulted from the public focus on the great problems of depression and then war. Popular literature on marriage tended to have an escapist quality, and at the same time there may have been a commonsense refusal on the part of the public to buy a professional point of view that ignored the massive problems of the outside world by telling couples that if they had problems it was their own fault. The emerging professional point of view was quite similar to what it was to be after the war, with the one exception that the prewar literature had a less massive sense of the general problem of aggression. Anger between spouses before the war was most often seen as the result of improper resolution of a few central issues, usually sex, money, and in-laws, and paragraphs or even chapters might be devoted to specific tips on handling these touchy issues.[35] After the war, the issues would more often be seen as subheadings under the general problem of marital adjustment and aggression. Tips focused not so much on issues per se as on general methods of conflict resolution.[36]

Another change in the marital advice literature has been mentioned by some writers as occurring in the late 1960s and early 1970s. Carol Tavris, for instance, has seen this as a period of renewed permissiveness to let all emotion hang out and, indeed, to feel and act angry.[37]

Where do we stand today in our view of marital anger? Is Tavris correct in claiming there has been a moderation of the constraints of the postwar years? Certainly, in the late 1960s and in the 1970s, a new interest in teaching people to assert themselves became prevalent among mental health professionals. During this period in which special interest groups began to assert themselves and even stridently and unapologetically to voice their anger, rage seemed such a predictable feature of the news that historians might judge that the public became desensitized to its frightening aspects. As the women's movement directed its attention to demanding rights, people began, inevitably, to talk about anger between the sexes and anger in marriage. Is it true that the mood of the late 1960s and 1970s really represented a change in the emotionology of anger in the home?

The Intimate Enemy by George R. Bach and Peter Wyden, published in 1968, proclaimed it would teach people how to fight fair in love and marriage. A popular success, it was excerpted in the *Ladies Home Journal* and became a Book of the Month Club selection. Assuring readers that screaming and even hitting one's spouse were not beyond the pale, the authors claimed that anger was inevitable between intimates and offered to teach readers to use it constructively.

Popular opinion did not immediately embrace this notion entirely, and it was not until the mid-1970s that one begins to see frequent evidence of it in the *Journal*. Dr. Theodore Rubin, a psychiatrist who wrote a monthly advice column, embraced this view wholeheartedly, assuring readers that in good marriages spouses did not always have to make up before bedtime[38] and that, in fact, they would be better off if they could express anger. "Too many of us convert the response of normal, healthy anger to what we believe is 'civilized' behavior. . . . if we freeze one emotion, we cannot expect to remain healthily responsive in other areas. . . . blocks of unexpressed anger actually inhibit the free flow of loving feelings."[39] Even "Can This Marriage Be Saved" picked up some of the new view. In one issue, the subheading read, " 'Quarreling is childish' says Steve. 'Apologizing is hypocritical' says Eve. But unless you express those angry and sorry feelings where are they supposed to hide?"[40]

Popenoe never expressed any sense of irony as he raced to the forefront of the new view: "Many intelligent men and women are under the mistaken impression that expressing anger is dangerous and destructive to a marital relationship. . . . If we could free our children from the fear that so many of us have of expressing our emotions, marriages would be better."[41] Strange, considering that this same expert had led the voices warning of the dangers of anger only a few short years before.

We argue, however, that it would be a mistake to make too much of the new encouragement toward anger, for it never totally changed the consensus, and insofar as it intended modification, that modification was very short-lived. Even those who spoke of the virtues of anger maintained the older point of view throughout.

Carol Tavris's fashionable book on anger takes a firm stance "in praise of civility" or, in other words, against the "free" expression of the anger she sees as widespread. Although she claims to be arguing against a prevalent view that anger needs to be expressed, her view is in fact the prevalent one and has been since the early nineteenth century.

If, in the early 1970s, there was some brief attention to the notion that anger in marriage should be expressed, even during that period and even among the main proponents of that idea plain limits were always stated. For instance, Bach and Wyden were concerned about teaching people to fight fairly rather than cruelly. For all their touting of self-expression, the purpose of the expression of anger, stated quite baldly, was to enhance intimacy.[42] Angry feelings were valuable because they directed spouses to the confrontation of problems, but problems could be solved. Permanent anger was not necessary. In sum, the new approach, while recognizing some new problems of domestic anger as suggested by feminism, introduced a newly labeled set of tactics to reach previously established goals.[43]

A *Journal* article on "How to Fight with a Man You Love," published in 1980, admitted that all good relationships would be punctuated by "rip-roaring fights." But once admitting this, it went on to warn that the fights were acceptable only if they generated an acceptable "solution" to a couple's problems and if people refrained from fighting "below the belt." The author also cautioned against shouting, for one cannot discern the meaning in an argument if one is shouting.[44] In other words, one could be angry if at the same time one could be under control! An autobiographical piece by a woman whose problem was a "slob husband" related how she had usually ended up screaming at her husband because of his messy habits until, seeing the light, she asked herself "if I had ever tried to iron out our differences in a calm, rational way."[45]

Rubin, who advised couples that it was all right to yell at each other, also insisted that such couples would be able to laugh at themselves.[46] Popenoe, for all his encouragement to expressing feelings, had not changed the tone of "Can This Marriage Be Saved" significantly. The counselor's 1980 account of how he handled Betsy, a wife who had tantrums, could have been published thirty years earlier. "The next time Betsy threw a tantrum, Guy followed my directions. . . . he grabbed his screaming, kicking, floor stamping wife, shoved her out of the door . . . and locked it. . . . he wouldn't let her back in until she was quiet. This sharp change in his response to unreasonable behavior was eventually effective. Betsy learned to manage her temper."[47] So much for the free expression of anger!

The new nod to anger was short-lived and always muted. Couples were advised that problems could be solved, that the purpose of anger management was to work out and then lessen the anger, and that anger between spouses, when handled properly, would be "short lived."[48]

The point of the advice on anger in marriage, even when there was some superficial encouragement to express the feeling, was that the marriage came first. It was not all right to admit that you might feel angry enough to leave the marriage. It was not all right to consider that, once the feelings were all expressed, the most profound feeling might be mutual antipathy. It was not all right to be angry if one lost control to the point of losing one's sense of humor. It was not all right to be angry if one lost control to the point of fighting "unfairly," of expressing hoarded up grievances, or even—tactical rationality triumphant—of neglecting to make an appointment before starting a quarrel.

It is hard to believe that people who feel really angry can manage to observe all these constraints, but the effort to constrain demonstrates that the new "permission" to be angry was not essentially novel. The new rhetoric, rather, was a nod to the assertive mood of the early 1970s, to the new feminism, and to the rising divorce rate. But a nod only. The new consensus that had arisen after the war was tempered only slightly.

It is also of note that, despite the claims of authors such as Bach and Wyden or Theodore Rubin that they were saying something dramatically new, there had been, even in the 1940s and 1950s, a spectrum of views on anger control in marriage. As early as 1945, Evelyn Duvall and Reuben Hill, in the widely cited *When You Marry,* had argued that some open conflict was permissible, preferable in fact to letting conflict smolder. They, like Bach and Wyden, deplored the fact that couples who came to them for counseling seemed to feel they were failures if they fought at all. Like Bach and Wyden, with their permission to quarrel, they offered many pages of advice on how to keep the quarrel in check.[49] James Peterson, in a textbook on marriage written in 1956, took as permissive a view as Bach and Wyden would on the desirability of some conflict, and even anger, in marriage and was unusual in offering no rules for containing fights.[50] We are arguing, in other words, that the new consensus acknowledged anger and tried to contain it but that from its inception there were some writers who put more emphasis on facing the anger and others who put more emphasis on managing it. For a brief period in the late 1960s and early 1970s, the pendulum may have swung slightly toward those who acknowledged anger, but this was a minor shift, and during this period, although the ostensible message was a new permission to be angry, the constraints were never lifted very far.

Thus even in the emotionology of the early 1970s one must still take quizzes, one must follow rules and techniques, one must set aside a regular time to quarrel. We cannot help noticing the obsessive-compulsive flavor in all this; and the flavor is hardly surprising, for the obsessive's desire is to be in constant motion in order to maintain control. His fear is that, if he lets up for a second, his true self will emerge, and that self is a lazy, sloppy animal dominated by lust, greed, anger, and other unacceptable feelings. We may note that the obsessive-compulsive style characterizing the new consensus was probably a healthier one than the prevalent Victorian styles of denial, conversion, projection, and reaction formation. Still, if the obsessive-compulsive did have some glimmer of reality, in this case the recognition that anger did exist, his emphasis was on the necessity for controlling that reality, controlling that anger.

Emotions and Expression

Was there more or less real anger felt and expressed in marriage during the period in which the new emotionological consensus took hold? We have argued that new emotional standards and their institutional implementation did have a demonstrable effect on work and may have encouraged some changes in modal personality in child rearing. In marriage, however, the disparity between standards and results so vivid since the Victorian era seems to have persisted, perhaps even increased, in the contemporary period. Of course there is no way to chart rates of anger or tactics actually used. But older themes continued, particularly the burdens placed on marriage by the increasing emphasis assigned to the institution as a source of emotional support and the tendency to judge oneself, at least in part, by one's emotional success as a spouse. And, given decreasing opportunity to express anger in the workplace, the temptation to use marriage as an outlet may even have increased.[51] There was some sense in the marriage manuals that men, particularly, did use their homes to vent the wrath that they had been forced to stifle at work. At least one sociological study found, in fact, that the degree of hostility expressed by men at home was directly related to the amount of frustration experienced on the job. Though most marriage manuals frowned on the practice of using the home to vent anger, they did acknowledge that the practice existed; at least one book, in fact, suggested that "providing a place where one can safely drain off hostility that has accumulated in the outside world is one of the important mental health functions of a good marriage." There must have been many men like Teddy, who, having absorbed the message that he must stifle temper on the job, "had no difficulty keeping his small-boy side locked away while he was at work." This meant he became angry at home: "To him, 'relaxing' at home had come to mean letting the small boy call the shots and bully everybody."[52]

Insofar as others, as well as Teddy, took their work problems out on their wives, there may well have been a new surge of angry behavior at home. The growing equality of women, at least financial equality, may well have been another cause of increased anger at home or at least of increased expression of anger; one sociologist, at least, has argued that in marriage it is only relative equals who fight.[53]

What of the quality of the experience of the couples exposed to the new consensus on anger? Again we are in the land of speculation, but some tentative suggestions may be offered. First, we may note that there is some evidence in the advice books that American couples, at least those seen by counselors, have remained uncomfortable with their own anger. From the 1940s on, those who wrote books insisting that some quarreling was only to be expected usually started by noting how many of their clients had been disturbed by the "myth" of conflict-free homes. Thus Duvall and Hill wrote in 1945: "We are burdened today with the vestiges of the self-righteous sweetness and light mode of thinking. The hundreds of couples who come to marital guidance clinics regularly to gain relief from guilty feelings of unworthiness because they quarrel at home are living proof of this assertion."[54] But the message remains unchanged in 1968 for Bach and Wyden, who argue that fight phobia is a common cause of divorce,[55] and in 1979 for Baldwin, who worries that too many people "just don't understand that much of their bickering and hostility is perfectly normal, understandable and appropriate. Their problem isn't that they are angry with each other; it's that they think they shouldn't be angry with each other."[56] It would appear that, however realistic the writers of the 1940s attempted to be in facing anger, readers never became entirely comfortable with the emotion.

One survey reported that an overwhelming majority of couples felt bad—increasingly angry, guilty, or unloved if they became emotional in quarreling with one another. In 1951, a Gallup poll showed that, of the traits people most disliked in their mates, bad temper was number one on the list for both sexes. The ambivalence of the emotionology was perhaps better understood and absorbed by the reading public than by the writers themselves.[57]

Working-class couples also report some discomfort with marital anger. "God, I was so scared," reported one wife, "I didn't know what to do. I felt sorry for him and I felt angry at him. It was like the two feelings were always there inside me, fighting with each other, until I got a terrible headache. Or else I'd get so upset, I'd throw up and not be able to eat." And a husband who wishes he could be like his single friends notes, "It's funny, the more I did that, the worse things got between us. I guess she kind of knew what I was thinking and that would make her mad. Then I'd get even madder because I couldn't even *think* what I wanted anymore without her starting up a fight." A wife worried that "I feel like I go crazy-angry sometimes. It makes me say and do things to Randy or the kids that I hate myself for." And a man is upset with his wife's anger: "When she comes after me like that, yapping like that, she might as well be hitting me with a bat. . . . It makes me feel like I'm doing something wrong, like I'm not a very good husband or something."[58]

Some observers of modern mores, particularly those with a strong feminist point of view, have claimed a gender difference in the internalization of anger-control standards in marriage. They argue that a Victorianism in this area persists that allows men to be more comfortable with rage while inhibiting these feelings in women.[59] Certainly, women continue to display some indirect expressions of anger that are less common in men, particularly their greater resort to crying when angry.[60] Without question, many women show a virtually Victorian inhibition from childhood on. Witness the case of Elizabeth: "I wasn't brought up to fight with my husband. My timid little mother never raised her voice to my loud-mouthed, bad-tempered father; she used to tell me patience was a woman's weapon."[61] But it is inaccurate to portray Victorianism as clearly authorizing male anger and inaccurate as well to ignore the confusions and inhibitions that men feel in dealing with anger in marriage. The men interviewed by Lillian Rubin were not noticeably more comfortable with marital anger than were the women. Husbands and wives, in the survey cited above, were equally uncomfortable after expressing anger.[62] In a case study of one family, Jean Baker Miller noted that both spouses were extremely anxious about becoming angry with one another.[63]

Discomfort with anger on the part of both sexes had been encouraged by family emotionology from the eighteenth century on. It is quite possible, however, that it has gained ground with time as the basic effort to control marital anger has sunk in, responding to successive generations of experts. Discomfort might certainly be increased by changes in the official standards of child rearing, which sought more fully to extirpate serious anger after 1940. If the causes of anger in marriage increased because of new constraints of work and the confusion engendered by women's new work roles, or even if they remained constant, a growing anxiety about anger in marriage might itself contribute to emotional discomfort. We are accustomed to expert renderings of the modern problem of divorce as resulting, in part, from the high expectations of love that form part of the modern ideal. An important addition to this must now be the realization of a high expectation of anger avoidance and a resulting vulnerability to anger actually expressed. As many marriages may end because of wounded feelings over anger in an institution supposed to be exempt from serious conflict as end from the realization that the bloom of love has withered.

In terms of actual experience, it may be speculated that the adaptation in the consensus introduced in the 1960s and 1970s led not only to some changes in behavior but also to enormous feelings of confusion. Carol Tavris has cited surveys showing that people who express anger often as a result feel bad and even more angry. We would argue that this is not the result of some universal in human nature to regret the expression of anger but rather that this follows from the fact that people who have been socialized in a culture that has for two hundred years urged repression cannot feel comfortable with a new permissiveness, particularly when the permissiveness is hedged and transient.[64] New tactical advice may have encouraged husbands and wives to do a bit more shouting in the 1970s, but the effect of this may have stimulated guilt and anger. The advice literature was hardly consistent in its permission to be angry, always urging that maturity demanded restraint and that loss of control would destroy a marriage. Anyone discussing marital anger as a topic with friends must be struck by the intensity of interest they express and by their visible relief in finding someone, at last, with whom they can discuss their personal experiences. This reflects a persistent anxiety that they are the only couple who scream at each other, who express deep anger—that all this anger means that the marriage is a big mistake. Although there have been some significant changes in the view on marital anger during the past two hundred years, it is clear that once the Victorian ideal was established it substantially endured and made realistic confrontation of anger in marriage exceedingly difficult. Even recently, a brief and modest foray into a more open discussion of anger, with Bach and Wyden, immediately produced the countersurge, represented by Carol Tavris and others, to warn that the floodgates were crumbling. And so, though we do not manage to avoid anger in marriage, we do largely manage to avoid talking about it frankly.

Despite the importance of the basic continuity in marital standards toward anger, some comment must be offered on the visible changes in actual behavior and, notably, the increase in divorce rates. The rising divorce rate does not of course prove an increase in marital anger—it may rather suggest a growing discomfort with existing levels—but it certainly demonstrates innovation in form. And it is certainly possible that the high divorce rate follows from an increase in the rate of anger between spouses; it unquestionably shows that anger was often present.

Another way to think about divorce and anger is to argue that, over the past century, the literature on anger in marriage was in some sense a response or, more precisely, a reaction to the recognition of marital fragility. The groping of the post-Victorian period represented an effort to deal with the new divorce statistics. The more recent managerial consensus, although formulated by professionals much earlier, became popular during a period when the divorce rate had risen higher than ever before. Conflict in marriage for the first time had become an issue, a topic that sold magazines and books. The public knew that, with women making some of the same claims to self-expression that had always belonged to men, conflict in marriage was inevitable. This was accommodated in the new literature, which admitted that fights did occur, but the literature then moved quickly to rescue the traditional standards by warning partners about keeping things from going too far. The brief flurry of books in the late 1960s and early 1970s that claimed to encourage mates to let it all hang out were also, in their way, a response to the widely publicized new surge in the divorce rate. Again, the purpose of this literature was to accommodate reality, but within a framework that tried to keep the institution of marriage intact.

Is it possible to think of this literature in any other way? Andrew Cherlin has written an excellent book on the marriage and divorce statistics of the last century, arguing that these express a fundamental trend toward the liberation of the individual. He sees the 1950s, the only period during which the divorce rate went down even slightly, as a strange exception that must be explained in terms of the particular events of the 1930s, most notably, the Great Depression. It might be possible to apply his argument to the expression of anger, claiming that individualism among other things manifests itself in increasingly untrammeled displays of temper.[65] Certainly, the rising divorce rate may reflect increasing levels of angry conflict, provoked by a need for individual expression after the constraints felt at work, the new role shifts on the part of women plus dispute over domestic chores, or simply a pleasure in being feisty as the spirit moves. But we argue that the relationship between divorce rates and anger remains more complex. Official standards and, to a considerable extent, the values individuals bring to actual marriages continue to urge anger control. Despite the emotionological blip of the 1970s, which might support an extension of Cherlin's argument that would see angry conflict as a manifestation of individual self-actualization, there was no fundamental trend toward greater acceptability of open expressions of anger. The strength of recent reactions, attacking a shift in standards that had not in fact occurred, demonstrates the power of emotionological continuity. Tactics changed, toward managerial strategies, but no new goal of individual emotional license emerged. Bach and Wyden's ideas represented only a brief flash in the pan, and even they had more in common with the managerial counselors than they realized. Today, most writers on marriage temper their advice to express anger with great caution.

Thus divorce trends do not follow from increased comfort with an idea that individual emotional freedom should take precedence over marriage. They may reflect more conflict, but still more clearly they reflect the sensitivity to anger, as well as the romantic idealization of marriage, promoted by the long-standing emotionology. Contemporaries still want marriage very badly, as recent increases in the marriage rate suggest, and they are still hungry for advice that will show them how to make it work in terms of their emotional standards—including advice on controlling anger.[66] Insofar as marital anger continues to be expressed, as during the past two centuries, it reflects both high expectations and emotional pressures from other aspects of life, and it creates fear and anxiety precisely because most people still seek in marriage an avoidance of anger. Thus divorce must be seen as resulting not simply from rampant individualism but from high, and in many ways unrealistic, ideals about the love that can be found in marriage and the anger that must be absent.[67]

Could the tensions between marriage and anger lessen? Acceptance of anger in marriage would have to result from a decrease in the emotional expectations of the institution or a greatly heightened confidence in its survivability. Neither seems likely. We may often need marriage as an outlet for anger, but we reject official recognition of the fact if only because we wish to foreclose the legitimacy of anger directed at ourselves. We recognize but resent the fragility of modern marriage and so remain afraid of the forces that might disrupt it. However much behavior may stray from the norm, most contemporaries agree with the experts that marital success or failure results primarily from the efforts of the partners involved: it is up to us. It is appealing to imagine a situation in which spouses recognize that anger is the inevitable and continuous product of the interaction of two human beings and cannot be "dealt with" or "solved" in the early years of marriage. It is appealing to imagine a situation in which people trust their own egos enough to express their emotions even when they are not rational and calm. We doubt, though, that, in a society that makes as strong a bifurcation between reason and emotion as our own, this will happen very soon.

In the meantime, we pay a heavy price for our illusions about anger. We worry that if we express ourselves we will irritate our spouses to the point that they will desert us or we will reveal ourselves as immature. We accept that it is legitimate, even necessary, to express some anger, but then we torture ourselves about whether we are doing it in the right way, at the right time, perhaps too little, perhaps too much. We strive for consistency. We seek to manage our tempers and adhere to the same goals in our relationships at home as in those at work. We raise our children to act the same way. But we are not comfortable with ourselves.

8 Conclusion
Keeping the Lid On

Continuities

At this point—the mid-1980s—in a complex evolution of American attitudes toward anger, it is important to stress the fundamental continuities. Since the desire to recognize and control anger arose—perhaps within some families in the colonial period, somewhat more widely by the later eighteenth century—advice literature and other forms of exhortation, including both religious and behavioral science tracts, have pursued the goal of limiting the expression of anger with considerable diligence. The goal of restraining anger thus forms an important part of the American character ideal over a two hundred year span. We have seen that recent attempts to portray American character as particularly angry or to criticize a presumed contemporary propensity for freewheeling ventilation of anger are off the mark. Such attempts, accurately picking up some cues from a few atypical sources and misreading the basic intent of some tactical advice, largely in fact continue the campaign begun by the predecessors of the early Victorians. The critics of "ventilation" have misread their recent history, which has, if anything, become less rather than more permissive, and they maintain anger as a central emotional enemy.

Reflecting the long campaign against anger, Americans rated anger control as one of the most important personal characteristics in an exhaustive late 1970s survey of national attitudes. Ability to keep one's temper was one of the five most commonly mentioned strengths—"When I get into an argument with someone, I know how to calm things down quickly"—and, among these five, one of the most detailed, least homespun-moralistic responses in the general category of personal strengths and weaknesses.[1] Thus has the prolonged battle to control anger borne fruit, not only in the goal of seeking internal restraint over anger and disapproving those who lack this restraint, but also in the intensity with which this goal is held.

Insistence on the durability of the basic campaign against anger is important for two reasons. First, in this important emotional respect at least, it qualifies efforts to define a brand-new, late twentieth-century

American character. While contemporary anger-control patterns do have some distinctive features, and possibly some ominous ones, they do not cast off entirely from previous modern patterns. Perhaps in other respects, also, contemporary character will prove to be a major variant on larger modern trends and not the entirely new animal that some critics have assumed.

Second, and more relevant to the examination of anger itself, the persistence of the attempt to control anger, despite significant variations in phrasing and tactics, makes particularly plausible the possibility that anger control has had real effects, either in reducing certain expressions of the emotion or in creating new levels of guilt and anxiety when the emotion breaks through. If basic standards for anger control altered every generation or two, the possibility that emotionology had serious effects on actual experience would be slight; behaviors, in intractable areas such as socialization, do not alter so quickly. Generational shifts might still be significant in describing cultural assessments of emotion or even some institutions set up to deal with or reflect emotion, but their reach would probably be limited. With anger control, we are dealing with a more basic modern phenomenon, which is why, by the twentieth century, one can discern some wide ramifications of the campaign beyond the individual, diary-entry concerns about temper control that dot the late eighteenth and the nineteenth centuries.

The durability of the basic interest in limiting anger reflects durable causes. We have seen that some factors shaping the campaign against anger did shift periodically, producing a distinctive articulation and some distinctive tactics. But the movement to control anger responds fundamentally to several factors running through the American experience (and in many respects, doubtless, the modern Western experience) over the past two centuries. Three sets of factors are involved.

1. The initial tendency to focus the anger-control effort on the family (though with the family often assumed to provide a more general formation of character) related to some changes in the definition and valuation of family functions from the late seventeenth century on. Initially, these changes owed much to the new esteem for familial warmth generated by Protestantism and other ideological forces peculiar to that period. In a larger sense, however, the concentration on anger control was a response to the decline of traditional church and community supervision of behavior and the desire to replace this supervision with internalized restraints. In a society that was beginning to change rapidly, with the expansion of market economic relationships and the dislocations caused by population growth, internal control seemed essential if social and personal life were not to become completely random. The importance of anger control in defining a home environment separate

from the buffetings of life in the marketplace was an extension of this felt need to inculcate personal emotional restraint. In the late eighteenth century and the early Victorian decades, of course, anger control was part of a broader pattern of internalized restraints. But anger control outlived this generalized campaign, remaining crucial in the development of personal mastery in a changing environment. More than other kinds of restraints, including sexual restraint, anger control has continued to be a vital tool in a society marked by a persistent need to deal with unpredictability and concourse with strangers in the absence of firm behavioral guidelines enforced by established community authorities. The growth of population and resultant crowding and particularly the experience of urbanization have provided consistent spurs to this emotional motif; unfettered anger became increasingly risky, as it had earlier, for example, in East Asian societies, where large numbers of people had to interact in a limited space.

2. Along with new needs for personal control came a culture that pressed increasingly for more democratic social behavior. From the Enlightenment on, and particularly in the United States, an egalitarian strain has affected at least superficial social behavior. In the eighteenth century itself, new egalitarian ideals contributed to the new standards of behavior preached to family members.[2] The love-up, anger-down motif concentrated directly on relationships between husband and wife and between parents and children, which had once been hierarchical, with anger a major prerogative of superior place, but which now were supposed to become more reciprocal. Of course equality was not achieved, either in families or in the wider society, and this is one reason that the modern emotionology of anger has had incomplete effects. But the cultural strand of egalitarianism remained vibrant, never fully displaced. In the twentieth century, it spread beyond family to the workplace and to other public relationships. Formal hierarchy was replaced in part by greater negotiation among theoretical equals, which in turn involved more consideration for others, more patience—and less tolerated anger.[3] The reduction of hierarchy added a new unpredictability to human relationships—and then another need for personal self-control. A democratic culture thus extended its effect, but the factor itself was not new.

3. The economic basis for anger control in the initial phases of the modern emotionology is not entirely clear. Certainly, the rise of market relationships and the sense of nonfamily members as competitors helps explain the new focus on a warm, anger-free family.[4] But it is probable that market dealings encouraged anger control more directly as well, as the necessity of dealing with and pleasing strangers imposed new constraints. Certainly, the extension of wage labor created pressures for

anger control in the proletarian segment of the population, though this same new hierarchy between employer and worker (or housewife and servant) created new possibilities for anger as well. In the twentieth century, the economic factor becomes clearer and more obviously important, in combination with the familial culture of anger control already established in the middle class and the pervasive egalitarian veneer in public relationships. With an increasingly intricate bureaucracy and then the expansion of people-dealing service occupations, the primacy of economic-organizational imperatives in restraining anger becomes increasingly patent.

While stressing the causal importance of ideology, economic organization, and the need to devise new emotional rules in a world filled with strangers, it is vital to see the complexity in the resultant emotionological and emotional products. We cannot always assert that basic causes led to new emotionology, which then resulted in changes in emotion and emotional perception, though this was often the case. At key points, as in the workplace in the early twentieth century or periodically in marriage, emotionology was also encouraged by apparently rising anger. Standards thus attempted to mediate between democratizing ideology and other environmental factors and levels of anger that did not always follow the same drumbeats. At times, indeed, the same forces that encouraged a restraining emotionology, such as more impersonal work organization, may also have sparked more visible anger, which in turn further encouraged the new emotionology. Emotionology, in other words, serves much as formal law does, reflecting changing social environment but sometimes also responding to countertrends in popular behavior; both cause and effect are complicated as a result.

Despite the complexity, it remains true that, while the environmental factors contributing to anger control have shifted in balance over time, their persistent intertwining forms the clearest basis for the substantial continuity in basic emotionological goals. Ideology, bureaucracy, and even population growth all pushed toward a reduction in violence and spontaneity in the emotionology of Western society, toward an increased emphasis on internal restraint—some sort of superego—or management devices that would conduce to the same end.[5] And of all the emotions or animal impulses that commanded attention over the longest span of time, anger turns out to head the list. At particular points, of course, attention focused heavily on a presumed need for sexual controls or, perhaps, for ways to limit the display of grief over death, but the need to keep the lid on anger has remained the most persistent motif in the emotional reconstruction of the American personality.

Complexities

Continuity established, it is obvious that there have been important variations on the theme. The importance of major chronological periods in the campaign against anger must be emphasized. Each period, from the early Victorian through the turn of the century to the contemporary, tossed up a distinctive style of advice and suggested some distinctive behavior patterns. The final two periods, at least, also created a number of institutions designed in part to implement the prevailing views on anger, like the boxing enthusiasm encouraged by the idea of channeling or the various personnel and counseling programs set up to translate the more recent management ideal. Each period, finally, emphasized an emotionology focused on a particular range of behaviors and a new attempt to redefine home/work relationships. The early Victorians concentrated of course on the family and character development; the latter was intended, but without great specificity, to apply to nonfamily situations, though the assumption of a marked emotional and moral contrast between the home and the outside world rather limited the extension. During the turn-of-the-century period the home/work dichotomy was preserved, but with an explicit willingness to recommend the use of anger-based zeal in public situations. This emphasis shifted in turn toward the middle of the twentieth century, with the more explicit extension of anger-control goals and mechanisms to public, and, particularly, to work, life. The variation in range of coverage, as well as in specific style, reflected important differences in each period's emotionology, though there was continuity as well. Within the three major periods certain minor changes must also be considered. For in each case, a new understanding of the home/work problem was being sought. Although our particular focus, of course, has involved one emotion, anger, it would be fruitful to examine other aspects of the history of mentalities in the context of this central problem of the industrialized West: how to develop personalities and standards suitable for these separate arenas in the context of a long tradition in which there had been no dichotomy between home and work.

Although the consistent effort to come to terms with the home/work problem was the most central thread defining our periodization, the larger periods also reflect shifts in the precise nature and balance of other factors determining the anger-control campaign. Democratic sentiment, for example, if of a somewhat patronizing sort, helped inspire the burst of reform activity around 1900, which in turn helped justify anger's utility in fueling moral outrage. Specific cultural factors also entered in: the idealistic optimism of mainstream religion for the early Victorians, social Darwinism for the emphasis on channeling, and various schools of behavioral science for the shift to the management approach. The effect of particular events, such as World War II, or of unusual currents in movements for private as opposed to public rights, as in the feminist periods of the early twentieth century and again the late 1960s and the early 1970s, left a mark on emotionology. The world war encouraged particular concern about aggression, which fit the larger period just beginning but produced a distinctive tone in the literature of the 1940s and 1950s. Feminist and, in the 1960s, other rights agitation produced some efforts to bend prevailing consensus toward a somewhat greater tolerance of personal anger, particularly in the marital advice literature.

The major periods are not simply analytical tools for understanding the complexities of change. They also organize important questions about effect. In particular, the abandonment of the channeling idea and its replacement with a more pervasive effort to manage anger leads inexorably to a fresh look at the widespread sense that some basic features of the American personality have been changing in recent decades. The continuity with earlier goals need not be neglected, but the potential gap between using the fighting instinct as goad for achievement and attempting to talk away any strong anger is so great that it demands recognition; it invites evaluation in terms of social and individual utility as well. New methods and goals in anger control become part of the challenging task of determining how deeply American personality characteristics are changing and whether these changes are for good or ill. In sum, the modern history of the emotionology of anger involves an ongoing tension between durable goals and causes and important shifts in direction, as each major period had a distinctive potential effect not only on outlook but also on emotional experience.

The second complexity in the modern history of anger standards, in addition to tension between periods and continuities, involves the persistent sense of ambivalence. In various ways—and the variety depended heavily on the period involved—the American campaign against anger seemed to leave loopholes, seemed indeed to court tension between controlling the emotion and seeking ways to express it.

Certainly, American emotionology did not produce the kind of single-minded concentration on reducing anger that anthropologists have discovered in some smaller cultures or that may exist even in more complex civilizations such as that of China.[6] Perhaps no Western society can do so if only because of the proximity of earlier traditions of greater spontaneity. It is tempting, moreover, to suggest a peculiarly American ambivalence even within a common Western frame. Frontier values; the kind of emotional distinction suggested in seventeenth-century Massachusetts between family and community, with anger restrained in one and released in the other, against relative strangers; the sheer diversity of the ethnic as well as class and gender cultures that had to be considered even in mainstream emotionology—all of these might suggest a particularly American tension.[7] We cannot insist on this conclusion yet, save for the comparative evidence on distinctive American socialization patterns regarding anger during the early decades of the twentieth century.[8] Until comparable work is done on the emotionology and experience of anger in other Western societies, and such work is eminently desirable, the "distinctively American" impulse must not be pressed too far.

But that there was tension and ambivalence in the American approach to anger cannot be denied. The ambivalence showed in the home/work dichotomy of the early Victorians, which reduced the explicit coverage of anger-control recommendations without formally diluting them. Ambivalence was of course built into the channeling ideas of the late nineteenth and early twentieth centuries, and it is hard to avoid the feeling, confirmed by the comparative child-rearing studies between 1920 and 1950, that channeling reflected a peculiarly happy American compromise in which anger could be attacked yet used. Ambivalence, though less enshrined by formal advice, showed also in the anger patterns of many American women, whose behavior as girls typically reflected a double emotional standard that did not, however, persist consistently into adulthood—with the result that many docile girls turned into morally indignant adult women, in the best traditions of male channeling advice, and many more turned into periodically angry wives. Even in the contemporary period, in which the anger-control campaign greatly expands its coverage and works for consistency in goal and method, ambivalence remains. If contemporary American values strive so vigorously for anger control—and in most ways they do— why the odd anomaly of the emotional context of many schools? The anomaly results in part, without question, from empirical problems, including the diversity of actual emotional approaches represented in student and teacher populations. Efforts have been made, at least in theory, to bring school approaches to anger in line with the general socialization approach. But the efforts have not only shattered when they run against empirical problems; they have not been massively promoted even in theory, as if Americans are still willing to see schools as places where older anger approaches can hold sway or teenagers as a group to which contemporary anger values cannot fully apply.

During each emotionological period, in other words, including to some extent the present period, Americans tolerated, and at points encouraged, some confusing signals about anger. The extent of the ambivalence varied with each period, and it has unquestionably been reduced—again at least in theory—in the most recent decades. But some sense remains that Americans, even in their formal standards, have combined a desire to constrain anger with some notion that the emotion is too useful, or simply too inevitable, to push constraint to the maximum. This theme, conjoined with a sense of the major periods in the anger-control campaign, must enliven and complicate any assessment of emotionology itself or of its effect.

The Results of Emotionology: The Theoretical Arena

A history of anger contributes particularly to an understanding of the evolution and effect of anger standards themselves. But it also feeds a discussion of some of the fundamental controversies about emotion that are raised more generally in the Introduction and that must be addressed before returning to the anger theme more explicitly.

The problem of determining the relationship between emotionology and emotion goes to the heart of the biological-social debate in emotion research, with the added though inescapable complexity of blending in the factor of change. We emerge from the historical consideration persuaded of the importance of both biological and social components of anger. The effect of emotionology—that is, of socially contrived standards—is striking. In considering the diary literature, replete with women who cry rather than become angry at their husbands, who "feel sick" but never "feel angry," or who never feel anger without at the same time experiencing guilt, we confront the overwhelming power that society has over individuals in giving them the very language by which they appraise situations and judge their responses. On the other hand, anger seems rarely to be excised entirely. The fact that such alternate expressions as crying and sickness commonly accompany protestations that an individual feels no anger, and that for the most part these expressions appear uncomfortable and indicative of unresolved conflict, argues that anger lurks beneath the attempt to bury it. The notion of defense mechanism is plausible here. One may, certainly, choose to reject the notion of the unconscious and to take the sad or sick Victorian woman at face value. However, one is left then with no explanation for her apparent conflict. We doubt that any student of emotion would find it necessary or helpful to take self-reports so literally. Some of the persistence of anger may reflect the genuine American ambivalence. Some may reflect the relative recency of the emotionological campaign: we can assume that new emotionology takes time to work its full effects, and two centuries may be a rather brief span in this process; pending additional studies of emotional change, we lack a precise temporal guide. But the idea of some basic anger remains plausible as well, even when it shows through defense mechanisms that cause people to plead loudly that they have no anger. Thus though modern social life has profoundly shaped anger, it has not produced all the results desired. Anger remains.

The ways in which societies shape emotion are also complex, as compared to some of the models available in both psychological and historical literature. Clearly, a simple Freudian hypothesis of frustration in childhood leading to increased anger in adulthood is inadequate to encompass the changes we have described. If this hypothesis were true, the modern period, one of increasing indulgence and permissiveness toward the infant, would see a clear-cut trend toward decreased anger and less of a need to express discomfort over that emotion. This, certainly, is far from what we have seen. Insofar as we have uncovered sources describing actual emotional experiences, we are struck by how much those experiences have been shaped and conditioned not simply by the unremembered and unconscious legacy of infancy but also by the conscious and cognitive structures of the emotionology dominant in each era. How striking it is that mid-Victorian women, taught not to feel anger or to feel it only with guilt, record just those experiences; that turn-of-the-century women, raised in a context in which humor is seen as a suitable defense within which to couch anger, often phrase and perceive their anger in humorous terms. We argue, then, that the child learns to deal with emotion, not only as a preconscious infant, but also as an observer of parental styles, which he may copy, and as a thinking entity who absorbs both conscious and unconscious emotionological prescripts through which he filters all his experience. And, of course, language shapes our experience. A tantrum in a society that has no word for the phenomenon is a different experience for both parent and child than is a tantrum that is labeled, and labeled with a judgmental connotation. We argue, then, that there may be such an entity as basic anger but that the experience of anger changes profoundly over time. We turn then to summarize our thoughts on what that change has meant over the last two hundred years.

The Results of Emotionology: The Social Arena

Continuities and changes in modern emotionology toward anger had results; this was not an isolated or purely hortatory strand in American culture. We have seen that emotionology clearly affected the perceptions of anger in contexts such as marriage or parenthood, producing new concerns. These concerns might feed back toward emotionology itself, producing changes in expert advice to accommodate practical anxieties about, say, angry children that earlier standards had promoted. More broadly, the development of new standards of anger control at work, reflecting in part the discomfort of middle-class managers bred to domestic values of minimizing conflict, showed the power of emotionology in affecting the evaluation of one's own emotions and the emotional behavior of others.

The emotionology toward anger also fed other kinds of cultural styles and expressions. The change in the imagery of the angry person from the nineteenth to the twentieth century, as anger moved from external enemy to internal foe, affected literary conventions. Shifts in the nature and vigor of villainy, in fiction, owe something to changes in emotionology. So, it might be suggested, do changes in humor. The period before the rise of the modern concern about anger saw a strong interest in satire, which in the seventeenth century was little more than insult dressed in clever garb. By the nineteenth century, literary and dramatic forms allowed less bitter, more thoroughly humorous por-trayals of negative social or personal traits; the satire of the eighteenth century would hold a middle ground in this tentative evolutionary sketch. A new ability and new need to poke fun may, then, follow from changes in anger values. Certainly the modern decline of creativity in vulgar insults and, more recently, even in the one principal exception in the United States, the ethnic insult, owes something to public restraints on anger. It is obvious, of course, that not all cultural outlets move neatly in tandem in this matter; in contemporary culture, anger-free violence popular in many teenage films and in science fiction has not fully per-meated villainy in adult popular culture. But some correspondence be-tween both substance and rhetoric and anger values explains important features of the evolution of modern Western fiction and drama.

A wider effort to assess the effect of anger emotionology involves also further inquiry into other areas of social action in which an emo-tional component, however intellectualized, inevitably came into play. The history of American values toward anger in this sense sheds new light on a variety of aspects of American social and political history.

As middle-class Americans became more conscious of anger as a problem, at least at the intellectual level, their understanding readily carried beyond pious advice about how to deal with children, spouses, or servants or literary ideals of femininity and the happy home. We have seen that the rising concern about anger intertwined with new definitions in mainstream religion—not only in preachers' family ad-vice but also in the rapid decline, from the early nineteenth century on, of the idea of an angry God and vengeful damnation. The extent to which most twentieth-century American Christians have come to dis-believe in hell is partly a reflection of their emotional reluctance to contemplate a wrathful God.

Rising concern about anger also entered into efforts to reduce spontaneity and conflict in leisure; the desire to impose rules and referees in sports, for example, clearly related to the attempt to use sports for channeled, rather than untrammeled, emotion. Growing sensitivity to certain kinds of crime, especially of the sort that might suggest particular anger, is another historical trend related in part to the evolving emotionology. Concern about juvenile delinquency and about adolescence as a period in which emotions were particularly suspect certainly tied into the worries about anger control and the need to find safe channels around 1900. Recurrent tendencies in the twentieth century to exaggerate crime trends, though they have several sources, owe something to the new perception of the unacceptability of expressions of anger. Certain kinds of crime, and anxiety about crime, have become to some extent methods of defining anger as deviance. This is most obvious, again, in the transformation of certain acts of youthful hooliganism, once regarded as acceptable (though probably annoying) letting off of steam, into criminal acts; but it feeds the more general preoccupation with crime as well.[9]

Even before this linkage became clear, the new emotionology of anger became linked with the changing definition of justice as it emerged in the late eighteenth and early nineteenth centuries. Like God, man was now supposed to punish without anger, which particularly led to a need to withdraw vengeance from the approved motivations of punishment. The withdrawal of punishment from the public arena, as well as the reduction of violence in punishment, were the main results of this clear attempt to revise the emotional basis of justice. As one student of the subject has noted, "The pleasure is gone from punishment"; modern Westerners might enjoy the process of detecting and even convicting criminals, but they liked to think of punishment as a matter of cool, institutional rationality. For in punishment, recognition not just of anger but of one's own anger might be uncomfortably vivid.[10]

In addition to persistent reciprocity between trends of this sort and the campaign against anger, there are important connections to seek within particular periods. The channeling emotionology of 1900, to use an obvious case, linked neatly with the Progressive approach to reform as well as to feminist agitation. The contemporary effort to repress anger more thoroughly links with widely noted changes in political style, particularly the rise of tolerance and the decline of the acceptable use of invective.[11]

Connections of this sort—the list could be lengthened and indeed deserves further inquiry—are in one sense obvious. This aspect of emotionology's effect leads, not thus far to new findings about justice or political tolerance, but to greater richness in the evaluation of trends or changes. Emotional style—in this case, anger standards—feeds into a large number of aspects of social or institutional behavior, in part because the style setters overlap. Standards of modern justice, for example, are shaped not by the populace at large so much as by a decision-making elite, itself particularly influenced by and eager to disseminate the dominant emotionology. The nature and durability of the resultant developments are better understood if the ingredient of emotional values is added. Of course the connection is partly cognitive. People who think that anger should be handled a certain way carry over similar thinking into considerations of crime, recreational regulation, or even God—and the cognitive interaction is mutual.

Emotionology affects our scientific inquiry no less than our fantasy lives as with literature or humor. Here too the relationship is mutual since scientific discoveries or dominant theory help shape the emotionology. But we have seen abundant evidence that many presumably scientific findings about marriage were affected in turn by the prevailing emotionology of anger. The effort since the 1940s to reprove anger thoroughly has certainly affected the tone of scientific inquiry. It becomes increasingly possible to attack behaviors seen as undesirable by labeling them ''angry'' or ''aggressive'' acts. Thus rape and other sexual crimes, as permissiveness made sexual reproof increasingly ineffective, even embarrassingly prudish, became acts of anger against women. Thus medical science in the twentieth century, particularly in the United States, emphasizes diseases that relate to choleric temperament and produces recommendations for personality change in the name of good physical health.[12] This is not to argue that these scientific findings are incorrect but only to point out that, conducted within a dominant emotionology hostile to anger, they may be colored by values as well as by data. The long campaign against anger, and its particular variants in each major period, affected the expertise applied to a variety of subjects and thus helped feed public perceptions and institutional remedies in ways more complex than carefully considered cognition alone. It has become increasingly difficult to study anger openly, to consider the emotion itself as opposed to hostile behaviors that can readily be reproved, or to view the emotion even when studied as anything but unpleasant, precisely because the emotionological values have so deeply penetrated intellectual inquiry.[13] This is one vital reason to add an evaluation of emotionology to the factors that enter into other value systems that are shaped by scientific research.

More generally, the extent to which emotionology relates to perceptions of justice or to religious thought also raises the possibility of direct emotional causation. The modern desire to avoid angry punishment, for example, is not simply an effort at intellectual consistency, though it is this in part. It is also visceral; an attempt to translate to systems of justice the same repression often agonizingly undertaken in oneself. To the extent that changing emotionology causes or mirrors actual emotional change, it helps translate this real alteration in experience—not just outlook—into other facets of social behavior. Americans have been fighting anger for two centuries. Their combat is easiest to trace at an intellectual level, but it has to some extent been an emotional experience as well. We can therefore look for symptoms of the campaign against anger in other reaches as extensions of emotional shifts, with the intensities these shifts imply, and not only in terms of ideological change. The battle against anger, with some of the ambiguities and tensions it has entailed, becomes a living factor in American history.

The Results of Emotionology: Experience and Perception

Has the changing emotionology toward anger altered, or reflected alterations in, actual emotional life? The answer is yes, but—which is better than no answer at all, though more complex than a ringing assertion that anger has declined in American life or that emotional repression has increasingly eviscerated American spontaneity.

As for the qualifications, it remains impossible to pretend to a full exploration of the actual emotional experience of ordinary people. The effort to detail a growing concern about anger has focused particularly on middle-class values, giving little entry to variations by class, region, or ethnic group. These variations are an important part of any actual emotional history, and they deserve further attention. We have seen them impinge even on middle-class perceptions in institutions such as schools or in condemnations of lower-class family life. But even for the Northern Protestant middle class, who most clearly generated and consumed the dominant emotionology in each major period, it remains difficult to fathom actual emotional change. Further work is desirable and possible, but as with other topics, such as actual sexual experience, the subject will always remain somewhat elusive.

Furthermore, the correspondence between emotionology and emotion was not necessarily consistent over time. We have argued that the correspondence probably increased with time, simply because of the intergenerational force of the basic campaign. Victorian emotionology thus may have effected experience less than did later versions. And a host of forces outside the emotionological realm—wars; protest movements, including feminism or the agitation of the 1960s—might have jostled the long-term relationship at critical points. Clearly, anger did not decline as neatly or as consistently as the emotionological evolution might suggest, and the eruption of particular events or pressures is partly responsible.

Many of the actual changes in anger, even when they did roughly parallel the emotionological thrust, may have involved more guilt or anxiety about anger than they involved the experience of anger itself. Sometimes, as we have suggested particularly in dealing with family life, concern about anger might heighten, rather than reduce, the emotion. It is clearest, particularly in the nineteenth century, that anger becomes an increasingly charged and difficult subject in actual experience. This was itself a change in emotional life, not just intellectual perception, but it was not precisely the same as a reduction in anger. It is particularly likely that efforts to socialize children toward avoidance of anger, including frequent parental anxiety about their own emotional displays coupled with an inability to avoid these displays entirely, produced confusion and anxiety about this aspect of emotional life;[14] it is much harder to show that the amount or nature of anger changed.

Finally, the emotionological trends, though they did parallel some changes in emotional experience, had an uneven effect, depending on context. Overall, we have suggested that the campaign against anger at work, though belated at least at the level of formal articulation and implementation, has had greatest success. There is considerable evidence to suggest that anger on the job is both less frequent and less acceptable, though not as infrequent and unacceptable as some authorities wished. The decline cannot fully be measured; it does not penetrate into anger felt on the job, about which evidence is not only obscure but contradictory. The emotional tone of work has changed, however, with the reduction of expressed anger and probably a reduction in the individual sense that anger is justified as central ingredients in the change.

The evidence for the family is quite different, even though it was here that the campaign against anger first began. Continued hierarchies within the family limited the effect of emotionology, though guilt and anxiety surely increased along with resentment at what now could be seen as unjustified emotional use of authority. The idea of family as emotional haven, though meant to produce an elimination of conflict, may actually, perversely, have encouraged angry outburst. Emotional intensification may have augmented anger as well as love; and the family was often used as a safety valve for emotions that could no longer be expressed elsewhere. In the twentieth century, even emotionological statements gave somewhat greater latitude to familial anger than to anger at work. They did not justify family anger, and they certainly sought to limit it rigorously; but they might be misread as suggesting that the family was a haven for, not from, hostility generated in the wider world.[15] Anger in the family may well have risen, and emotionology in this area may have been more an attempt to limit this tide than a formative factor in emotional experience. Even here, however, the experience of anger has become more complicated. Some families bought into the emotionology quite literally, like the couples reported by therapists since the 1940s who refused to fight lest expressed anger symbolize marital failure. In still other families, new perceptions of anger created heightened guilt when quarrels did break out and magnified resentment against angry outbursts by a spouse.

In child rearing, finally, a mixed picture emerges. There is little question that many parents did change their goals and methods to produce a reduction of anger. This involved some repression and considerable anxiety about their own emotional reactions to children. The purposes of socialization did shift, and this in turn caused some real-life changes. At the same time, not all agents of socialization moved in tandem with anger-controlling parents, which meant that children received some confusing signals from teachers and other sources. Children were obviously affected by the more intimate confusion between anger goals taught to them and the anger that erupted between their parents. In other words, while parental emotional styles did shift, they were partly countered by anger in other aspects of family life. Here was real-life ambivalence for children, which helps explain continued ambivalence in more formal standards. Finally, of course, even conscientious efforts to implement anger control might have unpredictable results, as the example of angry women emerging from apparently gentle girls has illustrated.

So has the experience of anger changed in modern American history? Yes, though with lags and variations. It has become popular in recent social history to begin to downplay the variations in private life that were discovered, with great fanfare, by researchers just a decade ago. Thus we learn that Victorian sexuality is not as different from its contemporary counterpart as was once believed—in part because what the Victorians said about sex was not taken literally by most people, even most respectable middle-class people. Or we are told that the essentials of child rearing have not really changed for some centuries, despite shifts in intellectual theories about children. With a subject as elusive as anger, it is important to try to strike a balance in this first historical probe: our anger does not differ as much from that of our pre-1750 ancestors as the shifts in formal preachments on the subject would suggest. But it does differ. We are less likely to express anger in certain contexts—most notably work but probably also parenting. We are more likely to be uncomfortable about anger when it is expressed by others or sensed in ourselves, a change that has brought particular complexity to married life. Our experience of anger has changed, and the range of outlets has become more restricted.[16]

Americans, as several historians have noted, have become a distinctly more orderly people since the early nineteenth century. Their work habits have been regimented by industrialization, but even other aspects of public behavior have yielded to greater self-control.[17] Some of this change is of course due to outside agencies, such as formal police forces. But some, we can now see, is due to emotional change itself. The campaign against spontaneous anger has corresponded to a real effort to limit the emotion in oneself. We have become in part, emotionally, what we have been advised to be.

The Problem of Outlets

I watched the Steelers lose football games every way you could think of and I never bitched. And I ain't no gambler neither. Never bet a penny on a football game. I just used to go to old Forbes Field every Sunday when the Steelers were home and it just brought out a lot of emotion in me I couldn't get rid of no other way.

Those are men. Giants. And they're down there strugglin' and sweatin' and bleedin' and doin' a little war right there between those chalk stripes on the grass and I just found out I could whoop and holler my guts out and nobody would think I was nuts. It didn't make no difference to anybody else what I was really hollering about. People around me were all hollering too. I mean, it really helps you, brother, to reach down to your toes and pull out a yell you been keepin' bottled up inside you for Christ knows how long.[18]

There is no way to be sure how constant the potential for anger is, in any grouping of people. The biological components of anger suggest considerable constancy;[19] certain psychoanalytic theories, used recently by some historians, do the same. Anthropologists have described societies in which anger is not just shunned in the value system but effectively blocked, though in some cases their argument seems overstated when one examines aggressive behavior toward animals or a sulking at frustration that might reflect the anger constant. Philip Greven, though inclined toward a belief in a primal anger in childhood, paints a picture of moderate evangelicals, in eighteenth-century America, whose anger seemed lower than usual, both in public and private, without resultant tension.[20] It is clear that various patterns of socialization affect not only the attitudes toward anger but also the frankness with which anger is expressed. Whether they actually reduce the emotion's force or divert it into indirect expression cannot at this point be determined.

Many Americans have been trying for some time to reduce anger, in themselves and in those with whom they deal. Expressions of anger have declined in a variety of contexts. It is certainly possible that the net effect is a reduction of the felt emotion in enough individual cases to have some effect on broader social experience. Thus while some airline stewardesses report tension and confusion, even outside the work setting, from the pressure and training directed at expunging anger, others may well carry a keep-smiling approach, however superficial, into other aspects of life, without the need to find some target for their anger. Crasser forms of training in docility, as in certain past slave systems, seem to have affected normal emotional response, so that resentments we think would be normal, even if covertly expressed, do not reach surviving record. So it is possible that the cumulative effect of a long campaign against anger, supplemented in recent decades by more extensive managerial devices, including efforts to avoid anger-provoking situations from childhood on, has really altered average emotional experience in the United States: with the result that there is less anger to vent.

Unquestionably, however, whatever the balance between social change and biopsychological constants, any alteration in anger levels has not gone as far as modern emotionology intended. Expressions of anger have been blocked or reduced without a corresponding reduction of angry sentiment. Damned in key channels, anger seeks outlet elsewhere. This results not only from diverse subcultures or incomplete penetration of mainstream emotional standards but also from the ambiguities in the emotionology itself. Americans have been and remain clearer on the inappropriateness of anger in certain settings than on the inappropriateness of the emotion itself. Thus an important aspect of the history of American emotional life involves the identification of outlets for an emotion that, though possibly genuinely reduced, nevertheless seeks expression.

The problem of outlets goes far back in the American past. John Demos described, though did not definitively prove, the use of anger against neighbors in Plymouth colony as a deliberate compensation for unusual attention to restraint of familial anger. During the Victorian period, when dominant emotionology hoped for a thorough restraint of anger based on good character, norms remained sufficiently novel in the actual experience of many families that the need for new outlets did not necessarily increase. Nevertheless, the recurrent fear that families were being used for the venting of anger developed but not expressed in the workplace suggests a new or increasingly important outlet that ran counter to public standards.

The idea of channeling fairly directly addressed the problem of outlets. In using sports to divert anger, and in developing new opportunities for spectatorship that may have vented anger as well through intense partisanship, the later nineteenth century developed a durable outlet for expressing anger and enthusiasm that could not be safely displayed in ordinary life. Historians have been inventive, in recent years, in developing reasons for the inclusion of the rise of modern sports in serious social and cultural history; at the risk of overburdening the categories of analysis, it seems obvious that emotional functions play a vital role in the origins and maintenance of sports interests. Protest also served as an anger outlet. This is not to argue that the need to vent anger caused protest or determined its incidence. But protest was an emotional expression, and protest ritual, the celebratory atmosphere of much protest, owed much to the need to find legitimate outlet for intense emotion. ''You ought to be out raising hell,'' said an old woman to a crowd of Colorado miners in 1916. ''This is the fighting age. Put on your fighting clothes.'' Feminists, temperance advocates, Progressive reformers, could also use the righteous cause to express anger that they tried to restrain in daily life. And the prerogative of anger was not one-sided. Employers, faced with insubordinate workers, often indulged their rage fully, and possibly they, too, drew some private pleasure from their outbursts.[21]

The problem of anger outlets for the late nineteenth and early twentieth centuries is not, to be sure, exhausted by the invocation of approved channels such as sports or even righteous indignation. The need to express anger may have been one of the ingredients of imperialist enthusiasm and other efforts to identify foreign enemies against whom unrestrained venom could be safely expressed. For women, certainly, despite the good causes that attracted some, the problem of safe outlets for anger was particularly acute. Many women doubtless found familial anger an essential escape valve, though it generated anxiety as well as relief. Others took out anger on servants and shopkeepers. Others displaced anger through hysteria and tears.

The rise of the managerial approach to anger, and its extension to the workplace, raised the problem of outlets to new levels, at least for men. The diminution of work-based protest was partly compensated, for some, by the rise of other protest outlets, including resurgent feminism, urban riots, single-issue political passions, and the youth movements of the 1960s. Yet Barrington Moore's sense of a decline in moral indignation, in recent decades, seems justified on the whole. Certainly, politics has declined as an opportunity for displays of passion, with declining voting levels and a tendency to downgrade the level and quality of vitriol in political rhetoric; symptomatically, a number of observers have noted the deterioration of the imaginativeness of insults exchanged in the halls of Congress.[22] Even youth movements reflected unusual ambivalence about using anger frankly, as they typically masked genuine rage with flowery invocations of love; this is one reason that radicals of an older tradition found their efforts wanting.[23] The question of outlets, endemic in the campaign against anger from its inception, takes on new contours in our own day.

Where can the contemporary American get mad? Are his or her opportunities adequate to the task? In sketching some lines of inquiry, we cannot pretend precision; nor are we claiming that the outlets are new to our own day (many are definitely not) or that their increased utilization is clearly measurable.

The importance of the family, and probably particularly the contemporary family, as an outlet has been a theme throughout our inquiry. Women may still require this outlet particularly, as they have been found particularly likely to initiate family conflict. Men's anger, in family settings, is more likely to be displayed in a disengaged grumpiness or attacks on material objects.[24]

An important subset of familial anger, measurably more intense in recent decades, is divorce itself as a ritual that legitimizes the expression of anger. As divorce has become both more common and more accepted, it clearly serves as one of the few occasions during which intense personal anger can be legitimately expressed and sympathetically listened to by friends and colleagues. This ritual ventilation, in a society that normally shuns the angry person or urges him to talk his anger out as quickly as possible, gives divorce—like protest in earlier decades—an important emotional function.

Outside the family, anger at strangers has also taken on new features. The rise of public canons of tolerance has reduced the acceptability of ritual attacks on large groups of strangers—particularly, identifiable minorities within our society, including groups once defined as deviant, but also foreign enemies to some extent. The tendency—admittedly not unqualified—to favor laid-back political styles, as opposed to the give-'em-hell rhetoric of earlier decades, both illustrates and furthers the decline of ritual outlet through identifying with angry attacks on others. But anger against unknown individuals has probably increased in importance. In rage (sometimes in the form of private cursing and shouting) against automobile drivers, sports fans, or service workers such as sales clerks and waiters, contemporary Americans may find an important safety valve. The need to vent anger against unknown strangers may also, by extension, help explain the otherwise puzzling twentieth-century increase in crimes of violence, including crimes against women, after several decades in which violent crime rates declined or stabilized. It may also help explain the popularity of media violence and our willingness, however reluctant, to tolerate its availability for young viewers. In various aspects of popular culture, we may implicitly recognize the need for some safe targets or symbols of violence since we seek to deny anger in so many daily interactions.

Are neighbors, also, still a semilegitimate outlet for anger, as they were in colonial society? The history of American neighborliness has yet to be written, but it would probably reveal a rise in superficial friendliness—the suburban veneer—in which anger was supposed to play no overt role. This trend, if substantiated, would simply fuel the need for targets among strangers, even targets who remain oblivious to the fury directed toward them from behind a steering wheel.

There is also anger in law. Americans, unusually litigious by tradition, have increasingly come to believe that the civil suit is a justifiable expression of anger. The establishment of small claims courts in most states during the 1920s and 1930s, justified by the need for consumer and labor protection, displays an interesting chronological correspondence to the development of the managerial approach toward anger that heightened the desirability of legitimate outlets.[25] Of course, lawsuits involve important factors other than emotions and probably even among emotions more commonly reflect greed than anger. Furthermore, the actual pattern of small claims court activity shows a dominance of organizational attacks on individuals, particularly for debt collection; only in a minority of cases have the courts allowed individuals to express anger at the wrongs done them by other people or by faceless corporations.[26] Yet there has remained some belief that the lawsuit gives the "little man" an opportunity to vent legitimate indignation.[27] Article titles on the American penchant for litigation, such as "So You're Mad Enough to Sue" and "Dial V for Vengeance," enhance this impression and may genuinely give contemporaries, even when not directly involved, some sense that appropriate emotional outlets do still exist.[28]

The search for outlets for anger helps describe some important trends in twentieth-century American life. Yet in another example of the pervasive American ambivalence about anger, many of the outlets have themselves become increasingly qualified. Sports still serve for emotional display. But the rise of largely noncompetitive, private sports such as jogging, often deliberately designed to drain emotional tensions without any direct manifestation as well as to promote physical health, suggests a growing aversion to the turn-of-the-century interest in using sports to channel anger without destroying it. Still more generally, the privatization of much American leisure—the tendency to do one's spectating at home, in front of the television—raises serious questions about the continued adequacy of sports enthusiasms as an anger outlet. Divorce continues to supply occasions for explosions of anger, but the spread of no-fault procedures qualifies the occasion, at least in theory, by reducing the extent to which the procedure pits the wronged against the villain. Other litigation, as an anger outlet, already limited in fact by the dominance of organizational suits and the drawn-out procedures, has shown interesting constraints. Here, too, a growing tendency to out-of-court settlement and formal, nonadversarial arbitration procedures demonstrates a public desire to reduce the opportunities for public displays of righteous anger. An interesting number of individual litigants—46 percent in a 1976 study—simply never show up for trial, finding the trial too much trouble or (most commonly) seeing the initiation of a suit as a sufficient way to let off steam.[29] "I was really angry. I'd been gypped and there was nothing I could do. I guess I knew that all along. I think that suing him made me feel better. I guess I did it just to let off steam."[30] Initial anger released, such plaintiffs often discovered an inability to sustain their anger. While this inability owed something to cumbersome procedures and the power of the opposition, it also reflected the entry of the dominant contemporary emotional style: force a person to repeat his grievance often enough, and he will retreat, embarrassed.

The effort to develop acceptable outlets for anger—acceptable because legitimate or private or both—forms an important thread in modern American history, particularly the history of the last half century. The campaign against anger may have reduced the emotion. It certainly reduced its normal, daily outlets or within the family made anger's expression increasingly uncomfortable. Compensations that did develop, such as sports, might be deeply cherished in part because of their emotional role, but they veered toward the peripheries of ordinary activity. Some of the outlets were themselves hedged by the spreading discomfort with anger, with an attempt even by the individuals directly involved to opt for unemotional mediation or to settle for brief and hollow display.

There remains, of course, a final outlet, aside from pathological cases in which anger is vented in violent crime, perhaps in part because of the absence of more general channels. Anger can be expressed against self. Many nineteenth-century women invalids used this option. A number of twentieth-century workers, both male and female, discuss the extent to which they are encouraged, and encourage themselves, to turn irritation at mistakes or frustrations against themselves. A study of patterns of violence in nineteenth-century Philadelphia finds that, while attacks on others decline per capita, suicidal attacks on self increase. The rise of the adolescent suicide rate might suggest, among other factors, a particular confusion and guilt about perceived anger and an inability to justify targeting the emotion against others. The anger-against-self theme must *not* be taken as a facile explanation of suicide rates or as an effort to see these rates as symbolic of larger social trends. But the tendency to use self as target for milder anger seems undeniable, as Americans (more indeed than Europeans) find it increasingly necessary to express discontent and frustration as psychic problems. In this tendency, particularly, the particular pressures of the contemporary version of the campaign against anger find vivid illustration.[31]

Clearly, anger forms a major problem in American history, and the problem has gained complexity in recent decades. The evaluation of anger has changed over time, at the level of academic expertise and popular outlook alike; particularly in recent decades, the ability to consider the emotion with any dispassion has declined. Emotional experience itself has changed for many Americans, and the changes form an important part of any definition of American character. Alterations in recent decades suggest a particular anxiety about anger, symbolized in the equation between anger and aggression. This relates in turn to other assessments of shifts in American personality traits, including Riesman's decline in individualism as well as Lasch's concern about parental softness and children's confusion, though our analysis places somewhat greater emphasis on continuity as well as change and less reliance on a particular psychoanalytic dynamic. Finally, the long campaign against anger, and its recent extension through managerial strategies, provides a central emotional component to a host of other developments in American life, developments that cannot be understood without inclusion of emotional history. How far this emotional component should be stressed, as a factor in changes in behavior ranging from divorce to flunking students in school to political styles and passions and, possibly, to our collective reactions to the diplomatic styles and rhetoric of other nations, cannot readily be determined. However tempting, it would be misleading to claim that in our concern over anger lies the touchstone of personal and public dilemmas in American life. It would be brash, for example, to assert that the disparity between dominant emotionology and the emotional context of contemporary schools should push this issue to the forefront of an educational reform agenda or that shifting emotional standards imply probable further changes in our sports preferences. But the complexity and confusion of our anger styles do suggest the need to confront this factor more openly in discussions of various public issues as well as in assessments of the private features of American character. The importance of the anger control motif in modern American history impels its inclusion in any attempt to assess future patterns of family life, work, or collective protest. Because our attitudes toward anger affect such a wide range of behavior and institutions, we can ill afford to continue to deal with the emotion implicitly or to assume we have handled it properly through facile condemnations of aggressive behavior.

Strengths and Weaknesses of the American Approach

One final aspect of the American history of anger demands assessment, though this produces its own ambiguities. While it would be inappropriate to turn from an analytical effort to an attempt at prescription, it is impossible to avoid some discussion of the advantages and disadvantages of the American campaign against anger and particularly its contemporary variant. The fashionable course would emphasize what we have lost through the attempt to limit emotional spontaneity. The attempt to control anger is, after all, unquestionably a form of social control, particularly when this attempt informs a host of manipulative devices in the workplace or a tendency to convert indignation into embarrassment. The correspondence between recent trends in child rearing and workplace goals concerning anger, which aim at creating emotional behaviors convenient for faceless bureaucracies and, it may develop, for the emotionless qualities of new communications machines, might lead to a reexamination of anger's merit in maintaining human individuality, though this same correspondence may induce some pessimism about the possibility of rolling back the emotional clock. It is conceivable that, more aware that anger is subject to change and various kinds of control, we may wish to modify certain contemporary trends, seeing aspects of the current antianger expertise as an undesirable artifact of recent history rather than the latest in scientific certainty.

Yet it is impossible to editorialize too stridently, and this is where we must part company to a degree with other recent critics of trends in personality ideals. The factors that have shaped the campaign against anger, even in its contemporary form, are not only powerful but also admirable, to a point. The goal of improving the democratic quality of family or work life, even when slightly superficial, is hard to reject entirely. Anger-control efforts have usefully compensated, or have attempted to compensate, for the decline of earlier community restraints in abusive behavior. By the same token, jeremiads against the antianger campaign as social control could easily be misleading; all societies engage in social control, and the attempt to limit anger may be no more objectionable than earlier efforts to enforce deferential behavior toward established hierarchies. Attempts to limit anger do have a potentially civilizing quality, improving personal relationships and work relationships alike. While some observers report a tension resulting from emotional manipulation on the job, others—even the politically radical—find the tenor of management improved by the recent attempt to smooth out aggressiveness. On the home front, it would certainly be difficult, and not only because of the evolution in values that we have traced, to argue for more anger in parental treatment of children. Nor can we contend, with Christopher Lasch, that the forces involved in the modern campaign against anger are readily personified as meddlesome experts who know not what mischief they create. For while experts have been involved in the campaign against anger, they have responded to popular concerns and to deeper forces in modern life. They are not even purely the servants of twentieth-century organizational imperatives, for roots of the anxiety about anger go farther back.

Many reasonable people, indeed, would argue that the modern campaign against anger, laudable in its civilizing intent, is open to criticism mainly because it has not gone far enough. The lingering ambivalence, not the anger-control goals, would here be the logical target. Evidence of child abuse suggests that we have not managed to spread parental inhibitions about displaying or inducing anger widely enough. School vandalism, marital conflict, the violent strands in American culture, the let-it-all-hang-out impulses in some schools of therapy—these remain tempting targets for people who, quite reasonably, seek greater dignity in personal and public life.[32]

Yet the dangers of the campaign against anger are real. Civilization can be carried too far. Mao Tse-tung recognized this in China when, as part of his attempt to rouse the peasantry from traditional passivity, he argued for the legitimacy of expressions of anger.[33] In a society becoming steadily more bureaucratized, with new technologies that threaten to depersonalize many aspects of life still further, it is hard to avoid the sense that some tolerance of anger, indeed some encouragements to its appropriate targeting, may provide vital counterweights. Certainly, without pretending unusual insight into the quality of modern life, it seems unlikely that the causes for legitimate annoyance have diminished as rapidly as the efforts to constrain anger have increased and as the range of legitimate expressions of anger has been reduced. Hence it is difficult not to feel some nostalgia for earlier periods in which the campaign against anger was less extensive or in which a certain balance was achieved through deliberately countenancing the emotion if suitably channeled.

Anger remains tricky. Attempts to balance its expression against the needs of family and social life must always be nuanced and complex. The quality of childhood, for example, has not improved as much as some optimists have claimed through the reduction of will-breaking techniques by means of injunctions against parental anger. Improvements are qualified by the fact that will breaking was not uniformly harsh or incompatible with real parental affection in the past, by the continued display of abusive parental anger in more recent times, and above all by the confusion that anger-control goals have brought to childhood, along with a very real extension of the claims to shape a child's personality. But if only because we are part of a value system that still commends restraint, it is hard not to conclude that there has been some gain in a culture that seeks to persuade parents to be more careful of their own hostilities in dealing with children. The relationship between anger and abusiveness is real, which is why we cannot conclude simply with a stirring appeal for a reversal of the modern emotional tides.

Yet some serious problems have emerged with the modern approach. The issue of targeting anger appropriately has become a real, and possibly an increasing, problem. The family has been unduly burdened by its service as an outlet for anger inhibited elsewhere. Other behaviors, including direction of anger against oneself, may be distorted by their service as channels for an anger that should be more evenly distributed. To be sure, the problem of selecting appropriate targets for anger could be reduced by more thoroughgoing success in extirpating the emotion. But we do not know, even theoretically, if such success can be achieved, and the long history of American ambivalence about anger creates particular doubts that this success is possible in our cultural context.

The campaign against anger certainly deserves evaluation in particular settings. We have noted the problems created by the guilt surrounding anger in family life and in the experience of childhood. In work, the manifold and expensive efforts to shape personnel procedures in the interest of reducing anger might profitably be subjected to new analysis. The cultural imperative of avoiding anger has been so strong that the anger-reducing institutions and philosophies have for the most part been assumed meritorious, lamented only when they failed to inhibit all outbursts. Yet not only are these efforts expensive, but they may also conceivably adversely affect the work environment by reducing useful emotional exuberance. Certainly turn-of-the-century expertise, persuaded of a link between anger and achievement, suggests one basis for a reevaluation. Even some ingredients of the ineffectiveness of contemporary politics may derive from the pervasive reluctance to express or confront public anger. A reevaluation of the emotional bases of politics might not produce results, might indeed confirm the desirability of emotional quiescence in politics. But here as in other cases a sensible verdict is possible only as we realize, and as we try to gain some objective distance from, the force of the emotional constraints that have altered the context of American life.

The manipulative aspects of the campaign against anger, though they do not describe the whole modern evolution, remain particularly noteworthy. Democratization of public and private life has not been complete. The emotionology as well as the hierarchical facts of work life, school, and marriage starkly reveal the danger of an approach that seeks to limit almost everyone's anger while allowing particular emotional prerogatives to those at the top of the heap.

Relatedly, the campaign against anger has left many Americans, particularly but not exclusively in recent decades, unusually sensitive to expressions of the emotion when they do occur. European observers have noted Americans' tendency to wounded feelings when confronted with anger—the counterpart of the impulse to be liked according to prevailing definitions that equate friendship with absence of anger. Within American society, reactions to angry protest may be complicated by prevailing middle-class embarrassment at naked expressions of the emotion. Family life has long been encumbered by the attempt to preach domestic anger control in a society that did not neatly follow the same emotional dynamic, perpetuating the impulse to use the family as an escape hatch from reality or to surround the family with a misleading suburban aura of emotional simplicity.[34] The family-society disparity has admittedly lessened in the contemporary period, but it has not disappeared; witness among other things the continued contrast between home and school emotional goals for many children. In sum: Americans, individually and collectively, may be particularly vulnerable to angry behavior by social superiors: if the boss is this mad, I must have done something wrong. Vulnerability can easily support hierarchy, when leaders find themselves authorized to use calculated expressions of anger to reinforce their control. Vulnerability certainly extends to family life, in creating the possibility of undue anxiety in the face of family members—including children—who learn that their anger has the power to confuse.

Vulnerability is confounded by our general ignorance of the long campaign to which Americans have been, and remain, subject. Experts, not deliberately manipulative, too readily ignore the complexities of anger, including its useful features, in favor of scientifically garbed warnings about its dangers to personal health and social well-being alike. It is legitimate to urge that experts, and those who consume expertise, be aware that current wisdom about anger is the artifact of a particular culture and not merely scientific wisdom. In particular, the linkage of emotional control to legitimate concern about the effects of outright aggression, in violent crime or the ultimate folly of total war, is not woven so tightly as we have been taught to believe.

For the most striking feature of the contemporary version of the campaign against anger is its disingenuous quality. We are told, by people who should know better, that we live in an age of emotional liberation, one in which—at last—the damaging forces of age-old repressions can be identified and reversed. This is not the case. The modern impulse to tolerate wider emotional expression is highly selective; it carefully excludes anger.[35] Perhaps we are freer to express tenderness, or sexual passion, or fear, than our ancestors were, though even in these areas permissiveness may sometimes be more superficial than real. But tolerance of anger is declining, not increasing, and the pretense of emotional liberation should not serve, as it has to date, as a smoke screen for this fact. Nor can we assume, despite two centuries of indoctrination, that love (or impersonal friendliness) conquers wrath. We might decide, or be compelled to decide, that the campaign against anger should continue anyway. But let us, at the least, be candid about the growing complexity of the emotional components of American life. Too many authorities, both conservative and radical, have during the past half century garbed their own revulsion against anger in permissive guise, by urging that workers or children who futilely talked away their anger were gaining new emotional freedom or by urging that people "get in touch with" their emotions while carefully ignoring the central emotional role of anger. The demands of objective appraisal and, particularly, the need to avoid vulnerability through excessive confusion about anger argue for rejection of this camouflage.

We can hope, at least, to understand more clearly what is changing in our emotional experience and in the emotional signals we receive in various contexts. Perhaps we cannot or should not do more. The campaign against anger can in many respects be justified in the name of civilized values, even aside from greasing the wheels of a managerial, service economy, and in any event it is motivated by such profound forces in our culture that it would be hard to reverse. But a knowledge that anger has a history has one final value: it allows us to explore alternative expressions as something other than an exercise in perversity. Family life might be relieved by more sensitive exploration of preindustrial willingness to use friendship and community as sources to talk over familial sources of anger—as against the modern tendency to believe that marital anger is somehow a sign of failure, best handled by silence or that angry consummation of failure, divorce. Personal emotional life might be clarified by a realization that in some cultures anger has brought pleasure—a pleasure that, according to contemporary research, only some athletes under the influence of amphetamines frankly recognize. It is certainly valid to recall that even the modern campaign against anger has taken some interesting twists, in which blanket condemnation has alternated with some recognition of anger's channeled usefulness. We may need to recall these twists in the future, for anger's utility as a goad to achievement or to moral indignation may certainly have to be summoned again. We need not, in other words, accept blindly the current wisdom that the only problem with anger in our lives is that the emotion, labeled aggression, still crops up too often. We may legitimately explore contexts in which the emotion has been otherwise perceived and on this basis consider situations in which anger may be too firmly stifled or its expression surrounded by too much guilt and anxiety, today or in the future.

The history of anger does not yield precise recommendations about how to handle the emotion, personally or socially. It does suggest more options and facets than current conventional and scientific wisdom allows. This can only aid creative thinking about an emotion whose recurrence (and for some, in certain periods, whose pleasures and uses) defies simplistic judgments. Anger can be dangerous; it must always be in some ways constrained; but it cannot and should not be eliminated.

The effort to control anger must be seen, in the political context, as part of a long-standing American tradition that places massive social responsibility on the individual. Did we trade in our earlier belief that differences in social standing were a justifiable reflection of differing levels of religious salvation for the Victorian belief that the discontented displayed failures of will, for the postwar faith that the unhappy were being justly punished for "immaturity," and for a more recent faith that all difficulties come from unwillingness to "communicate" honestly with others and seek "growth" for ourselves? Is anger, biologically programmed within us to help us respond appropriately to noxious outside stimuli, so easily to be dismissed as a failure of the self? Is it possible that, in rediscovering the social function of anger that the Progressive era identified in the channeling notion, we may also rediscover the Progressive insight into the necessity for a better balance between the responsibility of the individual to better society and the responsibility of society to come to the aid of the individual? In this manner, can we come to recognize that the angry individual may sometimes be rational and functional?

One of the most insidious features of the anger-control campaign, certainly, has been its potentially paralyzing insistence that anger is an internal problem rather than a normal response to external stimulus. Even in the nineteenth century, the domestic emphasis rested on an assumption that intrusions into familial tranquillity resulted from the perturbations of the marketplace. The rise of the managerial approach in the twentieth century even more clearly encouraged the view that anger responded either to no reality at all or to a reality outside the context in which it was expressed; thus anger at work reflected domestic disharmony, and anger in the family was brought home from work. Here was and is the basis for the pervasive attempt to convince people that what is after all a normal emotion was essentially a problem within themselves, the emotional equivalent of stomach gas.

We need to attend, also, to the problem of internal, emotional reality. One of the main links between the contemporary approach to emotion and nineteenth-century themes, for all the important differences in tone, is an assumption that emotions can be facilely manipulated, usually in the interest of promoting desired behavior. Feelings are not as plastic as Victorian injunctions at self-control or contemporary recommendations to defuse through verbalization suggest. The assumption of facile emotional control has had its greatest effect in making Americans feel uncomfortable and confused about many of their sharpest emotions; for the gains made in overall behavior, themselves not without disadvantages, we have paid a heavy price in the loss of emotional richness and clarity.

Finally, whatever one's conclusion about the balance between civilizing unruliness and oppressing the emotional basis for threats to the established order or between behavioral controls and emotional satisfactions, one point at least should be clear. Potshots against one or another aspect of anger are not in fact self-contained, whatever their apparent virtues in a narrow context. They form part of a large and significant effort at reshaping the American character, an effort that has definitely, in the twentieth century, turned to an attempt to undermine the emotional basis for grievance. We need greater self-consciousness, among experts in various disciplines, of the interconnectedness between their advice or findings and a wider, ultimately political, context of behavior. We may choose still to concentrate on a repression of anger, but we should know that we are choosing.

The history of anger, in sum, gives us some notion of why we are the way we are today and of how we may and may not change. Knowing where we come from emotionally, we may liberate ourselves from previously unquestioned compulsions of behavior and feeling and are able to make new choices. Here we meet as psychiatrist and historian, in the common belief that understanding the person and his past can enhance freedom.

Appendix A

Sample Periodization: Anger in American Child-rearing Norms (Emotionology)

I. Seventeenth Century
Will-breaking techniques; lack of specific concern about anger (Western Europe); evidence of considerable anger in relations between neighbors.

Possible Puritan variant.—Some adult anxiety about temper control; efforts to deflect anger with the family.

II. 1700/1750–1860
Disapproval of anger; varying child-rearing methods used to translate this disapproval; use of word *tantrum;* particular focus on adult behavior.

1830 and following.—Semisecular child-rearing manuals; anger control as part of character building; special maternal and female responsibilities.

III. 1860–1940
American ambivalence about anger: disapproval; efforts to discipline and control combined with strong approval of channeled anger (especially among males).

1860–90, 1890–1910, and 1910–30.—Several subperiods of fluctuating child-rearing advice and judgments of the nature of children in other respects.

IV. 1940 and Following
Rising concern about anger; more uniform disapproval; abandonment of channeling approach; efforts to avoid and defuse.

1940s through the late 1950s.—Permissive subperiod.
1960s and following.—Somewhat strict subperiod.

Appendix B

Table B1: Changes in Strike Patterns

	Average Number of Strikes Annually	Average Number of Workers Annually
1930–39	2,009	909,969
1940–49	3,205	2,247,845
1950–59	4,309	2,213,300
1960–69	3,534	1,809,100
1970–79	5,253	2,288,200

Source.—*Analysis of Work Stoppages* (Washington, D.C.: U.S. Department of Labor, Bureau of Labor Statistics, 1941–80); *Strikes in the United States, 1880–1936* (Washington, D.C.: U.S. Department of Labor, Bureau of Labor Statistics, 1937).

Table B2: Shop Conditions Issues and Union Organization Issues

	Average Percent of Strikes Annually	Average Percent of Strikers Annually
1940–49	36.0	29.2
1950–59	29.9	18.5
1960–69	28.7	30.2
1970–79	21.7	21.0

Source.—*Analysis of Work Stoppages* (Washington, D.C.: U.S. Department of Labor, Bureau of Labor Statistics, 1941–80); *Strikes in the United States, 1880–1936* (Washington, D.C.: U.S. Department of Labor, Bureau of Labor Statistics, 1937).

Notes

Chapter 1

1. Benjamin Franklin, *Autobiography* (New York, 1962), pp. 29–30; Studs Terkel, *Working* (New York, 1974), pp. 289ff.; William H. Whyte, Jr., *The Organization Man* (New York, 1956), p. 152.

2. William Alcott, *The Young Husband* (Boston, 1840), pp. 287ff.; *Peterson's Magazine* 47, no. 6 (1865): 405.

3. Paul Popenoe, *Marriage Before and After* (New York, 1943), pp. 210–17.

4. "Can This Marriage Be Saved," *Ladies Home Journal* 4 (April 1965): 36.

5. Hugh D. Graham and Ted R. Gurr, *Violence in America: Historical and Comparative Perspective,* rev. ed. (Beverly Hills, Calif., 1979). On particularly American anxieties about the association between democracy and violence, see David Brion Davis, *Homicide in American Fiction, 1789–1860: A Study in Social Values* (Ithaca, N.Y., 1957), 239ff., 312. For an interesting, though ahistorical, comment on stereotypical American aggressiveness, see Rupert Wilkinson, *American Tough: The Tough Boy Tradition and American Character* (Westport, Conn., 1984).

6. Carole Tavris, *Anger: The Misunderstood Emotion* (New York, 1982).

7. "The Sixth Deadly Sin," *New York Times,* 16 March 1983.

8. Christopher Lasch, *Haven in a Heartless World: The Family Besieged* (New York, 1977), passim; Ronald Tyrrell, Frederick McCarty, and Frank Johns, "The Many Faces of Anger," *Teacher* 94 (February 1977): 60.

9. W. Lloyd Warner, *American Life: Dream and Reality* (Chicago, 1962), p. 108. For a comment on the theme of emotional restraint in white-ruled America, see Ronald T. Takaki, *Iron Cages: Race and Culture in Nineteenth-Century America* (Seattle, 1979).

10. Henry Kellerman, "A Structural Model of Emotion and Personality," in *Emotion: Theory, Research, and Experience,* ed. Robert A. Plutchik and Henry Kellerman (New York, 1980), 1: 349–84.

11. Julian M. Davidson and Richard J. Davidson, eds., *The Psychobiology of Consciousness* (New York, 1980), p. 78.

12. Helmut Schoeck, *Envy: A Theory of Social Behavior* (New York, 1966); Robert A. Baron, "Aggression," in *Comprehensive Textbook of Psychiatry,* ed. H. I. Kaplan, A. M. Freedman, and B. J. Sadol, 3d ed. (Baltimore, 1980), pp. 412ff.; see also Jeffrey Gray, *The Psychology of Fear and*

Stress (New York, 1971), p. 17, on cultural differences even in facial expressions of anger.

13. Paul R. Kleinginna, Jr., and Anne M. Kleinginna, "A Categorized List of Emotion Definitions, with Suggestions for a Consensual Definition," *Motivation and Emotion* 5 (1981): 345–79. The work of Silvan Tomkins fits here as well, for Tomkins modifies the drive theory of Freud with a theory of affect that emphasizes the complexity of human motivation as opposed to animal drive. Unfortunately, Tomkins's application of this theory to anger has not yet appeared, though he does label it a negative affect. (Silvan S. Tomkins, *Affect, Imagery, Consciousness* [New York, 1962–63].)

14. Arnold H. Buss and Ann Burkee, "An Inventory for Assessing Different Kinds of Hostility," *Journal of Consulting Psychology* 21 (1957): 343–44; Albert Rothenberg, "On Anger," *American Journal of Psychiatry* 128 (1971): 454–60.

15. On abstract, almost scholastic definition efforts, see Kleinginna and Kleinginna; "A Categorized List"; and for a convenient summary of several such efforts, Theodore D. Kemper, "How Many Emotions are There? Wedding the Social and the Autonomic Components" (St. John's University, Department of Sociology, n.d., typescript).

16. Dolf Zillman and Jennings Bryant, "Pornography, Sexual Callousness, and the Trivialization of Rape," *Journal of Communication* 17 (1982): 10–21.

17. Stanley Schachter and Jerome E. Singer, "Cognitive, Social, and Physiological Determinants of Emotional State," *Psychological Review* 69 (1962): 379–99. Schachter's work, however, has been widely criticized (see Kemper, "How Many Emotions," pp. 21 ff.).

18. James R. Averill, "The Acquisition of Emotions during Adulthood," in *Emotion in Adult Development,* ed. Carol Zander Malatesta and Carroll E. Izard (Beverly Hills, Calif., 1984), pp. 23–44.

19. James R. Averill, "A Constructivist View of Emotion," in Plutchik and Kellerman, eds., *Emotion,* pp. 305–39, and *Anger and Aggression: An Essay on Emotion* (New York, 1982). But the Averill book is curiously lacking in overall theory, beyond the basic contention that anger is usually functional (though capable of running amok); it remains largely true that an overall theoretical approach with much direct application to anger remains to be developed, and recent literature has commented more on the absence of such approaches than on successful syntheses. See Kleinginna and Kleinginna, "A Categorized List," which uses a history of past definitions simply to produce some working definitions to guide further investigation. Representative of renewed sociological interest is Arlie Russell Hochschild, *The Managed Heart: Commercialization of Human Feeling* (Berkeley, Calif., 1983).

20. Jean L. Briggs, *Never in Anger: Portrait of an Eskimo Family* (Cambridge, Mass., 1970); Joel R. Davitz, *The Language of Emotion* (New York, 1969); Edwin I. Megargee and Jack E. Hokanson, eds., *The Dynamics of Aggression: Individual, Group and International Analyses* (New York, 1970); John W. M. Whiting and Irwin L. Child, *Child Training and Personality* (New Haven, Conn., 1953).

21. Briggs, *Never in Anger*.

22. Shula Sommers, "Adults Evaluating Their Emotions: A Cross-cultural Perspective," in Malatesta and Izard, *Emotion*, pp. 319–38.

23. The overwhelming influence of the work of Sigmund Freud is probably the main reason attention has concentrated on aggression as opposed to anger, for Freud dealt with anger only tangentially while devoting an immense amount of analysis to aggression. The problem is that he changed his evaluation of the sources and function of aggression over his own lifetime and that some of his confusions have been compounded by those of his followers in the analytic community. Until recently, no clear work on aggeession has appeared to sort out some of this befuddlement. On the one hand, aggression has been defined as a hostile drive that seeks to express itself by doing harm to others against their will. On the other hand, psychiatrists, particularly child psychiatrists, have seen aggression as a variety or a part of the libidinal life force, one of the sources of all active energy, the drive or wish the infant has to master himself and his environment. Such confusion in definition naturally led to very different views of the value of aggression and how it should be handled. In the midst of this confusion, analysts were not left with much of an intellectual framework with which to look at the separate subject of anger.

It is strange, perhaps, that the analytic confusion about aggression has befuddled American social science as a whole, but this, too, is not totally unexplainable. For one thing, those social scientists most interested in culture—and this is certainly true of historians—have been very slow to realize that there is more to psychiatry than Freud. Unfortunately, most psychohistory has been an attempt to fit historical facts into Freudian models—ironic, in view of the fact that the mainstream of modern psychiatry has strongly questioned the sanctity of those models and would probably welcome the help of other disciplines in exploring other approaches to the psyche. Without question, historical work on emotion can contribute to theoretical understanding in subjects inadequately grasped or synthesized to date.

But much of the theorizing about aggression has discouraged historical contribution, positing a changeless, pseudobiological model. Social psychologists admit an important social element in aggression, which is not viewed as a literal constant in human behavior. But the theories that were popular from the 1940s to the 1970s, focusing on the close, almost automatic relationship between frustration and aggression, removed the subject from much serious consideration of change. Conditions that produce frustration were thus seen to produce a predictable response, unless massive and improbable socialization intervenes. Even the possibility of catharsis was downplayed. At most, socialization may alter targets of aggression. And so a historian concerned with aggression was relegated to chronicling an established response, unable to participate in the actual interpretation of the phenomenon itself.

In fact, impressive historical work over the past decade has contributed to shaking the automatic frustration-aggression linkage, and when we move from aggression to anger, the theoretical field is open wider still. For the focus on aggression has led to some erroneous assumptions about anger. One basic reason that researchers have been concentrating on aggression rather than anger is that they have naturally been concerned with the obvious and dramatic problems of war and violence, problems that seem to demand public attention. Modern aggression research is the product of reactions to the evidence of modern war, genocide, race prejudice, and, more recently, machismo. Insofar as the analytic definition of aggression has been understood to be that of a hostile, destructive, and violent rather than a life-enhancing force, aggression has been seen to be a major national problem. After all, aggression defined in this fashion refers to a behavior we all want to control. Anger is just a feeling, and feelings are not as obviously dangerous as behaviors.

One result of the focus on aggression, and aggression defined in its most negative sense, has been to give anger a bad reputation. We all know that violence is a bad thing, and if violence comes from aggression, and if anger is also somehow aggressive, then anger must be bad. Right? Wrong. Because although many modern researchers have argued that anger is an uncomfortable emotion, one to be avoided, there is in fact no solid evidence to suggest that anger produces uniform discomfort, and as we will see, there is abundant historical evidence to suggest that anger has often been quite enjoyable. More generally, a focus on violent aggression, though a legitimate historical as well as social-scientific concern, distracts from the much more common experience of being angry—which is the primary topic of this study. The best discussion of the problem of defining "aggression" is Henri Parens, *The Development of Aggression in Early Childhood* (New York, 1979); on the lack of attention to anger as opposed to aggression, see Rothenberg, "On Anger." See also Leonard Berkowitz, ed., *Roots of Aggression: A Reexamination of the Frustration-Aggression Hypothesis* (New York, 1969); Lewis A. Coser, *The Functions of Social Conflict* (Glencoe, Ill., 1956); John Dollard et al., *Frustration and Aggression* (New Haven, Conn., 1939); Roger N. Johnson, *Aggression in Men and Animals* (Philadelphia, 1972); and on the rising sociobiological interest in the evolutionary functions of emotion itself, Robert Plutchik, *Emotion: A Psychoevolutionary Synthesis* (New York, 1980). On historians' findings, as against the classic frustration-aggression equation, see the works of Charles Tilly, including *From Mobilization to Revolution* (Reading, Mass., 1978). For an argument that language training is significant in socializing the expression of emotion, see Michael Lewis and Linda Michalon, "The Socialization of Emotion," in *Emotion and Early Interaction,* ed. Tiffany Field and Alan Fogel (Hillsdale, N.J., 1982), pp. 189–212. For two examples that apply rather than test the frustration-aggression hypothesis in history, see Michael Paul Rogin, *Fathers and Children: Andrew Jackson and the Subjugation of the American Indian* (New York, 1975), chap. 2. See also our discussion of premodern child rearing in chap. 2 below.

24. Lawrence Stone, *The Family, Sex and Marriage in England, 1500–1800* (New York, 1977); Jean-Louis Flandrin, *Families in Former Times* (Cambridge, 1979); Randolph Trumbach, *The Rise of the Egalitarian Family: Aristocratic Kinship and Domestic Relations in Eighteenth Century England* (New York, 1978); Edward Shorter, *The Making of the Modern Family* (New York, 1976).

25. Randolph Trumbach, "Review Essay: *The Family, Sex and Marriage in England, 1500–1800,*" *Journal of Social History* 13 (1979): 139.

26. Lucien Febvre, *A New Kind of History,* ed. Peter Burke, trans F. Folca (New York, 1973), pp. 13–26.

27. Gray, *Psychology of Fear* (n. 12 above).

28. Stone, *Family, Sex and Marriage,* p. 245.

29. For a fuller discussion of this concept, see Peter N. Stearns with Carol Z. Stearns, "Emotionology: Clarifying the Study of the History of Emotional Standards," *American Historical Review* 90 (1985): 813–30. An excellent overview of norms of love suggests a similar distinction (William Goode, "The Theoretical Importance of Love," *American Sociological Review* 24 [1959]: 38–47). Psychologists are also beginning to stress the distinction (Carol Malatesta and Carroll E. Izard, introduction to Malatesta and Izard, eds., *Emotion,* p. 19).

30. Hochschild, *The Managed Heart* (n. 19 above).

31. We do not, in this study, emphasize strictly high-culture sources; the most formal statements about anger in theology and later in behavioral and social science enter mainly as they penetrated more popularized literature. Our principal research thrust has been toward advice literature—for religious life, marriage, child rearing, teaching, and work and personnel activity. This kind of evidence provides the core of our data on the emotionology of anger and its evolution.

This advice literature raises several obvious problems. Much of it was rather ephemeral. It is difficult to be sure of representativeness, particularly for nineteenth-century materials, when evidence of "best-selling" popularity is largely wanting. We have controlled for this problem by taking the largest available sample; by relying on secondary studies, as in the child-rearing area, that have already dealt with popularity; and by using widely read periodicals to control the more scattered manuals (this is particularly important in the marriage category, where manuals have heretofore been studied only rarely for several key periods). We have also used other supplementary evidence, in child rearing, e.g., using children's stories along with advice to parents. And in all cases we have relied heavily on sheer repetition of key ideas in advice serving each of the main categories of behavior. When a basic approach to anger is indicated in one child-rearing manual after another and in popular family magazines as well, the inability to establish the exact representativeness of any given source becomes less agonizing than would otherwise be the case. All this is to admit at once that the evidence is less than exhaustive and is open to some criticism but that we have considerable confidence in it.

A further difficulty in the sources of emotionology of anger proved less onerous than we initially envisaged. Large tracts are rarely devoted to anger, though there are a few interesting exceptions. Often the reasearcher is forced to reason from brief comments on subtopics (such as temper tantrums in young children), from circumlocutions (a common problem in nineteenth-century marital and twentieth-century personnel advice), and from the outright absence of comment where it should logically occur. In all these respects the emotionology of anger is harder to study, in modern centuries, than that of love. But reasonably explicit comment is sufficiently abundant to make a coherent picture possible. In only a few cases, such as nineteenth-century work styles, must our argument be based so fully on the absence of remark that it becomes potentially vulnerable.

Discussion of actual emotion and of our third subject, the reaction to the experienced emotion in any given period, calls on a wider array of sources, and here we make far less of a claim to effectively exhaustive treatment. By using existing historical and, for the twentieth century, social-scientific studies of work or family, plus some direct evidence of institutions or practices established to implement accepted values, plus some additional primary data (from letters and diaries and statistics on divorces or protest activity), and, finally, by reading between the lines in the advice literature, we mean to suggest probable outlines of the actual history of anger—that is, the relationship between emotionology and some actual behavior and experience. But the impressionistic quality of these various data is admitted in advance and therefore also the often speculative quality of the generalizations drawn from them. Substantially more research should focus on the nature of past emotional experience in order to determine the historical role of emotions and the extent of actual emotional change, though this research must inevitably contend with impressionistic and incomplete data as well as, on an emotion such as anger, the smoke-screen effect of the dominant emotionology.

We intend, in sum, to cover the modern evolution of the emotionology of anger; to relate the major stages of its evolution to certain other aspects of American development, which, even when familiar, deserve exploration from the emotional angle; and to sketch some contours of the actual experience of anger. There is danger, to be sure, in presenting conclusions differentially researched, though the practice is hardly uncommon; but we believe that the risk is worth taking, having here been made explicit, given the importance of opening up a substantially new facet of historical inquiry.

32. Kleinginna and Kleinginna, "A Categorized List," p. 355.

33. Tomkins, *Affect, Imagery, Consciousness*. There is a controversy in the current study of emotion between those who seek unvarying definitions of a set number of "basic" emotions, innate in the infant, and those more concerned with the variations of emotion that depend on context; this latter group includes those with both biological and social orientations. The controversy follows familiar divisions between idealists and empiricists. As historians, our sympathies lie with the empiricists. We are unconvinced by the evidence accumulated thus far that there is a single fixed entity called "anger" or that the quest for such an entity after earliest infancy is particularly useful; we believe that more understanding of anger is possible by observing it more carefully than by defining it prematurely.

34. On the importance of class differentiation, even in emotionology, see nineteenth-century legal assumptions that middle-class couples were naturally more sensitive to anger than their working-class counterparts were and so more deserving of divorce on grounds of mental cruelty; here, and in many other respects, emotionology becomes a vital tool in understanding class rela-

tionships and perceptions. A focus on dominant emotionology is almost inevitable in an initial study of a topic like anger; it receives some additional support from the increasing homogeneity that has been noted in child-rearing norms (and, we will argue, work norms as well) since the mid-twentieth century. (Urie Bronfenbrenner, "Socialization and Social Class through Time and Space," in *Readings in Social Psychology*, ed. Eleanor Maccoby, T. M. Newcombe, and E. L. Hartley [New York, 1958], pp. 406–24.)

Chapter 2

1. On premodern-modern contrasts, see Edward Shorter, *Making of the Modern Family* (New York, 1975); David Hunt, *Parents and Children in History: The Psychology of Family Life in Early Modern France* (New York, 1970); for a recent revisionist statement ("Parental care would appear to have altered little from the 16th century to date" [p. 269]), Linda A. Pollock, *Forgotten Children: Parent-Child Relations from 1500 to 1900* (Cambridge, 1984); Steven Ozment, *When Fathers Ruled: Family Life in Reformation Europe* (Cambridge, Mass., 1983).

2. Eph. 4:26. For a good start on a sketch of the intellectual history of anger, including the ambivalent Christian view, see James R. Averill, *Anger and Aggression: An Essay on Emotion* (New York, 1982), chap. 1. Averill notes Aquinas's characteristic ambivalence, which we will see echoed often in later Western history: on the one hand fierce anger is wrong, but on the other it is vital to be angry against evil (*Summa theologica* 292ae.158.1, 8). On the angry God theme, see Norman Cohn, *Pursuit of the Millennium* (New York, 1970). For comments on saints and anger, we are grateful to suggestions by Andrew Barnes and particularly Ruldoph Bell (see Donald Weinstein and Rudolph M. Bell, *Saints and Society: The Two Worlds of Western Christendom, 1000–1700* [Chicago, 1983]).

3. John Robinson, *The Works of John Robinson, a Pastor of the Pilgrim Fathers*, ed. Robert Ashton (Boston, 1851), 1: 226–28.

4. John Demos, *Entertaining Satan: Witchcraft and the Culture of Early New England* (New York, 1982), esp. pp. 97–131; Jeffrey Russell, *Witchcraft in the Middle Ages* (Ithaca, N.Y., 1984).

5. Pollock, *Forgotten Children*.

6. Ruth Benedict, *Patterns of Culture* (New York, 1934), pp. 120–59, discussing the Island of Dobo. We are grateful to Wendy Wiener for suggesting this case.

7. John Demos, *A Little Commonwealth: Family Life in Plymouth Colony* (New York, 1970); David Brion Davis, *Homicide in American Fiction, 1798–1860: A Study in Social Values* (Ithaca, N.Y., 1968).

8. George Lakoff and Zoltan Kovesces, *The Cognitive Model of Anger Inherent in American English*, Berkeley Cognitive Science Report no. 10 (Berkeley, Calif., 1983).

9. John P. Demos, "Shame and Guilt in Early America," *Journal of Social History* (in press); on the larger emotional context, with some historical

reference, see Helen Lewis, *Shame and Guilt in Neurosis* (New York, 1971).

10. Homer, *Iliad*, 18.109. The quotation, abridged, is cited, with qualified approval, in G. Stanley Hall, *Adolescence* (New York, 1931).

11. George M. Shatton, *Anger: Its Religious and Moral Significance* (New York, 1923), p. 239; Weinstein and Bell, *Saints*.

12. Lawrence Stone, *The Family, Sex and Marriage in England, 1500–1800* (New York, 1977); Jean-Louis Flandrin, *Families in Former Times* (Cambridge, 1979).

13. Walter Ong, *Orality and Literacy* (London and New York, 1982). Ong plausibly argues that rising literacy causes new emotional standards, though he offers no direct evidence from actual emotionology. He almost surely errs in implying a uniform emotional style for preliterate peoples. (See Michael Mac-Donald, *Mystical Bedlam: Madness, Anxiety, and Healing in Seventeenth-Century England* [Cambridge, 1981]).

14. Charles Radding, "Evolution of Medieval Mentalities: A Cognitive Structural Approach," *American Historical Review* 82 (1978): 577–97.

15. Hunt, *Parents and Children*, p. 147.

16. Flandrin, *Families in Former Times*.

17. Herman W. Roodenburg, "The Autobiography of Isabella de Moerloose: Sex, Childrearing and Popular Belief in Seventeenth Century Holland," *Journal of Social History* 18 (1985): 521ff. De Moerloose was dearly loved as a child; her will not broken. But after infancy she was exposed to rather frightening examples of parental anger, without apparent apology. Her case thus suggests continuities (maternal affection is not simply modern) but also contrasts (in the unmitigated and therefore frightening display of anger) with characteristic modern standards.

18. Jerome Kagan, *The Growth of the Child: Reflections on Human Development* (New York, 1979). Current orthodoxy in child development circles insists on the adaptability of children to various parental styles rather than on automatically diverse outcomes to diverse styles.

19. Bertram Wyatt Brown, *Southern Honor, Ethics and Behavior in the Old South* (New York, 1982); Rhys Isaac, *The Transformation of Virginia, 1740–1790* (Chapel Hill, N.C., 1982), p. 344; Isaac makes it clear that Southern anger could occasionally misfire—when the power to back it up was lacking—but not because it was disapproved of per se.

20. On expectations that servants show anger at insults to their masters, see Sara Maza, *Servants and Masters in 18th-Century France* (Princeton, N.J., 1983).

21. Robert W. Malcolmsen, *Popular Recreation in English Society, 1700–1850* (Cambridge, 1973); Natalie Davis, *Society and Culture in Early Modern France* (Stanford, Calif., 1975). On southern brawling, see Isaac, *Transformation of Virginia*, pp. 95–96; and Elliott J. Gorn, " 'Gouge and Bite, Pull Hair and Scratch': The Social Significance of Fighting in the Southern Back-country," *American Historical Review* 90 (1985): 18–43. On anger in and against witchcraft, see Demos, *Entertaining Satan*. On changing rates of murder and violence, see Lawrence Stone, "Interpersonal Violence in English

Society, 1300–1980,'' *Past and Present* no. 101 (1983): 22–23; Roger Lane, *Violent Death in the City: Suicide, Accident and Murder in Nineteenth-Century Philadelphia* (Cambridge, Mass., 1979). On the revenge tradition, see Jacob Black-Michaud, *Cohesive Force: Feud in the Mediterranean and the Middle East* (New York, 1975); and Sarah Rubin Blanshei, ''Crime and Law Enforcement in Medieval Bologna,'' *Journal of Social History* 16 (1982): 121–38. For philosophical and literary references on the Western history of revenge, see Susan Jacoby, *Wild Justice: The Evolution of Revenge* (New York, 1983). Norbert Elias (*The Civilizing Process: The History of Manners,* trans. Edmund Jephcott [New York, 1978]) discusses the emotional vagaries of premodern European society, noting the frequency of flashes of temper. His discussion of the rise of more genteel manners, though focused primarily on habits of politeness in dining and so on, obviously relates to the disciplining of temper and the increasingly widespread view, by the eighteenth century, that emotional outbursts and lability were childish. (See esp. pp. 190–203.)

22. *Maladicta: The International Journal of Verbal Aggression* 1 (1977): 7; see also 3 (1979): 2. On the verbal aggression of peasant societies, see Lawrence Wylie, *Village in the Vaucluse* (New York, 1964): and J. T. Sanders, *Rainbow in the Rock: The People of Rural Greece* (Cambridge, 1962).

23. Demos, ''Shame and Guilt in Early America''; *Records and Files of the Quarterly Courts of Essex County, Massachusetts,* 8 vols. (Salem, Mass., 1911–21), 2:353, 1:275, 8:272. For similar southern insults, see Isaac, *Transformation of Virginia,* p. 95.

24. Edward Bever, ''Old Age and Witchcraft in Early Modern Europe,'' in *Old Age in Preindustrial Society,* ed. Peter N. Stearns (New York, 1983), pp. 150–90; Demos, *Entertaining Satan;* Carol Z. Wiener, ''The Beleaguered Isle: A Study of Elizabethan and Early Jacobean Anti-Catholicism,'' *Past and Present,* no. 51 (1971): 27–62.

25. Paul Monroe, *Thomas Platter and the Educational Renaissance of the Sixteenth Century* (New York, 1904); Elias, *Civilizing Process.*

26. MacDonald, *Mystical Bedlam.*

27. Stone, *Family, Sex and Marriage*; Demos, *A Little Commonwealth*; on the use of colonial courts to defuse anger, see David Konig, *Law and Society in Puritan Massachusetts* (Cambridge, Mass., 1979).

28. Nathaniel B. Shurtleff and David Pulsifer, eds., *Records of the Colony of New Plymouth in New England* (1861; reprint, Boston, 1978), 1:102.

29. William Thomas Davis, ed., *Bradford's History of Plimouth Plantation* (Boston, 1898), 1: 293–94; Demos, *A Little Commonwealth.*

30. Stone, *Family, Sex and Marriage;* Flandrin, *Families in Former Times.*

31. David Hackett Fischer, *Growing Old in America* (New York, 1977); Peter N. Stearns, *Old Age in European Society: The Case of France* (New York, 1979); Lutz Berkner, ''The Stem Family and the Development Cycle: An Eighteenth-Century Austrian Example,'' *American Historical Review* 77 (1972): 398–414; Keith Thomas, ''Age and Authority in Early Modern England,'' *Proceedings of the British Academy* 62 (1976): 233–48. Bever (''Old

Age and Witchcraft,'' p. 189) offers the fascinating suggestion that witchcraft trials may have altered the emotional image presented by the elderly, or at least elderly women, toward greater passivity and benignity.

32. Jack P. Greene, ed., *Diary of Colonel Landon of Sabine Hall,* 2 vols. (Charlottesville, Va., 1965), pp. 250, 310, 315, 763, 1004, 1102.

33. Peter Laslett, *The World We Have Lost: England before the Industrial Age* (New York, 1971). Faye E. Dudden (*Serving Women: Household Service in Nineteenth-Century America* [Middletown, Conn., 1983]) argues that preindustrial servants were treated ''more like family'' than were nineteenth-century servants, socially more distant, as immigrants or farm girls, from middle-class mistresses and therefore more likely to be targets for anger. This is of course possible, but dubious, as far as emotional style, including family style, is concerned, and the claim runs against available eighteenth-century evidence on servant conditions. Parents often bound children out as servants in harsh conditions, largely for economic reasons but in part to avoid conflict in the home as growth reduced the childish habit of obedience.

34. Laslett, *The World We Have Lost.*

35. Benjamin Franklin, *Autobiography* (New York, 1962), p. 30; see also Stephen Innes, *Labor in a New Land: Economy and Society in Seventeenth-Century Springfield* (Princeton, N.J., 1983), pp. 119, 140–48.

36. Johann Huizinga, *The Waning of the Middle Ages* (New York, 1962), p. 10. Robert Darnton (*The Great Cat Massacre* [New York, 1984]) suggests uses of animals as emotional outlets.

37. Edwards and Heaton are quoted in Philip J. Greven, Jr., *The Protestant Temperament: Patterns of Childrearing, Religious Experience and the Self in Early America* (New York, 1977), pp. 111, 113; see also Philip J. Greven, Jr., ed., *Childrearing Concepts, 1628–1861* (Itasca, Ill., 1973); Catharine Sedgwick, *Home* (Boston, 1841), p. 15 and passim.

38. Flandrin, *Families in Former Times;* Randolph Trumbach, *The Rise of the Egalitarian Family: Aristocratic Kinship and Domestic Relations in Eighteenth Century England* (New York, 1978); on more affectionate images of and roles for the elderly, see Fischer, *Growing Old.*

39. *Century Dictionary* (New York, 1909); Eric Partridge, *Dictionary of Slang and Unconventional English* (New York, 1937), p. 865; *Oxford English Dictionary.* Quotes come from Samuel Foote, *Knights* (London, 1748); and Mrs. Mary P. Delaney, *Life and Correspondence* (London, 1776). See *Oxford English Dictionary,* s.v. *tantrums.*

40. Flandrin, *Families in Former Times.*

41. Greven, *Temperament,* pp. 264–65; Stone, *Family, Sex and Marriage,* pp. 224, 237.

42. Greven, *Temperament.*

43. Reverend C. B. I. Hallock, *Fraternal Sermons and Addresses* (New York, 1931), p. 43.

44. Elmer H. Murdoch, ''Emotions—Their Rightful Place,'' *Alliance Witness,* 24 June 1970, pp. 3–4.

45. A statement made in 1913 by Albert Ellis, the evangelical founder of

rational emotive therapy (cited in David McLaughlin, *Modern Revivalism* [New York, 1959], p. 82).

46. Keith Thomas, *Man and the Natural World: A History of the Modern Sensibility* (New York, 1983).

47. Ong, *Orality and Literacy*. Ong's theory is, however, excessively generalized; he wrongly imputes a set emotionality to all preliterate societies when in fact his data bear on Western culture almost exclusively. Ong also fudges once literacy is achieved, again finding undue homogeneity. While some new concern about anger may describe literate society generally, as we think it does for Western society, it is definitely not an even concern. Ong tries to deal with this by claiming surprising persistence for the oral tradition. Thus the anger of the Lincoln-Douglas debate reflects the passion of an oral society, which cannot be reproduced in our more controlled, literate age. This is an erroneous use of orality for what was a quite literate nineteenth-century Illinois populace and cannot therefore guide emotional history too precisely. Other factors besides literacy enter in.

48. Edmund Leites, "The Duty to Desire: Love, Friendship and Sexuality in Some Puritan Theories of Marriage," *Journal of Social History* 15 (1982): 383–408; Flandrin, *Families in Former Times*.

49. Trumbach, *The Rise of the Egalitarian Family*.

50. Elias, *The Civilizing Process*; W. K. Jordan, *The Development of Religious Toleration in England from the Convention of the Long Parliament to the Restoration, 1640–1660* (Cambridge, Mass., 1938), pp. 316, 347ff.; Susie I. Tucker, *Enthusiasm: A Study in Semantic Change* (Cambridge, 1972), pp. 52–61.

51. Carole Shammas, "The Domestic Environment in Early Modern England and America," *Journal of Social History* 14 (1980): 3–24.

52. Max Weber, *The Protestant Ethic and the Spirit of Capitalism*, trans. Talcott Parsons (New York, 1958); R. H. Tawney, *Religion and the Rise of Capitalism: A Historical Study* (New York, 1947); for an updated statement of capitalism's propensity to remold personality, see Andrew Scull, ed., *Madhouses, Mad-Doctors and Madmen* (Philadelphia, 1981), pp. 105–15.

53. Ann Douglas, *The Feminization of American Culture* (New York, 1977); Elizabeth E. Skoglund, *To Anger, with Love* (New York, 1977): John Warwick Montgomery, "Getting Hold of Our Feelings," *Christianity Today* 25, no. 4 (1981): 92; Shattan, *Anger*; David W. Augsburger, *Anger and Assertiveness in Pastoral Care* (Philadelphia, 1979); George Hodges, *The Training of Children in Religion* (New York, 1917); Norman Hope, "How to Be Good—and Mad," *Christianity Today* 12, no. 1 (1968): 3–5; Jack O. Balswick and James W. Balkwell, "Religious Orthodoxy and Emotionality," *Review of Religious Research* 19 (1971): 308–19.

Chapter 3

1. Since the history of American marriage manuals has not been written, our choice of manuals has depended on the secondary works and bibliography

of the history of the family. Great help was provided by Michael Gordon, who allowed us to use his list of manuals compiled from the *American Catalogue of Books* and the *Cumulative Book Index*. Although it was impossible to read every manual printed, a sufficient number were used (approximately 115) to enable us to get a sense of variety as well as representativeness.

Choice of magazines was made by using Frank Luther Mott's assessment of what was most popular (*A History of American Magazines*, 4 vols. [Cambridge, Mass., 1957–68]). *Godey's Lady's Book* (hereafter cited as *Godey's*) was used from 1840–55 (see Mott, 1: 581). *Peterson's Magazine* (hereafter cited as *Peterson's*) was used for 1860–95 (see Mott, 1: 593, 2: 309–11). The *Ladies Home Journal* (hereafter cited as *LHJ*) was used for the twentieth century (see Mott, 4: 540ff.). Lest it be objected that these magazines were consumed by women only, Mott has demonstrated that they were widely read by men too, the *LHJ*, in fact, being the magazine third most in demand by soldiers during World War I (1: 590, 4: 550).

We have chosen to work with popular magazines because we feel that in some sense they are representative of or at least in line with popular opinion. For the same reason, we have utilized marriage manuals and, in later sections, manuals on child rearing and employee relations. We have not, except in passing, used great works of literature, for unlike scholars in the American-studies tradition, we doubt that such sources are especially representative of mass opinion. Many Victorian novels did express the dominant emotionology. In some historical periods, however, art expresses feelings not usually permitted—witness the romantic love themes of traditional Chinese or premodern European literature or, we will later argue, the symbolic anger expressed in twentieth-century American culture. The role of "art," then, in emotionology is complex, not only because of the issue of representativeness, but also because art can fill contradictory roles, depending on period (and, perhaps, the solidity of an emotionology): it can help install an emotionology, as in Victorian literature, or it can support it by providing outlets for emotions actually proscribed.

2. Nancy Cott, *The Bonds of Womanhood* (New Haven, Conn., 1977) pp. 63ff.; Barbara Welter, "The Cult of True Womanhood: 1820–1860," *American Quarterly* 18 (1966): 151–74; Barbara Berg, *The Remembered Gate: Origins of American Feminism: The Woman and the City, 1800–1860* (New York, 1978), pp. 30–59; Mary P. Ryan, *Womanhood in America* (New York, 1975), pp. 137ff.

3. Peter Gay, *The Bourgeois Experience: Victoria to Freud*, vol. 1, *Education of the Senses* (New York, 1984), pp. 42–70; Daniel Rodgers, *The Work Ethic in Industrial America, 1850–1920* (Chicago, 1978), pp. 1–29. Michael Paul Rogin, *Fathers and Children: Andrew Jackson and the Subjugation of the American Indian* (New York, 1975), pp. 13ff.

4. F. Saunders, *About Women, Love and Marriage* (New York, 1874), pp. 11, 19. Rogin sees this dream of a peaceful Eden as regressive and in some sense related to the wish of the adult to return to its infant symbiosis with the mother. For a discussion of the persistence of this sort of fantasy in contemporary life and a similar interpretation of its meaning, see James Mann, *Time-*

limited Psychotherapy (Cambridge, Mass., 1973), chap. 1. It is indeed of historical interest if such fantasies began to become widespread exactly when mother-infant relationships were first becoming intensified. That the Eden was so often contrasted with the work world, however, shows that the adult fantasy was a statement of present and conscious concerns with industrialism as well as unconscious wishes for a return to childhood.

5. Reverend Daniel Wise, *Bridal Greetings* . . . (New York, 1852), p. 122.

6. James Bean, *The Christian Minister's Affectionate Advice to a New Married Couple* (Boston, 1832), p. 17.

7. *Godey's* 22 (1841): 165.

8. *Godey's* 34 (1846): 5–7.

9. William Alcott, *The Young Husband* . . . (Boston, 1840), p. 231.

10. *Godey's* 26 (1843): 213–14. For a discussion of T. S. Arthur, see Helen W. Papashvily, *All the Happy Endings* (New York, 1956), pp. 49ff.

11. James R. Miller, *Home-Making* (Philadelphia, 1882), pp. 20–27.

12. Orson S. Fowler, *Fowler on Matrimony* . . . (New York, 1842), p. 105.

13. Ibid.; Bean, *Christian Minister's Affectionate Advice,* pp. 37–38.

14. Wise, *Bridal Greetings,* p. 23.

15. Reverend John L. Brandt, *Marriage and the Home* . . . (Chicago, 1895), pp. 123, 134.

16. *Godey's* 47 (1853): 138–39.

17. Ibid.

18. *Godey's* 47 (1853): 397.

19. *Godey's* 28 (1843): 214.

20. *Peterson's* 68, no. 3 (September 1875): 183–89.

21. *Peterson's* 47, no. 6 (June 1865): 405–7.

22. *Godey's* 30 (1845): 71–73.

23. *Godey's* 21 (1840): 77–81.

24. Miller, *Home-Making,* p. 294.

25. A classic statement of Victorian fear of sex is Peter Cominos, "Innocent Femina Sensualis in Unconscious Conflict," in *Suffer and Be Still* ed. Martha Vicinus (Bloomington, Ind., 1972), pp. 155–72. Recent work has modified the literalness with which the Victorian sexual ethic was translated into actual sexual behavior (see Gay, *Bourgeois Experience*; and Carl Degler, *At Odds: Women and the Family in America from the Revolution to the Present* [New York, 1980]). But this recent work, somewhat exaggerated in its effort to liberate middle-class sexual behavior, has not seriously altered the judgment of the official sexual ethic and indeed suffers from failing to integrate Victorian emotionology about sex with behavioral evidence. For a comment, see Carol Z. Stearns and Peter N. Stearns, "Victorian Sexuality: Can Historians Do It Better?" *Journal of Social History* 18 (1985): 625–34.

26. For an interesting discussion of what different periods define as the essential self, see Ralph H. Turner, "The Real Self from Institution to Impulse," *American Journal of Sociology* 81, no. 5 (1976): 989–1016.

27. *Godey's* 47 (1853): 395.

28. *Godey's* 40 (1850): 192.

29. Fowler, *Fowler on Matrimony*, p. 104.

30. Nelson Sizer, *Thoughts on Domestic Life* . . . (New York, 1858), p. 41.

31. *Godey's* 20 (1840): 31–32.

32. *Godey's* 44 (1852): 43.

33. *Godey's* 21 (1840): 74.

34. *Godey's* 31 (1845): 96.

35. *Godey's* 21 (1840): 128.

36. *Godey's* 23 (1841): 267.

37. *Godey's* 20 (1840): 30.

38. See, e.g., the advice that a husband "coax" his difficult wife (*Godey's* 43 [1851]: 6–7) or, more unusual, the story "Circumstances Alter Cases," in which a wife is praised for solving her marital conflicts by tricking her husband (*Godey's* 30 [1845]: 164).

39. Ebenezer Baily, *The Young Ladies' Class Book* (Boston, 1832), pp. 84–85.

40. Alcott, *The Young Husband*, pp. 289–91.

41. James Reed, *Man and Woman Equal but Unlike* (Boston, 1870), p. 29.

42. Fowler, *Fowler on Matrimony*, p. 105.

43. Wise, *Bridal Greetings*, p. 31.

44. G. Stanley Hall, "A Study of Anger," *American Journal of Psychology* 10 (1899): 615–91; Nina Baym, *Women's Fiction: A Guide to Novels by and about Women in America, 1820–1870* (Ithaca, N.Y., 1978), p. 241.

45. *Godey's* 31 (1846): 92–96.

46. *Godey's* 43 (1851): 6–7.

47. *Godey's* 30 (1845): 68, 71.

48. Brandt, *Marriage and the Home*, pp. 75ff., 102. See also Alcott, *The Young Husband;* and the phrenologists Hiram S. Pomeroy, *The Ethics of Marriage* (New York, 1888); and John Robins, *The Family* . . . (Chicago, 1896). Choice of a right spouse became especially important as a subject in the books written in the 1880s and 1890s, a trend that reflects a context of rising anxiety about divorce.

49. *Peterson's* 39, no. 6 (June 1861): 481–82.

50. *Godey's* 47 (1853): 397.

51. *Godey's* 21 (1840): 74.

52. *Godey's* 21 (1840): 16.

53. *Godey's* 22 (1841): 169.

54. *Godey's* 28 (1844): 214.

55. *Godey's* 23 (1841): 267; and *Godey's* 22 (1841): 75, 77, 109, 122.

56. Alcott, *The Young Husband*, pp. 287, 290–91.

57. *Peterson's* 47, no. 6 (June 1865): 405.

58. *Godey's* 21 (1840): 77, 80.

59. *Godey's* 44 (1852): 44.

60. *Godey's* 24 (1842): 2ff.

61. *Godey's* 30 (1845): 1–4.

62. *LHJ* 1 (March 1884): 7.

63. Baily, *Young Ladies' Class Book*, p. 85.

64. Reverend William M. Thayer, *Hints for the Household . . .* (Cleveland, 1853), pp. 43–44.

65. William A. Alcott, *The Young Wife . . .* (Boston, 1837), pp. 205ff.

66. Mrs. Chapone is cited in Baily, *Young Ladies' Class Book,* p. 84. On the *Ruth Hall* controversy, see Ann D. Wood, "The 'Scribbling Women' and Fanny Fern: Why Women Wrote," *American Quarterly* 23 (1971): 3–24.

67. Degler, *At Odds*; Stearns and Stearns, "Victorian Sexuality."

68. Peter G. Filene, *Him/Herself: Sex Roles in Modern America* (New York, 1975), pp. 78–79, 92.

69. Alcott, *The Young Husband*, pp. 231–32, 257–58.

70. Bernard Wishy, *The Child and the Republic* (Philadelphia, 1968); R. Gordon Kelly, *Mother Was a Lady: Self and Society in Selected American Children's Periodicals, 1865–1890* (Westport, Conn., 1974); Philip J. Greven, Jr., ed., *Childrearing Concepts, 1628–1861* (Itasca, Ill., 1973). Evaluation of the history of child-rearing advice on anger, in this and subsequent chapters, is based on a combination of studies of advice—often quite good, though not directed to the subject of anger—and primary materials. Inquiry into nineteenth-century approaches is facilitated by several excellent histories of child rearing in general, such as those cited above. These studies help establish the representativeness of the primary materials consulted. For the twentieth century, which period will be first broached in chap. 4, secondary treatments have focused primarily on infant care and on Dr. Spock (see Leone Kell and Jean Aldous, "Trends in Child Care over Three Generations," *Marriage and Family Living* 22 [1960]: 176–77; Jay Mechling, "Advice to Historians on Advice to Mothers," *Journal of Social History* 9 [1975]: 44ff.; Celia B. Stendler, "Sixty Years of Child Training Practices," *Journal of Pediatrics* 36 [1950]: 122–34; Thomas Gordon, *Parent Effectiveness Training* [New York, 1970]; and Martha Wolfenstein, "Trends in Infant Care," *American Journal of Orthopsychiatry* 23 [1953]: 120–30). Here we have undertaken wider reading, testing for representativeness by picking up major examples of "schools" such as the Watsonians and by using materials issued from major parent-guidance groups and publications, including the journal *Parents' Magazine*. Representativeness is also tested through analysis of internal consistency on key points within each period and through juxtaposition with some children's literature and school advice. There is no denying the fact that a study of child-rearing literature that goes beyond mere summary, to claims of changes in tone and of some connection with wider social values, exceeds the most rigorous standards of evidence. This limitation imposes caution on both researcher and reader. It is at least partially compensated for by the importance of advancing a richer historical context for the understanding of emotional life.

71. Fowler, *Fowler on Matrimony*, p. 21.

72. Alcott, *The Young Husband*, p. 285; Sizer, *Thoughts on Domestic Life*, pp. 19–20.

73. Baily, *Young Ladies' Class Book,* p. 84.

74. W. Lloyd Warner, *American Life: Dream and Reality* (Chicago, 1962).

75. Dorothy Canfield Fisher, *Mothers and Children* (New York, 1914), pp. 165ff.

76. Jean-Louis Flandrin, *Families in Former Times* (Cambridge, 1979), p. 149.

77. Philip J. Greven, Jr., *The Protestant Temperament: Patterns of Child-rearing, Religious Experience and the Self in Early America* (New York, 1977), pp. 111ff.

78. Martha Jane Jewsbury, *Letters Addressed to Her Young Friends* (Boston, 1829); John Angell James, *The Family Monitor, or a Help to Domestic Happiness* (Concord, N.H., 1829), p. 83; Louisa Hoare, *Hints for the Improvement of Early Education and Nursery Discipline* (Salem, Mass., 1826).

79. Horace Bushnell, *Views of Christian Nurture* (Hartford, Conn., 1847), pp. 47, 198; see also Greven, ed., *Childrearing,* p. 142. On the ongoing Calvinist theme, see Robert Sumley, "Early Nineteenth-Century American Literature on Child-Rearing," in *Childhood in Contemporary Cultures,* ed. Margaret Mead and Martha Wolfenstein (Chicago, 1955), pp. 150–67; Anne L. Kuhn, *The Mother's Role in Childhood Education: New England Concepts, 1830–1860* (New Haven, Conn., 1947), p. 78; thus Catharine E. Beecher devoted a whole chapter to "cheerfulness" in her *Treatise on Domestic Economy* (1841; reprint, New York, 1970). In much of the advice literature of this period, temper is discussed obliquely for men, on the assumption that it can be successfully disciplined in childhood, but not explicitly at all for girls or women. Thus Catharine Sedgwick notes that business cares may legitimately ruffle a man's temper but that "his wife was of a happier temperament. Her equal, sunny temper soon rectified the disturbed balance of his" (*Home* [Boston, 1841], p. 15).

80. Wishy, *Child and the Republic,* pp. 162ff.; Jacob Abbott, *Gentle Measures in the Management and Training of the Young* (New York, 1871).

81. Sedgwick, *Home;* Wishy, *Child and the Republic,* pp. 44ff.

82. Kelly, *Mother Was a Lady,* pp. 74–75; Wishy, *Child and the Republic,* pp. 43ff.; Sedgwick, *Home,* pp. 20ff.

83. John S. C. Abbott, *The Mother and the Home* (London, 1834), pp. 51, 63.

84. Ibid., p. 63; Hall, "Anger," p. 572.

85. Marion Marland, *Eve's Daughter, or Common Sense for Maid, Wife and Mother* (New York, 1882), p. 222.

86. On attacks on traditional discipline, see issues of the *LHJ* from 1880 to 1889; Grace Langdon and J. W. Stout, *The Discipline of Well-adapted Children* (New York, 1952), p. 11; and Dorothy Canfield Fisher and Sidonie M. Greenberg, eds., *Our Children: A Handbook for Parents* (New York, 1932). On women and anger, see G. Stanley Hall, *Adolescence* (New York, 1931), vol. 2, passim; and Marland, *Eve's Daughter.* On the reduction of outlets, particularly through efforts to prevent childish cruelty to animals (a subject

that, however, merits elaboration), see Fisher, *Mothers*, p. 39. On vagueness of specific advice, see T. S. Arthur, *Home Scenes* (Philadelphia, 1854), pp. 54–60, and *The Mother's Rule* (Philadelphia, 1858).

87. This process bears no small resemblance to the changes in mainstream American Protestantism that have been termed a "feminization." As women gained new religious influence and reflected their own new, Victorian standards, they helped attack traditional ideas of an angry God and angry punishments in the afterlife. (See Ann Douglas, *The Feminization of American Culture* [New York, 1977].) A more precise probable link also exists between the feminized emotionology at this point and the advent of increasingly maternally dominated child rearing during the middle decades of the nineteenth-century (see Mary Ryan, *Cradle of the Middle Class: The Family in Oneida County, New York, 1790–1865* [Cambridge, Mass., 1981], pp. 145–85).

88. Lloyd DeMause, ed., *History of Childhood* (New York, 1974); Greven, ed., *Childrearing Concepts*; Rena L. Vassar, ed., *A Social History of American Education* (Chicago, 1965), 1:5, 26, 180. Even Linda A. Pollock (*Forgotten Children: Parent-Child Relations from 1500 to 1900* [Cambridge, 1984]) notes some change on this score.

89. Beecher, *Treatise*, pp. 191ff. William G. McLoughlin, "Evangelical Child-Rearing in the Age of Jackson: Francis Wayland's View on When and How to Subdue the Willfuness of Children," *Journal of Social History* 9 (1975): 234.

90. Margaret Elizabeth Sangster, *An Autobiography* (New York, 1909), p. 44.

91. Charlotte (Howard) Gilman, *Recollections of a Southern Matron* (New York, 1852), pp. 296–98.

92. Robert Griswold, "The Evolution of the Doctrine of Mental Cruelty in Victorian American Divorce, 1790–1900," *Journal of Social History* (in press).

93. Greven, *The Protestant Temperament* (n. 77 above); Wishy, *Child and the Republic* (n. 70 above).

94. Elizabeth Parsons Channing, *Autobiography* (Boston, 1907); and Lydia Howard Sigourney, *Lucy Howard's Journal* (New York, 1858), pp. 6–7; DeMause, ed., *History of Childhood;* Patricia Branca, *Silent Sisterhood: Middle Class Women in the Victorian Home* (Pittsburgh, 1975), pp. 95–113.

95. See discussion in Ann Douglas Wood, "The Fashionable Diseases: Women's Complaints and Their Treatment in Nineteenth Century America," in *Clio's Consciousness Raised,* ed. Mary S. Hartman and Lois Banner (New York, 1974); Carroll Smith-Rosenberg, "Hysterical Women," *Social Research* 39 (1972): 652–78; Hannah S. Decker, "Freud and Dora: Constraints on Medical Progress," *Journal of Social History* 14 (1981): 449ff.

96. Jean Strouse, *Alice James: A Biography* (New York, 1980), pp. 130ff.

97. Fowler, *Fowler on Matrimony*, pp. 104–5.

98. James R. Averill, *Anger and Aggression: An Essay on Emotion* (New York, 1982), p. 295; Baym, *Women's Fiction*, p. 144; Ella W. Wilcox, *Men, Women and Emotions* (Chicago, 1894), p. 222.

99. Lillian Bell, *Why Men Remain Bachelors* (New York, 1906), p. 23.

100. Papashvily, *All the Happy Endings*, passim.

101. Wise, *Bridal Greetings*, p. 122.

102. *Peterson's* 48, no. 2 (August 1865): 119–25; see also Wilcox, *Men, Women and Emotions*, p. 222, on martyrdom; Beecher, *Treatise*, p. 122.

103. Ethan Smith, ed., *Memoirs of Mrs. Abigail Bailey* (1815; reprint, New York, 1980), pp. 14ff., 17.

104. Frances Anne Kemble, *Journal of a Residence on a Georgian Plantation in 1838–1839* (New York, 1863), passim.

105. *Godey's* 42 (1851): 193.

106. Gilman, *Recollections*, pp. 296–98.

107. Sangster, *Autobiography*, pp. 143ff. For a modern statement that anger not expressed causes self-alienation, see Jean Baker Miller, "The Construction of Anger in Women and Men," Stone Center for Developmental Services and Studies, Work in Progress no. 83-01 (Wellesley, Mass., 1983).

108. M. R. Yarrow, J. D. Campbell, and R. V. Burton, *Child-Rearing: An Inquiry into Research Methods* (San Francisco, 1968).

109. DeMause, ed., *History of Childhood*; Branca, *Silent Sisterhood*, pp. 95–113.

110. Elizabeth Cady Stanton, *Eighty Years and More—Reminiscences, 1815–1897*, ed. Gail Parker (New York, 1971).

111. Robert L. Griswold, *Family and Divorce in California, 1852–1890: Victorian Illusions and Everyday Realities* (Albany, N.Y., 1982), pp. 4, 43, 174.

112. Sidney H. Ditzion, *Marriage, Morals and Sex in America: A History of Ideas* (New York, 1953), p. 441. For the view that solace was found still in feminine friendships and extended kin, see Marilyn Ferris Motz, *True Sisterhood: Michigan Women and Their Kin* (Albany, N.Y., 1983).

113. Carol Tavris, *Anger: The Misunderstood Emotion* (New York, 1982), chap. 9.

114. Averill, *Anger and Aggression*, p. 167.

115. Jill K. Conway, *The Female Experience in Eighteenth- and Nineteenth-Century America: A Guide to the History of American Women* (New York, 1982), pp. 270, 272; Donald M. Scott and Bernard Wishy, *America's Families: A Documentary History* (New York, 1982), pp. 248–49; Cott, *Bonds*, pp. 80 ff.

116. Wise, *Bridal Greetings*, p. 119.

117. Michael Ryan, *The Philosophy of Marriage* (Philadelphia, [1850s?]), p. 71.

118. James R. Miller, *Home-Making*, p. 42. See also Wilcox, *Men, Women and Emotions*, p. 224; Thomas De Witt Talmage, *The Marriage Ring* (New York, 1886), p. 65; Sizer, *Thoughts on Domestic Life*, p. 44; E. J. Hardy, *How to Be Happy though Married* (New York, 1886), pp. 198ff.

119. *Peterson's* 40, no. 5 (November 1861): 397; *Peterson's* 57, no. 5 (November 1870): 391; *Peterson's* 67, no. 5 (May 1875): 374; and *Peterson's* 78, no. 4 (October 1880): 310.

120. For a discussion of the dual errors of equating emotionology and emotion and of ignoring their relationship, see Stearns and Stearns, "Victorian Sexuality." For an example of a woman who seemed comfortable ignoring the emotionology, see C. Richard King, ed., *Victorian Lady on the Texas Frontier: The Journal of Ann Raney Coleman (1830s–1880s)* (Norman, Okla., 1971), pp. 90–92. We are aware, certainly, of the fact that those who keep diaries are not necessarily typical.

Chapter 4

1. Herman Melville, *Billy Budd, Foretopman* (1891), in *Four Short Novels,* ed. William Plomer (New York, 1959), pp. 201–2. David Brion Davis has noted occasional sympathy for justifiably aroused anger and an equation of such anger with morality in other novels (see *Homicide in American Fiction, 1798–1860: A Study in Social Values* [Ithaca, N.Y., 1968], pp. 289–90).

2. E. Anthony Rotundo, "Body and Soul: Changing Ideals of American Middle-Class Manhood, 1770–1920," *Journal of Social History* 16 (1983): 23–38; Peter G. Filene, *Him/Herself: Sex Roles in Modern America* (New York, 1975), pp. 68–77.

3. Flora H. Williams, *You and Your Children* (Nashville, Tenn., 1946), pp. 40, 43; R. Gordon Kelly, *Mother Was a Lady: Self and Society in Selected American Children's Periodicals, 1865–1890* (Westport, Conn., 1974).

4. Gabriel Compayré, *Development of the Child in Later Infancy,* trans. M. Wilson (New York, 1902), and *The Intellectual and Moral Development of the Child,* trans. M. Wilson (New York, 1901).

5. G. Stanley Hall, "A Study of Anger," *American Journal of Psychology* 10 (1899): 615–91; American Institute of Child Life, *The Problem of Temper* (Philadelphia, 1914).

6. Ernest Groves and Gladys Groves, *Wholesome Childhood* (Boston, 1931).

7. A. H. Arlitt, *Psychology of Infancy and Early Childhood* (New York, 1930); Leslie B. Hohman, *As the Twig Is Bent* (New York, 1941); *Parents' Magazine* from 1927 to 1938; John B. Watson, *Psychological Care of Infant and Child* (New York, 1928), pp. 41–43. Child guidance workers, as noted above, reported great parental concern about tantrums in the 1920s and 1930s, exceeding what the experts recommended.

8. D. A. Thom, *Guiding the Adolescent,* U.S. Department of Labor, Children's Bureau Publication (Washington, D.C., 1935), and *Child Management,* U.S. Department of Labor, Children's Bureau Publication (Washington, D.C., 1925).

9. Reverend Andrew Morton, *The Family Circle* (Edinburgh, 1865); Louisa May Alcott, *Little Women* (1868–69) (New York, 1946), p. 98; see also p. 93.

10. D. G. Harris, H. G. Gough, and W. E. Martin, "Children's Ethnic Attitudes: Relationship to Parental Beliefs Concerning Child Training," *Child*

Development 21 (1950): 169–81; Albert Bandura and Richard Walters, *Adolescent Aggression* (New York, 1959), pp. 88–141; W. Lloyd Warner, *American Life: Dream and Reality* (Chicago, 1962), pp. 108, 210.

11. Garry Cleveland Myers, *Building Personality in Children* (New York, 1931), p. 190; M. H. Appel, "Aggressive Behavior in Nursery School Children and Adult Procedures in Dealing with Such Behavior," *Journal of Experimental Education* 11 (1942): 185–99.

12. Kelly, *Mother Was a Lady;* Abigail J. Stewart, David G. Winter, and H. David Jones ("Coding Categories for the Study of Child-Rearing from Historical Sources," *Journal of Interdisciplinary History* [1975]: 687–701) find some parallels in Britain, with reduction of references to obedience and mildness as virtues.

13. American Institute of Child Life, *Problem of Temper*, pp. 1–5; Hall, "Anger," p. 683.

14. Edwin Kirkpatrick, *Fundamentals of Child Study* (New York, 1919), p. 136; Alice M. Birney (Mrs. Theodore W.), *Childhood* (New York, 1904), pp. 66–67, 96.

15. Marion L. Faegre and John E. Anderson, *Child Care and Training* (Minneapolis, 1947); Percival M. Symonds, *The Psychology of Parent-Child Relationships* (New York, 1939), p. 151.

16. Howard R. Garis, *Uncle Wiggily's Story Book* (New York, 1921), p. 4. We are grateful to Clio Stearns, who called this passage to our attention.

17. Charlotte Gilman, *The Home, Its Work and Influence* (New York, 1903), p. 169; White House Conference on Child Health and Protection, *Growth and Development of the Child*, pt. 4, *Appraisement of the Child* (New York, 1932); U.S. Department of Labor, Children's Bureau, *Infant Care* (Washington, 1914).

18. Parents' Magazine, *The Mother's Encyclopedia* (New York, 1933), 1: 66, 2: 353.

19. Celia B. Stendler, "Sixty Years of Child Training Practices," *Journal of Pediatrics* 36 (1950): 122–34; A. Michael Sulman, "The Freudianization of the American Child: The Impact of Psychoanalysis in Popular Periodicals in the United States, 1919–1939" (Ph.D. diss., University of Pittsburgh, 1972); Clark Vincent, "Trends in Infant Care Ideas," *Child Development* 22 (1951): 199–210; Bernard Wishy, *The Child and the Republic* (Philadelphia, 1968).

20. Jay Mechling, "Advice to Historians on Advice to Mothers," *Journal of Social History* 9 (1975): 44–63; Martha Wolfenstein, "Trends in Infant Care," *American Journal of Orthopsychiatry* 23 (1953): 120–30; Leone Kell and Jean Aldous, "Trends in Child Care over Three Generations," *Marriage and Family Living* 22 (1960): 176–77.

21. Hall, "Anger," p. 638.

22. Ibid., pp. 670, 689; American Institute of Child Life, *Problem of Temper*, pp. 1, 10, 11; Dorothy Canfield Fisher, *Mothers and Children* (New York, 1914); John Anderson, *Happy Childhood: The Development and Guidance of Children and Youth* (New York, 1933), p. 101; Phyllis Harrison-Ross and Barbara Wyden, *The Black Child—a Parents' Guide* (New York, 1973), p. 180; Ruth W. Washburn, *Children Have Their Reasons* (New York, 1942),

pp. 8, 53. See also Smiley Blanton and Margaret Blanton, *Child Guidance* (New York, 1927); G. Stanley Hall, *Adolescence* (New York, 1931), 1: 221; William Healy, *Personality in Formation and Action* (New York, 1938).

23. C. Anderson and Marty Aldrich, *Babies Are Human Beings* (New York, 1938), pp. 115–16; see also M. S. Smart and R. C. Smart, *Living and Learning with Children* (Boston, 1949); Marion L. Faegre et al., *Child Care and Training* (Minneapolis, 1928), p. 146; Emily Post, *Children Are People* (New York, 1940), p. 259; George Lawton, *How to Be Happy though Young* (New York, 1949), p. 110; Esther Lloyd-Jones and Ruth Fedder, *Coming of Age* (New York, 1941), pp. 35, 40.

24. Ada Hart Arlitt, *The Child from One to Twelve* (New York, 1931), pp. 93–97; see also Robert B. Sears, Eleanor Maccoby, and Harry Levin, *Patterns of Child Rearing* (New York, 1957), pp. 268–69.

25. Julius Sachs, "Co-education in the United States," *Educational Review* 33 (1900): 300 and passim; Edward H. Cooper, *The Twentieth Century Child* (London, 1906).

26. William O'Neill, *Divorce in the Progressive Era* (New Haven, Conn., 1967), pp. 34ff.

27. Ibid., passim.

28. Madison C. Peters, *Will the Coming Man Marry?* (Philadelphia, 1905); Reverand E. J. Hardy, *Still Happy though Married* (New Haven, Conn., 1914).

29. Wilfred Lay, *A Plea for Monogamy* (New York, 1923), pp. 236, 276; Marie Stopes, *Married Love* (London, 1919); V. F. Calverton, *Bankruptcy of Marriage* (n.p., 1928); John Haynes Holmes, *Marriage and Divorce* (New York, 1913); Walter M. Gallichon, *The Psychology of Marriage* (New York, 1918).

30. William L. Howard, *Confidential Chats with Girls* (New York, 1911); Bernard MacFadden, *Marriage: A Lifelong Honeymoon* (New York, 1903), p. 71.

31. *Ladies Home Journal* (*LHJ*) (September 1905): 40.

32. O'Neill, *Divorce*, pp. 185–86; Ronald L. Howard, *A Social History of American Family Sociology, 1865–1940* (Westport, Conn., 1981), pp. 39, 43ff.

33. Frank Luther Mott, *A History of American Magazines*, 4 vols. (Cambridge, 1957–68), 4: 547.

34. *LHJ* (July 1915): 3, 4, 52.

35. *LHJ* (June 1915): 16, 60–61; see also *LHJ* (April 1920): 41, 168.

36. *LHJ* (August 1910): 80; see also the editorial in *LHJ* (1 January 1911): 6; and the editorial in *LHJ* (1 October 1911): 6.

37. *LHJ* (January 1905): 16.

38. *LHJ* (February 1915): 7.

39. Ella W. Wilcox, *Men, Women and Emotions* (Chicago, 1894), p. 83; Hardy, *Still Happy*, p. 245.

40. *LHJ* (June 1910): 42.

41. *LHJ* (June 1905): 8.

42. *LHJ* (March 1915): 18.

43. *LHJ* (August 1920): 110.

44. *LHJ* (February 1910): 10.

45. *LHJ* (June 1910): 6.

46. Hardy, *Still Happy*, p. 198.

47. *LHJ* (February 1925): 164; see also a mattress ad directed toward "keeping your temper, no one else wants its" in *LHJ* (October 1900): 21.

48. *LHJ* (November 1920): 132.

49. Hardy, *Still Happy*, p. 199; Lillian Bell, *Why Men Remain Bachelors* (New York, 1906), passim.

50. *LHJ* (June 1915): 20.

51. *LHJ* (March 1920): 139–40.

52. Arthur W. Spalding, *Makers of the Home* (Mountain View, Calif., 1928), p. 98.

53. *LHJ* (March 1905): 10.

54. *LHJ* (1 November 1910): 34.

55. *LHJ* (February 1910): 30.

56. *LHJ* (February 1915): 26.

57. *LHJ* (May 1930): 34.

58. Thomas Haskell, *The Emergence of Professional Social Science* (Urbana, Ill., 1977); Richard Hofstadter, *Social Darwinism in American Thought* (Boston, 1955).

59. Elaine Tyler May, *Great Expectations: Marriage and Divorce in Post-Victorian America* (Chicago, 1980); R. L. Howard, *American Family Sociology*; Filene, *Him/Herself*, p. 11.

60. Daniel T. Rodgers, "Socializing Middle-Class Children: Institutions, Fables, and Work Values in Nineteenth-Century America," *Journal of Social History* 13 (1980): 354–67.

61. Wishy, *Child and the Republic*; Rodgers, "Socializing Middle-Class Children."

62. Henry May, *The End of American Innocence* (New York, 1959).

63. For a general discussion, see William H. Chafe, *The American Woman: Her Changing Social, Economic and Political Roles, 1920–1970* (London, 1972), chap. 9. For specific examples, see also *LHJ* (April 1945): 131; *LHJ* (February 1945): 94ff., 141–44; and *LHJ* (October 1945): 183.

64. Arlitt, *The Child from One to Twelve*, pp. 93–97; for a secular approach even later, see also B. Von Haller Gilmer, *How to Help Your Child Develop Successfully* (New York, 1951), pp. 82–91, 149–50.

65. Andrew J. Cherlin, *Marriage, Divorce, Remarriage* (Cambridge, Mass., 1981), p. 22; Jeffrey K. Liker and Glen H. Elder, Jr., "Economic Hardship and Marital Relations in the 1930s," *American Sociological Review* 48 (June 1983): 343–59; E. T. May, *Great Expectations,* p. 162.

66. Melvin L. Kohn, "Social Class and the Exercise of Parental Authority," in *Personality and Social Systems,* ed. Neil Smelser and William Smelser (New York, 1963), p. 208.

67. Martha S. White, "Social Class, Child Rearing Practices, and Child Behavior," in Smelser and Smelser, eds., *Personality and Social Systems,* pp. 286–96; Sears et al., *Patterns of Child Rearing*; Appel, "Aggressive Behavior

of Nursery School Children''; Kell and Aldous, ''Trends in Child Care'';
Myra Musto and Doris Sharpe, ''Some Influential Factors in the Determination of Aggressive Behavior in Preschool Children,'' *Child Development* 18 (1947): 11–28; G. S. Gates, ''An Observational Study of Anger,'' *Journal of Experimental Psychology* 9 (1926): 325–36; D. R. Peterson et al., ''Child Behavior Problems and Parental Attitudes,'' *Child Development* 32 (1961): 151–62; Harold Orlansky, ''Infant Care and Personality,'' *Psychological Bulletin* 49 (1949): 1–48.

68. Phyllis Moen, E. L. Kain, and Glen Elder, Jr., ''Economic Conditions and Family Life: Contemporary and Historical Perspective,'' in *American Families and the Economy,* ed. R. Nelson and F. Skidmore (Washington, D.C., 1983), pp. 335–37.

69. Leigh Minturn and W. W. Lambert, *Mothers of Six Cultures* (New York, 1964), pp. 143 ff.; Margaret Mead and Martha Wolfenstein, eds., *Childhood in Contemporary Cultures* (Chicago, 1955), pp. 104, 223, 414; Sears et al., *Patterns of Child Rearing,* pp. 231ff.; Richard L. Rapson, ''The American Child as Seen by British Travelers, 1845–1935,'' *American Quarterly* 17 (1965): 524; Lawrence Wylie, *Village in the Vaucluse* (New York, 1964), pp. 49–51, 196–200. These studies use data from the 1930s through the 1950s. See also Jerome Kagan, ''The Child in the Family,'' in *The Family,* ed. A. S. Rossi, J. Kagan, and T. Hareven (New York, 1978), p. 39.

70. Hall, ''Anger''; Benjamin Rader, *American Sports* (Englewood Cliffs, N.J., 1983).

71. Sophie Ritholz, *Children's Behavior* (New York, 1959), pp. 60–61 and passim.

72. Lawrence A. Cremin, *American Education—the Colonial Experience, 1607–1783* (New York, 1970), p. 51; William Kilpatrick, *The Dutch Schools of New Netherland and Colonial New York* (Washington, D.C., 1912), p. 31. See also Helen Sobehart, ''Toward a History of Anger in the Schools'' (Carnegie-Mellon University, Department of History, December 1983, typescript). We are grateful to Sobehart and also to Joan Francis for many of the data that follow.

73. Cremin, pp. 368, 483.

74. Ibid., *American Education,* pp. 487–89 (taken from *The Diary of Cotton Mather* [New York, 1957], 1: 534–37).

75. J. Manning, ''Discipline in the Good Old Days,'' *Phi Delta Kappan* 41, no. 3 (1969): 96.

76. Rena L. Vassar, ed., *A Social History of American Education* (Chicago, 1965), 1:26 (taken from *The Autobiography of Reverend John Barnard* [Boston, 1766], pp. 178–87). See also Manning, ''Discipline—Old Days,'' p. 96; Philip J. Greven, Jr., *The Protestant Temperament: Patterns of Childrearing, Religious Experience and the Self in Early America* (New York, 1977), p. 278; Cremin, *American Education,* p. 500.

77. Thus a Boston committee in 1845 found an average of sixty-five floggings daily in a population of four hundred students, despite administration advice against any such punishments (Manning, ''Discipline—Old Days,'' pp. 94, 99; Otis Caldwell and Stuart Courtis, *Then and Now in Education* .

[New York, 1971], p. 20; Michael E. Katz, *The Irony of Early School Reform* [Cambridge, Mass., 1968], p. 129).

78. Charles E. Silberman, *Crisis in the Classroom* (New York, 1970), pp. 152–53.

79. Manning, "Discipline—Old Days," p. 96; Pennsylvania Retired School Employees Association, *So Your Children Can Tell Their Children* (Pittsburgh, 1961), pp. 101, 176, 210; Gerald L. Gutek, *A History of the Western Educational Experience* (New York, 1972), p. 383; Pittsburgh Public Schools, *Handbook for Counselors* (Pittsburgh, 1933), p. 34.

80. Daniel A. Prescott, *Emotion and the Educative Process* (Washington, D.C., 1938), pp. vi, vii, 29.

81. Vassar, ed., *American Education,* 2:219 (citing George Creel, "Hopes of the Hyphenated," *Century Magazine* 62 [January 1916]: 354–63).

82. Edwin I. Megargee and Jack E. Hokanson, eds., *The Dynamics of Aggression: Individual. Group and International Analyses* (New York, 1970), p. 106.

83. Ritholz, *Children's Behavior,* pp. 60–61; E. K. Wickman, *Children's Behavior and Teachers' Attitudes* (New York, 1928), pp. 17, 127, 161; Caroline B. Zachry, *Personality Adjustments in School Children* (New York, 1929).

84. Pittsburgh Public Schools, *Handbook of Personnel Procedures* (Pittsburgh, 1948), p. 37.

85. On mother-father differences, see Jerome Kagan, "Socialization of Aggression and the Perception of Parents in Fantasy," *Child Development* 29 (1958): 318; Jerome Seidman, ed., *The Child: A Book of Readings* (New York, 1958), p. 130; Arthur T. Jersild et al., *Joys and Problems of Child Rearing* (New York, 1949), pp. 212ff.

86. Hardy, *Still Happy,* p. 209.

87. Winnifred Babcock, *Me: A Book of Remembrance* (New York, 1915), pp. 231, 276, 349–50.

88. Filene, *Him/Herself,* pp. 44ff.

89. Christopher Lasch, *Haven in a Heartless World: The Family Besieged* (New York, 1977).

90. Margo Horn, "The Moral Message of Child Guidance, 1925–1945," *Journal of Social History* 18 (1984): 25–36.

91. Minturn and Lambert, *Mothers,* passim; Ritholz, *Children's Behavior* pp. 60–61; Wickman, *Children's Behavior;* White House Conference on Child Health and Protection, *The Young Child in the Home* (New York, 1936), p. 214.

92. Ethel Spencer, *The Spencers of Amberson Avenue: A Turn-of-the-Century Memoir,* ed. Michael P. Weber and Peter N. Stearns (Pittsburgh, 1983), p. 47.

93. Ibid., p. 121.

94. Thom, *Child Management,* passim; Pamela Holcomb, *The Pittsburgh Child Guidance Center* (Pittsburgh, 1986).

95. Daniel Miller and Guy Swanson, *The Changing American Parent* (New York, 1958), p. 223; Nancy P. Weiss, "Mother: The Invention of Ne-

cessity," *American Quarterly* 29 (1977): 553; Sears et al., *Patterns of Child Rearing*, p. 231.

96. Spencer, *The Spencers*, pp. 69, 78–79.

97. Filene, *Him/Herself;* Joe Dubbert, *A Man's Place: Masculinity in Transition* (Englewood Cliffs, N.J., 1979).

98. John W. M. Whiting and Irwin L. Child, *Child Training and Personality* (New Haven, Conn., 1953); James R. Averill, *Anger and Aggression: An Essay on Emotion* (New York, 1982); M. R. Yarrow, J. D. Campbell, and R. V. Burton, *Child-Rearing: An Inquiry into Research Methods* (San Francisco, 1968), p. 80; Orlansky, "Infant Care and Personality"; Jerome Kagan and H. A. Moss (*Birth to Maturity: A Study of Psychological Development* [New York, 1962]) argue that unpredictability is particularly salient for girls, whose anger is most fully repressed in childhood but who may turn out to be quite aggressive in later life.

99. Jed Dannenbaum, *Drink and Disorder: Temperance Reform in Cincinnati from the Washingtonian Revival to the WCTU* (Urbana, Ill., 1984).

Chapter 5

1. Herman Melville, *Billy Budd* (New York, 1972), pp. 215, 226.

2. The idea of periodic new anger, rather than sustained resentment, is indirectly suggested in James Cronin, *Industrial Conflict in Modern Britain* (Totowa, N.J., 1979). On the emotionality of worker protest, see Michelle Perrot, *Les Ouvriers en grève: France, 1871–1890,* 2 vols. (Paris, 1974); Stephen Meyer, *The Five Dollar Day: Labor Management and Social Control in the Ford Motor Company, 1908–1921* (Albany, N.Y., 1981).

3. Daniel J. Elazar, ed., "Working Conditions in the Early Twentieth Century: Testimony," *American Jewish Archives* 21 (1969): 163; L. G. Lindahl, "Discipline 100 Years Ago," *Personnel Journal* 28 (1949): 246.

4. Tamara K. Hareven and Randolph Langenbach, *Amoskeag: Life and Work in an American Factory City* (New York, 1978), pp. 352 and passim; see also Michael Santos, *Iron Workers in a Steel Age: The Case of the A. M. Byers Company, 1900–1969* (D.A. diss., Carnegie-Mellon University, 1981).

5. David Grimsted, "Ante-Bellum Labor Agitation: Violence, Strike, and Communal Arbitration," *Journal of Social History* 19 (1985): 1–27.

6. Duane A. Smith, ed., "Pike's Peak Fifty-Niner: The Diary of E. A. Breven," *Colorado Magazine* 47 (1970): 269–311; Robert R. David, Jr., ed., "An Ohioan's Letter from the California Gold Fields in 1850," *Ohio History* 76 (1967): 159–63.

7. On persistent traditionalism in other related aspects of the management approach, see Reinhard Bendix, *Work and Authority in Industry: Ideologies of Management in the Course of Industrialization* (New York, 1956); Peter N. Stearns, *Paths to Authority* (Urbana, Ill., 1978), pp. 107–9; Daniel Nelson, *Managers and Workers: Origins of the New Factory System in the United States, 1880–1920* (Madison, Wis., 1975), pp. 37ff. Of course, some industrial age employers extended serious concern for workers' moral behavior.

When this combined with attention to proper discipline, the result—at least in theory—could extend controls over angry behavior beyond the most blatant forms of troublemaking. Thus some railroad concerns sought to control fighting among its workers and gave instructions to foremen on how to settle disputes. Railroads were also concerned about civil behavior to passengers. Still, instruction manuals for workers and supervisors, though sometimes in these cases going beyond material discipline and technical matters, avoid specific comment on emotional style. It may be that growing industrial experience and moral and supervisory discipline did gradually alter or affect worker expressions of anger on the job—curtailing fighting, e.g., just as on-the-job drinking was gradually reduced. But this aspect of the disciplinary process has not been seriously studied and in any event is at some remove from explicit emotional control. (Walter Licht, *Working for the Railroad: The Organization of Work in the Nineteenth Century* [Princeton, N.J., 1983], pp. 100–106.)

8. David M. Katzman, *Seven Days a Week: Women and Domestic Service in Industrializing America* (New York, 1978); Daniel E. Sutherland, *Americans and Their Servants: Domestic Service in the United States from 1800 to 1920* (Baton Rouge, La., 1981); see also Leonore Davidoff and Ruth Hawthorne, *A Day in the Life of a Victorian Domestic Servant* (Winchester, Mass., 1976); Theresa McBride, *The Domestic Revolution: The Modernization of Household Service in England and France, 1820–1920* (New York, 1976).

9. Katzman, *Seven Days a Week;* Sutherland, *Americans and Their Servants.*

10. Catherine E. Beecher, *Treatise on Domestic Economy* (1841; reprint, New York, 1970), p. 134.

11. Ibid., pp. 122, 139–40.

12. Katzman, *Seven Days a Week,* pp. 250ff.

13. S. Weir Mitchell, *Wear and Tear, Or Hints for the Overworked* (1887; reprint, New York, 1973), p. 17; see also George M. Beard, *American Nervousness: Its Causes and Consequences* (New York, 1881).

14. On big business and white-collar growth, see Alfred Chandler, *The Visible Hand* (Cambridge, Mass., 1974); Daniel Bell, *The Coming of Post-industrial Society* (New York, 1973), pp. 121–64.

15. Daniel T. Rodgers, *The Work Ethic in Industrial America, 1850–1920* (Chicago, 1978), pp. 88ff.; Nelson, *Managers and Workers,* pp. 37ff.; Judith A. Merkle, *Management and Ideology: The Legacy of the International Scientific Management Movement* (Berkeley, Calif., 1980); Robert F. Hoxie, *Scientific Management and Labor* (1915; reprint, New York, 1966); Frederick W. Taylor, *Shop Management* (New York, 1911), and *The Principles of Scientific Management* (New York, 1911).

16. "Pugancity is a great driving force. It is a wonderful thing that under Scientific Management this force is aroused not against one's fellow workers but against one's work" (L. S. Gilbreth, *The Psychology of Management* [New York, 1919], p. 259).

17. Hareven and Langenbach, *Amoskeag*; see also the discussion below of the effect of World War II women workers on personnel counseling procedures.

18. Nelson, *Managers and Workers*, p. 152; John B. Miner, *Personnel Psychology* (New York, 1969), p. 194; Stanley M. Herman, *The People Specialists* (New York, 1968), pp. 245ff.

19. Hugo Münsterberg, *Psychology and Industrial Efficiency* (Boston, 1913), pp. 128, 205; Mary Smith, *Handbook of Industrial Psychology* (New York, 1944).

20. See, esp., the admirable discussion in Loren Baritz, *The Servants of Power: A History of the Use of Social Science in American Industry* (Middletown, Conn., 1960).

21. Meyer, *The Five Dollar Day*.

22. Helen Baker, *Employee Counseling* (Princeton, N.J., 1944), p. 56; Robert N. McMurray, *Handling Personality Adjustment in Industry* (New York, 1944).

23. Annette Garrett, *Counseling Methods for Personnel Workers* (New York, 1945); Baritz, *The Servants of Power*, passim.

24. Joseph Tiffin and E. J. McCormick, *Industrial Psychology* (Englewood Cliffs, N.J., 1965), pp. 90, 188; Theodore Hewlett and Olive Lester, "Measuring Introversion and Extroversion," *Personnel Journal* 6 (1928): 352–61; Baritz, *The Servants of Power;* Doncaster Humm, "Skill, Intelligence and Temperament," *Personnel Journal* 22 (1943): 80–90; Herman, *The People Specialists*, pp. 245ff.; R. A. Sutermeister, "Training Foremen in Human Relations," *Personnel* 20 (1943): 13.

25. Susan Porter Benson, "The Clerking Sisterhood: Rationalization and the Work Culture of Saleswomen in American Department Stores, 1890–1960," in *Worker's Struggles, Past and Present*, ed. James Green (Philadelphia, 1983), pp. 101–7; R. C. Borden and Alvin Busse, *How to Win a Sales Argument* (New York, 1926), p. 7.

26. Walter Dill Scott et al., *Personnel Management: Principles, Practice, and Point of View* (New York, 1941); Borden and Busse, *How to Win a Sales Argument;* Laurence Siegel, *Industrial Psychology* (Homewood, Ill., 1969), pp. 347–57; Benson, "The Clerking Sisterhood," pp. 107–16; Margery W. Davies, *Woman's Place Is at the Typewriter: Office Work and Office Workers, 1870–1930* (Philadelphia, 1982), p. 95.

27. Edward Kilduff, *The Private Secretary* (New York, 1915), pp. 50, 57 (see also later editions to 1935).

28. Davies, *Woman's Place Is at the Typewriter*, p. 146; see also pp. 155–210.

29. William H. Leffingwell and Edward M. Robinson, *Textbook of Office Management* (New York, 1950), pp. 386ff.; Daniel Katz et al., *Productivity, Supervision and Morale among Railway Workers* (Ann Arbor, Mich., 1951), p. 33; Harry W. Hepner, *Human Relations in Changing Industry* (New York, 1938), p. 355; C. Wright Mills, *White Collar: The American Middle Classes* (New York, 1953), p. 234.

30. Elton Mayo, *The Human Problems of an Industrial Civilization* (New York, 1933), pp. 84ff.; F. J. Roethisberger and William J. Dickson, *Management and the Worker* (Cambridge, Mass., 1941), pp. 180ff.; Scott et al., *Personnel Management*.

31. William J. Eisenberg, "Qualities Essential for Supervisors," *Personnel Journal* 27 (1948): 251ff.

32. Tiffin and McCormick, *Industrial Psychology,* p. 418; Mayo, *Human Problems,* pp. 84ff.; Baritz, *The Servants of Power,* pp. 105ff.

33. Hepner, *Human Relations,* p. 96.

34. Mayo, *Human Problems,* pp. 84ff.; Garrett, *Counseling Methods,* p. 39; Roethisberger and Dickson, *Management and the Worker,* p. 269.

35. Nathaniel Cantor, *Employee Counseling: A New Viewpoint in Industrial Psychology* (New York, 1945), p. 64.

36. Garrett, *Counseling Methods,* p. 71.

37. Cantor, *Employee Counseling,* pp. 64ff.; Baritz, *The Servants of Power,* pp. 159ff.

38. James Jackson, "Reprimanding Employees," *Personnel Journal* 15 (1937): 75.

39. Robert N. McMurray, "Mental Factors in Labor Disputes," *Personnel* 12 (1935): 153–56; Ross Stagner, "Psychological Aspects of Industrial Conflict," *Personnel Psychology* 1 (1958): 142; Robert F. Peck and John W. Parsons, "Personality Factors in Work Output," *Personnel Psychology* 9 (1956): 77.

40. Roethisberger and Dickson, *Management and the Worker,* pp. 207, 269.

41. Burleigh B. Gardner and David G. Moore, *Human Relations in Industry* (Homewood, Ill., 1955), p. 272.

42. Roethisberger and Dickson, *Management of the Worker,* p. 348.

43. Ibid., p. 212; Tiffin and McCormick, *Industrial Psychology,* pp. 188ff.

44. Rexford Hersey, *Better Foremanship* (Philadelphia, 1961), p. 10; Glenn Gardiner, *Better Foremanship* (New York, 1941), pp. 53–54; Charles C. Smith, *The Foreman's Place in Management* (New York, 1946), p. 119.

45. W. E. Baer, "Do's and Don't's in Handling Grievances," *Personnel* 43 (1966): 30.

46. Gardiner, *Better Foremanship,* p. 32; see also Brian Kay, "Key Factors in Effective Foreman Behavior," *Personnel* 36 (1959): 28; Ordway Teal, *Human Nature and Managers* (New York, 1933), pp. 35ff.; W. B. Dominick, "Let's Take a Good Look at the Foreman's Job," *Personnel* 21 (1944): 160–69; John M. Pfiffner, *The Supervision of Personnel* (Englewood Cliffs, N.J., 1958), pp. 223ff.

47. C. S. Slowcombe, "Good Technique in Negotiating," *Personnel Journal* 14 (1935): 49.

48. Lester Tarnopol, "Personality Differences between Leaders and Nonleaders," *Personnel Journal* 37 (1958): 57–62; Miner, *Personnel Psychology,* p. 194; Erwin H. Schell, *The Techniques of Executive Control* (New York, 1934), p. 101.

49. Teal, *Human Nature and Managers,* p. 40.

50. Schell, *The Techniques of Executive Control,* p. 101.

51. Baritz, *The Servants of Power,* passim.

52. Harry Hepner and F. B. Pettengill, *Perceptive Management and supervision* (Englewood Cliffs, N.J,, 1961); Scott et al., *Personnel Management*; William R. Spriegel, Edward Schultz, and William B. Spriegel, *Elements of Supervision* (New York, 1942), p. 22; George D. Halsey, *Handbook of Personnel Management* (New York, 1947), p. 270; Hepner, *Human Relations*, passim.

53. Roethisberger and Dickson, *Management and the Worker*, p. 199.

54. Ibid., pp. 207, 269.

55. Gardner and Moore, *Human Relations*, p. 272.

56. Pfiffner, *Supervision*, p. 223; Paul Pigors and Charles A. Myers, *Personnel Administration* (New York, 1951), pp. 151–72; Leffingwell and Robinson, *Textbook of Office Management*, p. 47.

57. C. R. McPherson, "Kid Gloves vs. Iron Fist," *Personnel Journal* 43 (1964): 43; R. A. Eman, "Three Ways to Humanize Your Handling of Workers," *Personnel Journal* 33 (1952): 62; Rexford Hersey, "Self-Analysis Quiz for Supervisors and Executives," *Personnel* 24 (1948): 454–74; Harvey Stowers, *Management Can Be Human* (New York, 1946), p. 94; Halsey, *Handbook*, pp. 577ff.

58. Dale Carnegie, *How to Win Friends and Influence People* (New York, 1940), pp. 2, 27, 68, 70, 156; Borden and Busse, *How to Win a Sales Argument*, p. 7.

59. Lyman W. Porter and E. E. Ghisells, "The Self-Perception of Top and Middle Management Personnel," *Personnel Psychology* 10 (1957): 397–407.

60. A. P. Burr, "Executive Selection," *Personnel Journal* 47 (1968): 785; Spriegel et al., *Elements of Supervision*, pp. 116ff.; Halsey, *Handbook*, pp. 257–72; Hepner and Pettengill, *Perceptive Management*, pp. 378ff.; Paul W. Johnson and J. C. Bledsoe, "Morale as Related to Perceptions of Leader Behavior," *Personnel Psychology* 26 (1973): 581–91.

61. Leffingwell and Robinson, *Textbook of Office Management*, p. 386; see also Rensis Likett, *New Patterns of Management* (New York, 1961); D. H. Brusch, "Technical Knowledge or Managerial Skills?" *Personnel Journal* 58 (1979): 771–75.

62. M. Smith, *Handbook*; see also D. K. Hardesty and W. S. Jones, "Characteristics of Judgement of High Potential Management Personnel," *Personnel Psychology* 21c (1968): 85–98, in which high-potential executives scored average or below in interpersonal relations.

63. Mary C. H. Niles, *Middle Management: The Job of the Junior Administrator* (New York, 1941), pp. 72–93.

64. Andrew W. Halpin, *The Leadership Behavior of School Superintendants* (Columbus, Ohio, 1956), pp. 27ff.

65. Burt Scanlan, "Management Leadership in Perspective," *Personnel Journal* 58 (1979): 168–71.

66. Carnegie, *How to Win Friends*, p. 156.

67. Baritz, *The Servants of Power*, p. 105; Baker, *Employee Counseling*, p. 56.

68. Roethisberger and Dickson, *Management and the Worker*, pp. 542ff.

69. Baker, *Employee Counseling*, p. 40; Meyer, *The Five Dollar Day*; Spriegel et al., *Elements of Supervision*, p. 116; Cantor, *Employee Counseling*, p. 66.

70. Garrett, *Counseling Methods* (n. 23 above), pp. 120, 151ff.

71. Ibid., p. 120.

72. Baker, *Employee Counseling*, p. 40.

73. Johnson and Bledsoe, "Morale," pp. 48–49; see also M. L. Gross, *The Brain Watchers* (New York, 1962), for a critique of testing as personality control; on limitations of use, see D. L. Kirkpatrick, "How to Select Foremen," *Personnel Journal* 47 (1968): 262–70; Guy W. Wadsworth, "Temperament Tests as Personnel Aids," *Personnel Journal* 15 (1937): 341–46; Leffingwell and Robinson, *Textbook of Office Management*, pp. 386ff.; Silas Warner, "Spotting the Neurotic—Helping the Maladjusted," *Personnel Journal* 36 (1957): 136–39.

74. G. W. Wadsworth, "How to Pick the Men You Want," *Personnel Journal* 14 (1935): 334.

75. "The Humm-Wadsworth Temperament Scale," *Personnel Journal* 13 (1934): 322.

76. Wadsworth, "Temperament Tests as Personnel Aids"; Humm, "Skill, Intelligence and Temperament," pp. 80–90; D. G. Humm and G. W. Wadsworth, "Temperament in Industry," *Personnel Journal* 21 (1942): 314–22; Baritz, *The Servants of Power*, pp. 155ff.; Hewlett and Lester, "Measuring Introversion and Extroversion"; Donald A. Laird, *The Psychology of Selecting Men* (New York, 1927).

77. Alfred Root, "A Short Test of Introversion-Extroversion," *Personnel Journal* 10 (1931): 250–54; Halsey, *Handbook*, pp. 251ff.; Scott et al., *Personnel Management*; Ludwig Huttner and D. M. Stone, "Foreman Selection in Light of a Theory of Supervision," *Personnel Psychology* 11 (1958): 403–9.

78. Gross, *Brain Watchers;* William H. Whyte, Jr., *The Organization Man* (New York, 1956), pp. 140, 276ff.; Robert M. Guion, *Personnel Testing* (New York, 1965); Huttner and Stone, "Foreman Selection"; Siegel, *Industrial Psychology*, p. 165.

79. John D. Cook et al., *The Experience of Work: A Compendium and Review of LYP Measures and Their Use* (New York, 1981); Guion, *Personnel Testing;* Tiffin and McCormick, *Industrial Psychology*, pp. 188ff.; Arnold H. Buss and Ann Durkee, "An Inventory for Assessing Different Kinds of Hostility," *Journal of Consulting Psychology* 21 (1957): 243–49.

80. Lester Tarnopol and Julia Tarnopol, "How Top-Rated Supervisors Differ from the Lower-Rated," *Personnel Journal* 34 (1955): 332; see also Sutermeister, "Training Foremen," p. 13; and Miner, *Personnel Psychology*, p. 194.

81. Mills, *White Collar*, pp. 186ff.; Herman, *The People Specialists*, pp. 245ff.; Jackson, "Reprimanding Employees," pp. 75–80; H. T. Rosenberg,

"A Supervisory Look at Human Relations," *Personnel Journal* 38 (1959): 292–94; Hepner, *Human Relations*, pp. 525ff.

82. Edwin Fleishman, "Leadership Climate, Human Relations Training and Supervisory Behavior," *Personnel Psychology* 6 (1953): 205–22; Baritz, *The Servants of Power,* pp. 164ff.

83. Sutermeister, "Training Foremen," p. 13.

84. Dominick, "Let's Take a Good Look."

85. T. M. Carron, "Human Relations Training and Attitude Change," *Personnel Psychology* 17 (1964): 403–24.

86. J. M. Greenwood and W. J. McNamara, "Leadership Styles of Structure and Consideration and Managerial Effectiveness," *Personnel Psychology* 22 (1969): 141–69; Quentin Guerin, "Focus on the Attitude Change Process," *Personnel Journal* 47 (1968): 95–99.

87. Kenneth D. Benne et al., eds., *The Laboratory Method of Changing and Learning* (Palo Alto, Calif., 1975); R. M. Hecht, J. E. Aron, and Sidney Wirtzman, "Let's Stop Worrying about Aptitudes and Look at Attitudes," *Personnel Journal* 44 (1965): 616–19.

88. Thomas Greening, "Sensitivity Training: Cult or Contribution?" *Personnel* 41 (1964): 22–25; Edgar Schein and W. G. Bennis, *Personal and Organizational Changes through Group Methods* (New York, 1965), pp. 286–96.

89. Burt Scanlan, "Sensitivity Training: Clarification, Issues, Insights," *Personnel Journal* 50 (1970): 549.

90. Ibid., pp. 549–52.

91. Chris Argyris, *Interpersonal Competence and Organizational Effectiveness* (Homewood, Ill., 1962), pp. 23ff.

92. Ibid., pp. 137ff.

93. Ibid., p. 137.

94. Ibid., pp. 174ff.

95. Ibid., pp. 255ff.

96. L. J. Schuster, "Needed: More Sensitivity, Less Thinking," *Personnel Journal* 48 (1969): 614–16.

97. A. A. Imberman, "Foreman Training," *Personnel Journal* 54 (1975): 222–25; P. L. Wilkens and J. B. Haynes, "Understanding Frustration-instigated Behavior," *Personnel Journal* 53 (1974): 770–74; Stuart M. Klein and R. R. Ritti, "Work Pressure, Supervisory Behavior, and Employee Attitudes," *Personnel Psychology* 23 (1970): 153–67.

98. Scanlan, "Managerial Leadership in Perspective"; Brusch, "Technical Knowledge?"

99. C. C. Smith, *The Foreman's Place* (n. 44 above), p. 119.

100. Cook et al., *The Experience of Work,* passim; John W. Coggers, "Are You a Skilled Interviewer?" *Personnel Journal* 61 (1982): 840–42; G. R. Carlson, "Check Backgrounds When You Hire—It Pays," *Personnel Journal* 48 (1965): 216–17; Kirkpatrick, "How to Select Foremen," pp. 262–70; Burr, "Executive Selection," p. 785; Arlie Russell Hochschild, *The Managed Heart: Commercialization of Human Feeling* (Berkeley, Calif., 1983).

101. Siegel, *Industrial Psychology*, p. 358; Richard A. Morano, "Managing Conflict for Problem-Solving," *Personnel Journal* 55 (1976): 353.

102. Carl Heyel, *Management for Modern Supervisors* (n.p., 1962), pp. 47ff.; C. A. Turner, *A Practical Manual of Effective Superivision* (New York, [1970s]); see also issues of *Personnel Psychology* from 1960 to 1980.

103. Otto Altorfer, "Emotional Job Fitness," *Personnel* 52 (1975): 33.

104. Louis E. Davis and Albert B. Cherns, *The Quality of Working Life* (New York, 1975), pp. 110ff.

105. S. R. Siegel, "Improving the Effectiveness of Management Development Programs," *Personnel Journal* 60 (1981): 771–73; "WHS Begins Assertiveness Course," *Women's Health Service Newletter* (Pittsburgh) (January 1984).

106. Hochschild, *The Managed Heart*, pp. 25, 33, 113; Leonard R. Sayles, *Behavior of Industrial Work Groups* (New York, 1958), p. 82.

107. Harvey Swados, *On the Line* (Boston, 1957), pp. 24, 48, 169.

108. Roethisberger and Dickson, *Management and the Worker*, p. 349.

109. D. A. Fleishman and E. F. Harris, "Patterns of Leadership Behavior Related to Employee Grievances," *Personnel Psychology* 15 (1962): 43–56; Katz et al., *Productivity, Supervision and Morale*; Woodruff Imberman, "Letting the Employee Speak His Mind," *Personnel* 53 (1976): 12–22; Turner, *A Practical Manual*.

110. Lindahl, "Discipline 100 Years Ago," p. 247; John S. Ellsworth, *Factory Folkways: A Study of Institutional Structure and Change* (New Haven, Conn., 1952), p. 204; Theodore V. Purcell, *The Worker Speaks His Mind on Company and Union* (Cambridge, Mass., 1953), pp. 108, 125; Sar A. Levitan and William B. Johnston, *Work Is Here to Stay, Alas* (Salt Lake City, Utah, 1973), p. 67.

111. Benson, "The Clerking Sisterhood"; Baritz, *The Servants of Power*; Hochschild, *The Managed Heart*.

112. Levitan and Johnston, *Work Is Here*, p. 66.

113. Tiffin and McCormick, *Industrial Psychology*, pp. 188ff.; Mills, *White Collar*, p. 184.

114. Levitan and Johnston, *Work Is Here*, pp. 67–68; Purcell, *The Worker Speaks*, pp. 188–230.

115. Herman, *The People Specialists*, pp. 245ff.; Baritz, *The Servants of Power*, pp. 134ff.

116. Santos, *Iron Workers in a Steel Age*; Hareven and Langenbach, *Amoskeag*.

117. Gardner and Moore, *Human Relations*, pp. 163ff. The process being described here closely relates to the description of a shift from management by compulsion to management by negotiation, provocatively analyzed by Abram de Swaan in "The Politics of Agoraphobia: On Changes in Emotional and Relational Management," *Theory and Society* 10 (1981): 359–85. De Swaan correctly notes that this process has reduced some predictability in human relations—the kind of predictability based on firm hierarchies—complicated protest, and created certain new anxieties. He also is correct in insisting on the

continued, indeed heightened, emotional control necessary in the new management style, despite permissive rhetoric—"controlled decontrol" is his term for the relaxation of manners in twentieth-century Western society. But de Swaan may exaggerate the egalitarian emotional climate, for he omits the continued emotional prerogatives of top management. We will take up elements of de Swaan's larger argument in the concluding chapter of this book. See also Richard Sennett, *The Fall of Public Man: On the Social Psychology of Capitalism* (New York, 1978), on the rise of bureaucratic promotion on grounds of cooperativeness and companionability rather than expertise.

118. Jai Ghorpade and J. R. Lackrits, "Influences behind Neutral Responses in Subordinate Ratings of Supervisors," *Personnel Psychology* 34 (1981): 511–22; P. J. Andersini and M. B. Shapiro, "Women's Attitudes toward Their Jobs," *Personnel Psychology* 31 (1978): 23; Charles W. Walker and Robert H. Guest, *The Man and the Assembly Line* (Cambridge, Mass., 1952), pp. 92ff., 143; Leonard Goodwin, "Occupational Goals and Satisfaction of the American Work Force," *Personnel Psychology* 22 (1969): 313–25.

119. Walker and Guest, *The Man and the Assembly Line*, p. 99.

120. See Appendix B; see also the 1941–80 vols. of *Analysis of Work Stoppages*, which is published annually by the Bureau of Labor Statistics of the U.S. Department of Labor (Washington, D.C.); and U.S. Department of Labor, Bureau of Labor Statistics, *Strikes in the United States, 1880–1936* (Washington, D.C., 1937). A full analysis of strike trends would require integration of anger control with more familiar factors such as political climate, unemployment rates, and pay trends; but the probability of an emotional factor is high.

121. M. D. Makel and A. J. Schuh, "Job Applicant Attributes," *Personnel Psychology* 24 (1971): 48–49.

122. W. K. Graham and J. T. Calendo, "Personality Correlation of Supervisory Ratings," *Personnel Psychology* 22 (1969): 483–87; K. R. Student, "Changing Values and Management Stress," *Personnel Journal* 53 (1976): 48–55; Porter and Ghisells, "Self-Perception," pp. 397–407.

123. George Thornton, "The Relationship between Supervisory and Self-Appraisals of Executive Performance," *Personnel Psychology* 21c (1968): 441–55; Hal Pickle and Frank Friedlander, "Seven Societal Criteria of Organizational Success," *Personnel Psychology* 20 (1967): 165–78; Hardesty and Jones, "Characteristics of Judgement," pp. 85–98; James H. Mullen, "The Leadership Dilemma in American Business," *Personnel Journal* 40 (1961): 290–94.

124. E. L. Miller, "Job Attitudes of National Union Officials," *Personnel Psychology* 19 (1966): 395–410; A. H. Cochran, "Management Tigers and Pussycats," *Personnel Journal* 50 (1971): 524–26; Greening, "Sensitivity Training," pp. 18–25; C. J. Lilley, "Supervisors Don't Criticize Enough," *Personnel Journal* 31 (1952): 209–12.

125. Studs Terkel, *Working* (New York, 1974), pp. 32, 81, 260, 285ff., 547, and passim.

126. Mills, *White Collar*, p. 184; Whyte, *The Organization Man*, p. 152.

127. Arthur M. Whitehill, Jr., *Personnel Relations: The Human Aspect of Administration* (New York, 1955), passim.

128. Harry Braverman, *Labor and Monopoly Capital: The Degradation of Work in the Twentieth Century* (New York, 1974), pp. 140–45.

129. Whyte, *The Organization Man*, pp. 276ff.; Ellsworth, *Factory Folkways*, pp. 204–19; on privatization, see J. Goldthorpe et al., *Affluent Workers in the Class Structure* (New York, 1969).

130. Benson, "The Clerking Sisterhood"; Mills, *White Collar*, p. 184.

131. Charles Tilly, *From Mobilization to Revolution* (Reading, Mass., 1978); Edward Shorter and Charles Tilly, *Strikes in France, 1930–1968* (New York, 1974). On an element of anger in recent protest, see Harry Maurer, *Not Working: Oral History of the Unemployed* (New York, 1979), pp. 295–96.

132. The personal element of early twentieth-century strikes is discussed in Peter N. Stearns, *Lives of Labor: Working in Mature Industrial Society* (New York, 1977), and *Revolutionary Syndicalism and French Labor* (New Brunswick, N.J., 1971); see also Perrot, *Les Ouvriers en grève*.

133. Jürgen Kocka, *White Collar Workers in America, 1890–1940: A Social-Political History in International Perspective* (Beverly Hills, Calif., 1980).

134. Baritz, *The Servants of Power*, p. 169.

135. See the previous chapter, on child rearing; on the tensions in American society over anger, see Jerome Kagan, "The Child in the Family," in *The Family*, ed. A. S. Rossi, J. Kagan, and T. Hareven (New York, 1978), p. 39–56; and W. Lloyd Warner, *American Life: Dream and Reality* (Chicago, 1962).

136. Daniel R. Miller and Guy Swanson, *The Changing American Parent* (New York, 1958).

137. Maurer, *Not Working*, p. 53.

138. Spriegel et al., *Elements of Supervision*, p. 116.

139. Hochschild, *The Managed Heart*, thus speaks of a "numbing" effect of emotional management on airline personnel, particularly women. She sees a rise in off-work concern for "authenticity" and implicit recognition of the new emotional constraints (the compelled falseness) at work—just as, several centuries ago, a new concern for "sincerity" paralleled the rise of more duplicitous commercial behavior as capitalist marketing practices spread. For Hochschild, indeed, emotional management is at once extensive and concealed enough to suggest that an Orwellian world has arrived without our being clearly aware of the fact. While some of these claims smack of hyperbole and are not confirmed by systematic research, there is no question that management has become increasingly explicit and far-reaching in its intentions of emotional control, at least for key personnel categories, and that these efforts do have a real effect on the work experience.

Chapter 6

1. Gladys Jenkins, W. W. Bauer, and H. S. Shachter, *Teenagers: A Health and Personal Development Test* (Chicago, 1954).

2. Phyllis Harrison-Ross and Barbara Wyden, *The Black Child—a Parent's Guide* (New York, 1957), p. 101 and passim; Dr. Benjamin Spock, *The Common Sense Book of Baby and Child Care* (New York, 1945), pp. 204, 252; Michael Zuckerman, "Dr. Spock, the Confidence Man," in *The Family in History,* ed. C. Rosenberg (Philadelphia, 1975), pp. 179–208.

3. Rhoda W. Bacmeister, *Your Child and Other People* (Boston, 1950), p. 68; M. Bruenberg, ed., *Encyclopedia of Child Care and Guidance* (Garden City, N.Y., 1954); Sophie Ritholz, *Children's Behavior* (New York, 1959), pp. 60–61; Elinor Verville, *Behavior Problems of Children* (Philadelphia, 1967), p. 287; Ira S. Wile, *The Challenge of Children* (New York, 1949).

4. J. C. Montgomery and M. J. Suydam, *America's Baby Book* (New York, 1951), p. 285.

5. "Mad," *Sesame Street 2: Original Cast Record* (New York, 1977). Anger was also forced out of many commercial cartoons from the 1960s onward, according to a March 1986 television interview with Bill Hanna and Joe Barbera, the prolific producers.

6. Stephen P. Banks and Michael D. Kahn, *The Sibling Bond* (New York, 1982), pp. 11, 224, and passim; Elizabeth Fishel, *Sisters: Rivalry and Love Inside the Family and Beyond* (New York, 1979), p. 111; Louise Bates Ames and Carol Haber (Gesell Institute), *He Hit Me First* (New York, 1982), p. 116.

7. Better Homes and Gardens, *Baby Book* (New York, 1974); Joseph Church, *Understanding Your Child from Birth to Three* (New York, 1973), pp. 119–20; *Infant Care* (Washington, D.C., 1963), p. 27.

8. Dorothy W. Baruch, *New Ways in Discipline: You and Your Child Today* (New York, 1949), pp. 7, 45, 61; Winnifred de Kok, *Guiding Your Child Through the Formative Years* (New York, 1935), pp. 78ff.; Joseph D. Teich, *Your Child and His Problems* (Boston, 1953), p. 142; Marion J. Radke, *The Relation of Parental Authority to Children's Behavior and Attitudes* (Minneapolis, 1946), pp. 11–12; Dorry Metcalf, *Bringing Up Children* (New York, 1947); Sidonie Gruenberg, *The Parents' Guide to Everyday Problems of Boys and Girls* (New York, 1958), p. 94.

9. Martin Bax and Judy Bermal, *Your Child's First Five Years* (New York, 1974); Irma S. Black, *Off to a Good Start* (New York, 1946), p. 140; Anna W. M. Wolf and Suzanne Szasz, *Helping Your Child's Emotional Growth* (New York, 1954); Grace Langdon and J. W. Staub, *The Discipline of Well-adapted Children* (New York, 1952). Langdon had earlier written in the channeling mode (*Home Guidance for Young Children* [New York, 1931]); her conversion to greater rigor, like Dr. Spock's a bit later, is particularly interesting.

10. Berthold E. Schwartz and B. A. Ruggieri, *You CAN Raise Decent Children* (New Rochelle, N.Y., 1971), p. 48.

11. Susan Aukewa and Marilyn Kostick, *The Curity Baby Book* (New York, 1977), pp. 12–13; Robert A. Baron, *Human Aggression* (New York, 1977), p. 269; Baruch, *New Ways,* p. 239; Florence Powdermaker and Louise Grimes, *Children in the Family: A Psychological Guide for Parents* (New York, 1940), p. 240; Fritz Redl, *When We Deal with Children* (New York, 1966).

12. Michael Gordon, "Infant Care Revisited," *Journal of Marriage and the Family* 20 (1968): 578–83.

13. Zuckerman, "Dr. Spock."

14. Spock, *Baby and Child Care*, pp. 13, 48, 349.

15. Harold W. Bernard, *Toward Better Personal Adjustment* (New York, 1951), pp. 170, 240; Community Service Society of New York, *The Family in a Democratic Society* (New York, 1949), p. 37; Harold H. Anderson, *Children in the Family* (New York, 1941), pp. 108ff.; Mary M. Thompson, *Talk It Out with Your Child* (New York, 1953), pp. 83, 240.

16. Thomas Gordon, *Parent Effectiveness Training*, (New York, 1970).

17. Violet Broadribb and Henry F. Lee, *The Modern Parents' Guide to Baby and Child Care* (Philadelphia, 1973), p. 204; see also William E. Martin and Celia Stendler, *Child Behavior and Development* (New York, 1959), p. 221; Schwartz and Ruggieri, *You CAN Raise Decent Children*.

18. See chap. 7 below, on marriage.

19. Lurre Nicholson and Laura Torbet, *How to Fight Fair with Your Kids . . . and Win!* (New York, 1980), p. 139; see also pp. 18, 22, 32–33, 130–31, 287, 296.

20. Boyd R. McCandless, *Children and Behavior Development* (Hinsdale, Ill., 1967), p. 546.

21. Angry fathers and anger-provoked and -provoking competition were central targets of male liberationists. For a convenient summary of views, see Joseph Pleck and Jack Sawyer, eds., *Men and Masculinity* (Englewood Cliffs, N.J., 1974); and Joseph Pleck and Elizabeth Pleck, *The American Man* (Englewood Cliffs, N.J., 1980).

22. Marie Wynn, *Children without Childhood: Growing Up too Fast in a World of Sex and Drugs* (Baltimore, 1984),

23. Christopher Lasch, *Haven in a Heartless World: The Family Besieged* (New York, 1977), and *The Culture of Narcissism: American Life in an Age of Diminishing Expectations* (New York, 1979).

24. Clara B. Stendler, "Sixty Years of Child Training Practices," *Journal of Pediatrics* 36 (1950): 122–34; Carole Tavris, *Anger: The Misunderstood Emotion* (New York, 1982); A. Michael Sulman, "The Freudianization of the American Child: The Impact of Psychoanalysis in Popular Periodicals in the United States, 1919–1939" (Ph.D. diss., University of Pittsburgh, 1972); Ronald L. Howard, *A Social History of American Family Sociology, 1865–1940* (Westport, Conn., 1981). See also William McCord et al. ("Familial Correlates of Aggression in Nondelinquent Male Children," *Journal of Abnormal and Social Psychology* 62 [1961]: 79–93), who argue that aggression can be either destructive or "fallow" (never good) and that the choice is up to culture and to family environment.

25. Tavris, *Anger*, passim.

26. Bernard, *Toward Better Personal Adjustment*, p. 170.

27. Seymour Fischbach, "The Catharsis Hypothesis and Some Consequences of Interaction with Aggressive and Neutral Play Objects," *Journal of Personality* 24 (1956): 460–61; Baron, *Human Aggression* (n. 11 above), p. 269.

28. Orville G. Brim, Jr., *Education for Child-Rearing* (New York, 1959), p. 162; Baruch, *New Ways*, p. 61; Verville, *Behavior Problems*, pp. 39, 287.

29. William C. Menniger, ed., *How to Be a Successful Teen-ager* (New York, 1954), p. 141; R. J. Havighurst and Hilda Taba, *Adolescent Character and Personality* (New York, 1949); Arnold Gesell et al., *Youth—the Years from Ten to Sixteen* (New York, 1956), p. 339.

30. Morris Fishbein and William A. White, eds., *Why Men Fail* (New York, 1943), pp. 54ff.; Baruch, *New Ways*, p. 61; Menniger, ed., *How to Be a Successful Teen-ager*, p. 141; Robert B. Sears, Eleanor Maccoby, and Harry Levin, *Patterns of Child Rearing* (New York, 1957), pp. 145ff.; Dorothy Canfield Fisher, *Our Young Folks* (New York, 1943), p. 24.

31. Zuckerman, "Dr. Spock," pp. 187–93; Daniel Miller and Guy Swanson, *The Changing American Parent* (New York, 1958), p. 143 and passim.

32. Leigh Minturn and W. W. Lambert, *Mothers of Six Cultures* (New York, 1964), pp. 143–91; P. E. Sears, *Doll Play Aggression in Normal Young Children: Influence of Sex, Age, Sibling Status and Fathers' Absence*, Psychological Monographs, vol. 65, no. 323 (1951).

33. Jay Mechling, "Advice to Historians on Advice to Mothers," *Journal of Social History* 9 (1975): 44–63; Paul J. Woods et al., "A Mother-Daughter Comparison on Selected Aspects of Child-Rearing in a High Socioeconomic Group," *Child Development* 31 (1960): 121–28; Ruth Staples and J. W. Smith, "Attitudes of Grandmothers and Mothers toward Child-rearing Practices," *Child Development* 25 (1954): 91–97.

34. John R. Seeley, R. Alexander Sim, and Elizabeth W. Loosley, *Crestwood Heights* (Toronto, 1956), p. 166.

35. Jean Baker Miller, "Conflict and Psychological Development," in *The Woman Patient*, ed. Malkal T. Notman and Carol C. Nadelson (New York, 1982), p. 292.

36. Mechling, "Advice to Historians," pp. 44–63.

37. Woods et al., "A Mother-Daughter Comparison," pp. 121–28; Lee Salk, *Preparing for Parenthood* (New York, 1974); Sears, "Doll Play"; Melvin L. Kohn, "Social Class and the Exercise of Parental Authority," in *Personality and Social Systems*, ed. Neil Smelser and William Smelser (New York, 1963), pp. 297–314.

38. Martha S. White, "Social Class, Child Rearing Practices, and Child Behavior," in Smelser and Smelser, eds., *Personality and Social Systems*, pp. 286–96.

39. Leone Kell and Jean Aldous, "Trends in Child Care over Three Generations," *Marriage and Family Living* 22 (1960): 176–77; Russell Green and Edgar O'Neal, eds., *Perspectives on Aggression* (New York, 1976), p. 117.

40. Leo Kanner, *In Defense of Mothers* (New York, 1944), p. 37.

41. Pamela Holcomb, *History of the Pittsburgh Child Guidance Center* (Pittsburgh, 1986).

42. Miller and Swanson, *Changing American Parent*; Havighurst and Taba, *Adolescent Character and Personality*; Menninger, ed., *How to be a Successful Teen-ager*.

43. Paula M. Rayman and Barry Bluestone, *Out of Work: The Consequences of Unemployment in the Hartford Aircraft Industry* (Washington, D.C., 1982); Phyllis Moen, E. L. Kain, and Glen Elder, Jr., "Economic Conditions and Family Life: Contemporary and Historical Perspective," in *American Families and the Economy,* ed. R. Nelson and F. Skidmore (Washington, D.C., 1983), pp. 335–37; Urie Bronfenbrenner, "Socialization and Social Class through Time and Space, *Readings in Social Psychology,* ed. Eleanor Maccoby, T. M. Newcombe, and E. L. Hartley (New York, 1958).

44. Kenneth Kenniston, *Youth and Dissent: The Rise of a New Opposition* (New York, 1971); Lewis Feuer, *The Conflict of Generations: The Character and Significance of Student Movements* (New York, 1969).

45. Peter Clecak, *America's Quest for the Ideal Self* (New York, 1983), pp. 179–228.

46. Dr. James R. Higgins, private interview at North Hills School District, Pittsburgh, Pennsylvania, 20 October 1983. (Dr. Higgins is a counselor education specialist and director of pupil personnel services at North Hills. Additionally, he has been active in both the national and the state Pupil Personnel Movement since its inception, coauthoring both the original and the 1983 Pennsylvania State Pupil Personnel Guidelines. He is currently president of the Pennsylvania Association of Pupil Personnel Administrators.) See also Robert W. Stoughton, James McKenna, and Richard P. Cook, "Pupil Personnel Services: A Position Statement" (Washington, D.C., April 1969, mimeographed); "Pupil Personnel Services in Pennsylvania: A Position Statement" (Pittsburgh, Pa., 1983, mimeographed); Victor Lipman, "Mr. Glasser's Gentle Rod," *American Education* 14 (1978): 28–31; Haim Ginott, "I Am Angry, I Am Appalled, I Am Furious," *Today's Education* 61 (1972): 23; Helen Sobehart, "Toward a History of Anger in the Schools" (seminar paper, Carnegie-Mellon University, December 1983). We are grateful to Sobehart and also to Joan Francis for many of the data that follow.

47. John R. Ban, "A Lesson Plan Approach for Dealing with School Discipline," *Clearinghouse* 55, no. 8 (April 1982): 345.

48. Robert Coles, *Children of Crisis: A Study of Courage and Fear,* 3 vols. (Boston, 1967–71), esp. vol. 3.

49. Edmund T. Emmer et al., *Classroom Management for Secondary Teachers* (Englewood Cliffs, N.J., 1984), p. 105; see also pp. 102–6.

50. Thomas Coates and Carl Thoreson, "Teacher Anxiety: A Review with Recommendations," *Review of Educational Research* 64, no. 2 (Spring 1976): 160.

51. Lipman, "Gentle Rod," pp. 28–29 (citing William Glasser, *Schools without Failure* [New York, 1968]); Ban, "Lesson Plan Approach," p. 345.

52. Ginott, "I Am Angry," p. 23.

53. Walter B. Kolesnick, *Educational Psychology* (New York, 1963), p. 458.

54. Robert Geiser, "What to Do If You Can't Stand That Kid," *Teacher* 91 (1973): 14–16, 19.

55. Fritz Redl, "Aggression in the Classroom," *Today's Education* 58 (September 1969): 30.

56. Ibid.; see also Ronald Tyrrell, Frederick McCarty, and Frank Johns, "The Many Faces of Anger," *Teacher* 94 (February 1977): 60.

57. John W. M. Whiting and Irwin L. Child, *Child Training and Personality* (New Haven, Conn., 1953).

58. Philip G. Zimbardo, *Shyness: What It Is and What to Do about It* (Reading, Mass., 1977), p. 211ff.

59. Marc Fasteau, *The Male Machines* (New York, 1976).

60. Barrington Moore, *Injustice: The Social Bases of Obedience and Revolt* (New York, 1978).

61. Ibid., pp. 500–502; "The Sixth Deadly Sin," *New York Times,* 16 March 1983. Note that a correlation between the decline of moral indignation as an approved category in child-rearing literature and the possible (admittedly, not proved) decline of such indignation in collective protest involves a much-debated link between personal and group anger. The correspondence is, we believe, striking, suggesting even a possible causation—from child-rearing standards to collective action—or a joint causation of both phenomena by the shift in desired work personality. The correspondence might even suggest that personal style of anger does indeed have a role in collective expressions of anger, though this has been disputed not only by some social psychologists but also by some of the more organization-minded students of protest. But the relationship suggested in this instance is tentative and should not obscure the varied and complex discussion of the role of personal emotionality in collective action (or, as in this case, inaction).

62. D. G. Harris, H. G. Gough, and W. E. Martin, "Children's Ethnic Attitudes: Relationships to Parental Beliefs Concerning Child Training," *Child Development* 21 (1950): 169–81.

63. Morris Janowitz, *The Last Half-Century: Societal Change and Politics in America* (Chicago, 1978), pp. 113ff. and passim.

64. David Riesman with Nathan Glazer and Reuel Denney, *The Lonely Crowd: A Study of the Changing American Character* (New Haven, Conn., 1973).

65. Zuckerman, "Dr. Spock."

66. Lasch, *Haven in a Heartless World*; but see also Jesse Batan, "The 'New Narcissism' in Twentieth Century America: The Shadow and Substance of Social Change," *Journal of Social History* 17 (1983): 199–220. Recent comparative studies of anger do not confirm Lasch's assumptions about monstrous fantasizing because of repressed rage. American youths generally remain somewhat more direct in their articulations about anger than do youths in more overtly repressive cultures, where Lasch's imagery would fit better. These results might suggest that the contemporary parental approach meets some success, normally, in limiting (though not in avoiding) anger. (See Joel R. Davitz, *The Language of Emotion* [New York, 1969].)

67. Whiting and Child, *Child Training*. In the wake of the Tavris book, various authorities have taken to the daily press to note the relationship between anger (excessive anger, to be sure), "whether vented or not," and heart disease as well as to bemoan the social effects of personal anger ("The Sixth Deadly Sin").

On the nineteenth-century concern about nervous tension—of which anger might be a product mentioned in passing—see Charles Rosenberg, *The Therapeutic Revolution* (Philadelphia, 1979), chap. 1; Woods Hutchinson, "Our Misunderstood Nerves," *Good Housekeeping* 61 (December 1915): 783; George M. Beard, *American Nervousness* (New York, 1881); F. Peterson, "The Effects of the Emotions upon the Body," *Good Housekeeping* 48 (March 1909): 371.

But recent popularized literature on the relationship between emotions and health focuses much more specifically both on anger and on the heart and vascular system. This is a point management enjoins on service employees as part of the discipline of niceness (see chap. 5 above). For the best general statement, see Meyer Friedman and Ray H. Rosenman, *Type A Behavior and Your Heart* (New York, 1981), pp. 17–24 and passim.

68. Edwin I. Megargee and Jack E. Hokanson, eds., *The Dynamics of Aggression: Individual, Group and International Analyses* (New York, 1970), passim.

69. Philip J. Greven, Jr., *The Protestant Temperament: Patterns of Child-rearing, Religious Experience and the Self in Early America* (New York, 1977); Jerome Kagan, "The Child in the Family," in *The Family,* ed. A. S. Rossi, J. Kagan, and T. Hareven (New York, 1978), p. 39. We may of course increasingly learn to vent anger in machine games, just as other anger-repressed cultures have de facto outlets against animals. Some managerial research has recently suggested that people communicating by computer are franker in expressions of anger than they are when speaking or when writing in longhand.

70. Baruch, *New Ways* (n. 8 above), pp. 239ff.

Chapter 7

1. *Ladies Home Journal (LHJ)* (Feburary 1960): 129.

2. Henry A. Bowman, *Marriage for Moderns* (New York, 1960), p. 298.

3. For examples of the earlier approach, see E. R. Groves, *Marriage* (New York, 1933); G. C. Meyers, *The Modern Family* (New York, 1934); Janet F. Nelson, *Marriages Are Not Made in Heaven* (New York, 1939). Compare Paul Popenoe's *The Conservation of the Family* (Baltimore, 1926) with his *Marriage Is What You Make It* (New York, 1950) to see the difference.

4. Leo Madow, *Anger* (New York, 1972), p. 115; Marcia Lasswell and Norman M. Lobsenz, *No Fault Marriage* (New York, 1976), in an argument that bad sex is just a symptom of a bad relationship. See also Theodore Isaac Rubin, *The Angry Book* (New York, 1969), pp. 99–100. On Freud, see Nathan G. Hale, Jr., *Freud and the Americans: The Beginnings of Psychoanalysis in the United States, 1876–1917* (New York, 1971), p. 430.

5. Ernest R. Groves and Gladys H. Groves, *Wholesome Marriage* (Boston and New York, 1927); Robert O. Blood, *Anticipating Your Marriage* (Glencoe, Ill., 1955), pp. 254–55.

6. *LHJ* (June 1960): 24.

7. Paul Popenoe, *Modern Marriage: A Handbook for Men* (New York, 1940), pp. 241–42.

8. Popenoe, *Marriage Is What You Make It*, p. 205.

9. John D. Baldwin, *Marriage without B.S.* (New York, 1979), pp. 145ff.; A. H. Chapman, *Marital Brinksmanship* (New York, 1974), p. 44; Herbert Fensterheim and Jean Baer, *Don't Say Yes When You Want to Say No* (New York, 1975), pp. 138ff.; Norman M. Lobsenz and Clark W. Blackburn, *How to Stay Married* (New York, 1968), pp. 103–4; Nena O'Neill and George O'Neill, *Open Marriage* (New York, 1972), p. 128; Charlie W. Shedd, *Letters to Karen: On Keeping Love in Marriage* (Nashville, Tenn., 1965), pp. 62ff.

10. *LHJ* (June 1970): 102.

11. *LHJ* (April 1965): 36.

12. *LHJ* (October 1955): 46.

13. Blood, *Anticipating*, pp. 209–10; Howard Clinebell and Charlotte Clinebell, *The Intimate Marriage* (New York, 1970), p. 51.

14. Paul Popenoe, *Marriage Before and After* (New York, 1943), pp. 210–11.

15. Popenoe, *Marriage Is What You Make It*, p. 71.

16. Blood, *Anticipating*, p. 253.

17. *LHJ* (March 1955): 47.

18. Popenoe, *Marriage Is What You Make It*, p. 205.

19. Lobsenz and Blackburn, *How to Stay Married*, p. 107; O'Neill and O'Neill, *Open Marriage*, p. 128.

20. Guilielma Bell Alsop and Mary F. McBride, *She's Off to Marriage: A Guide to Success and Happiness in Married Life* (New York, 1942), pp. 34, 232.

21. Popenoe, *Marriage Is What You Make It*, pp. 65–67.

22. *LHJ* (December 1947): 209.

23. Randolph Ray, *Marriage Is a Serious Business* (New York, 1944), p. 19.

24. Shedd, *Letters to Karen*, p. 64.

25. George R. Bach and Peter Wyden, *The Intimate Enemy* (New York, 1968), pp. 63–64, 71.

26. G. V. Hamilton and Kenneth MacGowan, *What Is Wrong with Marriage* (New York, 1929); Harriet R. Mowrer, "Marriage Conflict," in *Marriage and the Family*, ed. R. Hill and H. Becker (Boston, 1942), pp. 336–63; Popenoe, *The Conservation of the Family*; Louis M. Terman, *Psychological Factors in Marital Happiness* (New York, 1938).

27. *LHJ* (September 1950): 26.

28. *LHJ* (July 1950): 26.

29. *LHJ* (July 1965): 63; *LHJ* (August 1955): 61. For more on this sort of psychological optimism, see Hale, *Freud and the Americans* (n. 4 above), pp. 421ff.

30. *LHJ* (April 1950): 26.

31. *LHJ* (April 1945): 131; "Are You Too Educated to Be a Mother?"

LHJ (June 1946): 6; *LHJ* (November 1946): 29; *LHJ* (November 1945): 158–60, 170.

32. *LHJ* (February 1945): 94ff., 141–44; *LHJ* (October 1945): 183.

33. Ronald L. Howard, *A Social History of American Family Sociology, 1865–1940* (Westport, Conn., 1981), chap. 3, esp. p. 73; Christopher Lasch, *Haven in a Heartless World: The Family Besieged* (New York, 1977), pp. 132ff., 143. The interactionist blindness to larger social problems influencing the family is illustrated by the story that Ernest Groves apparently opposed the New Deal because it would not solve the fundamental problems of family life (Howard, *American Family Sociology,* p. 93, n. 107).

34. John H. Scanzoni, *Opportunity and the Family* (New York, 1970), p. 138.

35. For an example of the early approach, see Nelson, *Marriages Are Not Made in Heaven* (n. 3 above); and Edgar Schmiedeler, *Marriage and the Family* (New York, 1946).

36. For instance, Evelyn Millis Duvall and Reuben Hill, *Being Married* (New York, 1960).

37. Carol Tavris, *Anger: The Misunderstood Emotion* (New York, 1982), passim.

38. *LHJ* (March 1980): 90.

39. *LHJ* (November 1975): 32.

40. *LHJ* (June 1975): 18.

41. *LHJ* (April 1975): 12.

42. Bach and Wyden, *Intimate Enemy* (n. 25 above), chap. 1.

43. For additional examples of this approach, see also David Mace and Vera Mace, *We Can Have Better Marriages* (New York, 1974), esp. the manuals mentioned in n. 9.

44. *LHJ* (March 1980): 61–62, 66, 166–67.

45. *LHJ* (January 1980): 101.

46. *LHJ* (August 1970): 34.

47. *LHJ* (April 1980): 24, 28.

48. *LHJ* (April 1975): 72; *LHJ* (November 1975): 32.

49. Evelyn Duvall and Reuben Hill, *When You Marry* (New York, 1945).

50. James A. Peterson, *Education for Marriage* (New York, 1956).

51. See chap. 5 above, on the contemporary work constraints influencing private life. In fact, the emotionology of marriage, while retaining largely Victorian goals, did leave a slightly larger opening to anger than did the emotionology of work, particularly white-collar work. At work, the goal was no anger at all. In marriage, which was still viewed as an emotional experience, anger now had to be acknowledged if, it was hoped, tightly controlled. The correspondence in goals and tactics between work and marriage standards was real, as we have discussed. But it might be possible to misread these standards as suggesting that marriage was a more emotionally open outlet than contemporary work was. In this sense, which again preserved a perverse kind of Victorianism, marriage might still be seen as a refuge, now not from the unruliness of work but from its manipulative rationality.

52. Scanzoni, *Opportunity,* p. 139; Clinebell and Clinebell, *The Intimate*

Marriage, p. 98; Judson T. Landis and Mary G. Landis, *Building a Successful Marriage* (New York, 1953), p. 264; *LHJ* (April 1970): 145.

53. John Scanzoni, *Sexual Bargaining: Power Politics in the American Marriage* (Englewood Cliffs, N.J., 1972).

54. Duvall and Hill, *When You Marry*, pp. 186–87.

55. Bach and Wyden, *Intimate Enemy*, pp. 22ff.

56. Baldwin, *Marriage without B.S.*, p. 143.

57. Landis and Landis, *Building*, pp. 292ff.; George H. Gallup, *The Gallup Poll: Public Opinion, 1935–1971* (New York, 1972), p. 1028.

58. Lillian Breslow Rubin, *Worlds of Pain: Life in the Working-Class Family* (New York, 1976), pp. 76–78, 115–16, and passim.

59. Alexandra G. Kaplan et al., ''Women and Anger in Psychotherapy,'' *Women and Therapy* 2 (1983): 29–40. It is notable that this essay was not based on any interviewing of men.

60. Andrew J. Cherlin, *Marriage, Divorce, Remarriage* (Cambridge, Mass., 1981), p. 22. The rate fell, after a postwar peak through the late 1950s, but was still rising compared to the prewar rates.

61. *LHJ* (April 1975): 12.

62. See nn. 57 and 58 above.

63. Jean Baker Miller, ''Conflict and Psychological Development,'' in *The Woman Patient*, ed. Malkah T. Notman and Carol C. Nadelson (New York, 1982), p. 292. One of us who is a psychiatrist (CZS) is struck by the guilt both her male and her female patients suffer in acknowledging anger.

64. Tavris, *Anger*, chap. 5. For the same conclusion, see Landis and Landis, *Building*, pp. 292ff.

65. Cherlin, *Marriage, Divorce, Remarriage*, pp. 65ff., 75.

66. For a discussion of how much people want marriage today, even thinking of it as a path to salvation, see Jonathan Gathorne-Hardy, *Marriage, Love, Sex, and Divorce* (New York, 1981), pp. 296ff. Cherlin's statistics on remarriage also support this view.

67. Rex A. Skidmore and Anthon S. Cannon, *Building Your Marriage* (New York, 1951), p. 437.

Chapter 8

1. Joseph Veroff, Elizabeth Douvan, and Richard A. Kulka, *The Inner American: A Self Portrait from 1957 to 1976* (New York, 1981), pp. 106–21.

2. Randolph Trumbach, *The Rise of the Egalitarian Family: Aristocratic Kinship and Domestic Relations in Eighteenth Century England* (New York, 1978).

3. Abram de Swaan, ''The Politics of Agoraphobia: On Changes in Emotional and Relational Management,'' *Theory and Society* 10 (1981): 373 and passim; Richard Sennett, *The Fall of Public Man: On the Social Psychology of Capitalism* (New York, 1978).

4. Benjamin Nelson, *The Idea of Usury* (Chicago, 1969), pp. 139–63.

5. de Swaan, ''Politics of Agoraphobia,'' pp. 370–71.

6. Jean L. Briggs, *Never in Anger: Portrait of an Eskimo Family* (Cam-

bridge, Mass., 1970); Jeffrey Gray, *The Psychology of Fear and Stress* (New York, 1971); Richard Solomon, *Mao's Political Revolution and the Chinese Political Culture* (Berkeley, Calif., 1971): William Goode, "The Theoretical Importance of Love," *American Sociological Review* 24 (1959): 38–47.

7. Jerome Kagan, "The Child in the Family," in *The Family*, ed. A. S. Rossi, J. Kagan and T. Hareven (New York, 1978), pp. 33–56.

8. Leigh Minturn and W. W. Lambert, *Mothers of Six Cultures* (New York, 1953); Robert B. Sears, Eleanor Maccoby, and Harry Levin, *Patterns of Child Rearing* (New York, 1957); Joel R. Davitz, *The Language of Emotion* (New York, 1969); see chap. 4 above.

9. John R. Gillis, *Youth and History: Tradition and Change in European Age Relations* (New York, 1981); Joseph F. Kett, *Rites of Passage: Adolescence in America from 1750 to the Present* (New York, 1977); Stephen Humphries, *Hooligans or Rebels? An Oral History of Working Class Childhood, 1889–1939* (London, 1981); Anthony M. Platt, *The Child Savers* (Chicago, 1977); Robert D. Storch, ed., *Popular Culture and Custom in Nineteenth-Century England* (New York, 1982); Benjamin Rader, *American Sports from the Age of Folk Games to the Age of Spectators* (Englewood Cliffs, N.J., 1983).

10. Roger Wertheimer, "Understanding Retribution," *Criminal Justice Ethics* 21 (1983): 34; see also pp. 31, 33.

11. Morris Janowitz, *The Last Half-Century: Societal Change and Politics in America* (Chicago, 1978), pp. 113ff. and passim.

12. Susan Brownmiller, *Against Our Will: Men, Women and Rape* (New York, 1975); Dolf Zillmann and Jennings Bryant, "Pornography, Sexual Callousness, and the Trivialization of Rape," *Journal of Communication* 17 (1982): 10–21; Meyer Friedman and Ray H. Rosenman, *Type A Behavior and Your Heart* (New York, 1974).

13. Albert Rothenberg, "On Anger," *American Journal of Psychiatry* 128 (1971): 454–60; Paul R. Kleinginna and Anne M. Kleinginna, "A Categorized List of Emotion Definitions, with Suggestions for a Consensual Definition," *Motivation and Emotion* 5 (1981): 345–79.

14. See, e.g., the anger imagery discussed in William James's youthful notebooks (Howard M. Feinstein, *Becoming William James* [Ithaca, N.Y., 1984], pp. 117–45 and passim).

15. Some maverick marital manuals at various points in the twentieth century specifically urged this function; thus marriage "provides a man and a woman with somebody to quarrel with at times when they feel like it, without any loss of self-respect" (E. J. Hardy, *Still Happy though Married* [New Haven, Conn., 1914], p. 209). In the 1950s similar arguments were made with the idea of family fights as essential "drains" for hostility accumulated elsewhere, necessary to mental health (Judson T. Landis and Mary G. Landis, *Building a Successful Marriage* [New York, 1953], p. 264; Howard Clinebell and Charlotte Clinebell, *The Intimate Marriage* [New York, 1954]).

16. Carl Degler, *At Odds: Women and the Family in America from the Revolution to the Present* (New York, 1980); Peter Gay, *The Bourgeois Experience: Victoria to Freud*, vol. 1, *Education of the Senses* (New York, 1984);

Linda Pollock, *Forgotten Children: Parent-Child Relations from 1500 to 1900* (Cambridge, 1984). For an example of a wife seemingly comfortable with anger even at her husband, see C. Richard King, ed., *Victorian Lady on the Texas Frontier: The Journal of Ann Raney Coleman* (Norman, Okla., 1971), pp. 90–92 (the journal covers the period from the 1830s to the 1880s).

17. Roger Lane, *Violent Death in the City: Suicide, Accidents and Murder in Nineteenth Century Philadelphia* (Cambridge, Mass., 1979); Eric Monkennen, "A Disorderly People? Urban Order in the Nineteenth and Twentieth Century," *Journal of American History* 68 (1981): 539–59.

18. K. C. Constantine, *The Man Who Liked Slow Tomatoes* (New York, 1983), pp. 85–86.

19. Robert Plutchik, *Emotion: A Psychoevolutionary Synthesis* (New York, 1980); Robert A. Baron, *Human Aggression* (New York, 1977); Julian M. Davidson and Richard J. Davidson, eds., *The Psychobiology of Consciousness* (New York, 1980).

20. Briggs, *Never in Anger*; Philip J. Greven, Jr., *The Protestant Temperament: Patterns of Childrearing, Religious Experience and the Self in Early America* (New York, 1977).

21. *New York Times,* 6 October 1916 (quoted in Lawrence T. McDonnell, " 'You Are too Sentimental': Problems and Suggestions for a New Labor History," *Journal of Social History* 17 [1984]: 629–54); and see Tamara K. Hareven and Randolph Langenbach, *Amoskeag: Life and Work in an American Factory City* (New York, 1978), on employer anger.

22. Benjamin Barber, *Strong Democracy: Participatory Politics for a New Age* (Berkeley, Calif., 1984).

23. Christopher Lasch, *Haven in a Heartless World: The Family Besieged* (New York, 1977); Barrington Moore, Jr., *Injustice: The Social Bases of Obedience and Revolt* (New York, 1978), pp. 500–502.

24. James R. Averill, *Anger and Aggression: An Essay on Emotion* (New York, 1982); Mirra Komarovsky, *Blue-Collar Marriage* (New York, 1964); Jean Baker Miller, "The Construction of Anger in Women and Men," Stone Center for Developmental Services and Studies, Work in Progress no. 83-01. (Wellesley, Mass., 1983).

25. Robert E. Veto, "Anger in American Litigation" (seminar paper, Carnegie-Mellon University, Department of History, 1984); James F. Corbetter, "Activities of Consumers' Organizations," *Law and Contemporary Problems* 1 (1933): 61.

26. Barbara Yngvesson and Patricia Hennessey, "Small Claims, Complex Disputes: A Review of the Small Claims Literature," *Law and Society Review* 10 (1975): 221; Craig Wanner, "The Public Ordering of Private Relations: Initiating Civil Cases in Urban Trial Courts," *Law and Society Review* 10 (1975): 422–23; Jerold S. Auerbach, *Justice without Law?* (New York, 1983), pp. 13 and passim.

27. Bruce J. Graham and John R. Snortum, "Small Claims Court—Where the Little Man Has His Day," *Judicature* 29 (1977): 267; Marc Galanter, "Why the 'Haves' Come Out Ahead: Speculations on the Limits of Legal Change," *Law and Society Review* 10 (1975): 108.

28. "So You're Mad Enough to Sue," *Changing Times* (October 1953): 25–31; "Dial V for Vengeance," *Newsweek,* 26 January 1970, p. 63.

29. Austin Sarat, "Alternatives in Dispute Processing: Litigation in a Small Claims Court," *Law and Society Review* 11 (1976): 344.

30. Ibid., p. 346; see also Laura Nader, ed., *No Access to Law: Alternatives to the American Judicial System* (San Diego, Calif., 1980).

31. de Swaan, "Politics of Agoraphobia" (n. 3 above), pp. 373–85.

32. Carol Tavris, *Anger: The Misunderstood Emotion* (New York, 1982).

33. Solomon, *Mao's Political Revolution* (n. 6 above), passim.

34. Richard Sennett, *Families against the City* (Cambridge, Mass., 1970), deals with middle-class anxiety about lower class displays of anger; Kagan, "Child in the Family," pp. 33–56.

35. de Swaan, "Politics of Agoraphobia," passim; for an evaluation similar to our own, see Miller, "Construction of Anger."

Index

Absenteeism, 111, 115, 144
Adolescents. *See* Teenagers
Advice literature, 36, 48, 51, 52–53, 61–67, 71, 81, 85, 106, 191, 249–50, 256–57
Aggression, 6, 8, 75, 76, 80, 83, 114, 126, 131, 141, 147, 160, 166, 168, 169, 175, 179, 191, 194–95, 199, 200, 216, 222, 232, 237, 238
Agyris, Chris, 136–37
Alcott, Louisa May, 74
Alcott, William, 38, 47, 48
Alger, Horatio, 75, 94
Ambivalence, 3, 70, 99, 106, 109, 126–27, 154, 158, 171, 174–75, 178–79, 182, 189, 206, 216, 230, 234, 236
American Institute of Family Relations, 191, 193
Amphetamines, 238
Animals, 7, 27, 31, 33, 55
Anthropology, 6–8, 186, 216, 226
Apprenticeship, 27, 114
Art, 160
Arthur, T. S., 38, 40, 53, 56
Asia, 32, 213
Assertiveness training, 141
Attitude surveys, 116
A-type personality, 186
Averill, James, 6

Babcock, Winifred, 104–5
Baby boom, 172, 180
Bach, George, 195, 201–2, 204, 206, 209
Bailey, Abigail, 61

Beecher, Catherine, 58, 113
Behaviorism, 73
Bernreuter test, 131
Bible, 19
Billy Budd, 70, 110
Biology, 4, 220
Blacks, 16, 19, 159
Blood, Robert, 192, 193, 194
Blood pressure, 13, 186, 284
Boxing, 9, 14, 77, 100, 107
Briggs, Jean, 7, 13
Britain, 10, 29, 30, 33
Buddhism, 21
Bureaucracies, 153, 184, 214, 233, 234
Bushnell, Horace, 54

Calvinism, 54
"Can This Marriage Be Saved," 192, 196, 202
Capitalism, 34, 114, 119, 149
Carnegie, Dale, 117, 124, 133
Cartoons, 279
Catholicism, 32
Channeling, 75, 98, 114
Cherlin, Andrew, 209
Chicago, 111
Child abuse, 234
Child guidance, 106, 175, 179
Child rearing, 22–23, 31, 50, 71, 98, 152, 155, 157, 225, 238
Children's stories, 55, 75, 76
Christian gentleman, 72, 75
Christianity, 10–20, 21, 32, 75, 220
Civil War, 11, 75
Computers, 233, 284
Confucianism, 21, 27

Constructivism, 6
Consumerism, 93, 97
Corporate economy, 93, 113, 135,
    148, 152–53, 157, 170, 176
Counseling, 116, 118, 127
Crime, 168–69, 222
Crying, 60–61, 114, 207, 218
Curses, 24, 220, 229

Darwin, Charles, 4, 92
Darwinism, 73, 77, 92, 94, 100–
    101, 114, 215
Delinquency, 75, 170, 221
Demos, John, 20, 100, 227
Department stores, 116–17
Detroit, 155, 176
Diaries, 60, 173, 212, 218
Divorce, 57, 67, 70, 81, 93, 95, 97,
    105, 109, 177, 190, 191, 199,
    207, 208–10, 229, 231, 237
Dueling, 24, 100
Duvall, Evelyn, 204, 206

Eastwood, Clint, 178
Edwards, Jonathan, 28
Emotionology, 14, 38, 72, 115, 139,
    157, 191, 213
Employers. *See* Managers
Enlightenment, 33, 51, 153, 213
Europe, 7, 10, 20, 22, 24, 26, 31,
    99–100, 101, 232, 236
Evangelicalism, 30, 52, 72, 226
Executives, 126–27
Exit interviews, 129–30
Extroversion, 130–31

Fathers, 104
Feminism, 62, 80, 85, 94, 97, 109,
    174–75, 184, 201, 203, 216,
    221, 228
Filene, Peter, 49
Fischer, Dorothy Canfield, 52, 79,
    171
Football, 100, 226
Ford Motor Company, 115
Foremen, 112, 118, 121, 128–29,
    132, 143, 145, 146

France, 22, 100
Franklin, Benjamin, 1, 27
Franklin, James, 1, 4
Freudianism, 8, 12, 13, 23, 73, 83,
    119, 159–60, 161, 168–70, 186,
    191, 195, 196, 219, 247
Frontier, 2, 167, 216
Frustration-aggression, 8, 219

Gender, 46–47, 57, 62, 76, 80–82,
    95, 103, 105, 108, 114, 176,
    197, 206–7, 260
Germany, 24, 100
God, 21, 54, 220, 221, 261
Godey's, 39, 48, 61, 65, 98
Greeks, 7
Graven, Philip, 30, 31, 226
Griswold, Robert J., 65
Guidance counselors, 179

Hall, G. Stanley, 73, 75–76, 79,
    100, 102, 170
Hardy, the Rev. E. J., 87, 88, 89
Hawthorne works, 117–18, 122,
    127–28, 143
Hill, Rubin, 204, 206
Holocaust, 169
Homer, 7, 21
Home-work dichotomy, 36, 71, 94–
    95, 110, 142–43, 152, 155–56,
    157, 171, 172, 188–89, 212–13,
    215, 236
Humm, Doncaster, 116
Humm-Wadsworth personality test,
    116, 131
Humor, 86–87, 198, 219, 220
Humors, 20
Hutterites, 187
Hysteria, 60, 62, 67, 228

Illness, 60, 62, 97, 141, 186, 191,
    218, 284
Imperialism, 228
Industrialization, 17, 35, 38, 111,
    149
Infant Care, 78, 161
Insults, 24–25, 220, 229

Interviews, 129–30, 140
Introversion, 130–31
Invalidism, 60, 97, 231
Islam, 21

James, Alice, 60
Japan, 141
Jogging, 230
Judaism, 21

Kagan, Jerome, 188

Ladies Home Journal, 1, 83, 85, 95, 192–93, 194, 197, 198, 200, 201, 202–3
Lasch, Christopher, 3, 13, 36, 153–54, 186, 232, 234
Lawsuits, 230
Leadership Behavior Description Questionnaire, 132, 140
"Light-touch" Christianity, 54
Literacy, 32, 252
Locke, John, 50
Love, 10, 13, 28, 31, 34, 229, 237

"Making Marriage Work," 196–97
Male liberation, 169, 184
Managers, 120, 146–47, 154, 171, 176, 220, 228
Marriage and Divorce, 82
Marriage Counsellors, 191
Mather, Cotton, 102
Mayo, Elton, 114, 117–19, 120, 121, 149
Melancholia, 22
Melville, Herman, 70
Men, 39, 46–49, 57, 62, 72, 75, 76, 80–82, 103, 105, 108, 167, 196, 205, 206–7, 228, 229
Middle class, 16, 36, 85, 93, 98, 99, 100–101, 112–13, 114, 152, 175, 220, 223, 236
Mills, C. Wright, 148, 156
Modernization, 34, 83
Montessori schools, 179
Moore, Barrington, 184, 228

Mothers, 53–56, 76, 80, 104, 174–75, 188
Münsterberg, Hugo, 115
Murder, 24

Narcissism, 186
National Congress of Mothers, 76, 80
National Institute of Child Life, 73, 76
Neighbors, 21, 26, 27, 100, 227, 230
New Deal, 116
New England, 9, 19, 20, 24, 102
New York, 102
No-fault divorce, 231

O'Neill, William, 82
Ong, Walter, 32

Parsons, Mary H., 41, 43
Permissiveness, 158–59, 160, 164–65, 219, 237
Personnel departments, 115
Peterson, James, 204
Philadelphia, 231
Phrenology, 40, 42, 48, 50
Pillsbury Mills, 131
Pittsburgh, 175
Politics, 12, 228–29, 235–36, 239
Popenoe, Paul, 191, 193, 194, 196, 202–3
Population, 32
Pornography, 6
Prejudice, 139–42, 169
Privatization, 150, 231
Progressivism, 11, 101, 109, 200, 221, 238
Protest, 27, 111, 118, 151, 177, 181, 184, 228, 233, 236, 283
Protestantism, 16, 21, 25, 30, 31, 34, 50, 52, 72
Psychoanalysis, 8, 184
Psychology, 4–6, 9, 83, 114, 115, 118, 145, 152, 169–70, 184, 200

Punishment, 54, 58, 98, 99, 102, 175, 179, 221
Puritans, 2, 19, 33, 36, 102

Quakers, 30
Quarrels, 39–41, 50, 53, 59, 87, 191, 225

Rape, 222
Revenge, 24, 54, 102, 221
Reynolds, Debbie, 190
Riesman, David, 153, 185, 232
Robinson, John, 19, 20, 22
Rogers, Mr. (Fred), 160–61
Romanticism, 30
Rubin, Theodore, 202–3, 204

Sales personnel, 117, 147, 171, 239
Sangster, Margaret, 58, 63
Schachter, Stanley, 6
Schools, 11, 12, 51, 58, 79, 101, 158, 167, 175, 177, 179, 217, 232
Scientific management, 114
Secretaries, 117
Sedgwick, Catharine, 55
Servants, 29, 32, 55, 59, 88, 92, 112–13, 122, 214, 254
Service economy, 152–53, 214
"Sesame Street," 160, 161
Sexuality, 42, 49, 60, 78, 83, 97, 106, 130, 159, 160, 168, 191, 214, 225, 237, 257
Sibling rivalry, 74, 78, 161, 172
Small claims courts, 230
Social history, 10
Social science, 83–84, 92–93, 114, 169, 195, 222
Social Security Board, 128
Sociology, 167, 195, 199, 200
South, 2, 24, 30
Spencer family, 106–7
Spock, Dr. Benjamin, 159, 164–65, 169, 171, 185
Sports, 80, 100, 160, 175, 183, 221, 226, 228, 230–31, 232, 238
Stanton, Elizabeth Cady, 64
Steelers, 226

Stewardesses, 140, 141–42, 143, 227
Stone, Lawrence, 30
Strikes, 111, 113, 142, 146, 151, 155, 243
Suicide, 232
Supervisory and Peer Leadership test, 132
Swados, Harvey, 143

Tantrum, 22–23, 29, 36, 50, 73, 78, 79, 96, 98, 101, 161, 162, 164, 166, 174–75, 203, 219
Tavris, Carol, 201, 202, 207, 208
Taylor, Frederick, 114
Teachers, 80, 102, 167, 178
Teenagers, 56, 77, 167, 170, 176–77, 182, 217, 221, 229, 232
Television, 160, 175, 178, 231
Temperance, 62, 80, 97, 109, 228
Terkel, Studs, 1, 147
Testing, 116, 130–32, 140
T groups (sensitivity training), 134
Thayer, William, 48
Tolerance, 33, 169, 185, 221, 229
Tomkins, Silvan, 15, 246
Training programs, 132, 141–42
Trumbach, Randolph, 10
Turnover, 118, 134, 142, 144

Uncle Wiggily, 77
Unions, 113, 121, 139, 143–44, 146, 147, 151, 156, 180–81
Utkus, 7, 13, 161–62

Victorianism, 35, 36–68, 71–72, 89–91, 110, 158, 159, 162, 167–68, 197, 200, 213, 225, 227
Violence, 24, 79, 181, 214, 220, 229–30
Virginia, 26

War, 12, 168, 170, 194–95, 199, 237
War Industries Board, 116
War Manpower Commission, 132
Warner, Lloyd, 4, 75, 160, 178

Washington, George, 55
Watson, John B., 73, 78, 79
Wayland, Francis, 58, 64
White-collar labor, 113, 117, 127,
    130, 142, 146, 148–50, 151,
    154, 176
Will-breaking, 22–23, 51, 52, 55,
    71, 98, 235
Witches, 25, 30
Women, 30, 46–49, 53, 56, 57, 60,
    62–63, 65, 76, 80–82, 85, 91,
    97, 102, 103, 105, 108–9, 112,
    114, 116, 117, 120, 129, 145,
    159, 172, 196, 200, 205, 206–7,

208, 217, 218–19, 222, 225,
    228, 229, 231
Working class, 72, 98, 99, 113–14,
    119–20, 142, 150, 154, 155–56,
    175, 177, 200, 206
World War I, 115, 146
World War II, 116, 127, 131, 143,
    146, 169, 190, 216
Wyden, Peter, 195, 201–2, 204,
    206, 209

Youth. *See* Teenagers

Zuni Indians, 187